The Subject of Experience

The Subject of Experience is about the self, the person. It consists of a series of essays which draw on literature and psychology as well as philosophy. Galen Strawson discusses the phenomenology or experience of having or being a self (What is the character of self-experience?) and the fundamental metaphysics of the self (Does the self exist? If so, what is its nature? How long do selves last?), and develops an approach to the metaphysical questions out of the results of the phenomenological investigation. He argues that it is legitimate to say that there is such a thing as the self as distinct from the human being. At the same time he raises doubts about how long selves can be supposed to last, insofar as they are thought of as entities distinct from human beings. He also raises a doubt about whether a self (or indeed a human being) can really be said to lose anything in dying. He criticizes the popular notion of the narrative self, and considers the differences between 'Endurers' or 'Diachronic' people, who feel that they are the same person when they consider their past and future, and 'Transients' or 'Episodic' people, who do not feel this. He considers the first-person pronoun 'I' and a number of puzzles raised by the phenomena of self-reference and self-knowledge. He examines Locke's, Hume's and Kant's accounts of the mind and personal identity, and argues that Locke and Hume have been badly misunderstood.

Galen Strawson holds the President's Chair of Philosophy at the University of Texas at Austin. He is the author of *Freedom and Belief* (Oxford, 1986, 2nd edition 2010); *The Secret Connexion: Causation, Realism, and David Hume* (Oxford 1989, 2nd edition 2014); *Mental Reality* (MIT Press 1994, 2nd edition 2009), *Selves: An Essay in Revisionary Metaphysics* (2009, revised edition 2011); *Locke on personal identity: Consciousness and Concernment* (2011, 2nd edition 2014); and *The Evident Connexion: Hume on personal identity* (2011, 2nd edition 2014).

The Subject of Experience

Galen Strawson

OXFORD
UNIVERSITY PRESS

UNIVERSITY PRESS

Great Clarendon Street, Oxford, OX2 6DP,
United Kingdom

Oxford University Press is a department of the University of Oxford.
It furthers the University's objective of excellence in research, scholarship,
and education by publishing worldwide. Oxford is a registered trade mark of
Oxford University Press in the UK and in certain other countries

Published in the United States of America by Oxford University Press
198 Madison Avenue, New York, NY 10016, United States of America

British Library Cataloguing in Publication Data
Data available

Library of Congress Cataloging in Publication Data
Data available

ISBN 978–0–19–877788–5 (Hbk.)
ISBN 978–0–19–880158–0 (Pbk.)

To my friend Simon Halliday

Contents

List of Figures

Preface

This book collects most of the essays I have written on the self or subject of experience. I've omitted two—'The self' (2009)[1] and 'The minimal subject' (2011)—because for the most part they summarize, clarify, and reorder material presented in *Selves* (2009). I've also omitted four that appeared in a previous collection, *Real Materialism and Other Essays* (2008): 'Self, Body, and Experience' (1999); 'What is the relation between an experience, the subject of an experience, and the content of the experience?' (2003); 'Against narrativity' (2004); and 'Episodic ethics' (2007). Finally, I've omitted a 1996 Wolfson College lecture, 'The sense of the self' (1999), which is a variant of essay 1, and 'The phenomenology and ontology of the self' (2000), which is mostly a summary of themes in essays 1 and 2.

This book is not designed to be read through from beginning to end. The essays it contains were written as independent pieces of work, and regularly echo each other in clarificatory remarks about what I mean by some term—'materialism', for example (see e.g. §1.1, §2.5, § 3.13, §4.5, §9.3), or 'consciousness', or 'thin subject' (see e.g. §1.2, §8.3, §9.5, §10.2). They also overlap in other ways: sometimes one paper develops another by repeating and expanding its text. This is particularly true in the case of Chapters 2 and 3, because the latter is a response to a set of papers commenting on the former.

'Essays' is certainly the right word. They're attempts—attempts to make something clear about the subject, the I, the self, the 'first person'. I'm not sure Valéry is right when he says that a poem is never finished, only abandoned, but I'm sure this is true of works of philosophy.

I've made almost no substantive changes, but I have corrected a few mistakes and recast a small number of sentences in the interest of greater clarity. I've also added some new quotations, and a good number of cross references. So these versions supersede all earlier published versions.

I'm grateful to many people for philosophical help, and thank them severally in the footnotes to the essays that follow. Many thanks also to Peter Momtchiloff and Matthias Butler for all their editorial help and advice, to Raj, Clement in production, to Christine Ranft for her expert copyediting, and to Andrew Hawkey for his transcendental proofreading.

---

[1] This paper is quite different from '"The Self"', Ch. 2 in this book.

Conventions

When I cite a work I give the date of first publication or (occasionally) the precise or estimated date of composition, while the page reference is to the published version listed in the Bibliography. I refer to Locke's *Essay Concerning Human Understanding* as '*Essay*', to Berkeley's *Treatise Concerning the Principles of Human Knowledge* as '*Principles*', to Hume's *Treatise Of Human Nature* as '*Treatise*', to Hume's *An Enquiry Concerning Human Understanding* as '*First Enquiry*', and to Kant's *Critique of Pure Reason* as '*Critique*'. In the case of Hume's *Treatise* I give the paragraph reference in the Norton and Norton edition followed by the page reference in the Selby-Bigge and Nidditch edition; a typical *Treatise* reference is '1.4.5.5/233'. For the first *Enquiry* I give the paragraph reference in the Beauchamp edition followed by the page reference in the Selby-Bigge edition; a typical Enquiry reference is '12.34/163'. In the case of the Abstract and the Appendix and Introduction to the *Treatise*, I refer to their paragraphs by number followed by the page reference in the Selby-Bigge and Nidditch edition, e.g. 'Abs§17/652', 'App§17/634', 'Int§7/xvi'. Cross references to passages in this book take the form '§7.11', where this refers to Chapter 7, section 11.

Acknowledgements

(2) '"The Self"', *Journal of Consciousness Studies* 4: 405–28 (1997); (3) 'The Self and the Sesmet', *Journal of Consciousness Studies* 6: 99–135 (1999); (4) 'Against Corporism', *Organon F* 16: 428–48 (2009); (5) 'I have no future', *The Philosophers' Magazine* 38: 21–6 (2007); (6) '"We live…beyond any tale that we happen to enact"', *Harvard Review of Philosophy* 18: 73–90 (2012); (7) 'The Unstoried Life', in *On Life-Writing* ed. Z. Leader (Oxford University Press), pp. 284–301 (2015); (8) 'Self-intimation', *Phenomenology and the Cognitive Sciences* doi 10.1007/s11097-013-9339-6 (2013); (9) 'Fundamental Singleness: How to Turn the Second Paralogism into a Valid Argument', in *The Metaphysics of Consciousness*, ed. P. Basile et al. (Cambridge University Press), pp. 61–92 (2010); (10) 'Radical Self-Awareness', in *Self, No Self?: Perspectives from Analytical, Phenomenological, and Indian Traditions*, ed. M. Siderits et al. (Oxford University Press), pp. 274–307 (2010); (11) 'I and *I*: Immunity to Error through Misidentification of the Subject', in *Immunity to Error Through Misidentification: New Essays*, ed. S. Prosser and F. Recanati (Cambridge University Press), pp. 202–23 (2012); (12) 'The secrets of all hearts: Locke on Personal Identity', in *Mind, Self, and Person*, ed. A. O'Hear (Royal Institute of Philosophy), pp. 111–41 (2015); (13) 'When I enter most intimately into what I call myself: Hume on the Mind' (originally 'Hume on Personal Identity') in *The Oxford Handbook of David Hume*, ed. Paul Russell (Oxford University Press), pp. 269–92 (2015); (14) 'All my hopes vanish: Hume on the Mind', in *The Continuum Companion to Hume*, ed. A. Bailey and D. O'Brien (Continuum), pp. 181–98 (2012).

1

Introduction
'The I, the I'

1.1

'The I, the I is what is deeply mysterious!' That's how it seemed to Wittgenstein a hundred years ago (1916: 80). I'm not sure it's true, even though (as Wittgenstein later observed) 'the very things which are most obvious may become the hardest of all to understand' (1948: 17).

There's a way of reading Wittgenstein's remark that makes it true (see §1.3, p. 10), but I don't think this is what he had in mind. In fact I'm sure it isn't. He was soused in Schopenhauer at the time, and while this can be a very good thing at some point in a philosophical career, it's not good if it leads one to think that 'the thinking subject is surely mere illusion'—another entry that Wittgenstein made in August 1916—or, again, that 'the subject is not part of the world'.[1] This gets the world and the subject wrong. As a thinking human subject of experience one is wholly in the world, a product of evolution by natural selection.[2]

That's one reply to the allegation of mystery. Another is that there's a primordial respect in which one knows what a subject of experience is simply in being one. I think there's a sense in which this is true of absolutely all subjects of experience, however primitive. To be an experiencing subject is necessarily to experience being an experiencing subject, and in that sense to know what it is to be a subject of experience. This is so even if the condition of being a subject of experience is never in the focus of one's attention in any way, and even if one lacks the mental resources to make the condition an explicit topic of reflection—because one is, say, a spider (see e.g. §9.11, p.186). Knowledge doesn't have to be reflective. There's a primordial 'sense of "knowing" in which, when you have an experience, there is no difference between the experience and knowing that you have it' (Russell 1940: 49)—where this includes knowing what it is like.

---

[1] 1916: 79–80 (for citation conventions see 'Conventions', p. xiii above). These views survive in his *Tractatus Logico-Philosophicus*: 'The thinking, presenting subject; there is no such thing... in an important sense there is no subject'; for 'it could not be mentioned' in a 'book [called] The world as I found it' (1922: 121).

[2] Perhaps the thing to do with people who persist in the view that the subject isn't part of the world is to plug them into the 'total perspective vortex', an imaginary device that delivers a 'momentary glimpse of the entire unimaginable infinity of creation, and somewhere in it a tiny little mark, a microscopic dot on a microscopic dot, which says, "You are here"' (Adams 1980: 57). In Adams's story, 'the apprehension of insignificance on this scale is... so shocking that the subject instantly dies' (Kahane 2014: 762). A telling test, because those who believe that the subject is not part of the world will presumably be unaffected.

We ourselves are cognitively sophisticated creatures, and we're also fully self-conscious.[3] We're capable of explicit apprehension of what it is to be a subject of experience. We possess a fully-fledged concept of the subject of experience, and we can draw out the complexities of the phenomenon in philosophical reflection. There are real and absorbing complexities in it, but it's not at all clear that there's any mystery. Whenever one finds oneself thinking that the subject of experience is a mystery one should recall the respect in which fully self-conscious, sophisticated concept-exercising creatures like ourselves know what subjects of experience are just in being subjects of experience and in being conceptually sophisticated. There is, to repeat, a fundamental respect in which we know *exactly* what subjects of experience are. We know exactly what it takes to be a subject of experience, primitive or sophisticated. It's worth adding that human beings become fully self-conscious at a very early age—around eighteen months.

One mistake is to take the existence of a chair, say, as a paradigm case of something that isn't mysterious, and to find the existence of a subject of experience mysterious relative to the existence of a chair. This may seem natural at first, but it probably gets things the wrong way round.

What makes something seem a mystery? A radical failure to understand it—perhaps also a sense that it may be impossible to understand. But what is understanding— theoretical understanding of some feature of the world (linguistic understanding is not at issue)? When we consider this question I think we come up against the fact that understanding is at bottom just a feeling—a certain sort of feeling we can have or lack. And if understanding is just a feeling, so too is mystery. Nothing is objectively a mystery.

It may be doubted that understanding is just a feeling. It may be said that to achieve technical mastery of some feature of concrete reality x—to know how to use x to produce certain results, to be able to predict what will happen to x if one does this or that—is to understand it. But it isn't; technical mastery of x isn't a form of understanding that doesn't require a feeling of understanding; it isn't understanding at all. We can master the principles of quantum mechanics and apply them practically in extraordinarily effective ways without claiming to understand quantum mechanics at all. The same goes for an automatic drinks dispenser. A feeling of complete confidence about what x will do if one does A, or alternatively B or C, isn't any sort of evidence that one understands x. So too a feeling of confidence of this kind is not a feeling of understanding with respect to x.

I think, then, that understanding is just a certain sort of feeling. I also think that it's sometimes a justified feeling. Perhaps the paradigm case of understanding some occurrence in the world is the one in which one understands why someone is acting in a certain way because one knows what they want and what they believe. (Perhaps this is the only perfect case of understanding an occurrence in the world.) It is, however,

---

[3] In my use, 'fully self-conscious' has the meaning that 'self-conscious' standardly has in analytic philosophy: to be fully self-conscious is to be able to think of oneself specifically and simply *as oneself*. A kitten chasing its tail can think of itself, but it doesn't know that it is itself that it is thinking of; see §11.7, p. 225]. I add 'fully' because I think that there's an ineliminable sense in which all experiencing beings are conscious of themselves simply in having experience at all: see [4] and [5], §10.4, p. 193.

important that when one has a feeling of understanding with regard to something x, there is always and necessarily something else, y, that one knows or takes for granted, something else that grounds one's feeling of understanding. It's always and necessarily relative to some $y \neq x$ that x seems understandable. It is only relative to a large set of beliefs about physical objects that it seems intrinsically understandable that this billiard ball should go off in this direction when knocked in this way by this other billiard ball, instead of turning into a white-winged dove and flying away. So too, if x seems to be a mystery, it must be because there's something else y that one knows or takes for granted that makes x's existence seem a mystery.

Suppose x—the candidate mystery—is *the subject of experience*. What is y? One familiar candidate for y is *experience*—consciousness, conscious experience.[4] The existence of active, experiencing subjects of experience obviously presupposes the existence of experience, and one reason that has been given for thinking that there's something mysterious about subjects of experience is the idea that there is already something deeply—irremediably—mysterious about experience or consciousness.

The idea is widespread in philosophy, but I don't think it has any good foundation. We have conscious experience all the time when we're awake, and often when we're asleep, and there's a fundamental sense in which we know exactly what it is. This is because there's a fundamental respect in which, when it comes to experience, *the having is the knowing*. And it's not just that we know the particular phenomenological character of the experience we have just in having it—where the knowledge is a matter of direct acquaintance. It's also the case that we know quite generally what experience is, just in having it. There's a fundamental respect in which we know *exactly* what experience is. So why should we think it mysterious?

It's true that we can know exactly what something is and still find it mysterious that it exists at all; and Wittgenstein is right, as observed, when he says that 'the very things which are most obvious may become the hardest of all to understand'. Still, we can come to find familiar things hard to understand for good reasons or bad, and in the case of experience those who find it or its existence mysterious have bad reasons—no real reasons at all—for doing so.

Some think that *physics* gives us reason to find it mysterious, or a commitment to materialism, or naturalism. This is a mistake. Suppose we take it with the physicalists or materialists that concrete reality is wholly physical in nature, and hence that [1] we're wholly physical beings. I think this myself, along with a great many others. Suppose, next, that we grant that [2] our experience is wholly a matter of neural goings-on in the brain. Again I think this myself, along with many others.

This is the point at which some think that it follows that the existence of experience is a mystery—an astonishing mystery. For how, they ask, could [2] be true? How could experience possibly be wholly a matter of neural goings-on in the brain?

If one thinks this, one has already gone hopelessly wrong. One has already made the mistake that generates the appearance of mystery: the mistake of believing that [3] we have a pretty good grip on the basic nature of the physical, a grip given which

---

[4] I'll use the terms 'experience', 'conscious experience' and 'consciousness' interchangeably.

the very existence of experience—the very idea that experience should be wholly physical—is mysterious. This mistake is massively compounded by a further belief, the belief that [4] the physical is, in and of itself, something fundamentally *non-experiential* in nature. It's only relative to a prior conviction that [3] and [4] are true, which is widespread among philosophers, that [2] may appear deeply mysterious.

The correct move at this point is not to hold on to [3] and [4] and accept that experience is a mystery (i.e. a mystery to us; nothing natural is intrinsically mysterious). The lesson of [2]—and I think it's important to stress that [2] is far beyond reasonable doubt, and has been, in effect, for hundreds of years—is that [3] is certainly false (I think that [4] is also almost certainly false).[5] We don't have a good and in particular comprehensive idea of the fundamental nature of the physical, contrary to [3], and we certainly don't know enough to know that the physical is, in and of itself, something fundamentally *non-experiential* in nature, contrary to [4]. It's worth noting that there is in fact *no evidence* for the existence of anything non-experiential in reality.[6]

We should be clear, then, that the *nature* of conscious experience is not a mystery. We know exactly what it is. Nor do we have any good reason to feel that its *existence* is a mystery—given that anything exists at all. (The fact that anything exists at all may be a good candidate for being a mystery.)[7] If anything is rightly thought to be a mystery (a mystery to us), it's the fundamental nature of the physical—a point confirmed daily by physicists. Or rather, more accurately: if anything is rightly thought to be a mystery, it's the fundamental nature of the physical *insofar as the physical is not experiential*. The qualification is needed because we know the nature of the experiential.

I don't think we'll ever be able to integrate fully the vast number of things we know about experience from our direct first-hand knowledge of it with the knowledge of the nature of the physical we acquire from physics and neurophysiology, in a way that gives rise to a sense of understanding. There are a number of reasons why this is so.[8] The present point, however, is simply that we have no good reason to think, as so many do, that experience is a mystery while physical stuff in general is not.

Suppose one endorses physicalism, the view that concrete reality is entirely physical in nature, as I do. (It should be noted that all this endorsement of physicalism really amounts to, at this point, is the claim that there is only one fundamental kind of stuff in concrete reality plus the claim that this stuff is the subject matter of the science of physics, which tells us a great deal about it, albeit only in highly abstract structural-relational terms.) And suppose one is determined to take a fully and genuinely naturalistic approach to the question of the nature of the physical, as I am. In that case one must begin by fully acknowledging the reality of experience (conscious experience). One must do this because experience is the most certainly known general natural phenomenon, which must as such be fully acknowledged by

---

[5] On the falsity of [3], see e.g. Locke 1689–1700 §2.23, Chomsky 2015 ch. 4. For doubts about [4] see e.g. Strawson 2006, 2016.

[6] See e.g. Strawson 2012b.   [7] See Parfit 1998a.

[8] The fact that physics only delivers abstract mathematico-structural knowledge of the nature of concrete reality is one of them—although it might also be thought to be a reason for optimism. See e.g. Russell 1927a: Part 3.

genuine naturalists.[9] A genuine naturalist should also reject the idea that there is any 'radical emergence' in nature, for the principle that *natura non facit saltum*—that nature doesn't make radical ontological/qualitative jumps, of the sort that seems required if experience is to emerge from stuff that is in its basic nature wholly non-experiential—is a fundamental principle of naturalism (it is a key part of methodological naturalism). I think one is then obliged to admit that the most plausible general theoretical view of the nature of the physical is that experience—experientiality—is one of its basic or fundamental features; that experientiality in some form or other is a pervasive feature of physical stuff, whether or not all-out panpsychism or panexperientialism is true.[10]

On this view, the only sense in which the existence of experience and subjects of experience is mysterious is the sense in which the existence of any concrete reality at all is mysterious. If we could *per impossibile* acquire full knowledge of the ultimate intrinsic nature of concrete reality,[11] we might discover that there is no non-experiential reality in our universe. I think we need to take seriously the possibility that no other sort of concrete reality is even metaphysically possible.

I can't develop this point here (see Strawson 2016 §21). It's a pity that so many are still unable to shake free of [4], the fabulously unwarranted theoretical conviction that physical stuff is in its basic nature non-experiential, and of the accompanying sense that any other view is preposterous. Adherence to [4] shuts one off from making much progress in the metaphysics of mind.

Part of the problem—it is perhaps the hidden heart of the problem—is that this theoretical conviction is powerfully underwritten by something non-theoretical, pre-theoretical. It's deeply grounded in the entirely sensible basic distinction we make, among the things we encounter in everyday life, between animate or minded things and inanimate or non-minded things. This distinction is in place very early on. It has powerful innate support. It is in constant—permanent—use in daily life: stones

---

[9] Many self-styled naturalists today are not genuine naturalists at all. They're false naturalists, anti-naturalists who are so deeply in the grip of [3] and [4]—in spite of the fact that there is strictly speaking *no evidence* for the existence of any non-experiential reality—that they doubt or deny or otherwise discount the existence of the most certainly known natural phenomenon: conscious experience.

[10] See e.g. Eddington 1928 ch. 12. For some recent work, see e.g. Alter and Nagasawa 2015, Brüntrup and Jaskolla 2016. All-out panpsychism is the view that experience and subjects of experience are all there are to concrete reality. All-out physicalist panpsychism is accordingly the view that experience and subjects of experience are all there are to the physical. Panexperientialism is the view that experientiality is all there is to concrete reality. Physicalist panexperientialism is accordingly the view that experientiality is all there is to the physical. Since a subject of experience must exist if experience exists, panexperientialism entails that the existence of a subject of experience is not something ontically over and above the existence of experience. I put the case for this last view in Strawson 2003b. Note that physics could not possibly give reason to doubt panpsychism—panexperientialist or not.

[11] The point that this is impossible for us is routine: see e.g. Poincaré 1903, Russell 1927a. It's a matter of 'the silence of physics'—the fact that physics only tells us about structure and relations, not about the intrinsic nature of the stuff that has the structure and exemplifies the relations. It's true that we know something about the ultimate intrinsic nature in having experience, as Russell saw ('we know nothing about the intrinsic quality of physical events except when these are mental events that we directly experience'; 1950: 153), but even if all concrete reality is wholly a matter of experientiality it doesn't follow that we have 'full knowledge of the ultimate intrinsic nature of concrete reality', if only because we don't understand how the complex reality of the brain as revealed by physics and neurophysiology relates to the experiential qualitative character of experience whose nature we know simply in having it.

and tables and chairs and stairs and cups are entirely non-minded. They're not experiential beings.

The everyday distinction is fine as it stands, as is the certainty with which we deploy it in everyday life. The problem lies in what happens when this certainty transfers its weight, very naturally but wholly illegitimately, into a general theoretical—metaphysical—picture according to which all physical stuff is essentially and wholly non-experiential in its basic nature, and constitutes experiencing beings only in certain extremely special cases (animal life). It's hard to overestimate the power of this conviction, which is thought to be admirably naturalistic although it violates a fundamental principle of naturalism by requiring one to posit the radical emergence of the experiential from the non-experiential.[12] Here I simply want to record it. I think it's part of the base psychological explanation of why people believe that the existence of experience is mysterious, a belief that may lead them in turn to think that the existence of the subject of experience—the 'I'—is mysterious.

Note that those like myself who believe that panpsychism or something in the vicinity of panpsychism is the most plausible theory of physical reality agree that stones and tables and chairs aren't subjects of experience. Certainly they think that the stuff that stones and tables and chairs are made of is in some sense intrinsically experiential in nature—whatever its other properties. But it doesn't follow from this that a stone or table or chair is itself a subject of experience, an individual subject of experience with an individual point of view looking out on the world. I think this last view is entirely foolish, and I don't know anyone who holds it. In this sense a sharp distinction between experiencing beings and experienceless beings can be (is) fully valid, when it comes to the difference between chairs and dogs, even if some version of panpsychism is true.[13]

1.2

So much for those who think that the subject of experience is a mystery because they think experience is a mystery. They're on the wrong track.

The point is worth making, but I don't think this is why Wittgenstein found the notion of the subject of experience mysterious. One question is what he meant by 'the I'. He may have simply meant the subject of experience, i.e. any subject of experience. Alternatively, he may have meant the *fully self-conscious* subject of experience, where to be fully self-conscious is not only to be able to think or be conscious of oneself, but also (as remarked in note 3) to be able to think and be

---

[12] Some self-styled naturalists avoid the problem of endorsing radical emergence by doubting or denying the existence of experience. They choose the fire over the frying pan, for this means doubting or denying the existence of the most certainly known general natural fact.

[13] My understanding is that there aren't really any persisting fundamental particles in physical reality. But if there are, then the existence of each one involves experientiality, on the panpsychist view. It therefore also involves a subject of experience (you can't have experientiality without having a subject of experience—see e.g. §9.2, p. 167. It certainly doesn't follow that there is any sense in which stones are subjects of experience. It's no more true that any composite entity made of subjects of experience is (or must be) itself a subject of experience than it is true that any composite entity made of cubes is itself (or must be) a cube.

conscious of oneself specifically *as oneself*, and hence to be able to master a first-person pronoun ('I' in English).[14]

I think Wittgenstein did simply mean the subject of experience, although he was probably thinking specifically of a human subject of experience, and hence of a fully self-conscious subject of experience. But if he thought that fully self-conscious subjects of experience were particularly mysterious, more mysterious than other subjects of experience, then I disagree again. I don't think we have any good reason to find the existence of subjects of experience mysterious, and I don't think that fully self-conscious subjects of experience are any more mysterious than any other subjects of experience. It's worth recalling again that human children become fully self-conscious at around eighteen months, before they're much good at talking. It's an early, utterly routine cognitive achievement for human beings, and it's not particularly amazing, given the resources they already have to hand at that point.[15]

It doesn't follow, from the fact that there's no reason to think that the subject of experience is mysterious, that there isn't much of interest to say about subjects of experience in general, and about fully self-conscious subjects of experience in particular, and about the notion of the self, and about the sense of self, and the use of 'I', and so on. There's a very great deal to say that is of enormous philosophical interest. The present point is only that there's no mystery, that the questions are tractable—especially if we can put in place a theoretical apparatus that helps us to make the right sorts of basic distinctions.

I think it helps enormously—to take one example—to distinguish between three ways of conceiving of the subject of experience: the *thick* conception, the *traditional inner* conception, and the *thin* conception. These three conceptions of the subject feature at various points in the essays in this book. The first conception, the widely favoured *thick* conception, takes the subject of experience to be the whole organism, e.g. the whole human being. The second conception, the (no less familiar) *traditional inner* conception of the subject of experience, takes the subject of experience to be something less than the whole human being, e.g. the brain, or some system in the brain.[16]

Both these familiar conceptions of the subject of experience build in the highly natural idea that subjects can exist when they're not experiencing anything, e.g. in dreamless sleep. The third and currently much less familiar conception of the subject of experience drops this idea. This is the *thin* conception of the subject of experience according to which *a subject of experience exists only when there is experience going on*—experience of which it is the subject. On this conception, there is no subject of experience at all in a human being, say Lucy, when she is dreamlessly asleep. When she has an experience, the existence of the subject of experience is strictly speaking wholly a matter of the existence of the patch of brain activity which is her current experience. (As before I assume the truth of physicalism.)

---

[14] It's a familiar point that this is a distinctive way of thinking of oneself. See e.g. §11.7, p. 225.

[15] I argue for this in Strawson 1986: 130–3, 'An attempt at demystification'.

[16] See §9.5, p. 171. We can include under this heading the familiar conception of the subject of experience as a 'soul', an immaterial (non-physical) being—so long as we take 'inner' in a sufficiently loose sense.

Most find the thin conception of the subject of experience highly unnatural, but this is just a matter of unfamiliarity. It's perfectly clear, it's historically important in one form or another, and it has valuable theoretical uses.

It isn't as if one has to choose between the three conceptions. All three have legitimate and important uses, and all three acknowledge the necessary truth that 'an experience is impossible without an experiencer' (Frege 1918: 27), a necessary truth that we can represent by [1] [experience → a subject of experience], taking the '→' to signify the strongest possible sort of modal connection.[17]

With [1] in place it's convenient to say that the third, thin conception of the subject differs from the first two by adding the converse of [1]. It adds to [1] the claim that the existence of a subject of experience entails the existence of experience—[2] [a subject of experience → experience]—to produce the biconditional [3] [a subject of experience ↔ experience].

The fact that [3] holds true of the thin conception of the subject raises the question whether there is really any 'real distinction' between a thin subject of experience, considered at any given time, and its experience, considered at that time (there's a real distinction between two things, in Descartes's terms, only if they can possibly exist apart). This is turn prompts the initially startling hypothesis, already mentioned in note 10, that a thin subject of experience considered at a given time might simply be identical with its experience considered at that time. I make a case for this admittedly difficult view in a paper in my book *Real Materialism and Other Essays* ('What is the relation between an experience, the subject of the experience, and the content of the experience?') and return to it briefly in this collection in Chapter 10, pp. 195–6 (prop. [17]), finding support for it in a wide range of authors—Descartes, Spinoza, Kant, Nietzsche, James, and Whitehead among others. Whitehead puts it as follows: 'the soul [or mind] is nothing else than the succession of my occasions of experience, extending from birth to the present moment' (1938: 163).

Suppose one thinks, as I do, that the thin conception of the subject of experience is important, and is perhaps the most fundamental way of conceiving of the subject. Nothing follows about the duration of the subject (or indeed its substantial composition). Descartes, for example, endorses both [1] and [2], and therefore [3], while holding both [4] that subjects of experience are non-physical entities and [5] that they can exist for ever. He can hold [5] compatibly with [2] because he famously holds that a subject of experience is always conscious (always 'thinking', in his terminology).[18] So Cartesian thin subjects may be immortal.

Locke also holds [4], at least officially (he is clearly also open to the materialist hypothesis), but he denies [2], with Descartes explicitly in mind. He suggests that the subject of experience or soul 'thinks not always; for this wants [i.e. lacks] proofs' (1689–1700: 2.1.10). He's wise to restrict himself to saying that the claim 'wants

---

[17] [1] invites, but survives, the objection that even if the existence of experience entails the existence of subjectivity, it doesn't necessarily entail the existence of something as solid or 'substance-like' as a subject of experience. I consider this point in (e.g.) §9.2, pp. 167–8.

[18] He holds this because he thinks, most strikingly, that a subject of experience is in fact wholly constituted by consciousness. See e.g. Rozemond 1998 ch. 2, Strawson 2017.

proofs', because it's an unsettled empirical question whether anything (e.g. dreamless sleep) ever really interrupts consciousness in an undamaged living human being. If I had to bet, I'd bet that there is always some form of a relatively high-level form of consciousness going on in a normal human being, from the first mental quickening in the womb until death, quite independently of whether or not any kind of panpsychism is true. And if this were shown to be so, then a Lockean thin subject would last a lifetime.[19]

Many think that we're continuously conscious throughout each waking day but entirely lose consciousness at some point each night—in dreamless sleep. If they're right, then human thin subjects standardly only last a day. Another proposal is that the human process of consciousness is constantly 'refreshed' throughout the day, in the way in which a computer screen is refreshed, although it's experienced (at least by most people—but see e.g. §2.9 and §3.19 below) as continuous. In that case human thin subjects only last as long as the periods of continuous consciousness. How long are these? It's a question of fact, and there are various possibilities—perhaps a couple of seconds, perhaps there are forty a second... and so on. It's not important.

These proposals about the duration of thin subjects are straightforwardly metaphysical; they're completely independent of any phenomenological claims about duration. Considered phenomenologically, one's experience can seem perfectly continuous even if it is in fact metaphysically gappy. So too, it can seem gappy when phenomenologically considered even if it is in fact perfectly continuous metaphysically. It's striking that William James introduced the expression 'the stream of consciousness' to describe the phenomenological character of consciousness, even as he favoured the metaphysical view that consciousness comes in 'pulses'.

I suspect that many people will find the thin conception of the subject uncomfortable, as remarked, and think it theoretically unhelpful. They may prefer a very different conception of the subject of experience, defended by Barry Dainton, according to which a subject is most fundamentally a potentiality for consciousness which need not ever actually be conscious in order to count as a subject.[20] (Obviously this view preserves the standard assumption that a subject can exist when it is not experiencing anything.) Here I will just reiterate my conviction that the thin conception of the subject is theoretically important—indeed indispensable. I hope that the papers in this book will be found to lend some support to this view.

1.3

When Wittgenstein said that 'the I' is deeply mysterious he said it for the wrong reason. He was tied up in Schopenhauer's 'world-knot'. 'World-knot'—'*Weltknoten*'—is often taken to be Schopenhauer's term for the 'mind–body problem' understood more or less as it is today,[21] but this seems to be a mistake. As far as I can see, Schopenhauer's difficulty lies in his view that the subject of experience who truly says 'the world is my representation', and who is in that sense the *generator* of the world

---

[19] Locke appears to be a 'mortalist'; someone who believes that human consciousness doesn't continue uninterrupted after bodily death.

[20] See e.g. Dainton 2008.   [21] See e.g. Feigl 1963, Griffin 1998.

encountered in experience, is identical with the subject who is encountered in that world representation:

the identity of the willing subject with the cognizing subject, by means of which (and indeed necessarily), the word 'I' includes and indicates both, is the knot of the world [*Weltknoten*] and therefore inexplicable.[22]

Insofar as one is the will-constituted generator of the spatiotemporal world in which one experiences oneself as living, the spatiotemporal world which is in fact only a world of representations, one isn't oneself a representation and can't be located in that world in the way one ordinarily experiences oneself to be.[23]

Schopenhauer goes on to say that 'anyone who has clearly realized the inexplicability of this identity will agree with me in proclaiming it to be the ultimate miracle' (§42). But there's no reason to think that something inexplicable is miraculous. It's almost as if Schopenhauer knows that this particular feature of his transcendental idealist metaphysics is incoherent (there are other forms of transcendental idealism that do not fall into this difficulty).

In any case Wittgenstein was wrong. There's nothing metaphysically puzzling about the existence of the 'I' or the subject of experience, or the first-person perspective or indeed the phenomenon of subjectivity. There's nothing metaphysically puzzling about the fact that there are billions—trillions—of subjects of experience or first-person perspectives.

So why have I opened this Introduction with Wittgenstein's remark? Well, it has a good ring to it, and there's also one crucial and familiar respect in which it's true, at least in the human case. We are in fundamental respects self-mysterious—and correspondingly self-ignorant. 'We do not deal much in fact when we are contemplating ourselves', as Mark Twain noted (1902: 341). Many have made the point, including Nietzsche in a passage quoted in §6.2 below (p. 108): 'If the hare has seven skins, the human being can shed seven times seventy skins and still not be able to say: "This is really you, this is no longer outer shell"' (1874: 129).

This isn't just a matter of the so-called 'Freudian unconscious', important though that is. The non-Freudian unconscious, the so-called 'adaptive unconscious' discussed by Timothy Wilson in his book *Strangers to Ourselves*, is no less important.[24] As for our attempts to acquire self-knowledge—they're usually remarkably ill-judged and remarkably unsuccessful. Menander makes one point—'"Know thyself" is a good saying, but not in all situations. In many it is better to say "know others".' One might add that it is also better, in many situations, to know what others think of one.

Goethe is a clumsy aphorist, but he makes another useful point:

---

[22] Schopenhauer 1847 §42. As far as I know, Schopenhauer's only other use of the word '*Weltknoten*' occurs in a remark about sexual intercourse: 'the act of generation is the world-knot for it states "the will to live has affirmed itself anew"' (1851: 2.316–17).

[23] '"The world is my representation": this holds true for every living, cognitive being' (Schopenhauer 1819–59 §1); 'everything that there is for cognition, i.e. the whole world, is only an object in relation to the subject, [only] an experience of an experiencer [*Anschauung eines Anschauenden*], in a word [only] representation' (ibid.).

[24] Wilson 2002. See also Kahneman 2011 and Cassam 2014.

if we turn to that significant utterance *know thyself* we must not explain it in an ascetic sense. It is not at all the self-knowledge of our modern hypochondriacs, humorists, and self-tormentors. It simply means: pay some attention to yourself, take note of yourself, so that you may know how you come to stand towards those like you and towards the world. This involves no psychological torture; every capable person knows and feels what it means.   (1809–32: §442)

Iris Murdoch makes another, in the course of questioning the idea that self-knowledge might be liberating, and considering the 'fantasy mechanism' that, on her view, largely controls our ethical-emotional apprehension of the world:

'self-knowledge', in the sense of a minute understanding of one's own machinery, seems to me, except at a fairly simple level, usually a delusion. . . . It is an attachment to what lies outside the fantasy mechanism, and not a scrutiny of the mechanism itself, that liberates. Close scrutiny of the mechanism often merely strengthens its power.   (1969: 67)

It may be that the best one can do, in the pursuit of some deeper form of self-knowledge, is simply to note down, over a few months, what one most truly likes (or hates—but I think that what one likes is more revealing).

Some think that self-knowledge is a necessary condition of authenticity. In fact it's not clear that it has anything to do with authenticity. Perhaps the best way to achieve the good of authenticity that self-knowledge is supposed to bring is to 'wing it'—in spite of the real dangers of certain forms of self-ignorance. When Simon Gray says, late in life, that 'the truth is that I don't really know even quite elementary things about myself, my wants and needs, until I've written them down or spoken them' (2008: 114), I think he's doing OK.

Chapters 6 and 7 expand on these points in various ways and consider some of the consequences. It isn't, however, their principal subject, and after we have put all the marvellous illustrations of our astonishing self-ignorance in place we need to rebalance: we need to allow that a lot of the time we do know what we feel, and why we're doing what we're doing.

1.4

I'll conclude with brief descriptions of the chapters that follow. First, though, let me add a comment on what I take to be the principal misunderstanding of what I've written about the self or subject of experience over the years. I think the misunderstanding has arisen from one of the conditions I impose—for purposes of argument—on something's qualifying as a self or subject. In many places I proceed on the assumption that if something is to qualify as a self or subject it must qualify as a *thing or object or substance* or '*TOS*' in any metaphysics that admits the existence of TOSs at all. (The substitution of 'TOS' for 'thing', 'object', or 'substance' is an attempt to tune out some of the many different and potentially confusing theoretical associations these words have in everyday speech and philosophy.)

In the first instance I introduce the TOS condition on being a self or subject of experience in undiluted form. This is because it seems a good way to give clear structure to the initial discussion. It's also traditionally accepted as a condition on being a subject of experience. In due course, however, I weaken it. I propose that for something to be a subject of experience is for it to have *at least as good* a claim to be considered as a TOS as anything else. This fits with the qualification of the condition in the previous paragraph, according to which a subject of experience must qualify as a TOS *in any metaphysics that recognizes the existence of TOSs at all.*

I then do some further loosening work. First, I accept the increasingly widely held view that all concretely existing TOSs are best thought of as processes, the view that all matter is well thought of as 'process-stuff ' (relative to whatever conception of time is correct). Then (this may well be thought to be a more radical move) I reject the view that there is a fundamental ontological categorial distinction between the concrete being of a TOS, considered at any time, and the concrete being of its propertiedness, considered at that time.[25] Finally, I propose that for something *x* to be a TOS is, most fundamentally, just for *x* to be a unity of a certain kind, a dynamic unity, in Leibnizian phrase, a 'strong activity-unity'; however long or short its duration. On this view, it doesn't matter how *x* classifies according to the traditional object/process/property/quality/state/event cluster of metaphysical distinctions. It doesn't matter so long as it can be seen to qualify as a strong activity-unity in the required manner. Unity alone—activity-unity—is the key notion, and the word 'activity' carries no implication of intentional agency. It's an appropriate term not only when *x* is conceived of as initiating change, but also (departing from Leibniz) when *x*'s essentially active process-being has the particular character it has because of something we would naturally classify as its being passively affected.

I take it that Berkeley's characterization of the self as a 'thinking, active principle' (1713: 116) or as 'purus actus' (1707–8 §701) qualifies as a conception of the self as a TOS; so does Fichte's overtly processual conception of the I or self or subject as a *Tathandlung*—a 'deed-activity'. Kant makes a similar point, in his own way, I believe, when he sets out the sense in which it is correct to think of the subject of experience as a single thing and as a substance (a strong activity-unity), even as he insists on the validity of the theoretical perspective from which it is 'quite impossible to determine the manner in which I [i.e. the subject or soul] exist, whether it be as substance [object] or as accident [property]', and equally impossible to know whether it is not in fact multiple rather than single in its ultimate substantial nature (1781–7: B420, A353, A363).

On these matters, as so often, the key notions of metaphysics find their clearest and most vivid expression in the writers of the past. This is why most of the best writing on metaphysics today takes place in the domain of the history of philosophy.

1.5

Now for the chapters that follow. Chapter 2, 'The self', was written at a time when many analytic philosophers were inclined to deny that the expression 'the self'

---

[25] See Strawson 2009: 304–17. I think that Descartes, Spinoza, Kant, Nietzsche, Russell, Whitehead, Ramsey, and many others agree. The word 'property' is fine and valuable for many philosophical purposes, but there are areas of philosophical enquiry in which it contains almost irresistible incentives to metaphysical misunderstanding. One particularly poignant problem is that the fact that the word works fine in many philosophical contexts leads many to think that it must be fine in all contexts.

referred to anything at all. Others objected that its meaning was too unclear for it to be used in worthwhile philosophical discussion (see e.g. §3.1, p. 41). A third group thought that its only possible legitimate use was its use to refer to the human being considered as a whole. I reject these three views, and make a proposal about how to endow 'the self' with sufficiently clear meaning without simply taking it to refer to the whole human being: begin with the fundamental phenomenology of the self, the experience of there being such a thing as the self distinct from the whole human being, before going on to the metaphysics of the self. I have a shot at the phenomenological project and then proceed to the metaphysical investigation—questions about the existence and nature of the self.

I pursue this approach further in Chapter 3, 'The Self and the Sesmet', adjusting the proposals made in the first essay in response to a set of criticisms published in the *Journal of Consciousness Studies* in 1999 and reprinted in the same year in *Models of the Self*, edited by Shaun Gallagher and Jonathan Shear. I end with a straightforwardly metaphysical proposal: anything that is to count as a self must be a subject of experience that is a single mental thing' (hence the acronym 'sesmet') in a sense that requires a careful—and from some points of view rather liberal—specification of what is meant by 'thing': a specification that allows (for example) that all things are equally well thought of as processes, and (as above) that Fichte's characterization of the self as a *Tathandlung* or 'deed-activity' is a characterization of the self as a thing in the required sense.

The suggestion that a self is a 'single mental thing' sounds as if it supports the traditional picture of the self as an indivisible immaterial soul. It does, but in fact—I suggest—there aren't any such things as immaterial souls. I argue that although selves as we know them, human selves, are correctly said to be 'single mental things', they are nonetheless wholly physical entities, straightforward spatiotemporal parts of human beings considered as a whole. I also consider the suggestion that they are best thought of as relatively short-lived things.

'Against Corporism', Chapter 4, was written for a conference on the work of my father P. F. Strawson held in Prague in 2009. It considers his well-known advocacy of the 'primitiveness of the concept of a person', and questions his rejection of the claim that there are two distinct referring uses of 'I'. One of Strawson's aims was to correct a tendency to overspiritualize the subject of experience; I suggest that some now overcorporealize it, and that a further balancing correction is needed. Many philosophers also favour a picture of human awareness according to which it's always tightly locked on to external objects and events, effectively self-invisible, unaware of itself as such. I challenge this picture by considering some of the extraordinarily pervasive respects in which awareness of one's own mental life, apprehended specifically as such, is itself a more or less constant feature of one's experience.

In Chapter 5, 'I Have no Future', I argue that human beings—living creatures in general—are not entities of such a kind that they can be rightly said to be deprived of anything by death. More specifically: they can't be rightly said to be deprived of anything if they don't live as long as they would have lived if they hadn't died in an 'untimely' way. Does it follow that we're not entities of such a kind that death is bad for us? I think it may follow (I'm not sure); I don't, however, think that appreciation of the point can dissolve fear of death. I also consider the question whether death might be bad for potentially immortal creatures—creatures capable of living for ever, so long as no fatal accident befalls them—even if there were a sense in which it isn't bad for essentially mortal creatures.

Many say that human beings are naturally 'narrative'. The idea is that we naturally conceive of ourselves and our lives in a narrative way and in some manner live in and through this self-conception. Many add that we ought to be like this—that this sort of 'narrativity' is necessary if one is to live a good life. I disagree, and Chapters 6 and 7, '"We live…beyond any tale that we happen to enact"', and 'The Unstoried Life', develop the line of resistance to the narrativist view that was first sketched in §8 of Chapter 2 (p. 31) and subsequently elaborated in 'Against Narrativity' (2004) and 'Episodic Ethics' (2007). The heart of the objection to the narrative approach is simply an insistence on human difference, interpersonal difference, in the face of all those who claim that there is really only one good way for us to live. Among those whom I call on in my defence of the anti-narrativist position are Emerson, Proust, and Virginia Woolf.

Chapter 8, 'Self-intimation', takes sides in an old debate. It seems clear—in fact trivially true—that all genuine or full-on conscious awareness essentially involves awareness of that awareness. This raises the question whether conscious awareness always somehow involves two distinct mental states, one of which is directed at the other, or whether it standardly only involves one state, a state which is in some manner 'self-intimating' or 'self-luminous'. Aristotle backs the second view—self-intimation—as I do, along with many philosophers in the Indian philosophical tradition, the Phenomenological tradition, and indeed the mainstream Western tradition. There remains a puzzling question about how such self-intimation is possible, about what it is, exactly—about how it may be further characterized, which I try to address in this paper.

In the magnificent Paralogisms section of the *Critique of Pure Reason*, Immanuel Kant notes that [i] a thought is a unity in some absolute sense. He also grants that [ii] the 'logical unity of every thought' is inseparable from the 'absolute…logical unity of the subject' of that thought (A356). Nevertheless he denies—quite rightly on his own principles—that one can move from knowledge of the truth of [i] and [ii] to the conclusion that [iii] the subject of a thought is (knowably) some sort of true metaphysical unity. In Chapter 9, 'Fundamental Singleness: How to Turn the Second Paralogism into a Valid Argument', I consider how to adjust [i] and [ii] so as to be able to get to [iii], and argue that it can be done; not, again, within the Kantian frame, but nevertheless on the basis of considerations that are in effect articulated by Kant, as when he acknowledges 'that…the I in every act of thought is *one*, and cannot be resolved into a plurality of subjects, … is something that lies already in the concept of thought, and is therefore an analytic proposition' (B407).

'The eye can never see itself directly. So too the I of thought can never know itself directly—it can never apprehend itself immediately as it is in the present moment of awareness, never know itself as it is precisely in that very moment of knowing. The act of knowing forces it to become an object of inspection for itself in such a way that it can no longer be truly immediately aware of itself.' I challenge this ancient view directly in Chapter 10, 'Radical Self-awareness'. I argue first (relatively uncontroversially) that there's a fundamental sense in which a subject is, when conscious, necessarily aware of itself as it is in the present moment of awareness, at least in the sense of being aware of certain of its (experiential) properties, simply because such self-awareness is a precondition of any awareness at all. More controversially, I argue that the subject can under certain special conditions be immediately aware of itself as subject, aware of itself as subject grasped specifically as such and in a fully self-conscious express or explicit manner.

Chapter 11, 'I and *I*: Immunity to Error Through Misidentification of the Subject', picks up a line of thought that can be traced from Wittgenstein's *Blue and Brown Books* (1933–5), to Strawson's *Individuals* (1959) and *The Bounds of Sense* (1966), to Shoemaker's 'Self-Reference and Self-Awareness' (1968), Anscombe's 'The First Person' (1975), and Evans's *The Varieties of Reference* (1982), and on from there. I argue that all genuine uses of 'I' in language or of the concept I in thought are indeed absolutely immune to error through misidentification of their referent.[26] I suggest that this is so even though 'I' and I don't necessarily always refer to the same thing, or kind of thing, even in the speech or thought of a single person (an idea put forward in Chapter 3). This is one of a suite of further theses about 'I' and I defended in the chapter and listed in its opening section.

The last three chapters are historical. They attempt to correct a number of long-standing errors about Locke's and Hume's conceptions of personal identity. Objections to Locke's account of personal identity formulated by Butler (1736) and Reid (1785) have been widely endorsed and have structured much of the discussion of Locke's view. Chapter 12, '"The secrets of all hearts": Locke on Personal Identity', argues that Butler's and Reid's objections not only fail completely as objections to Locke but also constitute vivid illustrations of his fundamental point.

Chapter 13, '"When I enter most intimately into what I call *myself*": Hume on the Mind', finds three main errors in the standard view of Hume's account of the mind in section 1.4.6 of the *Treatise*, 'Of personal identity'. First, Hume doesn't actually endorse the 'bundle theory' that he so famously expounds in 1.4.6, according to which the mind or self is just a 'bundle' of perceptions, although he holds that it is the only clear conception of the mind available, and is to that extent theoretically defensible. Nor, secondly, does he deny the existence of subjects of experience, endorsing a 'no ownership' view of experiences. Nor, thirdly, does he claim that the subject of experience isn't encountered in experience.

In the appendix to his *Treatise* Hume notoriously repudiates the view that the bundle theory of personal identity is theoretically defensible—acceptable as a positively contentful account of the mind in specifically philosophical contexts. There have been many different attempts to explain this move on Hume's part. In Chapter 14, '"All my hopes vanish": Hume on the Mind', I propose that the best explanation starts out from Hume's own account of what the bundle theory fails to provide, which is very clear, and which rules out most of the attempted explanations. According to Hume, the trouble is that his official theory of ideas delivers an account of the 'true idea of the mind' (the bundle theory) that is incompatible with his overall theory of what the mind is.[27]

---

[26] I, for names of concepts.

[27] Thanks to Chris Janaway for his advice on Schopenhauer.

2

'The Self'

I know that I exist; the question is, what is this 'I' that I know?

(Descartes 1641: 18)

The soul, as far as we can conceive it, is nothing but a system or train of different perceptions.

(Hume 1740: Abs§28/657)

What was I before I came to self-consciousness? ... *I* did not exist at all, for I was not an I. The I exists only insofar as it is conscious of itself.... *The self posits itself*, and by virtue of this mere self-assertion it *exists*.

(Fichte 1794–5)

The 'Self'..., when carefully examined, is found to consist mainly of... peculiar motions in the head or between the head and throat.

(James 1890: 1.301)

The ego continuously constitutes itself as existing.

(Husserl 1931: 66)

Any fixed categorization of the Self is a big goof.

(Ginsberg 1963)

The self which is reflexively referred to is synthesized in that very act of reflexive self-reference.

(Nozick 1981: 91)

The self... is a mythical entity.... It is a philosophical muddle to allow the space which differentiates 'my self' from 'myself' to generate the illusion of a mysterious entity distinct from... the human being.

(Kenny 1988: 3–4)

A self... is... an abstraction..., [a] Center of Narrative Gravity.

(Dennett 1991: 426–7)

My body is an object all right, but my self jolly well is not!

(Farrell 1996: 519)

2.1 Introduction

The substantival phrase 'the self' is very unnatural in most speech contexts in most languages, and some conclude from this that it's an illusion to think that there is such a thing as the self, an illusion that arises from nothing more than an improper use of language. This, however, is implausible. People are not that stupid. The problem of the self doesn't arise from an unnatural use of language which arises from nowhere. On the contrary: use of a phrase like 'the self' arises from a prior and independent sense that there is such a thing as the self. The phrase may be unusual in ordinary speech; it may have no obvious direct translation in many languages. Nevertheless all languages have words which lend themselves naturally to playing the role that 'the self' plays in English, however murky that role may be. The phrase certainly means something to most people. It has a natural use in religious, philosophical, and psychological contexts of discussion, which are very natural contexts for human beings. I think there is a real philosophical problem about the existence and nature of the self, not just a relatively uninteresting problem about why we think there's a problem. It is too quick to say that a 'grammatical error . . . is the essence of the theory of the self', or that '"the self" is a piece of philosopher's nonsense consisting in a misunderstanding of the reflexive pronoun' (Kenny 1988: 4).

The first task is to get the problem into focus. I will recommend one approach, first in outline, then in slightly more detail. I will model the problem of the self, rather than attempting to model the self. I think the problem requires a straightforwardly metaphysical approach; but I also think that metaphysics must wait on phenomenology, in a sense I will explain. Most recent discussion of the problem by analytic philosophers has started from work in philosophical logic (in the large sense of the term).[1] This work may have a contribution to make, but a more phenomenological starting point is needed.

I will use the expression 'the self' freely—I am already doing so—but I don't want to exclude in advance the view that there is no such thing as the self, and the expression will often function as a loose name for what one might equally well call 'the self-phenomenon', i.e. all those undoubtedly real phenomena of experience that lead us to think and talk in terms of something called the self, whether or not there is such a thing.

2.2 The Problem of the Self

Many people believe in the self, conceived of as a distinct thing, and they're not clear what it is. They believe that there is such a thing as the self because they have a distinct *sense* of, or experience as of, the self, and they take it that it is not delusory. This sense of the self is the source in experience of the philosophical problem of the self. So the first thing to do is to track the problem to this source in order to get a better idea of what it is. The first question to ask is the *phenomenological question*:

What is the nature of the sense of the self?

---

[1] See for example the essays collected in Cassam 1994.

But this, in the first instance, is best taken as a question explicitly about human beings: as the *local phenomenological question*

(I)   What is the nature of the human sense of the self?

Whatever the answer to (I) is, it raises the *general phenomenological question*

(II)   Are there other possibilities, when it comes to a sense of the self? (Can we describe the minimal case of genuine possession of a sense of the self?)

The answers to (I) and (II) raise the *conditions question*

(III)   What are the grounds or preconditions of possession of a sense of the self?

and this question raises a battery of further questions. But progress is being made, at least potentially. For if one can produce satisfactory answers to (I), (II), and (III) one will be in a good position to raise and answer the *factual question*, the fundamental and straightforwardly metaphysical question

(IV)   Is there (could there be) such a thing as the self?

I think one has to answer (I) and (II), and probably (III), in order to answer (IV) properly.

2.3 The Local Question: Cognitive Phenomenology

I will now go through the plan in more detail, and sketch how I think some of the answers should go. The first question is the local phenomenological question: What is the nature of the ordinary human sense of the self? This raises a prior question: Can one generalize about the human sense of the self? I think the answer is Yes: when it comes to the philosophical problem of the self, the aspects of the sense of the self that are of principal concern are very basic. They are situated below any level of plausible cultural variation.[2] They are conceptual rather than affective: it is the *cognitive phenomenology* of the sense of the self that is fundamentally in question, i.e. the conceptual structure of the sense of the self, the structure of the sense of the self considered (as far as possible) independently of any emotional aspects that it may have. The cognitive phenomenology of the self is bound up with the affective phenomenology of the self in complicated ways, but emotional or affective aspects of the sense of the self will be of concern (e.g. in §2.8) only insofar as emotions shape or weight conceptions.

What, then, is the ordinary, human sense of the self, insofar as we can generalize about it? I propose that it is (at least) the sense that people have of themselves as being, specifically, a mental presence; a mental someone; a single mental thing that is a conscious subject of experience, that has a certain character or personality, and that is in some sense distinct from all its particular experiences, thoughts, and so on, and indeed from all other things. It is crucial that it is thought of as a distinctively mental

---

[2] Work in evolutionary psychology suggests that doubts about the possibility of generalization that derive from considerations of cultural difference can be easily dealt with. See e.g. Barkow, Cosmides, and Tooby 1992.

phenomenon, and I will usually speak of the 'mental self' from now on (the qualifier 'mental' may be understood wherever omitted).

Is the sense of the mental self, as so far described, really something ordinary? I believe so. It comes to every normal human being, in some form, in childhood.[3] The early realization of the fact that one's thoughts are unobservable by others, the experience of the profound sense in which one is alone in one's head—these are among the very deepest facts about the character of human life, and they found the sense of the mental self. It is perhaps most often vivid when one is alone and thinking, but it can be equally vivid in a room full of people. It connects with a feeling that nearly everyone has had intensely at some time—the feeling that one's body is just a vehicle or vessel for the mental thing that is what one really or most essentially is. I believe that the primary or fundamental way in which we conceive of ourselves is as a distinct mental thing—sex addicts, athletes, and supermodels included. Analytic philosophers may find it hard to see—remember—this, given their training, and it is easy to lose sight of the point in derision.

This not to deny that we also naturally conceive of ourselves as mental-and-non-mental things, human beings considered as a whole. We do. Nor is it to claim that the sense of the mental self incorporates some sort of belief in an immaterial soul, or in life after bodily death. It doesn't. Philosophical materialists who believe, as I do, that we are wholly physical beings, and that the theory of evolution by natural selection is true, and that animal consciousness of the sort with which we are familiar evolved by purely physical natural processes on a planet where no such consciousness previously existed, have this sense of the mental self as strongly as anyone else.

In more detail: I propose that the mental self is ordinarily conceived or experienced as:

(1) a *thing* or *entity*, in some robust sense
(2) a *mental* entity, in some sense
(3, 4) a *single* entity that is single both (3) *synchronically* considered and (4) *diachronically* considered
(5) *ontically distinct* from all other things
(6) a *subject of experience*, a conscious feeler and thinker
(7) an *agent*
(8) an entity that has a certain character or *personality*.

This is an intentionally strong proposal, and it may be thought to be too strong in various ways. Most of (1)–(8) can be contested, and the list may well contain redundancy, but it provides a framework for discussion. There are various entailment relations between the eight elements that need to be exposed; (1)–(6) are closely linked. (1) also raises the general question 'What is a thing?'—a question that will be important when the fundamental factual question ('Is there such a thing as the self?') is considered.

---

[3] It certainly does not require the special kind of experience recorded by Nagel (1986: 54–7) or Richard Hughes (1929, ch. 6), for this is by no means universal.

I don't think the list omits anything essential to a genuine sense of the mental self, even if it includes some things that are not essential. I will assume that this is true for the purposes of this paper: a primitive framework can show the structure of a problem even if it is not complete. It can be the best way to proceed even if the problem resists regimentation in terms of necessary and sufficient conditions. If an omission were identified, it could simply be added to the existing framework.

(2) is the only one of the eight properties that is not attributed as naturally to the embodied human being as to the putative mental self, and it may be suggested that the sense of the mental self is just a delusory projection from the experience of embodiment. Perhaps the so-called self is just the human being incompletely grasped and illegitimately spiritualized. This is a popular view in analytic philosophy, but I am not yet in a position to assess it.[4] Some argue from the fact that use of the word 'I' to refer to the supposed mental self does not ordinarily stand out as distinct from use of the word 'I' to refer to the human being considered as a whole to the conclusion that we have no good reason to distinguish them. To this it may be replied that appeal to facts about public language use is often irrelevant to facts about meaning and reference, and is nowhere more spectacularly inappropriate than in the case of the problem of the self.[5]

2.4 Phenomenology and Metaphysics

Equipped with an answer to the local question, one can go on to raise the general question: 'Are there other possibilities, so far as a sense of the mental self is concerned?' Given the assumption that the list of eight properties doesn't omit anything essential to a genuine sense of the self, this amounts to the question whether one can dispense with any of (1)–(8) while still having something that qualifies as a genuine sense of the mental self. It enquires, among other things, after the minimal case of a sense of the mental self. The answer is partly a matter of terminological decision, but for the most part not.

How might the answer go? I don't yet know, but if I had to commit myself it would be as follows: (4) and (8) are not necessary to a sense of the mental self, even in the human case (see §§2.8–9). (6) is secure, but a serious doubt can be raised about (7). (2) and (5) need careful qualification if they are to survive. (1) and (3) can be challenged but effectively defended.

—Objection: surely the phenomenological investigation loses something crucial at this point? It's no longer rooted in the human case, so it's no longer independent of specifically philosophical theories about what selves actually are or can be: such theories are bound to be part of what governs our judgements about whether some thinned down sense of the mental self can count as a genuine sense of the mental self once we go beyond the human case.

I believe that a detailed attempt to answer the general phenomenological question will show that this is not so: our basic judgements about whether anything less than

---

[4] For older versions of the view, see e.g. James (1890, ch. 10). See also Bermudéz et al. (1995).
[5] This point is developed in Chapter 4.

(1)–(8) can count as a genuine sense of the mental self can remain comfortably independent, in any respect that matters, of metaphysical philosophical theorizing about the nature of the self. In fact I think they can be sufficiently supported by reference to real but unusual human cases.

Suppose phenomenology is substantially independent of metaphysics. What about the other way round? Here I think there is a fundamental dependence: metaphysical investigation of the nature of the self is subordinate to phenomenological investigation of the sense of the self. There is a strong phenomenological constraint on any acceptable answer to the metaphysical question which can be expressed by saying that the factual question 'Is there such a thing as the mental self?' is equivalent to the question 'Is any (genuine) sense of the self an accurate representation of anything that exists?'[6]

This equivalence claim can be split in two:

(E1)   If there is such a thing as the self, then some sense of the mental self is an accurate representation of something that exists

(E2)   If some sense of the mental self is an accurate representation of something that exists, then there is such a thing as the self.

(E1) and (E2) may seem trivial, but both may be challenged. The first as follows:

(C1)   There is really no very good reason to think that if the self exists, then there is some sense of the mental self that is an accurate (if partial) representation of its nature. Perhaps the mental self, as it is in itself, is ineffable, quite unlike any experience of it.

(C1)   is Kantian in spirit. The second rejection is a response made when some particular sense of the mental self has been characterized:

(C2)   This sense of the mental self you have characterized is indeed an accurate representation of something that exists, but the thing of which it is an accurate representation does not qualify for the title 'the mental self' because it does not have feature F (e.g. it is not an immaterial, ± immortal, ± whatever, substance).[7]

The force of (E1) and (E2) is revealed precisely by the fact that they reject proposals like (C1) and (C2). In this way they impose a substantial constraint on metaphysical theorizing about the self. According to (E1), nothing can count as a mental self unless it possesses all the properties attributed to the self by some genuine sense of the mental self, whatever other properties it may possess. It rules out metaphysical claims about the self that fail to respect limits on the concept of the self revealed by the phenomenological investigation. It states a necessary condition on qualifying for the title of self. (E2), by contrast, rules that nothing can fail to count as a mental self if it possesses all the properties that feature in some sense of the mental self, whatever other properties it may possess or lack. It states a sufficient condition on qualifying for the title of self—it lays it down that there is no further test to pass.

---

[6] I take it that a representation R of a thing X is accurate if (and only if) X really has the properties R represents it as having. R need not be complete to be accurate.

[7] For a revision of this scheme see Strawson 2009: 55–6.

To make the equivalence claim, then, is to say that one must have well developed answers to phenomenological questions about the experience of the self before one can begin to answer metaphysical questions about the self. The equivalence claim excludes two forms of metaphysical excess—extravagance and miserliness. Extravagance is blocked by showing that we cannot answer the question 'Is there such a thing as the self?' by saying 'Yes there is (or may be), but we have (or may have) no understanding of its ultimate nature.' Miserliness is blocked by showing that we cannot answer by saying 'Well, there is *something* of which the sense of the self is an accurate representation, but it does not follow that there is any such thing as the self.'

If the answers to the phenomenological questions go well, we should be left with a pretty good idea of what we are asking when we ask the factual, metaphysical question 'Is there such a thing as the self?' Any metaphysical speculations that are not properly subordinate to phenomenology can be cheerfully 'commit[ted] . . . to the flames'.[8]

2.5 Materialism

In §§2.6–9 I will give examples of more detailed work within this scheme. Before that I must give a brief account of the sense in which I am a materialist.

Materialists believe that every thing and event in the universe is a wholly physical phenomenon. If they are even remotely realistic in their materialism they admit that conscious experience is part of reality. It follows that they must grant that conscious experience is a wholly physical phenomenon. They must grant that it is wholly physical specifically in its mental, experiential properties. They must grant that the qualitative character of the taste of bread, considered just as such and independently of anything else that exists, is as much a physical phenomenon as the phenomenon of an electric current flowing in a wire.

It follows that materialists express themselves very badly when they talk about the mental and the physical as if they were opposed categories. For, on their own view, this is exactly like saying that cows and animals are opposed categories. For all mental phenomena, including conscious-experience phenomena *considered specifically as such*, just are physical phenomena, according to them; just as all cows are animals.

So what are materialists doing when they talk as if the mental and the physical were different things? What they presumably mean to do is to distinguish, within the realm of the physical, which is the only realm there is, according to them, between the mental and the non-mental, and, more specifically, between the experiential and the non-experiential; to distinguish, that is, between mental (or experiential) aspects of the physical, and non-mental (or non-experiential) aspects of the physical.[9] This is

---

[8] Hume 1748: 12.34/165. I should say that I'm rejecting, and not claiming to refute, more unbridled approaches to the metaphysics of the self.

[9] I need to make the distinction between mental and experiential phenomena, because although all experiential phenomena are mental phenomena, not all mental phenomena are experiential phenomena, according to ordinary usage. Beliefs, likes and dislikes, and so on are mental phenomena, although they have no experiential character.

the difference that is really in question when it comes to the 'mind–body' problem, and materialists who persist in talking in terms of the difference between the mental and the physical perpetuate the terms of the dualism they reject in a way that is inconsistent with their own view.[10]

Let me rephrase this. When I say that the mental and the experiential are wholly physical I mean something completely different from what some materialists have apparently meant by saying things like 'experience is really just neurons firing'. I don't mean that all that is really going on, in the case of conscious experience, is something that can be discerned and described by current physics, or by any non-revolutionary extension of current physics. Such a view amounts to some kind of radical eliminativism, and is certainly false. My claim is quite different. It is that it is the experiential considered specifically as such—the portion of reality we have to do with when we consider experiences specifically and solely in respect of the experiential character they have for those who have them as they have them—that 'just is' physical. No one who disagrees with this claim is a serious and realistic materialist.[11]

A further comment is needed. As remarked, thoroughgoing materialists hold that all mental phenomena, including all experiential phenomena, are entirely physical phenomena. But triviality threatens when things are put this way. For now even absolute idealism (in one version, the view that only experiential phenomena exist) can claim to be a materialist position.

This possibility can be excluded by ruling that anything deserving the name 'materialism' must hold that there are non-mental and non-experiential phenomena as well as mental or experiential phenomena. One can also go further, and take materialism to incorporate what one might call 'the principle of the necessary involvement of the mental with the non-mental'. Most realistic materialists take it that the existence of each particular mental or experiential phenomenon involves the existence of some particular non-mental, non-experiential phenomenon. More strongly expressed: each particular mental or experiential phenomenon has, essentially, in addition to its mental or experiential character or mode of being, a non-mental character or mode of being.

One might call this 'mental-and-non-mental' materialism. When I talk of materialism in this chapter, I will take it to involve this view. (I have abandoned this restriction on materialism since writing this paper. I now take it that materialism is compatible with panpsychism. See e.g. Strawson 2006, 2016.) More needs to be said: given that we have knowledge of central aspects of the fundamental reality of the mental just in having experience in the way we do, we need to ask whether it is possible to give some basic positive characterization of the non-mental, perhaps in terms of properties like time, length, position, mass, electric charge, spin, 'colour', and 'flavour' in the quantum theory sense. But this is enough to make it clear that the

---

[10] There is tremendous resistance to abandoning the old mental/physical terminology in favour of the mental/non-mental, experiential/non-experiential terminology, even though the alternative is very clear and is exactly what is required. Cf. Searle (1992: 54), also A. Campbell (1994).

[11] Hurlburt et al. discuss a superficially 'zombie'-like subject who has 'no reportable inner experience' (1994: 391–2), but it becomes clear that he does have experience in the current sense.

present question about whether the self exists in the human case is not a question about whether we might possibly be 'Cartesian egos' or immaterial substances. It is the question whether the mental self exists given that we are ordinarily embodied, entirely physical living human beings.

2.6 Singularity

I have sketched how I think answers to the phenomenological questions should go, described the constraint that phenomenology places on metaphysics, and endorsed a form of materialism that is unequivocally realist about conscious experience. I will now give samples of more detailed work on the phenomenological questions.

The proposal for consideration is that the mental self is conceived or experienced as (1) a *thing*, in some sense, (2) a *mental* thing, a *single* thing that is single both (3) *synchronically* considered and (4) *diachronically* considered, (5) a thing that is *ontically distinct* from all other things, (6) a *subject of experience* and (7) an *agent* and (8) something that has a certain *personality*. In this section I will discuss (3) and (4) in the framework of the *local* phenomenological question, after very brief comments on (1) and (2). In §§2.7–9 I will discuss (4) and (8) in the framework of the *general* phenomenological question. In §2.10 I will say something about (5).

Thinghood and mentality: What about the claim (1) that the self is conceived of as a thing? In a way, this is the least clear of the eight claims, but the general idea is this: the self isn't thought of as merely a state or property of something else, or as an event, or process, or series of events. To that extent, there is nothing else for it to seem to be, other than a thing. It's not thought of as being a thing in the way that a stone or a cat is. But it is thought of as a thing of some kind. In particular, it is thought of as something that has the causal character of a thing; something that can undergo things and do things. Bishop Berkeley's characterization of the self as a 'thinking...principle' seems as good as any (1713: 116). A principle, in this old use, manages to sound like a thing of some sort without sounding anything like a table or a chair.

The second claim, (2), that the self is thought of as something mental, is also unclear. The idea is something like this: when the self is thought of as a thing, its claim to thinghood is taken to be sufficiently grounded in its mental nature alone. It may also have a non-mental nature, as materialists suppose, but its counting as a thing is not thought to depend on its counting as a thing considered in its non-mental nature: the self is the *mental* self. It's true and important that many people naturally think of themselves as possessing both mental and non-mental properties, but this doesn't affect the truth of (2).

Singularity: Clearly, to think of the self as a thing is already to think of it as single in some way—as *a* thing. But in what way? I have three main claims in mind.

First: insofar as the mental self is thought of as single, it is not thought of as having singularity only in the sense in which a group of things can be said to be a single group. Rather it is thought of as single in the way in which a single marble (e.g.) is single when compared with a single pile of marbles. Developing the Lockean point just made about the fundamental causal component in our idea of a thing, one might say that the mental self is conceived of as something that has the kind of strong unity of internal causal connectedness that a single marble has, as compared with the much weaker unity of internal causal connectedness found in a pile of marbles.[12]

Second: the mental self's property of singleness is thought of as sufficiently and essentially grounded in its mental nature alone. This closely parallels the idea that the self's claim to thinghood is thought of as sufficiently grounded in its mental nature alone, and the same moves are appropriate. We may suppose that the mental self has non-mental being (the brain-as-revealed-to-physics, say) as well as mental being, and also that it is believed to have non-mental being. The fact remains that it is thought of as having singleness in a way that is independent of its having singleness when considered in its non-mental nature.

One may express this by saying that its *principle of unity* is taken to be mental. What does 'principle of unity' mean? Well, it is arguable that everything that is conceived of as a single thing or object—electron, atom, neuron, sofa, nation-state—is conceived of as a single thing relative to some principle of unity according to which it *counts* as a single thing. An atom counts as a single thing relative to one principle of unity, and it counts as many things relative to other principles of unity—those which discern subatomic particles. Many associate this point with the view that there are no ultimate facts of the matter about which phenomena are things or objects and which are not; they hold that all *principles of objectual unity*, as one might call them, are ultimately subjective in character. But this is a further claim. In itself, the claim that everything that is taken to be a single object is so taken relative to some principle of objectual unity is compatible with the view that there are objective principles of objectual unity given which there are right answers to questions about which things are genuinely single objects.

Let me try to put the point about the self in another way: we may suppose that the mental self (the self-phenomenon) has non-mental being as well as mental being, and it may even be widely believed that this is so (few give the matter much thought). The fact remains that it is thought of as having singleness in its mental being in a way that is independent of any singleness that it may have in its non-mental being. In this sense it is taken to be single just as something mental.[13] I will illustrate this idea after introducing the third main point about singleness.

This is that the mental self is standardly thought to be single in the two ways just characterized both when it is considered (3) synchronically, or as a thing existing at a given time, and when it is considered (4) diachronically, i.e. as a thing that persists through time.

In what follows, I will stretch the meaning of 'synchronic' slightly, and take it to apply to any consideration of the mental self (or self-phenomenon) that is a consideration of it during an *experientially unitary* or *unbroken* or *hiatus-free* period of

---

[12] Cf. Campbell 1995. A marble, of course, is made of atoms, and is a collection of things from the point of view of an atom. An atom is a collection of things from the point of view of an electron, and perhaps the series continues. This is the point of the comparative formula 'single in the way in which a marble (e.g.) is single when compared with a pile of marbles'.

[13] Compare 'X is taken to be single just qua something physical (i.e. non-mental)'. The thought that this expresses is not problematic for ordinary thought, and the thought expressed by 'X is taken to be single just qua something mental' should not be thought to be more problematic.

thought or experience. The notion of a hiatus-free period of thought or experience is important for my purposes, and needs further description (see §2.9). For the moment let me simply assert that in the normal course of events truly hiatus-free periods of thought or experience are invariably brief in human beings: a few seconds at the most, a fraction of a second at the least. Our eyes are constantly engaged in saccadic jumps, and reflection reveals the respect in which our minds function in an analogous—if more perceptible—way. Research by Pöppel and others is said to provide 'clear evidence that... the experienced Now is not a point, but is extended,... that the [human] conscious Now is—language and culture independent—of the duration of approximately 3 seconds', and although this proves nothing about the existence of hiatuses, or about the nature of the self, it is undeniably suggestive.[14]

'Diachronic' complements 'synchronic' and applies to consideration of the mental self (or self-phenomenon) during any period of conscious thought or experience that includes a break or hiatus. Such periods may range from a fraction of a second to a lifetime.

Now reconsider the second claim—that the mental self is taken to be single just as something mental. This has a synchronic and a diachronic aspect. I will begin with the former. Suppose that someone fully convinces you (perhaps by hypnosis) that your current mental life with all its familiar characteristics, which incorporates your current sense of the single mental self, depends on the activity of three spatially separated brains in three different bodies. Will this immediately annihilate your natural sense of your mental singleness? Surely not. Your thought is likely to be 'Wow, I have got three brains—I, the single thing or person that I am.'[15] Your sense of the mental self is overwhelmingly likely to continue unchanged. It doesn't depend on your believing that you have a single brain or body. Suppose that you find out that there are three separate brains in your single body, collaborating to produce your experience. Again this will not override the experience of mental singleness.

It may be objected that in the case imagined you still have experience as of inhabiting a single body. This is true, given that you are an ordinary human being. But one can equally well imagine a three-bodied creature that naturally experiences itself as three-bodied, and as receiving information (perhaps via different sense modalities) from all three bodies, while still having a strong sense of the single mental self, and thinking of itself as 'I'. Here the experience of three-bodiedness is likely to make the sense of the singleness of the mental self particularly vivid. It is true that ordinary human experience of oneself as mentally single is deeply shaped by experience of having a single body, but it hardly follows that any possible experience of oneself as mentally single depends essentially on such experience.[16]

Now for the diachronic case. Suppose that one experiences one's mental life as something that has strong diachronic singleness or unity (some do much more than others). And suppose that one then finds out—or comes to be convinced—that it

---

[14] Ruhnau 1995: 168, Pöppel 1978. Citing this research in his essay 'The Dimension of the Present Moment', the Czech immunologist and poet Miroslav Holub writes that 'in this sense our ego lasts three seconds' (1990: 6).

[15] Kant (1781: A353–4) makes a related point.

[16] This is the kind of issue that arises when one asks (III), the 'conditions' question.

depends for its existence on the successive existence of a series of numerically distinct brains or neuronal entities. Will this annihilate one's sense of the mental self as a single thing persisting through time? It would be extraordinary if it did: for, by hypothesis, everything else is the same, experientially, as it was before one made this discovery. This suggests that confrontation with the fact of one's non-mental multiplicity will have no more force to undermine one's sense of the singleness of the mental self in the diachronic case than in the synchronic case.

There is a famous footnote in Kant's discussion of the Third Paralogism:

An elastic ball which strikes another similar ball in a straight line communicates to the latter its entire motion, and therefore its entire state (if we take account only of positions in space). If, in analogy with such bodies, we postulate substances such that the one communicates representations to the other together with consciousness of them, we can conceive a whole series of substances of which the first transmits its state to the second, the second its own state with that of the preceding substance to the third, and [so on]. The last substance would then be conscious of all the states of the previously changed substances as being its own states, because they would have been transferred to it together with consciousness of them   (1781: A363–4)

Kant's aim is to argue that no experience of the diachronic singleness of the mental self can possibly establish that the mental self or 'I' is in fact a diachronically single substance. My different, compatible claim is that even if one came to believe that the existence of the mental self did *not* involve the existence of a diachronically single substance, there is no reason to suppose that this would undermine one's experience of the mental self as so single.

To summarize: even if one takes it for granted that the mental self (or self-phenomenon) has a non-mental nature or being, one's experience of the mental self as single is independent of any belief that it is single—either synchronically or diachronically—in its non-mental nature or being. This, then, illustrates the respect in which the singularity of the mental self is conceived of as being essentially grounded in its mental nature alone.

It's also true—to diverge from merely phenomenological concerns—that thoughts that occur in a single body or brain (or substance of some other sort) may fail to seem anything like the series of thoughts of a single self or thinker, both when considered 'from the inside' (i.e. from the point of view of the thinker of any given one of the thoughts in question) and when considered from the outside (i.e. by someone who is not the thinker of any of the thoughts, but who has access to the contents of the thoughts, as in a novel). Consider the diachronic case first: imagine that a series of self-conscious thoughts or 'I-thoughts' occurs in the same brain, one at a time, while none of them ever involves any awareness of any thought earlier (or indeed later) than itself, and while no two of them ever stand in any of the relations (of content, temperamental coherence, etc.) in which temporally close pairs of thoughts often stand when they are the thoughts of a being that we naturally think of as a single thinker.

In this case, it may be said that we lack any mentally grounded reason for saying that there is a single thinker. Some may want to say that there is nevertheless a single thinker, simply because a single brain is the locus of all the thoughts. But why should the fact of non-mental diachronic singleness decisively overrule the natural judgement that there is no plausible candidate for a diachronically single mental self in this case? The fact of non-mental multiplicity in the three-bodies case had no power to defeat the natural judgement of mental singleness. Why should the fact of non-mental singleness in this case defeat the natural judgement of mental multiplicity (lack of mental singularity)?[17]

Now consider the synchronic case: imagine that a single brain is the site of experiential phenomena that are just like the experiential phenomena taking place simultaneously in the brains of three different people (the first thinking exclusively about Vienna, the second exclusively about menhirs, the third exclusively about DNA). Here it is natural to judge that there are three subjects of experience. If one counts the whole brain non-mentally considered as the non-mental being of each of the three apparently distinct thought-thinking selves, then one has multiplicity of selves in spite of non-mental singleness.

The judgement that there are three subjects of experience may seem natural in this case, but it can be cogently challenged. It is very difficult to draw firm conclusions about the number of subjects of experience associated with a single brain from facts about the contents of the experiences associated with that brain. As far as the synchronic case is concerned: it may be a fact about human beings that they can only genuinely entertain one conscious thought at a time, but it does not seem to be an a priori truth about conscious thinking in general. As far as the diachronic case is concerned: it is not clear that there is any lower bound on the connectedness of the successive thoughts and experiences of a single subject of experience, any point at which we can confidently say 'These experiences are too unconnected and disordered to count as the experiences of a single subject of experience.'[18]

Multiplicity? So far I have taken it for granted that human beings standardly have some sense of the singleness of the mental self. But some may claim to experience the mental self as fragmentary or multiple, and most of us have had experiences that give us—so we feel—some understanding of what they mean.

It seems, however, that the experience of multiplicity can at most affect (4), the sense of the mental self as diachronically single (recall that a sense of the mental self as diachronically single may well be concerned with short periods of time; when I want to consider longer periods of time—weeks, months, years, lifetimes—I will talk about 'long-term' continuity). It cannot affect (3), the sense of the mental self as synchronically single (single during any one 'hiatus-free' period of thought or experience). Why not? Because any candidate for being an experience of the mental self as synchronically multiple at the present moment will have to be an episode of explicitly self-conscious thought, and there is a crucial (trivial) respect in which no such episode could be experience of the mental self as synchronically multiple. Explicitly self-conscious thought need not always involve some explicit sense of the mental self as something present and involved, even when it has the form 'I *f*', or 'I am F' ('I forgot the key', 'I'm late for my exam'). But whenever it does—and it must if there is to be anything that is a candidate for being an *experience* of the mental self as

---

[17] The phenomena of dissociative identity disorder may also support the idea that non-mental single-ness is compatible with a multiplicity of mental selves, but the present example is much more extreme.

[18] See van Inwagen 1990: 196–202.

synchronically multiple at the present moment—there is a fundamental respect in which the mental self must be experienced as single, for the space of that thought at least.

This may seem obvious, but it can be disputed. It may be said that even experience of the mental self synchronically considered can seem to be experience of something shattered and multiple ('My name is legion', *Mark* 5.9). There seem to be forms of human experience that invite such a description. One may be under stress and subject to rapidly changing moods. One may feel oneself pulled in different directions by opposed desires. Human thought-processes can become extraordinarily rapid and tumultuous. But what exactly is being claimed, when it is said that the self may be experienced as synchronically multiple? There seem to be two main possibilities: either the experience is that there are many selves present, or it is (just) that the self is complex in a certain radical way. But in the second case, the experience of radical complexity that is claimed to justify the description 'synchronically multiple' clearly depends on a prior sense of the mental self as synchronically single: in this case 'multiple' is a characterization that is applied to something that must have already presented as single in order for the characterization to be applied at all.

What about the first case, in which the experience is that there are many selves present? Well, we may ask who has the experience that there are many selves present? To face the question is to realize that any explicitly self-conscious experience has to present as experience from one single mental point of view. (The word 'mental' is not redundant here, for the three-bodied person that has sensory experience of being three-bodied may have three sensory points of view while still having only one mental 'point of view'.) If so, the experience that there are many selves present is necessarily experience from some single point of view. Even if a single brain is the site of many experiences that there are many selves present, each such experience is necessarily experience from a single point of view. This is the trivial aspect of the claim that experience of the mental self as synchronically multiple is not really possible.[19]

It may be added that when one's mind races and tumbles, it is natural to experience oneself as a largely helpless spectator of the pandemonium. To this extent, experience of chaotic disparateness of contents may reinforce a sense of singleness rather than diminishing it. Nor can one experience conflict of desire unless one experiences both desires as one's own.

2.7 Personality

So much for a consideration of (3) and (4)—synchronic and diachronic singleness—in the framework of the local phenomenological question (What is the human sense

---

[19] See further Ch. 9. I take this to be compatible with the possibility of Husserlian '*splitting of the I*' in transcendental-phenomenological reflection (1929: 35), and also with a thought-experiment of Parfit's in which he imagines being able to 'divide his mind' in order to do two separate calculations in two separate streams of consciousness, and then reunite it. He considers his attitude to the process after several divisions and reunions: 'in each of my two streams of consciousness I would believe that I was now, in my other stream, having thoughts and sensations of which, in this stream, I was unaware' (1984: 246–8).

of the self?). I will now consider (4) and (8)—diachronic singularity and personality—in the framework of the general phenomenological question (What senses of the self are possible?). I will begin with personality, and, like William James, I will sometimes talk 'in the first person, leaving my description to be accepted by those to whose introspection it may commend itself as true, and confessing my inability to meet the demands of others, if others there be' (1890: 1.299).

It seems plain that (8) is not a necessary component of any possible sense of the mental self—that experience of the self does not necessarily involve experience of it as something that has a personality. Most people have at some time, and however temporarily, experienced themselves as a kind of bare locus of consciousness—not just as detached, but as void of personality, stripped of particularity of character, a mere (cognitive) point of view. Some have experienced it for long periods of time. It may be the result of exhaustion or solitude, abstract thought or a hot bath. It is also a common feature of severe depression, in which one may experience 'depersonalization'. This is a very accurate term, in my experience and in that of others I have talked to.

Sustained experience of depersonalization is classified as psychotic relative to the normal human condition, but it is of course experientially real, and one can imagine human beings getting stuck in this condition; some do. Equally, one can imagine aliens for whom it is the normal condition. Such an alien may still have a clear sense of the self as a specifically mental thing. It may still have an unimpaired sense of itself as a locus of consciousness, just as we ordinarily do—not only when we suffer depersonalization, but also in everyday life.[20]

A very strong form of what may be lost in depersonalization is recorded by Gerard Manley Hopkins, who talks of considering

my self-being, my consciousness and feeling of myself, that taste of myself, of *I* and *me* above and in all things, which is more distinctive than the taste of ale or alum, more distinctive than the smell of walnutleaf or camphor, and is incommunicable by any means to another man.... Nothing else in nature comes near this unspeakable stress of pitch, distinctiveness, and selving, this selfbeing of my own.[21]

My enquiries suggest that while some people feel they know exactly what Hopkins means, most find this claim deeply bewildering: for them, their personality is something that is unnoticed, and in effect undetectable, in the present moment. It's what they look through, or where they look from; not something they look at; a global and invisible condition of their life, like air, not an object of experience. Dramatic differences like these back up the view that we need a phenomenology of the sense of the self before we try to answer the factual question about whether or not there is such a thing.

---

[20] A friend who recently experienced depersonalization found that the thought 'I don't exist' kept occurring to him. It seemed to him that this exactly expressed his experience of himself, although he was aware of the force of Descartes's 'I think, therefore I am', and knew, of course, that there had to be a locus of consciousness where the thought 'I don't exist' occurred. The case of Meursault is also worth considering, in Camus's book *The Outsider*. So too is his remarkable description of his mother in *The First Man*. (Note added in 2015: I had not heard of Cotard's syndrome when I wrote this paper.)

[21] Hopkins 1880: 123, quoted in Glover 1988: 59.

2.8 The Self in Time: Effects of Character

So much, briefly, for (8). Must any sense of the mental self involve experience of the self as (4) something that has long-term diachronic continuity as a single thing? I think not. The sense of the single mental self may be vivid and complete, at any given time, even if it has to do only with the present, brief, hiatus-free stretch of consciousness, at any given time. Nor do I think that this is just some alien or logical possibility, though it is also that. It lies within the range of human experience. One can be fully aware of the fact that one has long-term continuity as a *living human being* without *ipso facto* having any significant sense of the *mental self* as something that has long-term continuity. One can have a vivid sense of oneself as a mental self, and a strong natural tendency to think that that is what one most fundamentally is, while having little or no interest in or commitment to the idea that the I who is now thinking has any past or future.

Human beings differ deeply in a number of ways that affect their experience of the mental self as diachronically continuous. Some people have an excellent 'personal' memory (i.e. memory of their own past life) and an unusual capacity for vivid recollection. Others have a very poor personal memory. And it may not be simply poor. It may also be highly quiescent, and almost never intrude spontaneously into their current thought. These deep differences of memory are matched by equal differences in the force with which people imagine, anticipate, or form intentions about the future.

These differences interact with others. Some people live deeply in narrative mode: they experience their lives in terms of something that has shape and story, narrative trajectory. Some of them are self-narrators in a stronger sense: they regularly rehearse and revise their interpretations of their lives. Some people, again, are great planners, and knit up their lives with long-term projects.

Others are quite different. They have no early ambition, no later sense of vocation, no interest in climbing a career ladder, no tendency to see their life in narrative terms or as constituting a story or a development. Some merely go from one thing to another. They live life in a picaresque or episodic fashion. Some people make few plans and are little concerned with the future. Some live intensely in the present, some are simply aimless.

Many things can encourage or obstruct a sense of the mental self as something that has long-term diachronic continuity. Most people are very consistent in personality or character, whether or not they know it. And this form of steadiness may in some cases strongly underwrite experience of the mental self's continuity. Others are consistent only in their inconsistency, and may for that reason feel themselves to be continually puzzling, and piecemeal. Some go through life as if stunned.

Neither inconsistency nor poor memory is necessary for the episodic experience of life. John Updike writes 'I have the persistent sensation, in my life and art, that I am just beginning' (1989: 239). These are the words of a man who has an extremely powerful personal memory and a highly consistent character. I have the same persistent sensation, and learn from Updike that it is nothing essentially to do with my extremely poor personal memory. I believe that it is an accurate description of how things are for many people, when it comes to that sense of oneself as a mental self that is—whether or not it is acknowledged—central to most people's self-conception.

I'm somewhere down the episodic end of the spectrum. I have no sense of my life as a narrative with form, or indeed as a narrative without form. I have little interest in my own past and little concern for the future. My poor personal memory rarely impinges on my present consciousness. Even when I am interested in my past, I'm not interested in it specifically insofar as it is mine. I'm perfectly well aware that it is mine, insofar as I am a human being considered as a whole, but I do not really think of it as mine at all, insofar as 'mine' picks out me as I am now. For me as I am now, the interest (emotional or otherwise) of my personal memories lies in their experiential content considered independently of the fact that what is remembered happened *to me*—i.e. to the me that is now remembering.[22] They're certainly distinctive in their 'from-the-inside' character, but this in itself doesn't mark them as mine in any emotionally significant sense. The one striking exception to this, in my case, used to be—but no longer is—memory of recent embarrassment.

I make plans for the future. To that extent I think of myself perfectly adequately as something that has long-term continuity. But I experience this way of thinking of myself as utterly remote and theoretical, given the most central or fundamental way in which I think of myself, which is as a mental self or someone. Using 'me*' to express this fundamental way in which I think of myself—or to denote me thinking of myself in this way, looking out on things from this perspective—I can accurately express my experience by saying that I do not think of me* as being something in the future. It is also accurate to shift the 'not', and say, more strongly, that what I think of as being in the future is not me*.

As I write these words, the thought that I have to give a lecture before a large audience in two months' time causes me some worry, which has familiar physiological manifestations. I feel the anxiety naturally and directly as pertaining to me even though I have no sense that it will be me* that will be giving the lecture. Indeed it seems completely false to say that it will be me*. And this is how it feels, not something I believe for theoretical reasons. So why do I feel any anxiety now? I believe that susceptibility to this sort of anticipatory anxiety is innate and 'hardwired', a manifestation of the instinct for self-preservation: my practical concern for my future, which I believe to be within the normal human range, is biologically grounded and autonomous in such a way that it persists as something immediately felt even though it is not supported by any emotionally backed sense on the part of me* now that me* will be there in the future. (Not even half an hour away—and certainly not tomorrow.) Insofar as I have any sense of me* (rather than the living human being that I am) as something with a history and future, it seems that this sense is a wispy, short-range product of, and in no way a ground of, my innate predisposition to such forward and backward looking things as anxiety or regret. And it dislimns when scrutinized, and it is more accurate to say that it does not exist.

---

[22] Here I am strikingly different from Campbell, who argues that 'fission' (in which one person is imagined to split into two separate people) 'would mean loss of the right to one's autobiographical memories, my memories of what I have seen and done' in some way that mattered (Campbell 1994: 189).

Now for an exception. You might expect me to say that when I think of my death at some unspecified future time, I think that it is not me* who is going to die, or at least that I do not think that it is me*. But I do think that it is me* that is going to die, and I feel fear of death. It's only when I consider future events *in life* that I do not think it's me*. This seems odd, given that my death necessarily comes after any future events in my life, and ought therefore to seem to have even less to do with me* than any future events in life. But it can be explained. This feature of my attitude to death is principally grounded in susceptibility to the following line of thought: When eternity—eternal nonexistence—is in question, the gap between me* and death that is created by the fact that I still have an indefinite amount of life to live approximates to nothing (like any finite number next to infinity). So death—nonexistence for ever—presents itself as having direct relevance for me* now even if me* has no clear future in life—not even tomorrow. On the vast scale of things that one naturally thinks in terms of when thinking of death, death is no significant distance away from me*, and looms as something that will happen to me*. This is not to say that I feel or fear that I am going to die now. The thought of eternity doesn't override common sense. But it has an emotional force that makes it seem plain that death faces me*. If this is Heideggerian authenticity, then Heideggerian authenticity is compatible with lack of any belief in the persisting self.

Note that this line of thought will have equal force for someone who *does* think of their me* as having a future in life: for if eternity of nonexistence is what you fear, a few years is not a protection. This idea was vivid for me as a young child combining an atheist upbringing with great difficulty in going to sleep. See further §5.9 below, pp. 99–100.

One indirect lesson of this case is important. It is that one's sense of one's temporal nature may vary considerably depending on what one is thinking about. But the general conclusion I draw is that a vivid sense of the self need not involve (4) a sense of it as something that has long-term continuity.[23]

2.9 The Self in Time: the 'Stream' of Consciousness

How does the moment-to-moment experience of consciousness relate to the sense of the self? Does it underwrite (4)? I will now consider this question.

I think William James's famous metaphor of the stream of consciousness is inept.[24] Human thought has very little natural phenomenological continuity or experiential flow—if mine is anything to go by. 'Our thought is fluctuating, uncertain, fleeting', as Hume said (1749–76: 194). It keeps slipping from mere consciousness into self-consciousness and out again (perhaps one can sit through a thrilling film without emerging into full I-thinking self-consciousness). It is always shooting off,

---

[23] Narrative personalities may feel there is something chilling and empty in the Episodic life. They may fear it, and judge that it shows lack of wisdom, conduces to lack of moral responsibility, and is 'deficient and empty' (Plutarch c.100: 214–17 (473B–474B)). This, however, is ignorance: even in its extreme form this life is no less intense or full, no less emotional and moral.

[24] James 1892: 145. Husserl is also heavily committed to the image of the stream, the '*flowing cogito*', the 'flowing conscious life in which the ... ego lives' (1929: 66, 31). For an excellent discussion of Buddhist uses of the metaphor of the stream see Collins (1982: §8.4).

fuzzing, shorting out, spurting, and stalling. William James described it as 'like a bird's life, ... an alternation of flights and perchings' (1890: 1.243), but even this recognition that thought is not a matter of even flow retains a strong notion of continuity, insofar as a bird traces a spatio-temporally continuous path. It fails to take adequate account of the fact that trains of thought are constantly broken by detours—byblows—fissures—white noise. This is especially so when one is just sitting and thinking.

Things are different if one's attention is engaged by some ordered and continuous process in the world, like a fast and exciting game, or music, or a talk. In this case thought or experience may be felt to inherit much of the ordered continuity of the phenomenon which occupies it. But it may still seize up, fly off, or flash with perfectly extraneous matter from time to time, and reflection reveals gaps and fadings, disappearances and recommencements even when there is stable succession of content.[25] It is arguable that the case of solitary speculative thought—in which the mind is left to its own resources and devices—merely reveals in a relatively dramatic way something that is true to a greater or lesser extent of all thought. There is an important respect in which James Joyce's use of punctuation in his 'stream of consciousness' novel *Ulysses* makes his depiction of the character of the process of consciousness more accurate in the case of the heavily punctuated Stephen Daedalus than in the case of the unpunctuated Molly Bloom. Dorothy Richardson, acknowledged as the inventor of the 'stream of consciousness' novel in English, remarked on the 'perfect imbecility' of the phrase to describe what she did.[26]

My claim is not just that there can be radical disjunction at the level of subject matter. Switches of subject matter could be absolute, and still be seamless in the sense that they involved no sensed temporal gap or felt interruption of consciousness. It seems to me, however, that such experience of temporal seamlessness is relatively rare.[27] When I am alone and thinking I find that my fundamental experience of consciousness is one of *repeated returns into consciousness as if from a state of complete, if momentary, unconsciousness*. The (invariably brief) periods of true experiential continuity are usually radically disjunct from one another in this way

---

[25] This is just a phenomenological report; but compare Dennett's discussion (1991: 189, 237–42) of the 'pandemonium' in the mind-brain as different words, ideas, thoughts, impulses vie for emergence into consciousness.

[26] This is Richardson's Miriam Henderson in church: 'Certainly it was wrong to listen to sermons... stultifying... unless they were intellectual... lectures like Mr Brough's... that was as bad, because they were not sermons.... Either kind was bad and ought not to be allowed... a homily... sermons... homilies... a quiet homily might be something rather nice... and have not *Charity*—sounding brass and tinkling cymbal.... *Caritas*... I have *none* I am sure...' (1915: 73). Compare Molly Bloom in bed: 'I want to do the place up someway the dust grows in it I think while Im asleep then we can have music and cigarettes I can accompany him first I must clean the keys of the piano with milk whatll I wear a white rose or those fairy cakes in Liptons at 7½d a lb or the other ones with the cherries in them and the pinky sugar 11d a couple of lbs of those a nice plant for the middle of the table Id get that cheaper in wait wheres this I saw them not long ago I love flowers...' (1922: 642). And Stephen Daedalus walking on the beach: 'Who watches me here? Who ever anywhere will read these written words? Signs on a white field. Somewhere to someone in your flutiest voice. The good bishop of Cloyne took the veil of the temple out of his shovel hat: veil of space with coloured emblems hatched on its field. Hold hard. Coloured on a flat: yes, that's right' (1922: 40).

[27] Molly Bloom might seem to be an example of seamlessness across radical change of content, but Shaun Gallagher argues that 'such radical disjunctions of content actually do disrupt the flow structure—content and form are not independent of one another' (private correspondence).

even when they are not radically disjunct in respect of content (it is in fact often the same thought—or nearly the same thought—that one returns to after a momentary absence). The situation is best described, it seems to me, by saying that it is as if consciousness is continually *restarting*. There isn't a basic substrate (as it were) of continuous consciousness interrupted by various lapses and doglegs. Rather, conscious thought has the character of a (nearly continuous) series of radically disjunct irruptions into consciousness from a basic substrate of non-consciousness. It keeps banging out of nothingness; it is a series of comings to. It's true that belief in the reality of flow may itself contribute to an experience of flow. But I think that the appearance of flow is undercut by even a modest amount of reflection.[28]

—But perhaps the experience of disjunction is an artefact of introspection. Perhaps unexamined consciousness has true flow, and the facts get distorted by the act of trying to observe what they are.

This seems highly implausible. Awareness of radical disjunction sometimes surfaces spontaneously and unlooked for. We can become aware that this is what has been happening; we do not see it only when we look. This is my experience, and the claim seems strongly supported by work described by Dennett (1991, see e.g. chapter 11). Even if the appearance of disjunction were partly an artefact of intentional introspection, this would be a striking fact about how consciousness appears to itself, something one needed to take account of when considering the underpinnings of the sense of the self. There's a sense in which this issue is undecidable, for in order to settle it one would need to be able to observe something while it was unobserved. Nevertheless, the view that there is radical disjunction might receive independent support from experimental psychology, and also, more indirectly, from current work on the non-mental neural correlates of consciousness.

I have been arguing—if that's the word—that the sense of the mental self as something that has long-term continuity lacks a certain sort of direct phenomenological warrant in the moment-to-moment nature of our thought processes. It is not supported at the level of detail by any phenomenon of steady flow. If there is any support for belief in the long-term continuity of the self in the nature of moment-to-moment consciousness, it is derived indirectly from other sources—the massive constancies and developmental coherencies of *content* that often link up experiences through time, and by courtesy of short-term memory, across all the jumps and breaks of flow. One (the human being, the mental-and-non-mental whole) walks from A to B, looking around, thinking of this and that. One works in a room for an hour. Examined in detail, the processes of one's thought are bitty, scatty, and saccadic in the way described; consciousness is 'in a perpetual flux', and different thoughts and experiences 'succeed each other with an inconceivable rapidity' (Hume 1739–40: 1.4.6.4/252). And yet one is experientially in touch with a great pool of constancies and steady processes of change in one's environment including, notably, one's body (of which one is almost constantly aware, however thoughtlessly, both by external sense and by

---

[28] This experience seems to be in affinity with the Buddhist theory of the way in which consciousness is an interruption of ongoing, unconscious *bhavaṅga* mind, although the Buddhist theory has many special further features. See Collins (1982: 238–47).

proprioception). If one does not reflect very hard, these constancies and steadinesses of development in the *contents* of one's consciousness may seem like fundamental characteristics of the *operation* of one's consciousness, although they are not. This in turn may support the sense of the *mental self* as something uninterrupted and continuous throughout the waking day.

This is a weak claim. It's not the claim that belief in the flow of consciousness is necessary to a sense of the self as something that has long-term continuity. One could think and feel that consciousness was gappy and chaotic and still believe in a mental self that had long-term continuity. Belief in the long-term continuity of the self is the most common position (among those who believe in the self at all), and the present suggestion is only that belief in the flow of consciousness may be one interesting and suspect source of support for this belief.

There is more to say, but not here. The central claim remains unchanged: one can have a full sense of the single mental self at any given time without thinking of the self as something that has long-term continuity. According to Reed 'our sense of self is intimately related to the subjective awareness of the continuity of life. Any break in personal time [or "time-gap experience"] is alarming, because it suggests some disintegration of psychic synthesis' (Reed 1987: 777). I believe that this is not generally true.

2.10 The Conditions Question

I have given examples of how one might set about answering phenomenological questions (I) and (II) in preparation for (IV), the factual question 'Does the self exist?' I have no space here to consider (III), the conditions question 'What are the grounds or preconditions of possession of a sense of the mental self?', but I think it is best approached by asking the more familiar question 'What are the grounds or necessary conditions of self-consciousness?', which has been widely discussed—e.g. by Kant, Fichte, Wundt, James, and their followers, and, more recently, by P. F. Strawson (1966: 97–112), Evans (1982: 7), and others (see e.g. the contributors to Bermúdez, Marcel, and Eilan 1995, and Cassam 1997). I believe that all discussions in the analytic tradition overestimate the strength of the conditions that can be established as necessary for self-consciousness, but this is a question for another time (I try to answer it in Strawson 1999c). I will now conclude with a wild sketch of how I think the factual question is to be answered.

2.11 The Factual Question

Suppose for the sake of argument that the answer to the general phenomenological question is as follows: any genuine sense of the self must involve a conception of the self as [(1) + (2) + (3) + (5) + (6)]—as a single, mental thing that is distinct from all other things and a subject of experience—but need not involve a conception of it as (7) an agent, or as having (8) character or personality or (4) longer-term dia-chronic continuity. If we couple this answer with the equivalence claim (§2.4, p. 21) we get the result that if there is such a thing as a mental self, it must at least fulfil conditions (1), (2), (3), (5), and (6)—one might call these the 'core conditions'.

It must be a distinct, mental thing that is correctly said to be a subject of experience and a single thing within any hiatus-free period of experience; whatever else it may be.[29]

Is there such a thing? If there is, is it right to call it a self? I can't legislate on how anyone should use the words 'self' and 'thing' (cf. note 8). It seems to me that the best answer is Yes, but many will think my Yes is close to No, because I don't think a mental self exists in any sense that will satisfy most of those who want there to be a self. I believe the Buddhists have the truth when they deny the existence of a *persisting* mental self, in the human case, and nearly all of those who want there to be a self want there to be a persisting self.

One could call this view the Pearl view, because it suggests that many mental selves exist, one at a time and one after another, like pearls on a string, in the case of something like a human being.[30,31] According to the Pearl view, each is a distinct existence, an individual physical thing or object, though they may exist for considerably different lengths of time. The Pearl view is not the view that mental selves are necessarily of relatively short duration—there may be beings whose conscious experience is uninterrupted for hours at a time, or even for the whole of their existence. (If I believed in God, this is how I'd expect God to be.) But we are not like this: we are lulled by the metaphor of the stream of consciousness, but the basic phenomenological form of our consciousness is that of a gappy series of eruptions of consciousness as if from a substrate of non-consciousness.

I don't suppose the Pearl view will be much liked. It sounds linguistically odd and counterintuitive. It offends against the everyday use of expressions like 'myself' to refer to enduring human beings, and nearly all theoretical speculation about the self incorporates a deep presumption that if one is arguing for the existence of the mental self one is arguing for something that exists for a substantial period of time.[32]

Sometimes we need to speak oddly to see clearly. I think it is important to defend the Pearl view, giving its linguistic counterintuitiveness a chance to diminish through familiarity so that one can judge it on its merits rather than on linguistic gut feeling. Perhaps the most that can be said for it is that it is the best we can do if we commit ourselves in advance to answering Yes to the question 'Is there any straightforward and metaphysically robust sense in which it is legitimate to talk of the mental self as a thing, something that really exists, like a chair or a cat, rather than merely as a "Humean" or Dennettian fiction?' In my view, that means that there is a lot to be said for it.

---

[29] Obviously the view that mental selves can have personality and can be agents and have longer-term continuity is not excluded by this proposal. Few agree that agenthood is dispensable with.

[30] It is unlike the 'bundle' theory of the self described but not endorsed by Hume, according to which the self, insofar as it exists at all, is a diachronically extended—but perhaps non-continuous—thing constituted of a series of perceptions (cf. Hume 1739–40: 1.4.6.1–23/251–63, App§§10–21/633–6, Abs§28/657–8).

[31] Note added in 1999. I have abandoned this name, which has proved misleading, in favour of 'the Transience view' (see e.g. §3.19, p. 72 below), because it leads people to think that it is important that there be a string on which the pearls are threaded; which was not at all my intention.

[32] Dennett's account of the self as an 'abstraction', a 'Center of Narrative Gravity' (1991: 426–7) may be the best one can do if one is determined to conceive the self as something that has long-term continuity.

The proposal, in any case, is this: the mental self—*a* mental self—exists at any given moment of consciousness or during any uninterrupted or hiatus-free period of consciousness.[33] In the human case, it exists only for some short period of time. But it is none the less *real*, as real as any rabbit or Z-particle. And it is as much a *thing* or *object* as any G-type star or grain of salt. And it is as much a *physical* thing as any blood vessel, jackhammer, or cow.

I can think of at least three overlapping tasks one has to undertake in order to develop the proposal. One has to say more about what it is to be a materialist; address the question 'What is a thing (or object)?'; and explain further what is meant by 'ontic distinctness'. I will make one comment about each.

(i) In saying that a self is an 'ontically distinct' thing, I mean—at least—that it is not the same thing as anything else ordinarily or naturally identified as a thing. But I don't mean that it is an 'independent or separately existing entity' (Parfit 1995: 18) relative to all other things naturally identified as things—such as atoms, neurons, and brains. Parfit takes a Cartesian immaterial ego to be a paradigm instance of such a separately existing entity, but I take it that a mental self's existence from time t_1 to time t_2 (suppose this to be a two-second interval) is identical with the existence from t_1 to t_2 of a set of neuron-and-neurotransmitter-(etc.)-constituting atoms or fundamental particles in a certain state of activation.[34]

Note that this is not any sort of reductionist remark, for the phrase 'a set of... particles in a certain state of activation', as used by a consistent and realistic materialist, does not refer only or even especially to non-mental phenomena that can be adequately described by current physics or something like it. It refers just as it says, to a set of neuron-and-neurotransmitter-(etc.)-constituting particles in a certain state of activation; and this existence and activity, as all genuine realistic materialists agree, is as much revealed by and constituted by *experiential* phenomena as by any non-experiential phenomena discernible by physics.

The plausibility of the claim that a mental self is a *thing*, given the way it is characterized in the penultimate paragraph, depends on the success of arguments sketched in (iii) below. But it is at least clear that ontic distinctness is not separate existence. Nor, it seems, is it what Parfit has in mind when he himself distinguishes distinctness from separate existence.

Consider a human being X. I will call the portion of physical reality that consists of X the 'X-reality'. This is a rough notion—as a physical being X is enmeshed in wide-reaching physical interactions, and is not neatly separable out as a single portion of reality—but it is serviceable none the less. Parfit offers two examples of things that stand in the relation of distinctness without separate existence: a statue and the lump

---

[33] The notion of uninterruptedness remains vague. Note that many will think that the period of consciousness must be one of explicit self-consciousness (cf. the opening quotation from Nozick), or must at least occur in a being capable of such self-consciousness. I am not sure that this is the best thing to say.

[34] See further Strawson 2003b. Compare van Inwagen's account (1990: 94–5) of how an atom may be 'caught up in the life of an organism' while existing both before and after it. One may equally well say that each member of the set of fundamental particles is 'caught up in' the life of a mental self.

of bronze of which it is made, and a nation and 'a group of people, on some territory, living together in certain ways'.[35] By contrast, I propose that there is an analogy between the following two relations: (1) the relation between one of X's little fingers and X considered as a whole, where X is considered statically at a particular moment in time; (2) the relation between a mental self that exists in the X-reality and the X-reality considered as a whole, where the X-reality is considered dynamically as something essentially persisting in time. In other words, I propose that there is some sort of part–whole relation to be discerned. It seems to me that selves are as real, and as much things, as little fingers (it is arguable that they have a better claim to count as things than fingers do).

(ii) Genuine, realistic materialism requires acknowledgement that the phenomena of conscious experience are, considered specifically as such, wholly physical, as physical as the phenomena of extension and electricity as studied by physics (§2.5). This in turn requires the acknowledgement that current physics, considered as a general account of the nature of the physical, is like *Hamlet* without the prince, or at least like *Othello* without Desdemona. No one who doubts this is a serious materialist, as far as I can see. Anyone who has had a standard modern (Western) education is likely to experience a feeling of deep bewilderment—category-blasting amazement—when entering into serious materialism, and considering the question 'What is the nature of the physical?' in the context of the thought that the mental (and in particular the experiential) is physical; followed, perhaps, by a deep, pragmatic agnosticism.[36]

(iii) The discussion of materialism has many mansions, and provides a setting for considering the question 'What is a thing or object?' It is a long question, but the answer suggests that there is no less reason to call the self a thing than there is to call a cat or a rock a thing. It is arguable that disagreement with this claim is diagnostic of failure to understand what genuine, realistic materialism involves.

—Come off it. Even if we grant that there is a phenomenon that is reasonably picked out by the phrase 'mental self', why should we accept that the right thing to say about some two-second-long mental-self phenomenon is (a) that it is a *thing* or *object* like a rock or a tiger? Why can't we insist that the right thing to say is simply (b) that an enduring ('physical') object—Louis—has a certain *property*, or (c) that a two-second mental-self phenomenon is just a matter of a certain *process* occurring in an object—so that it is not itself a distinct object existing for two seconds?

I think that a proper understanding of materialism strips (b) and (c) of any appearance of superiority to (a). As for (c): any claim to the effect that a mental self is best thought of as a process rather than an object can be countered by saying that there is

[35] 1995: 17. The statue just consists in the lump of bronze, and is therefore not a separately existing entity, but it is not the same as a lump of bronze: for example, we can melt down the statue and so destroy it without destroying the lump of bronze. The existence of the nation 'just consists in the existence of a group of people, on some territory, living together in certain ways': it is not a separately existing entity. But it is also 'not the same as that group of people, or that territory'.

[36] Cf. Chomsky 1995: 1–10; Russell 1927 ch. 37.

no sense in which a mental self is a process in which a rock is not also and equally a process. So if a rock is a paradigm case of a thing in spite of being a process, we have no good reason not to say the same of a mental self.[37]

—But if there is a process, there must be something—an object or substance—in which it goes on. If something happens, there must be something to which it happens, something which is not just the happening itself.

This expresses our ordinary understanding of things, but physicists are increasingly content with the view that physical reality is itself a kind of pure process—even if it remains hard to know exactly what this idea amounts to. The view that there is some ultimate stuff *to* which things happen has increasingly lost ground to the idea that the existence of anything worthy of the name 'ultimate stuff' consists in the existence of fields of energy—consists, in other words, in the existence of a kind of pure process which is not usefully thought of as something which is happening to a thing distinct from it.

As for (b): the object/property distinction is, as Russell says of the standard distinction between mental and physical, 'superficial and unreal' (1927: 402). Chronic philosophical difficulties with the question of how to express the relation between substance and property provide strong negative support for this view. However ineluctable it is for us, it seems that the distinction must be as superficial as we must take the distinction between the wavelike nature and particlelike nature of fundamental particles to be. Obviously more needs to be said, but Kant seems to have got it exactly right in a single clause: 'in their relation to substance, [accidents] are not in fact subordinated to it, but are the manner of existence of the substance itself' (1781–7: A414/B441).

2.12 Conclusion

So much for the sketch of my answer to the factual question. I think it expresses a difficult truth, but it is exiguous and probably looks very implausible. It is not designed to persuade, however; it simply marks a possible path. One can think it monstrously implausible without rejecting the approach to the problem of the self proposed in this paper: one can agree about the importance of answering (I) and (II), the two phenomenological questions and (III), the conditions question, even if one wants to give a very different answer to (IV), the factual question.[38]

---

[37] In saying this, I don't mean to show any partiality to the 'four-dimensionalist' conception of objects.

[38] I am grateful to Derek Parfit, Shaun Gallagher, Jonathan Shear, Keith Sutherland, and P. F. Strawson for their comments on a draft of this paper.

3

The Self and the Sesmet

3.1 Introduction

I am most grateful to all those who commented on '"The Self"'.* The result was a festival of misunderstanding, but misunderstanding is one of the great engines of progress. Few of the contributors to the symposium on 'Models of the Self' were interested in my project. Some (like Olson and Wilkes) were already highly sceptical about the value of talk about the self; others were committed to other projects centred on the word 'self' that made mine seem irrelevant at best and many worse things besides. Large differences in methodological and terminological habits gave rise to many occasions on which commentators thought they disagreed with me although they had in fact changed the subject. So I am not sure anyone found my paper useful. But I found some of the responses extremely useful, especially those that adverted to Eastern and phenomenological traditions of thought.[1]

I decided to take on the self—the self understood as an internal mental presence, a mental entity in the old, strong, classical-philosophical sense—as a lawyer takes on a client. I took my sadly maligned client's innocence and good standing on trust. I took it that there really are such things as selves in every sense in which there are dogs or chairs. I then committed myself to making the best case I could for them from a realistic materialist standpoint.[2] My starting assumption was that whatever a self is, it is certainly (a) a subject of experience, and it is (b) not a whole human being (so not a person, if a person is taken to be an entity like a whole human being).[3]

It seems to me that if one is going to take this brief seriously, as a materialist, and try to show that such selves exist, then one must aim to show that they are objects of some sort—concrete objects, not abstract objects—and hence, given materialism, physical objects.[4] This view strikes many people as obviously—even hilariously—false, and a

---

* This paper is a response to a set of commentaries on '"The Self"' (Ch. 2).

[1] Such as Forman 1998, Hayward 1998, Laycock 1998, Zahavi and Parnas 1998, Shear 1998. When I cite a work I give the date of composition or first publication, while the page reference is to the edition listed in the Bibliography.

[2] A realistic materialist standpoint does not much resemble some of the positions that claim to be materialist—see §3.13 below.

[3] This immediately separates me from Bermúdez, who, like many philosophers, chooses to use 'person' and 'self' interchangeably (1998: 459), and peels off into a different debate—along with Gendler in her well-balanced piece on thought-experiments (1998). It also separates me from all those in the analytic tradition who think that facts about language suffice to show that 'the self' is either a human being considered as a whole or nothing but a 'mythical entity' (e.g. Kenny 1988, 1989 ch. 6).

[4] Dennett's proposal that the self is a 'center of narrative gravity' (1991: 426–7) does not take the brief seriously in this sense: it denies that there really are such things as selves (and is I believe correct, insofar as

central aim of this paper is to argue that this reaction stems from a failure to think through what it is to be physical, on a genuine or realistic materialist view, and, equally, from a failure to think through what it is to be an object.[5] I think that one has to solve for three inadequately conceived quantities—*self, object, physical*—simultaneously, using each to get leverage on the others.

I confess that I was attracted by the counterintuitive sound of the claim that selves are physical objects, and was duly rewarded by the quantity and quality of the protests. But I would have made the claim anyway, because I think it is correct. It is unwise to be gratuitously provocative. In areas like this it is not enough to write so as to be understood; one must write so as not to be misunderstood. Problems of communication that afflict metaphysics in general proliferate like rabbits when the topic is the self.

I will, then, try to clarify what I understand by the words 'object' and 'physical', in the hope that to understand everything will be to forgive everything,[6] and that we can—together with the cognitive self, the conceptual self, the contextualized self, the core self, the dialogic self, the ecological self, the embodied self, the emergent self, the empirical self, the existential self, the extended self, the fictional self, the full-grown self, the interpersonal self, the material self, the narrative self, the philosophical self, the physical self, the private self, the representational self, the rock bottom essential self, the semiotic self, the social self, the transparent self, and the verbal self (cf. e.g. James 1890, Stern 1985, Dennett 1991, Gibson 1993, Neisser 1994, Butterworth 1995, 1998, Cole 1997, Gazzaniga 1998, Legerstee 1998, Gallagher and Marcel 1999, Pickering 1999, Sheets-Johnstone 1999), *none* of whom I object to, although I have not chosen to write about them—fall into each others' arms in a passion of mutual understanding and, like Bunyan's pilgrim, go on our way rejoicing.

This paper is only a report on work in progress, however. Much argument is omitted, and I have not thought enough about some of the proposals it contains. Nor have I had space to comment as fully as I would have liked on many of the contributions to the symposium on 'Models of the Self' (e.g. Blachowicz 1997, Edey 1997, Perlis 1997, Ramachandran and Hirstein 1997, Radden 1998, Tani 1998).

My brief for the self also led me to conclude that there are many short-lived and successive selves (if there are selves at all), in the case of ordinary individual human beings. Some find this conclusion disappointing—they think it amounts to saying that there is no such thing as the self, or at least no such thing as 'a self worth wanting' (Wilkes 1998: 154, 156, 159, 161). But if 'self' is so defined that its existence necessarily involves some sort of substantial long-term continuity, my aim is to disappoint.

William James also holds that there are many short-lived selves (1890: 1.360–3, 371, 400–1). I did not know this when writing '"The Self"' because I had never read

---

selves are taken to be things that persist over long periods of time). Brook's (1998: 590) reason for accepting the claim that the self is an object—i.e. that human beings are objects—is ruled out by my starting point as just described.

[5] For one thing, all physical objects are literally processes. If this is a 'category mistake', don't blame me, blame nature—or ordinary language.

[6] In spite of J. L. Austin's remark that to understand everything might only increase one's contempt.

to the end of his great chapter on 'The Consciousness of Self' and had participated in the common error of thinking that he held the self to *'consist mainly of [muscular] motions in the head or between the head and throat'*.[7] Now I know better, and am happy to be on the same side as James. I am also still hopeful of receiving the blessing of certain Buddhists, in spite of widespread scepticism about the validity of my claim to their support,[8] and I hope eventually to show that there is something right about the view of the self famously expounded by Hume in his *Treatise,* and equally famously rejected by him.

The claim that there are many short-lived selves and that they are physical objects may not only look disappointing. It may also look like one of those philosophical views that can perhaps be defended and made consistent and even shown to have certain theoretical advantages, but that remains ultimately boring because too far removed from what we feel and what we want (Olson (1998: 655) finds it 'absurd'). My hope and belief is that it can be made compelling and shown to be natural and true to life, although I suspect that deep differences of temperament will make this hard for some to see. My overall aim is not to produce a piece of irreducibly 'revisionary' metaphysics—one that shows that we are all wrong in our ordinary views.[9] It is to set out some rather ordinary and widely agreed facts in a certain way that I believe to be illuminating and true, although initially rebarbative.

3.2 The Problem

The notion of the self as we have it is much too baggy and unclear for us to answer questions like 'Do selves exist?', and Olson thinks we should stop speaking of selves altogether (1998: 645). But psychologists and philosophers and a host of others will never do as he says, and one alternative is to try to clarify and define the notion of the self in such a way that it is possible to answer such questions. Olson doubts that this can be done. He doubts, in fact, that there is any such thing as 'the problem of the self'. But there is a clear sense in which there is a problem of the self simply because there is thought to be a problem of the self; and the main reason why there is thought to be a problem of the self is that there is thought to be such a thing as the self; and the main reason why there is thought to be such a thing as the self—an inner, mental self, 'a secret self... enclosed within', a 'living, central,... inmost I'[10]—is simply that

---

[7] 1890: 1.301. This ostensibly ontological remark, which is often lifted out of context and misunderstood, is not a claim about what selves are. It is a claim about what gives rise to our sense or feeling of the self. The question James has asked himself, and is answering (1890: 1.299, 301–2, James's italics, my underlining), is 'Can we tell more precisely in what the *feeling* of this central active self consists,—not necessarily as yet what the active self *is*, as a being or principle, but what we *feel* when we become aware of its existence?' His final, somewhat tentative reply is that it may be that 'our entire *feeling* of spiritual *activity*, or what commonly passes by that name, is really a feeling of bodily activities whose exact nature is by most men overlooked'—the stress falling heavily on the words 'feeling' and 'activity'.

[8] Sheets-Johnstone quotes Epstein—'the distinguishing characteristic of Buddhist meditation is that it seeks to eradicate, once and for all, the conception of self as an entity' (1998: 250–1, quoting Epstein 1995: 138–9)—as evidence of the vanity of my aspiration, although I tried to make it clear (see e.g. §2.6 and §3.17 below) that there is no tension between this view and my claim that selves are physical objects.

[9] For the distinction between 'descriptive' and 'revisionary' metaphysics, see P. F. Strawson 1959: 9–10.

[10] Traherne (1637–74) and Clough (1862), quoted by Kenny (1989: 86).

we have experience that has the *character* of there being such a thing. And this is not, as some have suggested, because we have been misled by words or beguiled by bad religious, psychotherapeutic, or philosophical traditions.[11] Such experience— I called it 'the sense of the self' in '"The Self"' and will call it 'self-experience' in what follows—is fundamental to human life. I am puzzled by Steven Pinker when he talks (albeit sceptically) of 'the autonomous "I" that we all feel hovering above our bodies',[12] for if I had to say where I thought ordinary experience imagines the I or self to be, I'd say 'Two or three inches behind the eyes, and maybe up a bit.' But self-experience doesn't have to involve any particular sense of location in order to be vivid, and to give rise to a genuine problem of the self.

3.3 Phenomenology and Metaphysics

What is the central question to which we would like an answer—granted that there is a problem of the self? It is, I take it, the straightforward question of fact

(I)   Do selves exist, and if so, what are they like?

But we need to know what sort of things we are asking about before we can begin trying to find out whether they exist.

How should we proceed? Well, it is self-experience that gives rise to the problem— the vivid sense, delusory or not, that there is such a thing as the self. I think, in fact, that it is the whole source of the problem, in such a way that when we ask whether selves exist, what we are actually asking is: Does anything like the sort of thing that is figured in self-experience exist?[13]

I suggest that there is nothing more at issue than this. And this, just this, is my fundamental move in trying to bring order and a chance of progress into the discussion—in particular, the philosophical discussion—of the self.

Does anything like the sort of thing that is figured in self-experience exist? The first thing to do is to see what sort of thing is figured in self-experience. Before we ask the *metaphysical* question

(I)   Do selves exist?

we must ask and answer the *phenomenological* question

(II)   What sort of thing is figured in self-experience?

I think this is at first best taken as a question about human beings, as the *local* phenomenological question

(II.1)   What sort of thing is figured in ordinary human self-experience?

But once we have an answer to the *local* phenomenological question, we have to go on to the more fundamental question, the *general* phenomenological question

---

[11]   Kenny 1988, 1989.

[12]   1997: 20. Note that this remark is phenomenological; Pinker's (rather unclear) metaphysical proposal is that 'the "I" is ... a unity of selfness over time, a locus that is nowhere in particular' (ibid. p. 564).

[13]   I use 'figured' in a highly general sense, one that carries no implication of picturing.

(II.2)   Are there other possibilities, so far as self-experience is concerned? (What sort of thing is figured in the minimal form of genuine self-experience?)

Once we have an answer to this second question we can go back to the metaphysical question 'Do selves exist?', which we can now address in two versions: 'Do selves exist as figured in ordinary human self-experience?' and 'Do selves exist as figured in the minimal form of self-experience?' But we have to begin with phenomenology.[14]

Some cultural relativists doubt that we can generalize about human experience, but it should become clear that the aspects of self-experience that concern me are situated below any level of plausible cultural variation. Even if there is some sense in which it is true that

the Western conception of the person as a bounded, unique, more or less integrated motivational universe, a dynamic centre of awareness, emotion, judgement, and action organised into a distinctive whole and set contrastively against other such wholes and against its social and natural background, is...a rather peculiar idea within the context of the world's cultures[15]

it doesn't constitute grounds for doubt about the present project.

I should stress that the expression 'self-experience' is just a phenomenological term: it is a name for a certain form of *experience* that does *not* imply that there actually are such things as selves. My use of the word 'self' is like William James's when he says that we must first try 'to settle...how this central nucleus of the Self may *feel*, no matter whether it be a spiritual substance or only a delusive word'. He uses the word 'self' freely as if it refers, while allowing that it may turn out to be 'only a delusive word', and I do the same.[16] Every time I use the phrase 'experience of the self' it can, if desired, be read as 'experience (as) of the self'.[17]

Some object that what I call 'phenomenology' is no such thing.[18] It is, however, a matter of the study of certain structures of experience considered just as such, and so fully qualifies for the name 'phenomenology'. I use the term in the standard non-aligned sense, which is widespread in analytic philosophy and has no special connection with the use that derives specifically from Brentano and Husserl.

---

[14] Brook (1998: 583) agrees that we must begin with phenomenology, but his reason differs from mine. His basic idea, which deserves serious consideration, is that the self considered as a metaphysical entity is a kind of phenomenologically constituted entity: 'the self is simply what one is aware of when one is aware of oneself [and specifically of one's mental features] from the inside' (ibid. p. 585). Zahavi and Parnas make a related move when they say that 'there is no difference between the...phenomenon of self and its metaphysical nature. Reality here is the same as appearance' (1998: 697). I think that we have to suppose that there is more to a self than is phenomenally given in this sense (see, however, the discussion of the 'Experience/Experiencer Identity thesis' in §13.2–3 below, pp. 254–5), and this seems to put me at odds with Zahavi and Parnas; but not necessarily with Brook.

[15] Geertz 1983: 59, quoted in Watson 1998.   [16] James 1890: 1.298.

[17] See §2.2. Wilkes (1998: 154) misses this point, taking it that I must suppose there to be a self, in talking of a sense of the self.

[18] Cf. e.g. Sheets-Johnstone, who criticizes my 'so-called "phenomenological" approach' (1999: 231), and Zahavi and Parnas (1998: 688).

3.4 Phenomenology: Self-experience

But what do I mean by 'self-experience'? (What, in '"The Self"', did I mean by 'the sense of the self'?) I don't (didn't) mean the 'sense of self' that is discussed in books about 'personal growth' and that is meant to be a good thing. Nor do I mean something that involves one's sense of oneself considered quite generally as a human being. I intentionally avoided the common phrase 'sense of self', using 'sense of *the* self' instead, and giving it an explicit definition: 'the sense that people have of themselves as being, specifically, a mental presence; a mental someone; a single mental thing that is a conscious subject of experience' (§2.2 above, p. 17). This definition was widely ignored, however, and the move from 'sense of the self' to 'sense of self' caused much misunderstanding.

Jonathan Cole, for example, shifted to 'sense of self' on his first page and contributed an excellent paper, on neurophysiological problems that affect the face, with which I have no disagreement (Cole 1997). Pickering also dropped the 'the' and also changed the subject, choosing to define the self as 'a semiotic process that emerges in a web of relationships'.[19] Maxine Sheets-Johnstone also changed the subject in her agreeably hostile paper. Oscillating freely between 'the sense of the self' and 'sense of self', she detailed a number of important facts about normal human experience and mental development. She was wrong, however, to think that these facts conflict with my views either about self-experience (especially the minimal, non-human case of self-experience) or about the nature of selves.[20]

By 'self-experience', then, I mean the experience that people have of themselves as being, specifically, a mental presence; a mental someone; a single mental something or other. Such self-experience comes to every normal human being, in some form, in early childhood. The realization of the fact that one's thoughts are unobservable by others, the experience of the sense in which one is alone in one's head or mind, the mere awareness of oneself as thinking: these are among the deepest facts about the character of human life.[21] They are vivid forms of self-experience that are perhaps most often salient when one is alone and thinking, although they can be equally strong in a room full of people. Many psychologists and anthropologists are quite rightly concerned to stress the environmentally embedded, embodied, ecological or 'EEE' aspects of our experiential predicament as social and organic beings located

---

[19] Pickering 1999. This is another interesting paper. Once again my only major disagreement is that there is something he and I disagree about.

[20] Thus I am not 'denying...a *developing* sense of the self', or that 'the conceptual sense of self has any foundation in affectivity' (Sheets-Johnstone 1999: 248). I am not committed to 'an instant self fabricated on the spot' (ibid.), and don't contradict myself (ibid.) when I say (1) that a self is as much a physical object as a cow, and (2) that it is not thought of as being a thing in the way that a stone or a cat is ((1) is a metaphysical claim, (2) is phenomenological). Similarly, my only disagreement with Legerstee's (1998) paper on infant self-awareness is on the question whether we disagree. Nor do I disagree with Butterworth's (1998) views about 'ecological' aspects of self, given the way he chooses to use the word 'self', although I am sorry to see that psychology has not yet abandoned the false view that children can't attribute false beliefs to others, and don't acquire a 'theory of mind', until they are four (they can be adept at the age of two).

[21] I do not identify them with 'the origin of the sense of mental self', as Pickering suggests (1999: 73), and can accept the various claims about the development of self-experience made in this symposium.

in a physical environment, but they risk losing sight of the respect in which self-experience—the experience of oneself as a specifically mental something—is, none the less, the central or fundamental way (although it is obviously not the only way) in which human beings experience themselves.

I hear the objection that this is a Western, academic, deskbound, perspective, but I have in mind something that becomes clear after one has got past such objections, something that has now become relatively hard to see. It is, in large part, a simple consequence of the way in which our mental properties occupy—and tend to dominate—the foreground, when it comes to our apprehension of ourselves. It is not only that we are often preoccupied with our own thoughts and experiences, living with ourselves principally in our inward mental scene, incessantly presented to ourselves as things engaged in mental business.[22] It is also that mental goings on are always and necessarily present, even when we are thoroughly preoccupied with our bodies, or, generally, with things in the world other than our own mental goings on. Obviously we can be the subjects of mental goings on without being explicitly aware of them as such. Our attention can be intensely focused outward. But even then we tend to have a constant background awareness of our own mental goings on—it is usually inadequate to say that it is merely background awareness—and a constant tendency to flip back to some explicit sense of ourselves as minded or conscious.

Many lay heavy stress on our constant background awareness of our bodies, but this awareness is fully compatible with our thinking of ourselves primarily or centrally as mental things, and those who stress somatic awareness may forget that it is just as true to say that there is constant background (as well as foreground) awareness of our minds. Kinaesthetic experience and other forms of proprioceptive experience of body are just that—experience—and insofar as they contribute constantly to our overall sense of ourselves, they not only contribute awareness of the body, they also contribute themselves, together with background awareness of themselves. The notion of background awareness is imprecise, but it seems plausible to say that there is certainly never *less* background awareness of awareness (i.e. of mind) than there is background awareness of body, and unprejudiced reflection reveals that awareness of mind, background or foreground, vastly predominates over awareness of body. Nothing hangs on this quantitative claim, however. For whether or not it is true, the constantly impinging phenomena of one's mental life are far more salient in the constitution of one's sense that there is such a thing as the self than are the phenomena of bodily experience.

Shear, in his contribution to the symposium, points out that it is common to have no particular sense of oneself as embodied when dreaming, although one's sense of one's presence in or at the dream-scene is extremely vivid. Such dream-experience is probably part of our experience from infancy, and doubtless contributes profoundly

---

[22] Russell Hurlburt made random samplings of the character of people's experience as they went about their daily life by activating beepers that they carried with them: 'it was striking that the great majority of subjects at the time of the beep were focused on some inner event or events, with no direct awareness of outside events at that moment' (Hurlburt et al. 1994: 387). Obviously such disengaged thoughts may themselves be focused on outside events—e.g. past events or possible future events. The fact is none the less of considerable interest (it is instructive to watch people in the street). See further Ch. 4 below.

to our overall sense of the self as a mental something. To consider its experiential character is, as he says, to get an idea of 'how discoordinated a basic aspect of our deeply held, naive commonsensical notions of self [is] from anything graspable in terms of body, personality, or, indeed, any identifiable empirical qualities at all'.[23]

Independently of this point there is, as Shear says, 'an important sense in which we conceive of ourselves purely as experiencers' (1998: 676) in a way which is certainly not just a recent and local product of modern (Western) man's 'hyperreflexivity'.[24] We may allow Gallagher's and Marcel's phrase 'hyperreflective consciousness' as a description of such self-experience, but only if we explicitly cancel any suggestion that it is recent and Western and in some way marginal, rather than something that has always been an essential part of the human experiential repertoire—and not restricted to solitary shepherds, spinners, trappers, messengers, farmers or fishermen, or times of 'philosophical reflection and certain limit situations like fatigue and illness'.[25] Many of those who are anxious to dissociate themselves from any 'taint' of 'Cartesianism' and to emphasize their EEE 'enthusiasm for the body'[26] have overcompensated. They have become unable to give a proper place to—clearly see—some of the plainest, most quiet, and most fundamental facts of ordinary human experience.

I am not saying that we don't also naturally experience ourselves as embodied human beings considered as a whole. Obviously we do.[27] Nor am I claiming that self-experience involves any belief in a non-physical soul. It doesn't. It is as natural and inevitable for atheists and materialists as for anyone else.

3.5 Phenomenology: the Local Question

Let me now add some detail to this general description of self-experience. In ordinary human self-experience, I propose, the self tends to be figured as

[1] a *subject of experience*, a conscious feeler and thinker
[2] a *thing*, in some interestingly robust sense
[3] a *mental* thing, in some sense[28]
[4] a thing that is *single* at any given time, and during any unified or hiatus-free period of experience
[5] a *persisting* thing, a thing that continues to exist across hiatuses in experience

---

[23] Shear 1998: 678. To say this is not to say that one could dream in this way if one didn't have (or hadn't once had) normal experience of embodiment. Nor is it to say that there is any sense in which one is or even could be independent of one's body, as Shear stresses (p. 677).

[24] Sass 1998: 545. Sass claims that we must look to 'the [modern] era of western intellectual history' to find the time 'when consciousness first comes to know itself as such', but—waiving objections based on ancient western and non-western traditions of thought—I would say that this happens, in a deep, plain, unqualified sense, in the case of every normal human being.

[25] Gallagher and Marcel 1999: 289.

[26] Shoemaker 1999a. Shoemaker is a 'friend of the body', as I am, but he senses that we live in a period of excessive reaction to the 'spectre' of 'Cartesianism'.

[27] Gallagher and Marcel (1999) give some outstanding descriptions of this phenomenon.

[28] A sense that is which is wholly compatible with materialism or physicalism.

[6] an *agent*

[7] as something that has a certain character or *personality*.[29]

I offer this as a piece of *cognitive phenomenology*: it aims to articulate the basic *conceptual structure* of our sense of the self, insofar as the self is experienced specifically as an inner mental presence. It does not advert to *affective* elements in our self-experience, which require separate discussion, but it does not thereby cast any doubt on their profound importance to the overall character of self-experience, or on the (phylogenetic and ontogenetic) importance of affect in the development of consciousness and self-consciousness, or on the view that 'affects constitute the core of being for many of our higher faculties' (Panskepp 1998: 579). It just focuses for purposes of discussion on one aspect of the phenomenon that is in question.[30]

All of [1]–[7] need explanation or argument, but here I will add only two brief illustrative comments to what I said in '"The Self"'. First, as far as [4] is concerned, I take the idea of a strongly experientially unified or hiatus-free period of thought or experience as primitive. The conscious entertaining of a thought like 'the cat is on the mat', in which the elements *cat*, *on*, and *mat* are bound together into a single thought, is a paradigm example of such a period of experience. So is looking up and seeing books and chairs and seeing them as such. Like Dennett, I take it that such periods are almost always short in the human case, and I believe that there is strong experimental support for this view.

Condition [2], the proposal that a self is experienced as a thing in some sense, is generally doubted, and I defend it in §3.7 below. The general idea is that self-experience does not present the self as (merely) a state or property of something else, or as an event, or some sort of process. To that extent, *there is nothing else for a self to seem to be*, other than a thing of some sort. Obviously it is not thought of as being a thing in the way that a stone or a chair is. But it is none the less figured as a thing of some kind—something that can *undergo* things and *do* things and, most simply, *be in some state or other*. None of these things can be true of processes as ordinarily conceived of.

3.6 Phenomenology: the General Question

Conditions [1]–[7] constitute the answer to the *local phenomenological* question, and deliver the following version of the *metaphysical* question: 'Do selves exist as figured

---

[29] I have dropped one of the eight conditions (the ontic distinctness condition) given in §2.3, p. 19, on the grounds that it is redundant, and have renumbered the others, giving first place, as seems appropriate, to the subject-of-experience condition.

[30] The term 'cognitive phenomenology' confused many. It is in no sense true that I have a 'determinedly cognitivist' conception of the self (Butterworth 1998: 132), or attempt to 'define a self in purely "cognitive rather than affective terms"' (Hayward 1998: 621), or think that 'the self is made up of cognitive phenomena' (Legerstee 1998: 640), or have 'a strictly cognitive view of the self' (Cole 1997: 467). More generally, it is in no sense true that I am not interested in, or discount, the affective aspects of self-experience. (I took up the term 'cognitive phenomenology' in 1980 when discussing the experience of freedom, which is clearly not just a matter of sensory experience: see Strawson 1986: 30, 55, 70, 96, 107–9. It also applies to the experience of thought and understanding language: see Strawson 1994: 5–13, 182–3; see also Ayers 1991: 244–54, and Pitt 2004. I have grown accustomed to the term, and should have realized that it invited misunderstanding.)

in ordinary human self-experience?' I think the answer is No, and on this I agree with James, Dennett, many if not all Buddhists, and probably with Hume, and even with Fichte. The related question 'What is the very best one can come up with, if one's brief is to argue that selves do exist as figured in ordinary human self-experience?' is well worth pursuing, but I am going to bypass it and go on to the *general phenomenological* question: 'What is the minimal form of self-experience?'

I think that [5], [6], and [7]—long-term continuity, agenthood, and personality— can be dispensed with (remember that we are no longer restricted to the human case), and that the minimal form of self-experience is a sense of the self as

[1]   a *subject of experience*
[2]   a *thing*, in some interestingly robust sense
[3]   a *mental* thing, in some sense
[4]   *single* at any given time, and during any hiatus-free or strongly experientially unified period of experience.

Many doubt whether any of [5], [6], and [7] can be dropped, and their dispensability needs to be argued for at length. But I think that they can be seen to be absent even in certain human cases.

Some hold that [7], the personality condition, is clearly ineliminable, because to think in terms of self just is to think in terms of individual personality. But self-experience is just: the specific experience of being a mental subject or inner mental presence; and even if this can involve a sense of oneself as having personality, it need not.

One way to make this vivid is to appeal to the fact that nearly everyone has at some time experienced themselves as a kind of bare locus of consciousness, void of personality, but still for all that a mental subject. Equally important, however, is the respect in which lack of any sense of the self as having personality is normal, in the human case. One tends to see personality clearly when one considers other people, but not when one considers oneself. One's personality is usually built so deeply into the way one apprehends things that it does not present itself to awareness in such a way as to enter significantly into one's self-experience. Obviously one may experience oneself as being in certain moods, but it certainly does not follow that one experiences oneself as having a certain personality. One's own personality is usually something that is unnoticed in the present moment. It's what one looks through, or where one looks from; not something one looks at.

What about [6], the agency condition? One of the great dividing facts about humanity is that some people experience their mental lives in a Rimbaud-like or Meursault-like fashion, i.e. almost entirely as something that just happens to them, while others naturally think of themselves as controllers and intentional producers of their thoughts.[31] The latter group are particularly likely to doubt whether [6] can be dispensed with, even in non-human cases, and I will not try to convince them here.

---

[31] Rimbaud 1871: 249, 250: 'It's false to say: I think: one ought to say it thinks [in] me...for *I* is an other...It's obvious to me that I am a spectator at the unfolding of my thought: I watch it, I listen to it'. Cf. also Camus 1942, 1960, and the description of the 'Spectator subject' and the 'natural Epictetans' in Strawson 1986: chs. 12 and 13. Bruner, referring to Happé 1991, notes that 'autists give typically

What does need to be said, in the context of the symposium, is that there is no tension between the claim that [6] can be dispensed with and facts about the crucial role of the experience of agency in human mental development, the importance of kinaesthesia to human self-awareness, and so on.[32]

3.7 Phenomenology: Diachronics and Episodics

Condition [5], the long-term persistence condition, engages with another of the great dividing facts about humanity. Some people have a strongly narrative or (more neutrally) *Diachronic* way of thinking about themselves, a strong sense that *the I that is a mental presence now* was there in the past and will be there in the future. Others have a very different, *Episodic* way of being in time. Episodics, looking out from the present, have very little sense that the I that is a mental presence now was there in the past and will be there in the further future. They are, perhaps, like John Updike when he writes that he has 'the persistent sensation, in my life . . . , that I am just beginning' (1979: 239). They relate differently to their autobiographical memories. In my own case, the interest (emotional or otherwise) of my—rather sparse—autobiographical memories lies in their experiential content considered quite independently of the fact that what is remembered happened *to me*. In fact I am strongly inclined to say that the events in question didn't happen to me—to *me**, i.e. to that which I feel myself to be, in having self-experience—at all (*me** is an essentially phenomenological notion, see §2.8, p. 32 above). These memories are of course distinctive in their 'from-the-inside' character, and they certainly happened to the human being that I (also) am; but it simply does not follow that they present, or are experienced, as things that happened to me* as just characterized.

Many are surprised by this last claim. They take it that having a 'from-the-inside' character immediately entails being experienced as something that happened to me*. But this is not so. The 'from-the-inside' character of a memory can detach completely from any lived identification with the subject of the remembered experience. My memory of falling out of a punt has, intrinsically, a from-the-inside character, visual (the water rushing up to meet me), kinaesthetic, proprioceptive, and so on, but it does not follow that it carries any sense or belief that what is remembered happened to me*.[33]

---

nonagentive accounts of themselves and their lives' (1994: 48), and autism is clearly of great interest when considering whether [5], [6], and [7] are necessary parts of human self-experience.

[32] So I have no disagreement with Legerstee (1998). The appearance of disagreement arises from three things: her reading of phenomenological claims as metaphysical claims; her focus on the human case; and her assumption that I *argue* 'that the "self" is a purely mental entity' (p. 627), whereas in fact I *define* the notion of self in this way in order to see what can then be made of it. Nor do I disagree with Sheets-Johnstone here. She finds my 'treatment of agency—or rather non-treatment of agency— . . . near astounding' (1999: 239), but the principal explanation, apart, perhaps, from differences in the way we experience things, is simple: I am not particularly concerned with the ordinary human case, or indeed with any human case, and certainly not with human developmental necessities.

[33] For the visual aspect, imagine two video recordings, one from the river bank, one from a camera placed between my eyes.

It does not follow even when the remembered event is experienced from the inside in emotional respects. I can have a memory that incorporates emotional concern felt from the inside without in any way feeling that what I remember happened to me*. So the inference from (a) 'The memory has a from-the-inside character emotionally considered' to (b) 'The memory is experienced as something that happened to me*' is not valid, although (a) and (b) may very often be true together (especially in the case of certain kinds of memory). I find this to be a plain fact of experience. Those who do not may gain a sense of it if they know what it is to be emotionally involved, by sympathy or empathy, in the life or outlook of another person or a fictional character without having any sense that one is that other person or character (the common phrase 'empathetic *identification*' can be misleading).

This is obviously not enough to show that self-experience need not involve [5], experience of the self as having long-term diachronic continuity. Large issues are involved. One concerns another great dividing fact about humanity which can be briefly described as follows. Many think it beyond question that we can and inevitably do (and in any case should) 'create and construct our "selves"'.[34] Others find such a claim bewildering, insofar as it implies that one's development as a person involves (or should involve) any significant amount of conscious planning, any need for studied reflection on where one has come from or where one is going, any preoccupation with one's life considered specifically *as one's own life*, rather than as a source of understanding and possible deepening whose instructiveness does not depend internally and constitutively—even if it depends causally—on the fact that it is one's own life.[35] For members of the second group the process is effectively automatic and unpondered; and they may observe that a person could develop just as valuably by empathetic participation—involuntary, unplanned, never consciously mulled over, not a matter of identification in any strong sense—in the experiences of the protagonists of great novels. In general, we can all learn deeply from experience, and from vicarious experience, and develop in various ways, without any particular autobiographical concern with ourselves, and indeed with little reflection on ourselves. The less conscious reflection the better, in many cases. The 'examined life' is greatly overrated.

Diachronics may feel there is something chilling and empty in the Episodic life, but the principal thing about it is simply that it is more directed on the present. The past is not alive in memory, as Diachronics may find, but it is alive—Episodics might say more truly alive—in the form of the present: insofar as it has shaped the way one is in the present. There is no reason to think that the present is less informed by or responsible to the past in the Episodic life than in the Diachronic life. It is rather that

---

[34] Wilkes 1998: 164. For a powerful statement of this position, see Schechtman 1996 ch. 5, 'The Narrative Self-Constitution View': 'baldly... stated', her view is that 'a person creates his identity by forming an autobiographical narrative—a story of his life' (p. 93).

[35] Hirst (1994) shows how there can be personal development in people who have severe anterograde or retrograde amnesia or both, and are to that extent incapable of 'narrative self-construction' of the sort that some believe to be necessary to such development. It is clear that such people have no deficit in their basic capacity for self-experience, and the same is true of 'W. R.', in spite of the fact that damage to his dorsolateral prefrontal cortex means that he is 'locked... into the immediate space and time' (Knight and Grabowecky 1995).

the informing and the responsiveness have different mechanisms and different experiential consequences.

3.8 Phenomenology: Me* and Morality

There is one other issue relating to [5] that is worth a comment. I claim in a footnote (Chapter 2, note 23) that the Episodic life may be 'no less intense or full, emotional or moral' than the Narrative or Diachronic life, and Wilkes argues forcefully that this cannot be so:

Morality is a matter of planning future actions, calculating consequences, experiencing remorse and contrition, accepting responsibility, accepting praise and blame; such mental phenomena are both forward- and backward-looking. Essentially.... Emotions such as love or hate, envy or resentment, would not deserve the name—except in some occasional rare cases— if they lasted for but three seconds, and were thereafter claimed, not by any me*, but by some former self.... The Episodic life could not be richly moral and emotional; we must have a life, or self, with duration. We are, and must consider ourselves as, relatively stable intentional systems. Essentially.   (1998: 155)

Well, it's true that the moral life of Episodics is not the same as that of Diachronics, but that is not to say that it is less moral or less emotional. There are strikingly different 'varieties of moral personality' in the human species,[36] and members of one variety tend to have an incorrectly dim view of the moral nature of members of another. The question is very complicated, and here the following brief points will have to suffice.

The main problem is that Wilkes exaggerates my position. In '"The Self"' I note that I make plans for the future, although I am somewhere down the Episodic end of the human spectrum, and in that sense 'think of myself perfectly adequately as something that has long-term continuity'. I add that 'I'm perfectly well aware that [my past] is mine, insofar as I am a human being considered as a whole', observe that there are certain things in the future—such as my death—and equally certain things in the past—such as embarrassment—that I can experience as involving me*, and stress the point that 'one's sense of one temporal nature may vary considerably depending on what one is thinking about' (§2.8, p. 33).[37] There is, then, no reason why some Episodics may not apprehend some of their past dubious actions as involving their me*, and accordingly feel remorse or contrition.

This is not to concede that remorse and contrition are essential to the moral life.[38] There is a great deal more to say, and Wilkes confuses an ontological proposal about the normal duration of human selves (up to three seconds) with a phenomenological description of Episodic experience that nowhere suggests that the present me*

---

[36] Cf. Flanagan 1991. One particularly striking difference is between those for whom the moral-emotional categories of resentment and humiliation are central, and those for whom they are hardly visible.

[37] One may link up to various discrete, non-narratively apprehended sections of one's past in exactly the way that Locke envisages in his massively misunderstood theory of personal identity (for the correct understanding, see Schechtman 1996: 105–9; see also Ch. 12 below).

[38] Note, for example, that matter-of-fact self-criticism—or indeed self-anger—that lacks the character-istic phenomenology of remorse or contrition (or self-reproach, or self-disgust) need not be a morally inferior way of experiencing one's own wrongdoing.

is always experienced as lasting only three seconds.[39] The Episodic life is not absolute in the way she supposes. Human beings fall on a continuous spectrum from radically Episodic to radically Narrative, and may move along the spectrum in one direction or another as they age.

Episodics are less likely to suffer in Yeats's way—

> Things said or done long years ago,
> Or things I did not do or say
> But thought that I might say or do,
> Weigh me down, and not a day
> But something is recalled,
> My conscience or my vanity appalled   (1933: 284)

—even if their lives have been as imperfect as everyone else's. But if they are faced with criticisms from Diachronics who see their lightness as a moral failing, they may observe, correctly, that there is a point (perilously close in some cases) where vanity and conscience—what appears to be conscience—turn out to be a single phenomenon. And this line of thought has striking continuations. It is, for example, arguable that *guilt* (also mentioned by Wilkes as important) is a fundamentally self-indulgent—selfish—moral emotion, as well as a superficial one; although *sorrow* about what one has done is neither selfish nor superficial. Some may suggest that this view of guilt is itself evidence of moral failing, and that someone who holds it cannot fully participate in the moral form of life (although one can hold it while continuing to feel guilt), but they are surely wrong.

This last suggestion shows a serious lack of feeling for human difference, but it isn't as bad as an objection that some (not Wilkes) have made, according to which Episodics cannot be properly moral because, in feeling unconcerned in their past, they lack a vital moral constraint on action. This is clearly false. One doesn't have to care about one's past (considered as such) in order to want to act rightly, and in order to do so. One doesn't have to be governed by prudential concern about one's *future past*—the past one will have to live with in the future. One's present commitments—outlook—feelings—awareness of the situation—can be wholly sufficient. Many find concern about the future past completely absent from the phenomenology of moral engagement. Their concern is to do what should be done simply because it is what should be done, or (without the Kantian loop) simply to do what should be done. To be guided by concern about one's future past when making decisions is not to have a distinctively moral motive at all, nor indeed a particularly admirable motive.

I want to finish with phenomenology and get on to metaphysics, but I still haven't discussed the widely rejected[40] phenomenological claim that self-experience (necessarily) involves [2] experience of the self as a thing in some sense. My optimistic view is that no one will disagree once I have adequately explained what I mean.[41]

---

[39] Half an hour is offered as one possible candidate—subject to the point, mentioned above, that 'one's sense of one temporal nature may vary considerably depending on what one is thinking about'.

[40] See for example Forman 1998: 191, Hayward 1998: 611, 624, Laycock 1998: 142, Pickering 1999: Sheets-Johnstone 1999: 249.

[41] I give a further independent argument in Strawson 2009: 65–7, 169–73.

3.9 Phenomenology: the Experience of the Self as a Thing

The objection to [2] is clear. Why couldn't a self-conscious creature's self-experience involve experiencing the self as just a property or set of properties of something else (perhaps a human being), or just as a process of some sort?

It depends, of course, on what you mean by 'thing', 'property', and 'process', and by 'experience something as a thing…or property…or set of properties…or process'. I take the words 'thing', 'property', and 'process' to have their ordinary, imprecise pre-theoretical force when they are used phenomenologically to characterize forms of experience. (The issue of how they are best used in metaphysics remains to be considered.)

The question recurs. Must genuine self-experience really involve [2], experience of the self as a thing of some kind?

It may seem very hard to be sure, given the vagueness of the word 'thing', and after the discussion of the question 'What is a thing?' in §§3.14–18 below some may feel that little hangs on the answer. What I have in mind is simply this: there is a key sense in which Kant is right that 'everyone must necessarily regard himself', the conscious subject, 'as [a] substance', and must regard all episodes of thought or conscious episodes 'as being only accidents of his existence, determinations of his state'. As he says, 'the "I" who thinks or is conscious must always be considered in such thought or consciousness as a *subject* and as something that does not merely attach to thought or consciousness like a predicate'.[42]

Kant's main aim in the Paralogisms is to show that one cannot argue from this phenomenological fact to any corresponding metaphysical fact. He points out that it does not follow, from the fact that we must *experience* or regard the 'I' or self as a substance or thing, that it actually *is* a substance or thing, or that we can know that this is so. We cannot, he says, rule out the possibility that the 'I' of thought or consciousness may in the final analysis be just a property of something else, 'a predicate of another being'. It is, he says, 'quite impossible' for me, given my experience of myself as a mental phenomenon, 'to determine the manner in which I exist, whether it be as substance [or object] or as accident [or property]'.[43] As a theorist one may believe (as I do) that there is a sense in which the phenomena that constitute selves (if they exist) are 'just' processes in the brain;[44] and one may also think (as I do not) that this view of selves is incompatible with the view that they are things in any worthwhile sense; and so conclude that they are definitely not things (insofar as they exist at all). So be it, Kant will reply. None of this constitutes an objection to the fundamental phenomenological claim that if one has self-experience at all, one must experience the self as a 'substance' or thing of some kind.

I agree. I have little to add to Kant's arguments and the last paragraph of §3.5 above, where it was suggested that the fundamental respect in which the self is apprehended under the category of thing is already manifest in the way in which it

---

[42] A349, B407. I read 'must' with Pluhar rather than 'can' with Kemp Smith.
[43] B419–20.   [44] For the trouble with 'just' see §3.17 below.

is experienced as something that can *have* or *undergo* things like sensations and emotions, something that can *be in some state or other*. No experience that presents something as something that *has experience* or even just as something that can *be in some state or other* can figure it merely as a property of something else, or as a mere process, or event.[45] This is the primary intuition.

It is worth thinking an explicit I-thought like 'I am reading an article' or 'I am present, here, now, thinking that I am present here now'; not simply apprehending the content of some such thought by reading, but stopping to think one through. If, overcoming one's natural contrasuggestibility, one accepts to do this, one encounters, in a vivid way, the inescapable respect in which self-experience—experience of oneself as a mental subject of experience—must involve figuring the self as a thing in a sense sufficient for the truth of [2].

—But how can you rule out a priori the idea that an alien might have self-experience that figured the self as just a process?

Well, if it really does have self-experience, and really does experience itself, when it apprehends itself as a mental self, as a subject of experience that has thoughts and experiences and is in certain mental states, then it experiences the self as a thing in a sense sufficient for my purposes. Kant got it right. If someone says that I have not really given an argument for this, and have merely presented an intuition in a certain way, I will not take it as a criticism. If someone says that I have taken a long time to say something obvious that Kant said long ago, I will accept it as a criticism but I will not mind. If someone says the whole section is a laborious statement of the obvious, I will be rather pleased. If, finally, someone says that any sense of the self as a thing may dissolve in the self-awareness of meditation, I will agree, and reply that in that case self-experience of the kind that is at present of concern will also have dissolved (this being, perhaps, and after all, the aim of the meditation).

3.10 Phenomenology: Eyes and *Is*

The preceding sentence raises an important issue. Self-experience is defined as experience that has the character of being of a—the—mental self. But it is not clear that any genuine experience of *what one is considered as a whole and specifically as a mental phenomenon*—call this 'M-experience'—must *ipso facto* be a form of *self-experience*. It is not clear that all genuine M-experience must have the full structure of self-experience. By the same token, it is not clear that the minimal case of self-experience is ipso facto the minimal case of M-experience. I suspect that the minimal case of M-experience may be some kind of 'pure consciousness' experience, of the kind discussed by Buddhists and others, that no longer involves anything that can usefully be called 'self-experience' at all.[46]

I will take this suggestion a little way, in combination with a point about the notion of an object of thought, for some contributors to the symposium focused on such

---

[45] Here 'property', 'process', and 'event' have their ordinary pretheoretical sense, and 'mere' and 'merely' are added to match.

[46] In this symposium, see e.g. Forman 1998: 186ff., Hayward 1998, Shear 1998. See also Parfit 1998b.

matters, and may feel that their central doubts have not yet been addressed, let alone answered.

When I claim that self-experience must involve [2] experience of being a (mental) thing of some sort, the sort of self-apprehension that I have in mind need not and typically does not involve targeting oneself as an *object of thought* in a way that opens a path to the well-known view that the I or self or subject is 'systematically elusive' to itself and cannot ever truly take itself—i.e. itself as it is in the present moment—as the object of its thought.[47] I think this view is false, in fact, but the first point to make is that it would not matter to [2] if it were true, for the root thought behind [2] is simply this: if you have self-experience, you can't *live* yourself, experienced as mental *subject*, as somehow merely a process or property or event. (This thought is, I suppose, very close to triviality, which is often, in philosophy, a good place to be.)[48] In this regard I agree with Sass when he says that 'the most fundamental sense of selfhood involves the experience of self not as an *object* of awareness but, in some crucial respects, as an unseen point of origin for action, experience, and thought', and again when he says that 'what William James called...the "central nucleus of the Self" is not, in fact, experienced as an entity *in the focus of our awareness*, but, rather, as a kind of medium of awareness, source of activity, or general directedness towards the world'.[49] This is well expressed, and I take it to be fully compatible with the lived sense in which the self is [2] experienced as a thing of some sort. [2] does not require experience of self that is experience (as) of 'an entity in the focus of awareness'.

Is the I or subject none the less systematically elusive? Is there some sense in which genuine self-presence of mind is essentially impossible? The matter requires reflection, but it seems to me that Lonergan, for one, is right when he says that

objects are present by being attended to, but subjects are present [to themselves] as subjects, not by being attended to, but by attending. As the parade of objects marches by, spectators do not have to slip into the parade to be present to themselves.[50]

Deikman makes the same point: 'we know the internal observer not by observing it but by *being* it...knowing by being that which is known is...different from perceptual knowledge', as do Zahavi and Parnas, introducing the notion of 'the basic self-awareness of an experience', which they describe as 'an immediate and intrinsic self-acquaintance which is characterized by being completely irrelational'.[51]

Certainly the eye cannot see itself (unless there is a mirror), and the knife cannot cut itself (unless it is very flexible), and the fingertip cannot touch itself, and one

---

[47] Cf. Ryle 1949: 186.

[48] Once, after having given a paper, Brian McGuinness was faced with the objection that one of his claims was trivial. He paused, looked worried for a moment, and then replied 'I *hope* it's trivial.'

[49] 1998: 562, my italics.

[50] Lonergan 1967: 226, quoted by Forman (1998: 193). It is interesting to note how this parallels some of Gallagher's and Marcel's remarks about the experience of agency (1999), notwithstanding the strong EEE emphasis of their discussion.

[51] Deikman 1996: 355, Zahavi and Parnas 1998: 696. Note that we certainly do not have to suppose that (1), 'knowing by being that which is known', or rather, perhaps, knowing (oneself) by being that which is knowing, entails (2), knowing everything there is to know about that which is known. On a materialist view, one may grant that that which is known, in the case of self-presence of mind of the sort envisaged in (1), has non-experiential being that is not known.

cannot jump on to the shadow of one's own head.[52] It is a very ancient claim, with many metaphorical expressions, that the I cannot take itself as it is in the present moment as the object of its thought, that 'my ... present ... perpetually slips out of any hold of it that I try to take',[53] and several contributors to this symposium concur. Laycock expresses the claim in dozens of different ways in his extremely rich Husserlian-phenomenological paper 'Consciousness It/Self', and observes that it is part of 'perennial Buddhist wisdom'.[54] And so it is, considered as a truth about the limitations of a certain form of self-apprehension. But it is as such fully compatible with a claim to which it appears to be opposed, according to which there is another form of self-apprehension in which the I or subject—or just consciousness, if you wish—*can* be directly or immediately explicitly aware of itself in the present moment. I think this is true, and will try to say why. First, though, note that it doesn't matter whether it is true or not when it comes to [2], the claim that self-experience involves experience of the self as a thing of some sort; for even if the I or subject cannot be explicitly aware of itself as it is in the present moment, [2] remains unaffected as a claim about how one must *live* oneself in having self-experience.[55]

The view that the mental subject can be aware of itself as it is in the present moment may be challenged as vague and mystical. The systematic elusiveness objection—according to which one cannot after all directly apprehend oneself as mental self or subject or thinker in the present moment—may be redeployed. You may think *I am now thinking a puzzling thought*, or *I'm looking down on India*, or just *Here I am*, in an attempt to so apprehend yourself, but in entertaining these contents you necessarily fail to apprehend the thing that is doing the apprehending—the entertainer of the content, the thinker of the thought, i.e. yourself considered as the mental self at that moment. Any performance, as Ryle says, 'can be the concern of a higher-order performance'—one can think about any thought that one has—but it 'cannot be the concern of itself'. When one thinks an I-thought

this performance is not dealt with in the operation which it itself is. Even if the person is, for special speculative purposes, momentarily concentrating on the Problem of the Self, he has failed and knows that he has failed to catch more than the flying coat-tails of that which he was pursuing. His quarry was the hunter.[56]

It is arguable, however, that to think *This very thought is puzzling*—or *I am now thinking a puzzling thought*, or *The having of this thought is strange*—is precisely to engage in a performance that is concerned with itself; so that a certain kind of immediate self-presence of mind is possible even in an intentional, designedly self-reflexive, and wholly cognitive act, quite independently of the truth of the

---

[52] Ryle 1949: 187. But perhaps it is high noon. One leans one's head forward and makes a small jump while slightly drawing back one's head.

[53] Ryle 1949: 187.

[54] 1998: 142. Cf. also Deikman (1996: 350): distinguishing between experiencing and 'seeing', which presumably stands for any sort of experientially mediated operation, he says that the 'I' can be experienced, but cannot be 'seen'.

[55] So I need not disagree with Edey, for example, when he claims (1997: 528) that 'the subject is not an object'.

[56] Ryle 1949: 188–9.

considerations adduced by Lonergan, Deikman, Forman, Shear, and others. It is only when one tries to apprehend that one has succeeded that one triggers the regressive step. It may be added that there does not seem to be any obvious reason why a hunter cannot catch the quarry when the quarry is himself. A detective with amnesia, sitting in her chair and reasoning hard, may identify herself as the person who committed the crime she is investigating. Wandering in the dark, I may get increasingly precise readings regarding the location of my quarry from a Global Positioning System, activate my grabber arms to move to the correct spot and grab, press the grab-function button, and get grabbed.

Actually one can allow, if only for the sake of argument, that concentration on cognitively articulated thoughts like *I am now thinking a puzzling thought* or *Here I am* cannot deliver what is required, or provide a successful practical route to appreciation of the point that it is possible to have genuinely present self-awareness of oneself as the mental subject of experience. For the best route is more direct, and does not involve any such cognitively articulated representations. It is simply a matter of coming to awareness of oneself as a mental presence—as mental presence— in a certain sort of concentrated but global—unpointed—way. It can be done; the object of one's awareness doesn't have to be a content in such a way that it cannot be the thing that is entertaining the content. On this point Ryle and others are simply wrong. There is no insuperable difficulty in the matter of present or immediate self-awareness. I can engage in it with no flying coat-tails time-lag. The case is just not like the case of the eye that cannot see itself, or a fingertip that cannot touch itself. A mind is, rather dramatically, more than an eye. If Ryle had spent more time on disciplined, unprejudiced introspection, or had tried meditation, even if only briefly, and in an entirely amateur and unsupervised way, like myself—he would have found that it is really not very difficult—although it is quite difficult—for the subject of experience to be aware in the present moment of itself-in-the-present-moment. As far as the level of difficulty is concerned, it seems to me that is like maintaining one's balance on a bar in a way that is quite hard but not extremely hard. One can easily lose one's balance—one can fall out of the state in question—but one can also keep it. No doubt it is something one gets better at if one practises certain kinds of meditation, in which such self-awareness has the status of a rather banal first step (about which there is extremely wide consensus) towards something more remarkable.

The direct evidence for this, and for 'pure consciousness' experience, is and can only come from introspection and meditative practice. Each must acquire it for himself or herself. This does not mean it is not empirical; clearly it is. It does mean that it is not publicly checkable, and it will always be possible for someone to object that the experience of truly present self-awareness is an illusion—produced, say, by Rylean flashes of 'swift retrospective heed'.[57]

Whatever one thinks of this, there is another mistake, which may tempt those who carry EEE thinking (§2.4) too far, that can be decisively blocked. There is no good argument from the true EEE fact that naturally evolved forms of consciousness are

---

[57] Ryle 1949: 153. These thoughts are developed in Ch. 10 below.

profoundly, and seemingly constitutively, and, in the natural course of things, almost incessantly, in the service of the interoceptive and exteroceptive perceptual and agentive survival needs of organisms[58] to the conclusion that Forman (e.g.) must be wrong to claim that 'consciousness should not be defined in terms of perceptions, content, or its other functions'.[59] Forman holds that in certain meditative states 'awareness itself is experienced as still or silent, perceptions as active or changing. Therefore instead of defining awareness in terms of its content, we should think about awareness and its mental and sensory *functions* as two independent phenomena or processes that somehow interact.' I think that this notion of interacting processes may be too separatist, and that the contentual features of states of awareness—more precisely, the contentual features of states of awareness that involve content other than whatever content is involved in simple awareness of awareness—should rather be seen as modifications of awareness. But the basic idea of pure awareness or consciousness is not in tension with anything in the theory of evolution by natural selection.

This is a topic that needs a lot more discussion. Here let me say that even if consciousness is not a primordial property of the universe, and came on the scene relatively late, there is no good reason—in fact it doesn't even make sense—to think that it first came on the scene because it had survival value. Natural selection needs something to work on and can only work on what it finds. Consciousness had to exist before it could be exploited, just as non-conscious matter did. I take it that natural selection moulded the consciousness it found in nature into adaptive forms just as it moulded the non-conscious phenomena it found. From this perspective, the task of giving an evolutionary explanation of the *existence* of consciousness is just like the task of giving an evolutionary explanation of the existence of non-conscious matter (there is no such task). And the evolution by natural selection of various finely developed types of consciousness (visual, olfactory, cognitive, etc.) is no more surprising than the evolution by natural selection of various finely developed types of body. Finally, even if evolved forms of consciousness came to be what they were because they had certain kinds of content that gave them survival value and that were (therefore) essentially other than whatever content is involved in simple awareness of awareness, it doesn't follow that pure consciousness experience is some sort of illusion or mere surface effect: even if pure consciousness experience as we can know it becomes possible only after millions of years of EEE-practical forms of consciousness, it does not follow that it is not uniquely revelatory of the fundamental nature of consciousness.

3.11 Transition: Phenomenology to Metaphysics

I have made a negative claim about self-experience and a positive claim with a rider. The negative claim is that self-experience does not necessarily involve [5]–[7]: it need

---

[58] Damasio (1994 ch. 10) gives a powerful description of the profundity of the connection between the mind and the rest of the body. Cf. also Panskepp (1998) on what he calls 'equalia...the most ancient evolutionary qualia', Ramachandran and Hirstein 1997, and Balleine and Dickinson 1998.

[59] Forman 1998: 197.

not involve any experience of the self as an agent that has long-term diachronic continuity and personality, even if it can do so. The positive claim is that any genuine form of self-experience must involve [1]–[4]: it must present the self as a subject of experience that is a mental thing that is single at any given time and during any unified or hiatus-free period of experience. The meditative rider to the positive claim is that genuine 'M-experience'—genuine experience of what one is considered as a whole and specifically as a mental phenomenon—need not involve self-experience.

I turn now from phenomenology to metaphysics, for the phenomenological investigation of self-experience has duly delivered two versions of the metaphysical question. (1) 'Do selves exist as figured in ordinary human self-experience?', (2) 'Do selves exist as figured in the minimal form of self-experience?' I am inclined to answer No to (1) and Yes to (2), but here I will consider only (2).

3.12 Metaphysics: Sesmets

Do selves exist as figured in the minimal form of self-experience? Are there [1] subjects of experience that are [4] single [3] mental [2] things? I think there are, and for the moment I will call them sesmets (subjects of experience that are single mental things), for this will allow me to put the case for their existence while leaving the question of whether it would be right or best to call them 'selves' entirely open.

In essentials I agree with William James, who holds that 'the same brain may subserve many conscious selves' that are entirely numerically distinct substances. Using the word 'thought' in the wide Cartesian sense to cover all types of conscious episodes, he claims that each '"perishing" pulse of thought' is a self, and in a famous phrase, says that 'the thoughts themselves are the thinkers'.[60] I think it is clearer to say that the existence of each thought involves a self, or consists in the existence of a self or sesmet or subject of experience entertaining a certain mental content, but the basic idea is the same. The apparent continuity of experience, such as it is,[61] and the consistency of perspective across selves, derives from the fact that sesmets 'appropriate'—in James's word—the experiential content of the experiences of their predecessors in a way that is entirely unsurprising insofar as they arise successively, like gouts of water from a rapidly sporadic fountain, from brain conditions that have considerable similarity from moment to moment even as they change. Given short-term or 'working' memory, the immediately preceding contents form part of the context in which new contents arise in every sense in which features of the external environment do.

'The I', James says,

is a *thought*, at each moment different from that of the last moment, but *appropriative* of the latter, together with all[62] that the latter called its own. All the experiential facts find their place in this description, unencumbered with any hypothesis save that of the existence of passing thoughts or states of mind.

---

[60] 1890: 1.401, 1.371; 1892: 191.   [61] For doubts see §2.9, pp. 33–5.
[62] This is surely too strong.

I take it, then, that there are many sesmets, in the case of a human being, and that for the most part they exist successively, although I agree with James that there is no theoretical difficulty in the idea that they may also exist concurrently.[63] Each one is an 'indecomposable unity', and 'the same brain may subserve many conscious selves' that 'have no *substantial* identity'.[64] James expresses himself loosely when he says that the self consists in 'a remembering and appropriating Thought incessantly renewed', for this phrase suggests that selves are things that have some sort of long-term continuity, but his more careful statement of his view explicitly cancels any such suggestion. He knows it is intensely natural for us to think of the self as something that has long-term continuity, and is accordingly prepared to speak loosely in sympathy with that tendency, while holding that it is in fact quite incorrect:

My present Thought stands ... in the plenitude of ownership of the train of my past selves, is owner not only *de facto*, but *de jure*, the most real owner there can be ... Successive thinkers, *numerically distinct*, but all aware of the past in the same way, form an adequate vehicle for all the *experience* of personal unity and sameness which we actually have.[65]

A sesmet, then, is a subject of experience as it is present and alive in the occurrence of an experience. It is as EEE—as embedded, embodied, and ecological—as anyone could wish. There cannot be a sesmet without an experience, and it is arguable that there cannot be an experience without a sesmet.[66] I take it that sesmets exist and are part of (concrete) reality. I think, in fact, that they are physical objects, as real as rabbits and atoms. It is true that this unpopular view depends on taking the words 'object' and 'physical' in an unfamiliar way, but I think that we have to take them in this way when we do serious metaphysics from a materialist standpoint. I will say something about this now, beginning with a brief account (repeating and expanding §2.5 above) of how realistic materialists must understand the physical.

3.13 Metaphysics: Realistic Materialists and the Physical

Step one. Materialism is the view that every thing and event in the universe is physical in every respect. It is the view that 'physical phenomenon' is coextensive

---

[63] 1890: 401. Note that there is no more metaphysical difficulty in the idea that a thing that lasts for two seconds can know Latin, be exhausted, kind, and in love, than there is in the idea that an ordinary human being considered during a two-second period of time can be said to have these properties during that time.

[64] 1890: 1.371, 1.401; 1892: 181.

[65] 1890: 1.362–3, 1.360; 1892: 181; my emphasis. Compare Damasio 1994: 236–43: 'at each moment the state of self is constructed, from the ground up. It is an evanescent reference state, so continuously and consistently *reconstructed* that the owner never knows that it is being *remade* unless something goes wrong with the remaking' (p. 240). Damasio goes on to say the same about what he calls the 'metaself' (p. 243), which is more closely related to the phenomenon currently under discussion.

[66] If this is so then sesmets—and hence possibly selves—exist even in the case of unself-conscious beings (cf. Damasio 1994: 238, 243). This is my view; see e.g. Strawson 2009: 101, 108. Many, however, will prefer to say that sesmets exist only in self-conscious beings, or (even more restrictedly) only in the case of explicitly self-conscious experiences. I note this issue in order to put it aside for another time.

with 'real phenomenon',[67] or at least with 'real, concrete phenomenon'.[68] Step two. If one thing is certain, it is that there is conscious experience: it is that *experiential phenomena*—by which I will mean the phenomena of conscious experience considered just in respect of the qualitative character that they have for those who have them as they have them—exist. Step three. It follows that genuine or *realistic* materialists (realistic anybodys) must fully acknowledge the reality of experiential phenomena. Step four. It follows in turn that they must hold that these experiential phenomena are wholly physical phenomena, and are wholly physical considered specifically in respect of their qualitative-experiential character.

Many find it odd to use the word 'physical' to characterize experiential phenomena. Many self-declared materialists talk about mental and physical as if they were opposed categories. But this, on their own view, is exactly like talking about cows and animals as if they were opposed categories. For every thing in the universe is physical, according to materialists. So all mental phenomena, including experiential phenomena, are physical, according to materialists; just as all cows are animals.

So why do materialists talk as if mental and physical were different? What they presumably mean to do is to distinguish, within the realm of the physical, *which is the only realm there is*, according to them, between the mental and the non-mental, or between the experiential and the non-experiential. But their terminology is flatly inconsistent with their own view, and they are in danger of forgetting the first lesson of realistic materialism—which is that if materialism is true, then qualitative-experiential phenomena must be wholly physical, strictly on a par with the phenomena of extension and electricity as characterized by physics. I use the words 'mental' and 'non-mental' where many use 'mental' and 'physical' simply because I assume, as a (wholly conventional) materialist, that every thing and event in the universe is physical, and find myself obliged to put things in this way.

So when I say that the mental and (in particular) the experiential are physical I mean something completely different from what some materialists have apparently meant by saying things like 'experience is really just neurons firing'. I don't mean that all features of what is going on, in the case of conscious experience, can be described by physics (or some non-revolutionary extension of physics). Such a view amounts to radical 'eliminativism' with respect to consciousness, and is mad. My claim is quite different. It is that it is the experiential (considered just as such) that 'just is' physical. No one who disagrees with this claim is a *realistic* materialist.[69]

The next step in realistic materialism is to undercut the common view that the mind–body problem is a problem about how mental and in particular experiential phenomena can possibly be physical phenomena *given what we already know about the nature of the physical*. If one thinks this one is already lost. The fact is that we have

---

[67] I use 'phenomenon' as a completely general word for any sort of existent, abstracting from its meaning of *appearance*, and without any implication as to ontological category.

[68] Some say numbers are real things, but it is agreed that they are abstract objects, not concrete objects in spacetime, if they exist.

[69] In the longer run, I think that the mental/non-mental distinction may need to give way to the—clearer—experiential/non-experiential distinction, but I will continue to operate with the former for the moment.

no good reason to think that we know *anything* about the nature of the physical world (as revealed by physics, say) that gives us any reason to find any problem in the idea that experiential phenomena are physical phenomena, strictly on a par with the phenomena of extension and electricity as characterized by physics. Why do so many think otherwise? Because they are, as Russell says, 'guilty, unconsciously and in spite of explicit disavowals, of a confusion in [their] imaginative picture of matter'.[70]

They think they know more than they do. They think, quite wrongly, that they have a pretty good fix on the nature of matter, and are naturally led thereby, as Zahavi and Parnas remark, to suppose that 'a better understanding of physical [i.e. non-mental] systems will allow us to understand consciousness better'; thereby ignoring the more plausible view 'that a better understanding of consciousness might allow us to understand the metaphysical nature of physical reality better'.[71]

I think that these points about realistic materialism (or whatever you want to call it) are extremely important. Once understood, they suffice to dissolve many people's intuitive doubts about materialism. But I will say no more about them here.[72]

3.14 Metaphysics: Particles, Simples, U-fields

I have claimed that sesmets have as good a claim to be thought of as physical objects as stars, cats, and bosons, and I have tried to check some of the doubts that this claim arouses by giving a brief sketch of what it is to be a realistic materialist. But it also raises a very general metaphysical question about which phenomena are properly said to be things or objects, and it is to this that I now turn.[73] As in '"The Self"' I will appoint Louis as a representative human being, and call the portion of reality that consists of Louis the 'L-reality'. The notion of the L-reality is rough—as a concrete physical being Louis is enmeshed in wide-reaching physical interactions and is not neatly separable out as a single portion of reality—but it is serviceable and useful none the less.

I will assume that every candidate for being a concrete thing or object is either a fundamental 'particle' or a 'simple' or 'field' or as I will say *U-field* ('U' for *Ur* or ultimate) or is made up of some number of U-fields in a certain relation. Accordingly I will take it that sesmets are either single U-fields or made up of U-fields.[74] I agree with van Inwagen[75] that the Leibnizian term 'simple' is preferable to 'fundamental particle' as a term for the ultimate constituents of reality, first because the term 'fundamental particle' has potentially misleading descriptive meaning, provoking a

---

[70]   1927a: 382.   [71]   1998: 702.

[72]   I discuss the question in Strawson 1994, chs. 3–4, 1999a, 2003a, following Locke (1689–1700: 311–14, 539–43), Hume (1739: 1.4.5.29–30/246–8), Priestley (1777: 103–32), Kant (1781/5, A358–60, A380, B427–8), Russell (1927a ch. 37, and 1927b chs. 12–16), Foster (1982 ch. 4), Lockwood (1989 ch. 10), and Chomsky (1995: 1–10)—among others.

[73]   I often use 'thing' rather than 'object', but I make no distinction between these terms. I am not trying to make things easier for myself by using the former rather than the latter.

[74]   I will also take it that 'virtual' particles (or U-fields) and 'antimatter' particles (or U-fields) are objects; and that spacetime itself may be best thought of as an object (one view worth serious consideration is that it is the only object there is).

[75]   1990: 72.

picture of tiny grains of solid stuff that has no scientific warrant, second because many of the things currently called 'fundamental particles' may not be genuinely ultimate constituents of reality.[76] I prefer to use 'U-field' because 'simple', too, carries implications—of radical separateness, non-overlappingness and indivisibility—that are best avoided.[77]

3.15 Metaphysics: Subjectivism, Objectivism, Universalism

What, then, is a physical object? It is, no doubt, *some kind of physical unity*. But this is vague, and some philosophers—the *subjectivists*—think that judgements about which phenomena count as objects are never objectively true or false. On this view, there are *no metaphysical facts of the matter*, and whenever we judge something to be an object we (explicitly or implicitly) endorse an ultimately *subjective* principle of counting or individuation relative to which the phenomenon *counts* as a (single) object: we are endorsing an ultimately subjective *principle of objectual unity*.

It is true that many judgements of objecthood—many principles of objectual unity—are so natural for us that the idea they are in any sense subjective seems preposterous. (Nearly all of us think that cups, saucers, meerkats, jellyfish, fingers, houses, planets, and molecules are individual objects, and there are clear pragmatic and evolutionary reasons why this is so.) But the subjectivists are unimpressed by this. They deny that the fact that some judgements of objecthood are very natural for human beings entails that those judgements are objectively correct, or record metaphysical facts. If we were electron-sized, they say, our natural judgement about a stone might be that it was a collection of things, a loose and friable confederacy, and not itself a single object. And although it seems uncomfortable at first to think that merely subjective principles of objectual unity underlie our judgements that chairs and stones are objects, the idea becomes increasingly natural as we move away from such central cases. Thus although nearly everyone thinks a chair is a single object, not everyone does.[78] And although many think cities, newspapers, galaxies, and flutes (assembled from parts) can correctly be said to be single things, quite a few do not. Some think a body of gas is an object, but many do not.

Very few (to move to a distinctively philosophical example) think that three spoons, one in Hong Kong, one in Athens, and one in Birmingham, constitute a single thing, but some do sincerely believe that the three spoons' claim to be

---

[76] One view is that the fundamental particles currently recognized—leptons and quarks—are not strictly speaking elementary and are to be 'explained as various modes of vibration of tiny one-dimensional rips in spacetime known as strings' (Weinberg 1997: 20). Whether this leaves strings in place as ultimates, or only spacetime, I do not know.

[77] For purposes of discussion I am taking it that it makes sense to speak of individual U-fields, perhaps by reference to certain particle-like observational effects, and in spite of the phenomenon of quantum entanglement. But nothing much hangs on this. There aren't any U-fields if there is 'structure all the way down' (a view that seems profoundly counterintuitive, but that may have to be taken seriously), and Post (1963) famously suggested that even if there are U-fields, they may have to be seen as 'non-individuals' in some way. Cf. also Lockwood 1989: 253, French 1998.

[78] Van Inwagen (1990) does not.

considered an individual object is as good as any other. According to one form of *universalism*, an extreme version of this view, any collection of U-fields in the universe, however scattered, counts as a single object in every sense in which a table does. A lepton in your amygdala, a quark in my left hand, and the U-fields that make up the rings of Saturn jointly constitute a single object just as surely as your pen or pet duck does. No collection of U-fields has a better claim to be an object than any other.

Whatever you think of this form of universalism, it has the merit of being a wholly objectivist theory of objects. It endorses a principle of objectual unity that delivers a clear principle of counting. It tells you that if there are n U-fields in the universe then there are exactly (2^n-1) objects in the universe. But it also has, in a way, a highly subjectivist or 'post-modern' aura, for it tells you that anything goes and everybody wins, that there is no real issue about whether any particular collection of U-fields is an object or not. It is, accordingly, arguable that genuinely objectivist positions emerge clearly only when more specific and limited principles of objectual unity are endorsed, e.g. by dogmatic common sense, which rules in favour of tables and chairs and against the three spoons; or by Spinoza, who holds that there is, as a matter of fact, only one thing or substance (God or nature, or spacetime, as we might now say); or by van Inwagen, who argues forcefully that only individual U-fields and living beings—and not, say, tables and chairs—are material objects.

This debate has many mansions, and the many mansions have many rooms, but I think I can avoid them. It doesn't matter which side you are on. If you think that there are indeed objective principles of objectual unity, and therefore that there are indeed metaphysical facts about which phenomena are genuine objects and which are not, then you can take me to be arguing that sesmets (and thus perhaps selves) are among the genuine objects. If, alternatively, you think that the subjectivist view is best, and that there are no ultimate metaphysical facts about which phenomena are genuine objects, then you may take me to be trying to convince people who are disposed to think of certain but not all collections of U-fields as objects (jellyfish and chairs, but not arbitrarily selected cubic feet of the Pacific Ocean or the three newspapers) that it is at least equally reasonable to think of the collections of U-fields that I choose to refer to by the expression 'sesmets' (or indeed by the expression 'selves') as objects. Practically speaking, my task is the same.

3.16 Metaphysics: the Nature of Objects

A concrete object, then, is a certain kind of physical unity. More specifically, it is either an individual U-field (subject to the doubt expressed in note 78) or a number of U-fields in a certain relation. I take it, anti-universalistically, that there are various grades and types of physical unity, and that some candidates for objecthood have a (much) better claim than others; that a human being, say, has a (much) better claim than your lepton + my quark + the rings of Saturn, or the three spoons, or a pile of bricks.

With this in place, consider the following suggestion. As one advances in materialism, deepening one's intuitive grasp of the idea that mental phenomena and non-mental phenomena are equally physical phenomena, one of the things that becomes apparent is that when it comes to deciding which things count as objects and which do not *there are no good grounds for thinking that non-mental criteria or principles of unity*—of the sort that we use to pick out a dog or a chair—*are more valid than mental criteria or principles of unity.*

It is arguable, in fact (here I repeat and expand §2.11 above), that there is no more indisputable unity in nature, and therefore no more indisputable physical unity, than the unity of a sesmet—the unity of a subject of experience that is the subject of, say, a single, unified experience of looking up and seeing books and chairs and seeing them as such, or the subject of the binding or seizing together in thought of the concepts GRASS and GREEN in the conscious thought *Grass is green.*[79] The only comparable candidates that I can think of are spacetime, and individual U-fields—if indeed there are any. I agree with the physicist Richard Feynman and the philosopher Peter van Inwagen that things like chairs are distinctly inferior candidates for being objects, when one gets metaphysically serious, and it is arguable that sesmets are about the best candidates there are for the status of physical objects.

—Hold on. I am prepared to grant, for the sake of argument, that there is a real phenomenon picked out by your use of the word 'sesmet'. And I am prepared to accept that sesmets are short-lived. A sesmet, let us say, is: the whole (and wholly material) phenomenon of the live-aware presence of the subject of experience in the present moment of consciousness or in the present hiatus-free period of experience. But why on earth should I also accept that the right thing to say about a sesmet is (A) that it is a *thing* or *object* like a rock, or a mayfly? Why isn't the correct thing to say simply (B) that an enduring object of a familiar sort—viz. Louis, a human being—has a certain *property* at a certain time, in having a certain unified, one-or-two-second-long, subject-of-experience-involving episode of experience? Why, alternatively, can't we say (C) that the occurrence of such an episode is just a matter of a certain *process* occurring in an object at a certain time, and does not involve any further distinct *object*?

Well, here the canyons of metaphysics open before us. The object/process/property conceptual cluster—the whole object/process/property/state/event cluster—is structured by strongly demarcatory, ontologically separatist habits of thought that are highly natural and useful and effectively inevitable in everyday life, but deeply misleading when taken to have a claim to basic metaphysical truth. I think a little thought strips (B) and (C) of any appearance of superiority to (A), whether or not one is a materialist. I will start with (C), but I can give only brief reasons where others have written books.

3.17 Metaphysics: Object and Process

Any claim to the effect that a sesmet is best thought of as a process rather than an object can be countered by saying that there is, in the light of physics, no good sense in which a sesmet is a process in which a rock is not also and equally a process. So if a rock is a paradigm case of an object in spite of being a process, we have no good

---

[79] This is a materialist version of an old thought. I am not suggesting that the subject of experience is the *agent* that *brings about* the binding or seizing, and in fact I do not think that this is so.

reason not to say that a sesmet is an object even if we are inclined to think of it as a process.[80]

In saying this, I don't mean to show any special partiality to the *four-dimensionalist* or *4D* conception of objects as opposed to the *three-dimensionalist* or *3D* conception. I think I can overfly this dispute—noting in passing that there are contexts in which the 4D conception of objects is more appropriate than the 3D conception, and contexts in which the 3D conception of objects is more appropriate than the 4D conception. This debate has its own elegant internal dynamic, and creates contexts in which its disagreements have importance, but it does not really matter to the present question about the existence of mental selves.[81]

It may be said that if there is a process, then there must be something other than it in which it goes on, something which is not just the happening itself—so that it can't be right to say that everything is a matter of process. I think this objection has no force. We already know that things are unimaginably strange, relative to our ordinary understanding of them. The general lesson of physics (not to mention a priori reflection) is that our pre-theoretical conceptions of *space*, *time*, and *matter* are in many respects hugely and provably wrong. So we already have a general reason to be cautious about the claim—which is, after all, a very general claim about the nature of *matter* in *spacetime*—that it is a hard metaphysical fact that the existence of a process entails the existence of an object or substance that is distinct from it.

Physics also provides a more specific reason for doubt. For it is of course one acceptable way to talk—to say that if there is a process then there must be something in which it goes on. But physicists seem increasingly content with the view that physical reality is itself a kind of pure process—even if it remains hard to know exactly what this idea amounts to. The view that there is some ultimate stuff to which things happen has increasingly ceded ground to the idea that the existence of anything worthy of the name 'ultimate stuff' consists in the existence of fields of energy—consists, one might well say, in the existence of a kind of pure process which is not usefully or even coherently thought of as something which is happening to a thing distinct from it.[82]

Physics aside, the object/process distinction lives—covertly—off a profoundly 'staticist' intuitive picture of objects and matter: an unexamined, massively influential and massively misleading picture of objects and matter as things whose essential nature can be fully given at an instant. This is one of the main confusions in what Russell called our 'imaginative picture of matter'.[83] For matter is essentially dynamic, essentially in time. All reality is process, as Whitehead was moved to observe by his study of twentieth-century physics, and as Heracleitus and others had already remarked long ago. We might be well advised to call matter 'time-matter' in contexts

---

[80]   The claim is not that everything that is naturally thought of a process is legitimately thought of as an object. (There is no good reason to think of the yellowing of a leaf as an object.) It is only that everything that is naturally thought of an object is legitimately thought of as a process.

[81]   For an outstanding piece of arbitration, see Jackson 1994: 96–103.

[82]   Unless, perhaps, that something is spacetime itself. But in this case the point remains: for now it looks as if all the more limited phenomena that we think of as paradigmatic objects—stars, tigers, and so on—are to be thought of as local *processes* occurring in the only genuine substance there is: spacetime.

[83]   See §3.13, pp. 63–4.

like the present one, so that we never for a moment forgot its temporality. We think of it as essentially extended, but we tend to think only of extension in space. But space and time are interdependent. All extension is necessarily extension in spacetime.

It follows from this alone, I think, that there is no ontologically weighty distinction between an object and a process. There is no need to invoke relativity theory. For even if relativity theory is false there is no metaphysically defensible concept of an object—a 'spatio-temporal continuant', as philosophers say—that allows one to distinguish validly between objects and processes by saying that one is an essentially dynamic or changeful phenomenon in some way in which the other is not. Nor is there anything in the 3D conception of objects that supports such a view.[84] The source of the idea that there might be some such valid distinction lies in habits of ordinary thought, usually harmless, that are highly misleading in certain crucial theoretical contexts. I believe that we continue to be severely hampered by this; even when we have, in the frame of theoretical discussion, fully agreed and, as we think, deeply appreciated, that objects are entirely creatures of time, process-entities.

3.18 Metaphysics: Object and Property

It seems to me that these (partly a posteriori, partly a priori) points about the superficiality of the object/process distinction find a different, irresistible, and wholly a priori expression when one considers the object/property distinction.[85] Our habit of thinking in terms of this second distinction is ineluctable, and there is a clear respect in which it is even more deeply entrenched than the object/process distinction. And it is perfectly correct, in its everyday way. But ordinary thought is no guide to strict metaphysical truth or plausibility, and one has already gone badly wrong, when discussing what exists in the world, if one draws any sort of ontologically weighty distinction between objects and properties according to which there are objects on the one hand and properties on the other hand.

Clearly there can no more be objects without properties than there can be closed plane rectilinear figures that have three angles without having three sides (the strength of the comparison is intentional). Objects without properties—*bare particulars*, as they have been called—things that are thought of as having properties but as being in themselves entirely independent of properties—are incoherent. For to be is necessarily to be somehow or other, i.e. to have some nature or other, i.e. to have properties.[86]

Some, rebounding from the obvious incoherence of bare particulars, suggest that the only other option is to conceive of objects as nothing but collections or 'bundles' of properties. But this option seems no better. Mere bundles seem as bad as bare

---

[84] Nor anything in the 4D view that challenges it—for the fourth dimension is, precisely, that of time, theorize it how you will.

[85] Also known as the distinction between particulars and universals, between the particular and the general, between individuals and universals, and so on.

[86] I take it that this point is not touched by the claim that one can distinguish between the essential and the contingent properties of individuals, and I am restricting attention, in this discussion, to 'intrinsic', 'non-relational' properties of objects.

particulars. Why should we accept properties without objects after having rejected objects without properties?

But this is not what we have done. The claim is not that there can be properties without objects; it is that objects (just) are collections of properties. This debate is as troublesome as it is ancient, conducted as it is against the insistent background rhythm of everyday thought and talk, but the idea is that adequate sense can be given to the admittedly odd-sounding claim that objects are nothing but collections of instantiated properties.

It sounds hugely peculiar, even so, to say of a child or a refrigerator that it is strictly speaking nothing but a collection of instantiated properties. In fact it sounds little better than the claim that there are bare propertyless objects. So it is fortunate that there is no need to put things in such troublesome terms. Philosophers have managed to find other ways of describing the object/property topos correctly. When Kant says that 'in their relation to substance, [accidents or properties] are not in fact subordinated to it, but are the way of existing of the substance itself', he gets the matter exactly right, and nothing more needs to be said.[87]

Armstrong puts the point as follows. We can, he says, '*distinguish* the particularity of a particular from its properties', but

the two 'factors' are too intimately together to speak of a *relation* between them. The thisness [*haeccitas*] and the nature are incapable of existing apart from each other. Bare particulars are vicious abstractions...from what may be called states of affairs: this-of-a-certain-nature.[88]

And states of affairs, one might add, are already static abstractions, vicious or not, from the world-in-time, the essentially dynamic or processual nature of reality.

So the distinction between an object or 'substance' or particular, considered at any given time, and its properties at that time, is, in Descartes's terms, a merely 'conceptual' rather than a 'real' distinction (hence the strong comparison with triangularity and trilaterality). Obviously we want to be able to say, in everyday life, that an object can stay the same while its properties change. Nothing here forbids that way of talking; and there are also theoretical contexts in which one can put things in this way without going wrong. In some theoretical contexts, however, it is essential to maintain a tight grip on the metaphysics of the object/property topos, and to keep Kant's phrase constantly in mind: 'in their relation to the object, the properties are not in fact subordinated to it, but are the way of existing of the object itself'.[89] This, I think, is another point at which philosophy requires a form of meditation, something considerably more than disengaged theoretical assent: cultivation of a shift in intuitions, a learned ability to hold a different stress-dynamic in place in the background of thought, at least for a certain period of time.

---

[87]   Kant 1781/7: A414/B441. Note that this point entails—I would say reveals—the incoherence of 'property dualism', insofar as this is understood to be a doctrine that is compatible with 'substance monism'—e.g. with being a materialist.

[88]   Armstrong 1997: 109–10. Compare P. F. Strawson's philosophical-logical use (1959: 167–78) of the metaphysically suggestive phrase 'non-relational tie' in his discussion of the way in which subject terms and predicate terms are combined in the description of reality. Lewis's account of 'things qua truthmakers', in his paper of that name, also chimes in well (Lewis 2002).

[89]   I have substituted 'object' and 'property' for 'substance' and 'accident' respectively.

—All this is very fine. But when one considers a human experience, and hence, on the present terms, an instance of a sesmet, it still seems intensely natural to say (B) that there is just one object in question—namely, a human being like Louis who is a subject of experience and who has the property of having an experience of a certain kind—rather than saying that there are really two objects in question, a human being, on the one hand, and a sesmet, on the other.

True. And yet I think that the two objects claim is correct, although I haven't yet given much of an argument for it, because the objection to the everyday object/property distinction doesn't bear directly against (B) in the way that the objection to the object/process distinction bears against (C).

The direct argument against (B) goes as follows. Consider a human being—Louis—in the light of materialism. Louis is identical with (or is constituted at any time by) a set of U-fields in a certain relation.[90] The same is true of an undetached human hand or pimple. The same is true of a sesmet—the phenomenon of the live-aware presence of the mental subject of experience in the present moment of consciousness or present hiatus-free period of experience. Thus far, then, they are all the same.

Now one may grant this similarity, while still wishing to say that a sesmet is a process occurring in a human being, or an aspect of a property—the property of having a certain experience—of a human being. But as one advances in materialism, deepening one's conception of the nature of a physical object, and one's intuitive grasp on the point that mental phenomena and non-mental phenomena are equally physical phenomena, one of the things one comes to see, I believe, is that there are in fact no better candidates in the universe for the title 'physical object' or 'substance' than sesmets.[91] Certainly it seems that there is, in nature, as far as we know it, no higher grade of physical unity than the unity of the mental subject present and alive in what James calls the 'indecomposable' unity of a conscious thought.

Unity, you say, proves nothing about ontological category. Let me re-express the claim. Negatively put, it is that if we consider the phenomenon of the living presence of the subject of experience during an episode of experience, and agree to speak of this phenomenon by saying that a sesmet exists, and make it explicit that we are adopting this (admittedly substantival) form of words without prejudice to any metaphysical conclusions that we may draw regarding its ontological category, then we have no more reason to say that it is really just a property (or state) of some other object, or just a process (or event) occurring in some object, than to say that it is itself an object—an instantiated-property-constituted process-object like any other physical object.

Positively put, it is that it is simply correct to say that the sesmet-phenomenon is an object, a physical object. Not only do we have reason to say this given its intrinsic character as a mental unity, and hence a physical unity, in spacetime. It is also hard to see that there are any better candidates for the status of physical objects than sesmets or selves—no better candidates, at least so far as this universe is concerned, and as far as our knowledge extends, for the title 'substance'.

---

[90] I am using the word 'set' without any theoretical load.

[91] The stress is on 'better'; I'm not saying one can't abandon the category *object*.

—This is charming, but it amounts to very little. You have taken the word 'object' and stripped away the features ordinarily thought to distinguish objects from properties and processes in such a way that it is then very easy—not to say empty—for you to call whatever phenomenon you finally identify as the self an object.

The only thing wrong with this objection is that it misdescribes my route and motivation. True, I think that the phenomenon I am proposing to call a sesmet, and am putting forward as a candidate for the title 'self', is an object. I also think that there is, in nature, no better example of an object.[92] But I do not start from that point and then adjust the metaphysics until it allows me to say this. The metaphysical moves that dismantle the standard frontiers in the object/process/property conceptual cluster seem irresistible in any case.

3.19 Metaphysics: the Transience View

According to the Transience view,[93] many sesmets exist in the case of something like a human being like Louis. Each one is an individual physical thing or object, and a sesmet exists in the L-reality (cf. §3.14) whenever there is an episode of conscious experience in the L-reality. How long does a given sesmet last? As long as the experientially unitary period of experience of which it is the subject. How many are there? There are exactly as many sesmets in the L-reality as there are experientially unitary periods of experience. For each experientially unitary period of experience must have a subject for whom it is a unitary, bound experience, a subject that holds it together in such a way that it constitutes an experientially unitary experience—the grasping of a thought-content, the seeing of a bird and the seeing of it as a bird, and so on. If distinguishing and counting such experientially unitary periods of experience is an irreducibly uncertain business, epistemologically speaking, the same goes for the counting of sesmets. It certainly does not follow that there is any metaphysical indeterminacy when it comes to the question of how many there are (though it may well be rather unimportant how many there are). Either way the facts remain what they are: there are many of these sesmet-involving bindings, in the case of a human being, and the conscious experience—the mental life—of a human being is just the living—the internal inhabitings—of these bindings.[94] When we consider a human being as a persisting psychophysical whole, we can perfectly well speak in terms of there being just one subject of experience. It is only when we decide to think about the Problem of the Self—to press the theoretical, metaphysical question of the existence of the self—that we do better to say that there are many subjects of experience—or selves.

---

[92] It is also, perhaps, the deep original of our active grasp of the notion of unity and objecthood (note that such a view is entirely compatible with experimental evidence for the innateness of our ordinary concept of a physical object). Nietzsche also makes this suggestion.

[93] Formerly known as the Pearl View (see §2.11, p. 37).

[94] Hayward is wrong to think that I offer 'the image of a string of pearl-like things as an image of the self', or claim that a self is 'a string of momentary things' (1998: 611, 624). Sheets-Johnstone makes the same mistake, for I do not claim that we experience the self 'gappily', or that 'the self is something that comes and goes' (1999: 251).

The Transience view is so called because of its application to the human case. It does not say that sesmets are necessarily of relatively short duration. It is only relative to everyday human standards of temporal duration that they appear short-lived, in any case,[95] and it is not a necessary feature of their nature. There may be beings whose periods of hiatus-free experience extend for hours, or for the whole of their existence.[96] We, however, are not like this. The basic form of our consciousness is—I believe—that of a gappy series of eruptions of consciousness out of non-consciousness, although the gaps are not usually phenomenologically apparent.[97]

There is no sesmet in the L-reality when there is no conscious experience in the L-reality. A sesmet is present only when there is actual experience or consciousness, and is I believe always short-lived in the human case. So it cannot be identified with a human being considered as a whole, or with a brain, or with a relatively enduring brain structure: it has quite different identity conditions. Most philosophers use the term 'subject of experience', which forms part of the term 'sesmet', in such a way that a subject of experience can be said to exist in the absence of any experience, and many have grown so accustomed to this use, and to identifying subjects of experience with human beings (or other creatures) considered as a whole, that they can no longer hear the extreme naturalness of the other use, according to which there is no subject of experience if there is no experience; according to which a subject of experience cannot exist at a given time unless *experience* exists at that time for it to be a *subject of*. I hope that those who find this natural use of 'subject of experience' strained can accustom themselves to it. It is only a matter of terminology, after all, and it is only this indubitably real phenomenon—the subject of experience considered as something that is alive and present in consciousness at any given moment of consciousness and that cannot be said to exist at all when there is no experience or consciousness—that concerns me here.

I take it, then, that there are many sesmets in the L-reality, and that for the most part they exist successively, and in a non-overlapping fashion, although I agree with William James that there is no theoretical difficulty in the idea that they may sometimes exist concurrently in the L-reality.[98] A sesmet may be short-lived, but it is none the less real, and it is as much a physical object as any piano. Modern physics says nothing about it, or rather, says nothing about its mental being considered specifically as such; but the fact that modern physics says nothing about something is a very poor reason for thinking that the something in question is not physical, or does not exist.

---

[95] Although 10^{-34}th of a second is a short time by human standards, it 'seems by the standards of early-universe physics as interminable as an indifferent production of *Lohengrin*' (Ferris 1997: 237).

[96] Perhaps meditation can engender longer periods of hiatus-free thought in human beings (cf. Pickering 1999: 64).

[97] See §2.9. My talk in §2.9 of an 'irruption into consciousness from a basic *substrate* of non-consciousness' was misleading in this connection (see Shear 1998: 684 for some effective criticism), for I had no metaphysical-substance-like substrate in mind.

[98] James 1890 (p. 401); cf. also Gallagher and Marcel (1999: 16). Wilkes's cases of 'synchronous [multiple] selves' (1998: 161–2) seem to me to support, rather than undercut, my claims (in §2.6) about the necessary singleness of a self at a time.

3.20 Metaphysics: 'I' and 'I'

But what then am I?—to repeat Descartes's question. What am I if the mental subject of experience is not the same thing as the human being? What is the relation between Louis and a sesmet (or self) that exists in the L-reality?

Am I a sesmet, or short-lived self? In one sense No. I am a human being. In another sense Yes, that is precisely what I am, as I speak and think now.

But what then am I? Am I two different things, I^H ('H' for human being) and I^S ('S' for sesmet) at a given time? Surely that is an intolerable conclusion?[99]

Not at all. It is simply a reflection of how 'I' works. 'I' is not univocal, and can refer to two different things. Or rather, its referential reach can expand outwards in a certain way, so that it can refer to more or less. The same is true of 'here' and 'now', but the phrase 'the castle' provides a better analogy for 'I', given the present concern with objects. Sometimes 'the castle' is used to refer to the castle proper, sometimes it used to refer to the ensemble of the castle and the grounds and buildings located within its outer walls. Similarly, when I think and talk about myself, my reference sometimes extends only to the sesmet that I then am, and sometimes it extends further out, to the human being that I am. The castle proper is not the same thing as the castle in the broad sense, but it is a (proper) part of the castle in the broad sense.[100]

The same is true in the case of a sesmet and a human being. Louis is identical with (or is constituted at any time by) a set of U-fields in a certain relation, and a sesmet S existing in the L-reality for a period of time t (a two-second interval, say) is identical with (or is constituted at any time by) a set of U-fields in the L-reality in a certain relation.[101] S is a peculiarly shaped thing (it is peculiarly shaped when considered spatially or non-mentally, but not when considered mentally) that has mental being and (I am presuming) non-mental being, and the relation between S and Louis, the human being (an object with, say, a seventy-year existence) is a straightforward part–whole relation, like the relation between Louis and one of his toes—or the relation between a morning glory plant and one of its flowers, or between Louis and one of his pimples. That, I believe, is how things are, physically and metaphysically.[102]

---

[99] Olson (1998: 654) asks why we should 'suppose that you and I are [sesmets]? Why couldn't we be human beings?' Without expecting to satisfy him, I reply that we are both.

[100] Some philosophers refuse to accept that 'I' is not univocal, and appeal to the court of 'ordinary language'. Others have different reasons for insisting on univocality. I will not pursue this here—no contributor to the symposium pursued such objections—except to note that the non-univocality of 'I' is plainly marked in the ordinary use of language (see e.g. ch. 11).

[101] The phrase 'a set of U-fields in a certain relation' does not, when used by realistic materialists, refer only or even especially to non-mental, non-experiential phenomena that can be described by current physics or something like it. It refers just as it says: to a set of U-fields in a certain relation, U-fields whose existence in relation is, in the case of a sesmet, and as all realistic materialists must agree, as much revealed and constituted by experiential phenomena as by any non-experiential phenomena characterizable by physics. (I am not optimistic about our chances of pinning the U-fields down one by one, for reasons given in Hornsby 1981, and for reasons deriving from physics; but the claim remains.)

[102] The organization of the set that constitutes S will change during t, i.e. during S's existence, not only because each atom will change internally, but also because there will be vast numbers of macroscopic changes, as electromechanical, metabolic, and other processes continue. The set's membership may well also change during t, and in this respect sesmets will be like objects of more widely recognized sorts—dogs,

Some may feel that it is unhelpful to claim that S is a part of Louis, because 'part of' so strongly suggests a persistent spatial part like a finger, but there is no good reason why 'part of' should be restricted to such cases, and no clear lower bound on the period of time required to earn the title 'persistent'. A pimple that lasts for a day is a part of Louis, a flower that lasts an hour is part of a plant, and a carbon atom that takes the following path through Alice is part of Alice:

Alice drinks a cup of tea in which a lump of sugar has been dissolved. A certain carbon atom that is part of that lump of sugar is carried along with the rest of the sugar by Alice's digestive system to her intestine. It passes through the intestinal wall and into the bloodstream, whence it is carried to the biceps muscle of Alice's left arm. There it is oxidized in several indirect stages (yielding in the process energy, which goes into the production of adenosine triphosphate, a substance that, when it breaks down, provides energy for muscular contraction) and is finally carried by Alice's circulatory system to her lungs and there breathed out as a part of a carbon dioxide molecule. The entire process—Alice began to do push-ups immediately after she had drunk her tea—occupied . . . only a few minutes   (1990: 94–5)

The thought or experience of which S (and thus Louis) is the subject is like a highly transient flower growing rapidly from nothing into full maturity and fading as rapidly to nothing, or like one sudden arcing jet of water—one of an indefatigable but essentially distinct series of such jets—from a powerful fountain with air bubbles in the system. This is the Transience view.

If necessary, I can do without the word 'self' and its plural. Others can use these words for whatever they like. They can say, if they like, that selves do not exist at all. I will be happy to make do with sesmets—objects whose existence is as certain as the existence of experience, which is certain; things whose existence can and must be as fully acknowledged by Buddhists as by anyone else.

That said, I remain strongly inclined to call sesmets 'selves', because I believe that sesmets are located at the centre of what we must mean to be talking about when we talk about the self, or selves, in a way that trumps all other claims to the word 'self'. Talk of sesmets leaves out a great deal of what some have in mind when they talk of selves, but the central component of the idea of the self is the idea of an inner subject of experience, and in the human case, or so I believe, the existence of inner subjects of experience is, as a matter of empirical fact, just the existence of sesmets. I think it is a deep and difficult truth, fundamental to the Buddhist tradition and prepared for, in the Western tradition, by Hume, that these short-term selves are what we are really talking about when we talk about the self.

Many agree that the central component of the idea of the self is the idea of an inner subject of experience, but insist that this inner subject is or can be something that has long-term diachronic continuity. On my view, though, this amounts to claiming that a many-membered set or series of sesmets in a certain relation can be a single subject of experience. But a many-membered set of sesmets in a certain relation is simply not

human beings, trees, socks—in as much as they are naturally (this is the 'three-dimensionalist' way of describing them) said to be made up of different U-fields at different times.

the kind of thing that can itself be a subject of experience.[103] So there is no place for the persisting self, on the present view. So there is no place for the self at all, as many conceive it.

3.21 Conclusion

Olson is right that 'self' is used in many different ways (1998: 645), but wrong to claim that we should give it up for this reason. Interdisciplinary discussion throws up a chaos of uses, but this turns out to be part of its value.[104] To read all the contributions to this symposium is to see that it is possible to navigate coherently among the many uses and to pursue one's own use fruitfully in the light of one's knowledge of the others. It can be painful at first—one brings cherished habits and sensitivities to the task—but the fall-out from the misprision is, as it accumulates, enlightening. And if one looks down on the debate from high enough, and in a sufficiently pan-dialectical spirit, I think one can see that there is, in spite of everything, a deep consensus about what is being talked about when the self is talked about, shapeshifting though it may be, and structured about various poles (e.g. the high-metaphysical pole and the Ecologically-Embedded-and-Embodied *Lebenswelt* pole) that unite it only by virtue of their dynamic opposition.[105]

---

[103] This is not a philosophico-grammatical point about the word 'set', which I am using without any theoretical load, for a set of U-fields in a certain relation can indeed be said to be or constitute a subject of experience, on my view.

[104] In the course of our disagreements we learn as much about striking differences in human self-experience as about striking differences in theoretical orientation.

[105] I am grateful to Derek Parfit, Edward St. Aubyn, and the editors of the *Journal of Consciousness Studies* for their comments.

4

Against Corporism

4.1

In February 1997 my father P. F. Strawson gave me a copy of his newly published collection of papers, *Entity and Identity and Other Essays*.* It was inscribed 'from a crypto-Platonist to a Cartesian materialist'. His crypto-Platonism—realism about universals without any sort of heavy Platonic heaven—will be familiar to many of you. Its roots lie, I think, in his long and in my opinion successful campaign against the even longer-running Quinean project of ontological desertification.

'Cartesian materialism' is a more paradoxical phrase. I'd previously endorsed 'naturalized Cartesianism', which 'couples belief in materialism with respect for the idea that the only distinctively mental phenomena are the phenomena of conscious experience (respect is not yet acceptance)' (1994: xii). By 1997 I'd added the claim that the subject of experience, conceived of as something that is non-identical with the human being considered as a whole, is a proper object of reference.

We may call the subject of experience so conceived (as something that is non-identical with the human being considered as a whole) 'the self'. The claim, then, is that the self is a proper object of reference considered independently of the whole human being. This sounds Cartesian, but the self that I take to be a proper object of reference considered independently of the whole human being is a wholly physical entity. It's a straightforwardly spatiotemporal part of the whole human being, and this is evidently not a Cartesian view.[1] So the Cartesian element in this paper is simply the idea that there are two proper objects of reference—the self and the whole human being. It's this that seems directly contrary to the account of the primitiveness of the concept of a person expounded by Strawson—as I will henceforth call him—in Chapter 3 of *Individuals*.

The conflict may be less than it seems. In *Individuals* Strawson is prepared to grant what he called a 'logically secondary existence' even to a classical Cartesian mind, a 'pure individual consciousness' (1959: 115)—subject to the Kantian requirement that this mind continues to experience itself as located in space, if only as a mere point of view, and continues to think of itself as having formerly had a body. Might not this concession, enlarged on in *The Bounds of Sense* in the passage on criterionless self-ascription of experiences (pp. 162–9), be developed in ways that will allow us to

---

* This paper was written for a conference on the work of P. F. Strawson held by the Academy of Sciences of the Czech Republic in Prague, 21–4 April 2009.

[1] I won't go into the reasons for saying that Descartes in his private thought by no means ruled out the view that materialism may be true, although this was clear to Regius, and I think also to Spinoza, the Vatican, and many philosophers in the eighteenth century.

make some sense of the view that the self is a proper object of reference that is non-identical with the whole human being?

Perhaps. But Strawson seems unequivocal when he writes that

both the Cartesian and the no-ownership theorists are profoundly wrong in holding, as each must, that there are two uses of 'I', in one of which it denotes something which it does not denote in the other   (1959: 98).

Strawson includes Wittgenstein among the 'no-ownership theorists', albeit somewhat tentatively, and I fully agree with him that the distinction between two uses of 'I' explicitly proposed by Wittgenstein—the use 'as object' and the use 'as subject' (1958: 65–9)—is unsound, because there's an absolutely fundamental sense in which all genuine uses of 'I' are 'uses as subject'.[2] At the same time, I think that the word 'I' does have two wholly legitimate uses: that it can and regularly does refer to different things in the thought and speech of an ordinary human being. So the difference of opinion between us remains.

Is there also a difference of method? When I do metaphysics I favour what Strawson called 'revisionary' metaphysics, rather than the 'descriptive' metaphysics he advocated himself.[3] So perhaps we can resolve the conflict by locating my claim that there is such a thing as the self (distinct from the whole human being) firmly on the revisionary side, in such a way that it isn't in any conflict with claims about the primitiveness of the concept of a person made on the descriptive side. But I think not. It seems that the conception of the distinct self that Strawson challenges in Chapter 3 of Individuals isn't just a philosophical confection, a piece of revisionary metaphysics. It's arguable, in fact, that it's a part of the fundamental human conceptual scheme in such a way that a satisfactory descriptive metaphysics needs to accord it some real validity, and not just explain its existence as a form of error.

This is the principal idea behind what I'm going to say today. But my aims are modest and essentially indirect. I simply want to try to provide some background material that may be useful to those who think that the idea of the subject of experience (the self) distinct from the whole human being should be allowed to have some metaphysical respectability. I'll first defend the notion of the self against a broadly speaking Wittgensteinian attack. Then I'll engage in some phenomenology, offering an account of some of the sources of our natural *experience* of there being such a thing as a self distinct from the whole human being. My main aim in so doing will be to criticize *corporism*, where by 'corporism' I mean an excessive fixation on the body which is currently fashionable—almost to the point of hysteria—in the philosophy of mind. The argument for the primitiveness of the concept of a person was principally aimed at those who tended to overspiritualize the subject of experience. Now, I think, some corrective work needs to be done on the other side, against those who overcorporealize the subject of experience (compare *Selves* §§2.2–2.4).

---

[2] See Ch. 11 below and Strawson 2009: 140, 150–1, 331–7.
[3] See Strawson 1959: 9–10.

The criticism of corporism will be simply a collection of platitudes about our experience of mind in everyday life, so this is not a 'Homeric struggle' (Strawson 1969: 172), if I'm right. It's more of a turkey shoot—whether or not it involves some 'straw men'.

4.2

Some philosophers think that the idea that there is such a thing as the self is an illusion that arises from an improper use of language, and it's true that the use of the word 'self' is unnatural in many speech contexts. But people (non-philosophers at least) aren't that stupid. The problem of the self doesn't arise from an unnatural use of language that arises from nowhere. Use of the word 'self' arises from a powerful, prior, and independent sense that there is such a thing as the self. The word may be unusual in ordinary speech, and it may have no obvious direct translation in some languages, but all languages have words or phrases that lend themselves naturally to playing the role that 'self' plays in English, and such words and phrases certainly mean something to most people.[4] They have a natural use in religious, philosophical, and psychological contexts, and these are very natural contexts for human beings.

'This may be so', says a philosopher,

but it's of little importance. The fact remains that the 'problem of the self' can be painlessly solved by sober attention to a few facts about language. If there really is such a thing as the self, one thing that's certain is that it's what we refer to when we use the word 'I'. So we should start by considering the behaviour of 'I' in some detail. If we are to understand the philosophical import or content of words like 'I', and so understand the nature of the things we use them to think and talk about, we must begin by paying close attention to the way in which we use such words in ordinary, everyday communication. This procedure won't help much in the case of words for natural kinds, like 'gold' and 'proton', whose nature is a matter for investigation by science, but it's vital in the case of all other words that raise philosophical problems.

So to begin. We certainly use the word 'I' to refer to ourselves considered as human beings, embodied human beings taken as a whole, things that essentially have both mental properties and large-scale bodily properties. Even if there is some special use of the word 'I' to refer to the putative self, this use doesn't ordinarily stand out as distinct from use of the word 'I' to refer to the whole human being. When we're talking to other people we never think 'Aha! Now they're using "I" with the special *inner-self* reference', or 'Now they're using "I" with the standard *whole-human-being* reference.' Nor do we ever think this about ourselves when we're talking. It's *no* part of ordinary thought that 'I' has two meanings, or that 'I' can have two different referents as used by a given single person either at a single time or at different times (I'm putting aside cases of 'dissociative identity disorder'). We have no reason to doubt that it's univocal whenever it's used—no reason to think that it's ambiguous or indefinite in some way.

This is good news, because it follows that the so-called 'problem of the self' has a quick and complete solution. It doesn't require any high metaphysical exertions, because it's certain, as just remarked, that use of 'I' to refer (or apparently refer) to the putative self doesn't stand out

---

[4] For the case of the ancient Greeks, see e.g. Sorabji 2006: 5.

as distinct from use of 'I' to refer to the human being in ordinary talk, and it follows from this that we don't in fact draw this distinction in ordinary thought, unwarped by philosophy.

More strongly, it follows that we can't legitimately draw it, and that we're talking a kind of nonsense when we think we do. But if this is so—and it is so—then we can prove that *my # self*, the putative inner self, is either nothing at all, or is simply *myself*, the living, embodied, publicly observable whole human being. For we've already established that the term—'I'—that allegedly refers to the putative former thing, 'the self', undoubtedly refers to the latter thing, the whole human being. But this means that the self is either the whole human being, or nothing at all. There is, by the inexorable logic of identity, no other possibility. So the self, considered as something distinct from the human being, 'is a mythical entity', in Kenny's phrase. 'It is', Kenny says, 'a philosophical muddle to allow the typographical space which differentiates *my self* from *myself* to generate the illusion of a mysterious entity distinct from…the human being.… Grammatical error… is the essence of the theory of the self… "The self" is a piece of philosopher's nonsense consisting in a misunderstanding of the reflexive pronoun' (1988: 4, 1989: 87, 1999: 39–40)

4.3

I think this argument is worthless—a *reductio ad absurdum* of the principles on which it relies. The appeal to facts about the use of language in ordinary everyday public communication, in the attempt to solve a philosophical problem, is perhaps nowhere more inappropriate than in the case of the problem of the self—precisely because such language use reflects the public, third-personal perspective on things. Suppose it's true that the referring term 'I' is rarely used in ordinary communication in such a way as to reflect any distinction between the putative inner self and the whole human being. What does this prove? It proves that the public, third-personal (non-first-personal) perspective on things is built into the everyday public use of language. And what does this fact about the everyday public use of language prove regarding the nature of reality and the scope of intelligible thought about it? Precisely nothing. It may be that the best thing to say, in the end, is that there's no such thing as the self, considered as something distinct from the human being, but this is certainly not the right way to try to establish such a conclusion. Even if referring terms like 'I' were *never* used in ordinary communication, as opposed to private thought, in a way that indicated awareness or acceptance of a distinction between the self and the whole embodied human being, this would have no interesting consequences for the question whether or not there are such things as selves.

Some hold that the force or content of the word 'I' in private thought can't possibly differ from the force or content of its use in public communication. They hold, further, for reasons already given, that the reference of 'I' in public communication can only be to the whole human being. Suppose, again, that they're right about this. The fact remains that there are no easy or guaranteed inferences from facts about ordinary public language use to facts about how we fundamentally—or really—think about things. Facts about ordinary public language use and its typical interpretation can't establish that the belief or feeling that there is such a thing as the self involves an illusion. Metaphysics is not that easy. And when we think in private, nothing stops us from doing what we (or vast numbers of us) naturally do: which is to think of ourselves, using 'I' in as much as we use language at all, as, primarily or fundamentally, inner conscious entities that are not identical with the embodied human beings that we are considered as a whole. Consistent and thoughtful materialists do this as much as anyone else: it doesn't involve any sort of belief that anything non-physical exists.

So clubbable assertions about ordinary public language use can't break in on our 'sessions of sweet silent thought'[5] to tell us that we're not really doing what we think we're doing, not really thinking what we think we're thinking. To suppose that they can is to make the great Wittgensteinian (or 'Wittgensteinian') mistake about the nature of language and thought and metaphysics, the career-swallowing mistake that makes it look (for example) as if a word like 'pain' can't be what it so simply and obviously is—a word for a publicly unobservable or 'private' sensation, a word that picks out and means the private sensation considered just as such—considered entirely independently of any of its behavioural or other publicly observable causes and effects.[6]

So I reject the basic presupposition or procedure of this argument from the public use of language. And it's arguable that it fails even on its own terms. It's arguable that the distinction between 'I' the (inner) self and 'I' the human being is in fact clearly marked in ordinary thought and talk. People sometimes naturally and sincerely report their experiences to each other by saying things like 'I felt completely detached from my body', or 'I felt I was floating out of my body, and looking down on it from above'. Experiences of this sort are particularly vivid and common in adolescence, occurring spontaneously in about 1 in 300 individuals. It doesn't matter that the floatings and detachings don't actually happen. What matters is that there are experiences of this sort, and that reports of this kind are natural forms of talk about real experiences in which the intended reference of 'I' is not to the whole human being and is understood not to be to the whole human being.[7] There's plainly no difficulty—no problem of communication stemming specifically from the use of 'I'—in using language in this way to describe one's experiences to others. Defenders of the argument from the public use of language may dismiss these cases as marginal and 'degenerate', misleading and 'parasitic', but this is to beg the question.

It may be that when we listen to another person's report of an out-of-body experience we most naturally take the report to be about the whole human being in front of us, or at the other end of the telephone connection, in spite of its express content. Perhaps we nearly always apprehend or construe *each other* primarily or solely in this way—as Strawsonian persons, human beings considered as a whole—when we communicate with each other. The fact remains that the distinction between the use of 'I' to refer to the self or 'inner someone' and the use of 'I' to refer to the embodied human being is sometimes clearly marked in ordinary thought and talk.

I propose, then, that there are two natural uses of 'I': the *inner-self use* and the *human-being-considered-as-a-whole use*. If there's any parasitism, it's arguable that

---

[5] Shakespeare, Sonnet 30.   [6] See e.g. G. Strawson 1994: ch. 8, esp. 219–25.
[7] See *Selves* §7.2. The way we experience ourselves in dreams is also important—see §4.8 below.

the latter is parasitic on the former, rather than the other way round. (I think this may be so even if there is a respect in which some grasp of the latter is a condition of acquisition of the former.) It's arguable, in other words, that the central or fundamental way in which we, or many of us, experience/conceive ourselves,[8] much of the time, is precisely as an inner entity, an inner presence that isn't the same thing as the whole human being. This applies as much to sex addicts, manual labourers, athletes, and supermodels as to the rest of us. In fact people may be more rather than less likely to experience themselves in this way if they are, for whatever reason, preoccupied with their bodies.

4.4

It may be that a capacity for such inner self-reference is impossible without experience of oneself as located in an ordered world of relatively enduring objects. Platner, Kant, and Strawson all think that this is so.[9] I doubt it, but I won't pursue the matter here, because it doesn't matter to my present purpose.[10] Instead I'll turn to the 'corporists'—those present-day philosophers and psychologists who, following and perhaps overextending Wittgenstein, Heidegger, Merleau-Ponty, Gibson, and others, have come to find it hard to admit the innerness of so much of our experience. Many of them think that it's precisely such claims about innerness that give philosophy a bad name and direction, an ivory-tower problem, and skew it away from the truth of the everyday consciousness of real fleshly human beings incessantly engaged in practical intercourse with the world and each other. But it's these philosophers, I think, who are up in the blind tower. They are of course right to follow Platner in 1772, Herbart in 1816, Feuerbach in 1843, Wundt in 1874, Nietzsche, James, Peirce, Bradley, the Phenomenologists, and all the many others who preceded them (I omit Descartes from this list only because he's so widely misunderstood that his inclusion would be misleading) in drawing attention to and stressing the profoundly environmentally embedded, embodied, 'enactive', 'ecological', or (for short) EEE aspects of our experiential predicament as organic and social beings situated in a physical world. But they're victims of theoretical overreaction. The EEE character of our existence must be thoroughly recognized—the point is as remarked an old one—but there must be equal recognition of the (entirely compatible) fact that one of the most important things about human life is the respect in which one experiences oneself as an inner entity distinct from the whole human being.

---

[8] [Note added in 2015] i.e. how we experience ourselves in an essentially conceptually informed manner. The expression, although clumsy, marks something extremely important—the fact that there is cognitive phenomenology in addition to sensory phenomenology. I introduced the term 'cognitive phenomenology' in my book *Freedom and Belief*, which is 'centrally concerned with . . . the . . . "cognitive phenomenology" of freedom . . . with our beliefs, feelings, attitudes, practices, and ways of conceiving or thinking about the world, insofar as these involve the notion of the freedom' (1986: v, new edn vi). Here I am centrally concerned with the cognitive phenomenology of self.

[9] Kant's and Strawson's views are well known. Platner writes that 'we are conscious of ourselves, that is of our existence, if we know the spatial, temporal and other relations of our condition. If we do not know where we are and when we are, then we are not conscious of ourselves' (1772 §193).

[10] For arguments see Strawson 1999c, 2009 Part 3.

Nietzsche shows penetration in 1883 when he writes that

I am body entirely, and nothing else; and 'soul' is only a word for something about the body. The body is a great intelligence.... Your little intelligence, my brother, which you call 'spirit', is...an instrument of your body.... You say 'I' and you are proud of this word. But greater than this—although you will not believe in it—is your body and its great intelligence, which does not say 'I' but performs 'I'.... Behind your thoughts and feelings, my brother, stands a mighty commander, an unknown sage—he is called Self. He lives in your body, he is your body...   (1883–1885: 61–2)

for reasons that have become increasingly apparent in the century since he wrote. He follows Feuerbach, writing forty years earlier in the sophisticated tradition of German materialism that followed German idealism:

whereas the old philosophy started by saying, 'I am an abstract and merely a thinking being, to whose essence the body does not belong', the new philosophy, on the other hand, begins by saying, 'I am a real sensuous being and, indeed, the body in its totality is my self (*Ich*), my essence itself'   (1843: 54)

but neither questions the present claim that we regularly figure or experience ourselves primarily as inner conscious entities or selves. Their remarks take their point precisely from the fact that it is true.

4.5

Why—how—do we come to experience ourselves in this way, given the EEE aspects of our existence? Part of the answer seems plain. It's a consequence of something that it has become hard for some to see in recent analytic philosophy of mind. I mean the way in which awareness of ourselves as mentally propertied is, to varying degrees, constantly present when it comes to our overall apprehension of ourselves. It's not just that we're often expressly taken up with our own conscious thoughts, living with ourselves principally in our inward mental scene, incessantly presented to ourselves as things engaged in mental business, even while aware of our external surroundings. This point now needs considerable emphasis, given the current body-heavy, 'corporist' climate of discussion. But the further and larger point is that awareness of our own conscious mental goings on is very often—arguably always—present, to varying degrees, even when we're thoroughly taken up with our bodies, or, generally, with things in the world other than our own mental goings on.

It's instructive to watch people in the street. Russell Hurlburt made random samplings of the character of ordinary people's experience as they went about their daily life, by activating beepers that they carried with them: 'it was striking that the great majority of subjects at the time of the beep were focused on some inner event or events, with no direct awareness of outside events at that moment'.[11] Such inturned thoughts may be almost exclusively concerned with external matters; they may, for

---

[11] See Hurlburt et al. (1994: 387) and Hurlburt 2011. For more experimental evidence see also Baars (1996), Hurlburt and Schwitzgebel (2007).

example, be memories of past events or anticipations of future events. The present point is simply that their occurrence involves an experienced contrast between one's inner mental goings-on, on the one hand, and one's external surroundings, of which one usually remains more or less aware, on the other hand. The experience of this contrast is rarely in the focus of attention: it's rarely 'thetic', in the Phenomenologists' (and in particular Sartrean) sense of the term. It is none the less there.

Plainly we can be the subjects of conscious mental goings on without being expressly aware of them considered specifically as such; our attention can be intensely focused outward. But even then we have a constant background awareness of our own conscious mental goings on (it's usually inadequate to say that it is merely background awareness) and a constant tendency to flip back, however briefly, to some more salient, non-background sense of ourselves as minded or conscious.

It isn't as if there isn't enough mental space—or time—for this. Conscious apprehension is extremely fast and rich. 'Thought is quick', as Hobbes says (1651: 1.3). What is the 'lifeworld', the *Lebenswelt*? There's a fundamental sense in which it is primarily an inner (or mental) world, even when one is preoccupied with the outer world, sailing a yacht, climbing a mountain, using a hammer, jogging, or running for one's life.[12] Silent thoughts hit people in a roaring football crowd, and they're aware of this happening, and of the strange detachment—but unarguable reality—of the 'place' in which this thought is present; not just of the content of the thought. What is the shepherd on the hill thinking about, or the woman at the loom, or the child lying awake in the dark? Writing this, I can see a man collecting garbage from the side of the road with tongs. He's not locked exclusively on the details of his immediate task and surroundings and bodily feelings. It's not as if there is nothing more to the content of his current experience than the external environment which he directly perceives, plus awareness of his bodily state. There are many things going on in his (conscious) mind, and he's not only aware of their content. He's also aware, however non-thetically, of himself as minded. This is not just the view of a dreaming philosopher.

Which stand out most for us, in daily life: our mental features or our bodily features? Most of us find that our moods and emotional feelings are a great deal more present to our attention than our bodies, most of the time.[13] These mental conditions profoundly colour our experience of outer things, and we're not so fiercely world-focused as to be generally unaware of this fact. Why is it important for philosophers to stress the EEE aspects of existence? Precisely because of the dominant position of mental as opposed to non-mental[14] features in our overall experience of ourselves.

---

[12] Moments of crisis can precipitate extraordinary innerness. For an extreme example, see Oliver Sacks's description of his mental state as he ran down a mountain in Norway, fearing pursuit by a bull (1984).

[13] Their causes may lie in our bodies in such a way that representationalists as different as Descartes and Tye want to say that they are about our bodies, but that is a separate point.

[14] I use the term 'non-mental' where many would use 'physical' for important reasons set out in *Selves* §6.6 (see also G. Strawson 1994: 57–8). Briefly, materialists hold that everything is physical. So if they admit the existence of the mental, they can't legitimately distinguish the physical from the mental. The only relevant distinction available to them is the distinction between the mental physical and the non-mental physical.

So it's not a fatal philosophical aberration, as some have supposed, to focus on the mind as opposed to the body, when considering the human condition. It's not an aberration at all. Even if it were an aberration, it wouldn't be a distinctively philosophical aberration. It would, rather, be an aberration intrinsic to the human condition. We are, in a sense, strangely—astonishingly—rarefied creatures. We don't make any mistake in being this way or in experiencing ourselves in this way. We are what we are. Our mentality is a huge, absorbing, and utterly all-pervasive fact about us. It's a natural object of attention for us. We're constantly aware of it even when we're not focusing on it. We live constantly at or on or over the edge of express awareness of our own mental goings on, considered specifically as such. Those who think that in normal human experience the external world wholly occupies the field of consciousness in such a way that we normally have no sort of awareness of the phenomenon of our awareness, those who think that the sensations and feelings that give us experience of the world are like invisible glass, so that we're generally wholly unaware of them, utterly falsify the extraordinarily rich, rapid, nuanced, complexly inflected, interdipping flow of everyday experience. In their fury to be 'anti-Cartesian' or philosophically 'street' they utterly forget what it is like to live an ordinary human life. They forget the profound and constant innerness of so much of everyday experience, its felt hiddenness and privacy. They forget that inner mental goings on *experienced as such* are constantly present in all our engagement with the world, however little they're dwelt on—as we move around thinking of this or that, swim, take a bath, play a fast sport, or argue with someone.

4.6

Note in passing that there's no conflict between this point and whatever is true in 'direct realism' about the perception of objects in the world. Direct realism stresses the important respect in which, when one sees a desk in normal conditions, one may be said to be in direct perceptual contact with the desk, and not merely in indirect perceptual contact with it via some mental representation of it. There is, of course, and necessarily, a conscious mental representation of the desk involved in one's seeing the desk—a conscious mental representation with a distinctively visual qualitative character. No conscious mental representation entails no sensation, hence no seeing.[15] But having the right sort of conscious mental representation *just is* seeing the desk; it's what being in direct visual perceptual contact with the desk is. You don't see the desk indirectly 'through' the mental representation. And there's a fundamental respect in which one's sense experience is in the normal case entirely 'transparent' or 'diaphanous' for one, when one perceives the world: that is, one's sense experience is not taken into account considered specifically as such.

---

[15] Seeing as ordinarily understood is an essentially conscious phenomenon, although we can of course give sense to a notion of unconscious seeing.

This is particularly apparent when one considers vision (it's much less compelling in the case of the other senses, where awareness of the medium by which one perceives the world is very often more patently present, even if not in the focus of attention). But even in the case of vision it doesn't follow, and isn't true, that one isn't aware of the sensory-qualitative character of the sensory experience—as Thomas Reid points out. One is always and necessarily aware of the sensory-qualitative character of the sensory experience. Otherwise one wouldn't see the desk at all! But, again, one needn't have any significant sense of the sensory experience considered specifically as a process of sensory experience.

But nor is this excluded. I can directly see—be in 'direct perceptual contact' with— the desk while also being clearly non-thetically aware of my awareness of the desk. Correctly formulated, direct realism doesn't involve the false claim that one has to be entirely unaware of the occurrence of the process of experience when one perceives something, and many very ordinary everyday circumstances bring awareness of it to the fore. Awareness of awareness is built into such simple things as changing positions to see something one cannot see from where one is.

In general, our experience is saturated with experience of ourselves as experiencing. Aron Gurwitsch is very accurate when, speaking of perception, he says that

consciousness . . . is consciousness of an object on the one hand and an inner awareness of itself on the other hand. Being confronted with an object, I am at once conscious of this object and aware of my being conscious of it. This awareness in no way means reflection: to know that I am dealing with the object which, for instance, I am just perceiving, I need not experience a second act bearing upon the perception and making it its object. In simply dealing with the object I am aware of this very dealing.   (1941: 330)

His closing formulation in this passage—'in simply dealing with the object I am aware of this very dealing'—is less likely to mislead than the earlier 'I am . . . aware of my being conscious of [the object]', because the phenomenon in question doesn't require any thought of oneself as such, i.e. as subject considered as such. This is in fact Gurwitsch's main point, which he has already made three pages earlier: 'the subject in his dealing with the object, aware as he is of this dealing, is nevertheless in no way aware of his ego, much less of his ego's involvement in his dealing' (1941: 327). He is none the less aware of the dealing, the mental going on, and—of course—the sensation that it involves.

We need to keep these sorts of facts very clearly in mind if we are to resist corporism, which is a kind of philosophical *body-fever*. The particular evil of corporism is that it recruits all sorts of interesting, reasonable and indeed true thoughts—the EEE points, direct realism as correctly formulated, the so-called object-dependence of perceptions, and the fact that the experiential-qualitative character of our experience is standardly 'transparent' for us in the sense just described—to back up a view to which they give no support at all, according to which we're so utterly engaged with the outer world that the outer world is all we have in our heads, so that we have, as it were, no mental life at all, as traditionally understood, and no sense of having a mental life. The result is an astonishing misrepresentation of the actual character of human life, with its constant innerness. Having a vivid and constant sense of having a mental life is itself an *essential and constitutive part of having a human mental life.*

4.7

Consider interpersonal communication. Awareness of one's own hidden, inner mental goings on is one of its most salient and unremitting features. Consider bargaining, negotiating differences, making plans for cooperation, playing chess. These activities provide one vivid set of cases. Awareness of the possibility of concealment, deception, hypocrisy, both on one's own part and on the part of others, is integral to our communication and ancient in our psychological phylogenesis.[16] Humans are full of hidden conscious intentions to keep secrets or omit details, both when they seek to cheat and betray and when they seek to surprise, to help, to exercise tact, to avoid upsetting others. They're constantly thinking things that they decide to say or not say. All this feeds a pervasive and ever-present awareness of the fundamental privacy of mental life, a sense of privacy that we must clearly recognize, and allow to be in certain fundamental respects accurate, even as we also recognize that many aspects of our mental lives are directly observable to others in our eyes, facial expressions, and larger-scale observable behaviour. And whatever is morally negative in what we hide, much is morally neutral or positive; we hide feelings of love or sadness, or conceal kind intentions behind sharp words.

Note, though, that this vast arena of intentional concealment from others, good or bad, is only a tiny part of what feeds the sense of the innerness of mental life when communicating with others. When one describes a remembered scene, one is aware of a great deal that is present to one's mind—some of it in sketchy, fleeting, quasi-sensory form—but unavailable to one's interlocutor. There is conscious experience of selecting from material that comes to mind. One is routinely aware of what one is not saying because one has to keep things short. There is, in conversation, the experience of one's thought wandering off the other's words, of something else coming vividly and privately to mind. There is the experience of realizing in a flash *in foro interno* what one wants to say in reply to someone while he or she is still speaking. All these things are real, concretely occurring phenomena of which we are aware, just as we're aware of phenomena in our external environment. We're built to be aware of many things going on around us, and this, unsurprisingly, includes our own mental goings on. Heideggerian cobblers absorbed in their work, nails in mouth and hammers in hand, are bathed in the reality of their mental innerness.

4.8

Why has it become hard for some philosophers and psychologists to give these facts their proper weight? Many, as remarked, are so anxious to dissociate themselves from a view they call 'Cartesianism', when discussing the nature of mind, that they tend to throw out everything that is right about Cartesianism along with anything that is wrong. Attraction or habituation to the idioms and ways of thinking of experimental psychology is also influential. But there's no conflict here, no either/or. Our back-ground awareness of our bodies is important, but it co-exists effortlessly with our

---

[16] It's one of the fundamental grounds of our intelligence, for reasons well set out by Trivers (1985) and Frank (1988) among others.

regularly experiencing ourselves primarily or centrally as inner conscious presences who are not the same thing as human beings considered as a whole. And although background awareness of body is indeed experience of the body, this doesn't prevent it from feeding or grounding experience of oneself as an inner mental presence distinct from the body, a sense of self, which I'll call 'self-experience', that presents the self primarily as a distinctively (and in some sense purely) mental entity. Granted that background awareness of body is indispensable to a sense of the self in creatures like human beings, indispensable to what Damasio calls 'the feeling essence of our sense of self' (1999: 171), indispensable both to its development in each individual and to its continuing existence, it doesn't follow, and isn't true, that any such sense of the self must figure the self *as* embodied in any way. This, after all, is precisely Wundt's point, and Nietzsche's, and Dewey's, and Feuerbach's before them, and arguably Fichte's before Feuerbach, and Platner's before Fichte.[17] Bradley has no doubt that the inner core of feeling, resting mainly on what is called Coenaesthesia, is the foundation of the [sense of the] self.[18] He follows William James, who writes that 'the nucleus of the '*me*' that the present thinking subject takes itself to be 'is always

---

[17] Dewey inveighs famously against the 'spectatorial' conception of the knowing human subject (see e.g. 1929: 215). Fichte's argument is indirect: I cannot have self-awareness without awareness of an external world, and by implication a body for the world to act upon (see Beiser 2002: 309–13, 325–33). Wundt is worth quoting at some length:

> In this development (of consciousness) one particular group of percepts claims a prominent significance, namely, those of which the spring lies in ourselves. The images of feelings we get from our own body, and the representations of our own movements distinguish themselves from all others by forming a *permanent* group. As there are always some muscles in a state either of tension or of activity it follows that we never lack a sense, either dim or clear, of the positions or movements of our body.... This permanent sense, moreover, has this particularity, that we are aware of our power at any moment voluntarily to arouse any one of its ingredients. We excite the sensations of movement immediately by such impulses of the will as shall arouse the movements themselves; and we excite the visual and tactile feelings of our body by the voluntary movement of our organs of sense. So we come to conceive this permanent mass of feeling as immediately or remotely subject to our will, and call it the *consciousness of ourself*. This self-consciousness is, at the outset, thoroughly sensational,... only gradually the second-named of its characters, its subjection to our will, attains predominance. [As this happens] our self-consciousness begins both to widen itself and to narrow itself at the same time. It widens itself in that every mental act whatever comes to stand in relation to our will; and it narrows itself in that it concentrates itself more and more upon the inner activity of apperception, over against which our own body and all the representations connected with it appear as external objects, different from our proper self. This consciousness, contracted down to the process of apperception, we call our Ego [or self. But this] abstract ego..., although suggested by the natural development of our consciousness, is never actually found therein. The most speculative of philosophers is incapable of disjoining his ego from those bodily feelings and images which form the incessant background of his awareness of himself. The notion of his ego as such is, like every notion, derived from sensibility, for the process of apperception itself comes to our knowledge chiefly through those feelings of tension which accompany it (1874, quoted in James 1890: 1.303 n.).

[18] 1893: 68. Coenaesthesia (pronounced *seeneestheesia*) is the 'general sense or feeling of existence arising from the sum of bodily impressions' (*Oxford English Dictionary*); 'the totality of internal sensations by which one perceives one's own body' (Dabrowski 1972: 292), 'the general sense of bodily existence; the sensation caused by the functioning of the internal organs' (*Stedman's Medical Dictionary for the Health Professions and Nursing*).

the bodily existence felt to be present at the time'; 'the "I" meaning' for the present thinking subject is 'nothing but the bodily life which it momentarily feels':

We feel the whole cubic mass of our body all the while, it gives us an unceasing sense of personal existence. Equally do we feel the inner 'nucleus of the spiritual self', either in the shape of physiological adjustments, or (adopting the universal psychological belief), in that of the pure activity of our thought taking place as such....The character of...warmth and intimacy...in the present self...reduces itself to either of two things—something in the feeling which we have of the thought itself, as thinking, or else the feeling of the body's actual existence at the moment,—or finally to both.[19]

Nearly everyone, perhaps, agrees that background interoceptive or somatosensory awareness of one's body is the foundation of self-experience, whatever place they also rightly give, with James, to 'the feeling which we have of the thought itself, as thinking'. It's a further point that background awareness of one's mind, of one's experiential goings on, is no less constant than background awareness of one's body. Background awareness that experiential goings on are going on is as much part of the overall field of experience as background somatic awareness. The notion of background awareness may be imprecise, but we can for the moment sufficiently define it as all awareness that is not in the focus of attention, all awareness that is not 'thetic' in the Phenomenologists' sense of the term. It then seems plausible to say that there is never *less* background awareness of awareness or experience than there is background awareness of body. I suspect there is more; that so far one's overall awareness of oneself is concerned, background awareness of awareness predominates over background awareness of body.[20]

When we're fascinated by the outer scene, our awareness of ourselves and our mental lives may seem dim. The outer scene may seem to flood consciousness. But even in these cases we're likely to be as aware of ourselves as mentally aspected— our fascination is itself such a property, and we feel it—as we are of ourselves as embodied.[21] When we have sufficiently digested the Platner-Feuerbach-Nietzsche-Wundt point that somatosensory awareness has a foundational role both in our acquisition of self-consciousness and in our continuing sense that there is a self, we need to register—or re-register—the obvious but fashion-occluded point that awareness of one's mind and mental goings on is no less important.

Dreams are also very important, when it comes to understanding the naturalness of the sense of the self as a mental entity. For when one dreams one often has no particular sense (or no sense at all) of oneself as embodied, although one's sense of

---

[19] James 1890: 1.400, 1.341 n., 1.333. Note that James uses 'thought' in the Cartesian way as a completely general word for conscious experience (1890: 1.224). In the first quotation I've put 'present thinking subject' in place of James's capitalized 'Thought' in accordance with his explicit terminological provision (1890: 1.338, 400–11).

[20] C. O. Evans traces the sense of the self to 'unprojected consciousness' which 'can only be experienced as background', and consequently identifies this unprojected consciousness as the best candidate for the title 'self' (1970: 149).

[21] It depends what we're doing. If we watch athletics we may tense up empathetically and may be to that extent more aware of the body. If we're walking by the sea or watching shooting stars, we're more likely to be aware of our mentality.

one's presence in the dream-scene is as vivid as can be. Such dream experience is part of our experience from infancy, and persists throughout life. It isn't necessary to appeal to it to make the present case, but I suspect that it contributes quite profoundly to our overall susceptibility to experience of ourselves as being, in some sense, and most centrally, conscious presences that are not the same thing as a whole human being.[22] As Shear remarks, the experiential character of such dreams shows 'how discoordinated a basic aspect of our deeply held, naive commonsensical notions of self [is] from anything graspable in terms of body, personality, or, indeed, any identifiable empirical qualities at all'.[23]

To say that one central way (arguably the central way) in which we conceive of or experience ourselves is as an inner conscious entity that is not identical with the whole human being is certainly not to say that we're ever right to do so—although I think we are. And to think of oneself in this way is certainly not to adopt any sort of dualist or immaterialist position. One can and does naturally think of oneself in this way even if one is an out-and-out materialist. Nor is it to deny that we also have a strong natural tendency to think of ourselves as human beings considered as a whole, 'Strawsonian' persons, essentially unified, indissolubly mental-and-non-mental single things to which mental and bodily predicates are equally and equally fundamentally applicable.[24] Nor is it to deny that the primary way in which we ordinarily think of people other than ourselves is as Strawsonian persons. The point is simply this: whatever else is the case, the sense that there is such a thing as the self, and that it is not the same thing as the whole human being, is one of the central structuring principles of our experience. The Strawsonian conception of persons as nothing more than essentially unified single things that have both mental and bodily properties is stamped deep into our ordinary apprehension of others and our normal use of language in communication, but it is not similarly stamped into the fundamental character of our private thought about ourselves—even though we standardly express our thought to ourselves in language.

It's a merely phenomenological remark—to say human beings naturally have a sense that there's such a thing as the self, and that it isn't the same thing as the whole human being. Once again, nothing follows about whether this sense of things is metaphysically reasonable or correct. I think that it is reasonable, and indeed correct. But if I'm going to argue for this I'll have to move on from the claim that our natural dual use of 'I' (to refer to ourselves both as Strawsonian persons and as inner mental selves) reflects the way we often think, to the stronger claim that it reflects the way things are.

---

[22] An alternative hypothesis is that the susceptibility is independently grounded, ease of dream disembodiment being just one manifestation of it.

[23] Shear (1998: 678). This is not to say that one could dream in this way if one didn't have (or hadn't once had) normal experience of embodiment, nor (as Shear stresses) that there is any sense in which one is or even could be independent of one's body. One possibility is that the experience of disembodiment in dreams might have something to do with the decoupling mechanism that ensures that we do not actually make the movements we make in dreams. (This might be so in spite of the fact that this decoupling is necessary precisely when we are experiencing ourselves as embodied in our dreams.)

[24] Strawson 1959: 101–10. These are also Cartesian persons, in fact, but current misunderstandings of Descartes make the point opaque.

I won't attempt this now. Instead I'll conclude with a brief remark about the two uses of 'I', using *I* to refer indifferently to the word or the concept or thought-element. It seems that the reference of *I* can contract inwards or expand outwards in a certain way in normal use. *I* is often compared with *here* and *now*, but it's not like *here* and *now* in this particular respect, because they expand and contract in a more or less continuous fashion (it's a familiar point that 'here' can denote this room, this villa, this city, this country, 'the West', the planet, and so on). *I*, by contrast, clicks between two more or less fixed positions, and bears comparison in this respect with *the castle*. Sometimes *the castle* is used to refer to the castle proper, sometimes it's used to refer to the ensemble of the castle and the grounds and buildings located within its outer walls. Similarly, when I think and talk about myself, my reference sometimes extends only to the self that I am, and sometimes it extends further out, to the human being that I am. Often my thought or semantic intention is unspecific as between the two.

Note that this claim is not the same as Wittgenstein's suggestion that there are two legitimate uses of 'I': the use 'as object' and the use 'as subject' (1958: 65–9). It is, rather, the proposal that there are two uses 'as subject': the use to refer to oneself considered as a whole human being and the use to refer to oneself considered as a self. The claim is that both are legitimate because there really are two distinguishable things in question (there's really no such thing as the use 'as object').[25]

This, now, is an outright metaphysical claim, and it brings me to the brink of the outright metaphysical project of arguing for the existence of an entity that is properly called 'the self'. This, though, is a task for another time (see e.g. Strawson 2009, 2011d).

---

[25] More mildly: 'the use "as object"' is a misleading name for what it is used to denote. See Ch. 11 below.

5

I Have no Future

5.1

If, in any normal, non-depressed period of life, I ask myself whether I'd rather be alive than dead tomorrow morning, and put aside the fact that some people would be unhappy if I were dead, I find, after reflection, that I have no preference either way. The fact that I'm trying to finish a book, or about to go on holiday, or happy, or in love, or looking forward to something, makes no difference. When I put this question to myself and suppose that my death is going to be a matter of instant painless annihilation, completely unexperienced, completely unforeseen, it seems plain to me that I lose nothing. I/GS, the human being that I am, lose/loses nothing. My future life and experience (the life and experience I will have if I don't now die) don't belong to me in such a way that they're something that can be taken away from me. I'm simply not a thing of such a kind that its future life and experience (the life and experience it will have if it doesn't now die) can be rightly thought of as its possession, hence as something that can be taken away from it in such a way that it is harmed. One might as well think that life could be deprived of life, or that something is taken away from an existing piece of string by the fact that it isn't longer than it is. It's simply a mistake, like thinking that Paris is the capital of Argentina.

I'll call this view *No Ownership of the Future*.

If one believes that what one is most essentially, considered as a self or subject of experience or person, is a fleeting or transient thing, a short-lived entity—and I think this *Transientist* view must be taken very seriously—then No Ownership of the Future may seem to follow immediately. One might put the point by saying that *Transience* entails *No Future* (no future beyond the present moment of experience), and No Future entails No Ownership of the Future. In this paper, however, I'm going to try to put aside the Transientist view and consider the proposal that No Ownership of the Future holds good even if the almost universally accepted conception of persons as relatively long-lived things is correct. I'll consider the proposal that No Ownership of the Future is true independently of any view about the temporal extent of persons—even if, as some believe, we are immortal.

If No Ownership of the Future is true, then it's true however we die. But I'm going to restrict attention to instant, painless, unexperienced, completely unforeseen annihilation—*instant annihilation* for short. There is in this case no fear, no suffering. Everything is completely normal up to the instant of extinction; nothing bad is experienced. One's life may be radiant up to or at that moment, and in that sense end perfectly.

The first thing to say, perhaps, is that it may be difficult to imagine the case in a sufficiently accurate way. It may be difficult to imagine one's death to be completely unforeseen given that one's death is part of what one is imagining. It's easy to figure it intellectually, but emotional interference may prevent one from grasping it properly. This may contribute to the explanation of why some people find No Ownership of the Future obviously false. I suspect that one can be confident that one is imagining it fully and be wrong.

Certainly nearly all the philosophers I have talked to have thought that No Ownership of the Future is false, and indeed obviously false. But some people seem to know immediately what I mean, and think it obviously true. Here I just want to record some—perhaps not entirely coherent, and in any case diverse—reflections.*

5.2

Epicurus' and Lucretius' famously unsatisfying view that death is not an evil has two main parts, roughly as follows. First, you don't mind in the least that you didn't exist for an eternity before you were born, so you shouldn't mind if you don't exist for an eternity after you're dead; so death is not a harm. Secondly, death can't constitute a harm to a person—Louis, say—before it occurs, up to the point of death (in the case of instant annihilation, everything is fine up to that point). Nor can it constitute a harm to Louis at or after that point, because he is no longer there to experience harm. So death is not a harm.

I mention the Epicurus–Lucretius view to put it aside. Not because it's not important (it is important), nor because it's been so widely discussed, nor because it's interpreted in too many different ways, but because I'm not sure it has anything essentially to do with No Ownership of the Future. (One reply that is made to Epicurus–Lucretius is that I can be harmed by loss of my future even though I can't suffer when dead. This, however, is precisely what No Ownership of the Future denies.) And even if there is a connection between the two views, I don't think that Epicurus–Lucretius has anything essentially to do with what makes No Ownership of the Future seem right to those, like myself, for whom No Ownership of the Future is a natural, untutored, pre-philosophical given.

Perhaps this is because we're already naturally inclined to experience the self as transient. I don't know. I don't think this is essential to our attitude, but, either way, endorsement of No Ownership of the Future seems to be fully compatible with fear of death—I've felt fear of death even when believing No Ownership of the Future to be true.

This may be a further reason for thinking that No Ownership of the Future has nothing essentially to do with Epicurus–Lucretius, given that their argument is meant to be a palliative or cure for fear of death. No Ownership of the Future isn't meant to

---

* This is a revision of a short piece written in 1998 without any familiarity with the current debate about death among analytic philosophers. A short version was published in 2007 in *The Philosophers' Magazine*. I'm out of my depth in this topic, and would have to rewrite the paper completely in the attempt to turn it into something comprehensively argued, so I've left its main lines untouched in the hope that it will be suggestive.

make anyone feel better about death—much as I'd like to. In the first instance it's simply a report of a conviction that some encounter when they contemplate instant annihilation.

It may be difficult to gauge one's fundamental reaction to the idea of instant annihilation when reading a paper like this, or when feeling dissatisfied or unfulfilled. One may do better to bring it to mind when one is in a more neutral state, not directly engaged in any tightly focused pursuit; perhaps when walking to work or going downstairs. Obviously the truth of No Ownership of the Future doesn't depend on such circumstances, but it may be easier to see in some circumstances than in others.

5.3

No Ownership of the Future appears to be an aspect of a broader view which can be stated independently of the thesis about no-ownership. This is the view that *my life doesn't go worse for me* in any sense if at any time I cease to exist in instant annihilation. This is because of the kind of thing I am—even when I'm considered in the normal manner as a thing of a kind that normally enjoys relatively long-term diachronic continuity.[1]

In one development, the view is this: *given that I'm alive, and must die*, my life doesn't go worse for me in any sense if I cease to exist in instant annihilation. More is not better: *there is no entity of which it is true to say that, for it, more life is better than less life*. One has already gone wrong if one has a conception of what one is that makes it seem that more could be better. This conception of what one is already incorporates the deep mistake. No appeal to what we naturally desire that makes it seem that more could be better can constitute an objection to No Ownership of the Future, because those natural desires also already incorporate the mistake.

If this is right, one can presumably delete the words 'and must die' in the previous paragraph. Given that I'm alive, my life doesn't go worse for me if I cease to exist in instant annihilation, even if I might have lived for ever. In this case too, any conception of the subject of experience that has the consequence that the subject of experience can be deprived of something by death is incorrect.

This claim may seem even harder to believe than the previous claim. I need to try to say something more in its defence. Let me first introduce a distinction between two ways of conceiving of oneself that may be useful in avoiding a possible misunderstanding.

5.4

Human beings are capable of self-consciousness in the following strong sense, which I'll mark with the term 'full self-consciousness': they can conceive of themselves specifically *as* themselves. They're not self-conscious only in the sense that they're

---

[1] I won't mention this qualification again.

capable of being conscious of what is in fact themselves. A kitten chasing its tail can do this, and I believe there's a fundamental sense in which any experiencing creature is conscious of itself just in being conscious at all.[2]

Given this definition of self-consciousness, I can express the distinction I have in mind as follows. Sometimes, when one is thinking of oneself in the fully self-conscious way, one experiences/conceives oneself as a human being considered as a whole. At other times one experiences/conceives oneself primarily as an inner mental presence or 'self'. One has what I'll call 'self-experience'. In both cases one is thinking of oneself, and one is thinking of oneself specifically as oneself in the fully self-conscious way, but the second inner-mental-presence way of thinking of oneself is importantly different from the whole-human-being way. I'll mark this difference by saying that in the second case one is thinking of oneself specifically as oneself*.

Some of the time one is conscious of oneself without thinking of oneself clearly in either of these ways. One is thinking of oneself, and one is fully aware of oneself as existing, and one is apprehending oneself specifically as oneself, in the fully self-conscious way, but one seems to feature in one's thought and experience in a fundamentally indeterminate manner: neither in the whole-human-being way nor in the inner-self way.

The inner-self way of thinking of oneself, which appears to be primary for most people in most circumstances (it's a distinctively philosophical mistake to think that this way of thinking of oneself is usually a product of philosophical or otherwise theoretical speculation), is closer to the indeterminate way of thinking of oneself than the whole-human-being way. But we can shift fast and effortlessly between the whole-human-being way and the inner-self way, and we often do. Sometimes the two ways seem to co-exist in a kind of unresolved superposition. This, however, is probably just another way of describing the state in which one is thinking of oneself in an essentially indeterminate way.

The difference between the two ways of experiencing/conceiving of oneself remains real, and there's a lot to be said about it.[3] All I want to do here, however, is to mark the importance of the second, inner-mental-presence way of experiencing oneself: experience of oneself specifically as oneself*.[4] Living human beings last from conception to death. As an ordinary adult human being one knows this and one knows one is a living human being. But when one thinks of oneself as a self or inner person one may well not think of oneself as something that began at birth and will end only at death. When Henry James writes about one of his early books

I think of.... the masterpiece in question.... as the work of quite another person than myself.... a rich relation, say, who.... suffers me still to claim a shy fourth cousinship   (1915: 562–3)

he knows perfectly well that he's the same human being as the author of that book, the human being Henry James that lasts from birth to death, but he doesn't feel he's the same *person* or *self*.

---

[2] See §10.7.   [3] See e.g. Strawson 2004, and § 4.3 above.
[4] Some philosophers have questioned it.

This feeling is familiar to most of us, in one form or another, when we have self-experience; but we differ greatly in how it affects us. We lie on a long psychological spectrum which stretches from strongly *Diachronic* people or *Endurers*, at one end, to strongly *Episodic* people or *Transients*, at the other. Those who are Diachronic—Endurers—naturally and ordinarily experience themselves* as something that was there in the further past and will be there—assuming life goes on—in the further future. Those who are Episodic—Transients—do not. They experience themselves* as something that was not there in the further past and will not be there in the further future ('further' is intentionally indeterminate).[5]

It seems that people differ greatly in this respect. An Endurer, a strongly Diachronic person, may have a vivid sense that the self (the he*) that he now feels himself to be is there throughout life. A strongly Transient or Episodic person may have no significant sense that the self (the she*) that she now feels herself to be exists outside the present moment. But people need not occupy rigidly fixed positions on this fundamental psychological spectrum. Human beings' sense of their* temporal extent can vary considerably according to their age, their mood, their state of health, their current preoccupations.

5.5

I've introduced this distinction in order to deflect an objection that I've already mentioned. I'm pretty strongly Transient or Episodic, on the whole, and this may be thought to be part of the explanation of why I naturally feel that No Ownership of the Future is true. And perhaps it is. But my aim is still to suggest that a Diachronic person has as much reason as I do to think—feel—that No Ownership of the Future is true.

Suppose Lucy thinks of herself* Diachronically, as something that will be there in the further future so long as Lucy (the human being that she is) doesn't die. It doesn't follow that there's any sense in which she thinks of her future as something that can be taken from her*. And one can drop the asterisk, because the same is true if Lucy is thinking of herself as a whole human being rather than as a self. Even if Lucy is an Endurer, strongly Diachronic, there needn't be any sense in which she thinks of herself as something which is such that there is something of which it can be deprived by death. Granted that one is a living human being, it doesn't follow that one is a thing of such a kind that one is or can be deprived of anything if one doesn't live as long as one would have lived if one hadn't died in an untimely way.

I like to think, then, that the doctrine of No Ownership of the Future is true for all people, not only for Transients who have little or no sense that they themselves* will exist in the future. Whether I'm Transient or Diachronic, my future can't be thought of as my property in a way that creates the possibility that it's something I can be deprived of. This is not to say that one can't have strong preferences about how one's life goes, given that one is going to go on existing. One can, though, have such preferences without having any preference for continuing to exist as opposed to ceasing to exist.

---

[5] See Strawson 2004. All four terms—'Diachronic' and 'Endurer', 'Episodic' and 'Transient'—are strictly *phenomenological* terms. They denote ways in which one experiences things when one is having self-experience, not ways one is independently of that experience.

Nor is it to say that one can't viscerally wish not to die—to continue to exist. Plainly one can. One can wish not to die, wish to continue to exist, even though one doesn't think that one is a thing of such a kind that one's future is something that can be taken away from one, a thing of such a kind that one can be harmed by instant annihilation.[6]

Roman Altshuler asks (email, 2016) how my opening claim—that I have no preference whether I live or die—is compatible with my fear of death. All that I can say is that this is a truthful report of how I feel—even if it involves some sort of inconsistency. Consideration of the case of instant annihilation seems to me to make it easy to see how the fear and the lack of preference are compatible. It may be, however, that knowledge that one is potentially immortal would change the situation. I will consider this shortly.

5.6

But what does 'one's future' mean, if it's not something one can be deprived of? I think it's sufficiently clear. It's enough to take it to refer to the future one will have if one doesn't cease to exist on account of something like instant annihilation. I'll call this one's *Future*, and rephrase the central claim in a stilted way that may be helpful.

Suppose Louis lives for forty years from 1976 until 2016, when he dies accidentally under anaesthetic. Suppose he would otherwise have lived for forty more happy years. Consider [A] the bounded portion of reality that consists of Louis from 1976–2016, and [B] the bounded portion of reality that would have existed from 2016–56 if Louis hadn't died. According to No Ownership of the Future, the existence of [A] involves nothing, no thing, no entity, which can be said to have had anything in [B] taken away from it. This is so although the existence of [A] involves the existence of Louis ([A] just is Louis).

Again this is not to say that people can't feel strongly that their future is theirs in such a way that it does make sense to say that it can be taken from them; many have just such a feeling. It's just to say, again, that thinking in this way involves a mistake. Many things that may seem to presuppose this way of thinking, such as fear of death, don't do so in fact. I can be frightened by the prospect of eternal future non-existence without thinking of my *Future*—the life that I will live if my life doesn't cease upon the midnight with no pain—as something which is mine in such a way that it can be taken from me (something which is such that I can be harmed if it doesn't occur). What is frightening is not losing something; it's just not being there. This, perhaps, is what Updike has in mind when he writes that 'it is not our selves in our nervous tics and optical flecks that we wish to perpetuate; it is the self [considered simply] as window on the world that we can't bear to think of shutting'.[7] One can be fairly strongly Episodic or Transient and still feel this viscerally on occasion.

---

[6] So too one can feel 'ultimately' morally responsible for one's actions even though one is convinced that the notion of 'ultimate' moral responsibility is incoherent. But the cases are not of the same kind.

[7] 1989: 206. Compare Dostoyevsky's preferring eternity in hell to non-existence. More mildly, Nagel agrees with Richard Wollheim (1984: 267) that 'death is a misfortune even when life is no longer worth living' (1986: 225).

5.7

Someone who wanted to argue for No Ownership of the Future might appeal to the theory of relativity, the 'block-universe' or 'four-dimensionalist' ('4D') view of reality, according to which (very roughly) time isn't really a matter of flow, and one's whole life is already laid out as a whole in the great pattern of concrete reality. I don't want to do this, because No Ownership of the Future doesn't depend on the 4D view of things any more than attraction to it depends on attraction to the 4D view of things. Nor is there anything in the ordinary everyday three-dimensionalist ('3D') view of things that supports the rejection of No Ownership of the Future. It doesn't follow, from the fact that I will be wholly there in the future (as three-dimensionalists suppose) if I don't undergo instant annihilation, that my *Future* is something that I can be deprived of by death in such a way that my life goes worse on account of that death.

The 4D view seems worth mentioning nevertheless. One way of expressing the central idea is by saying that time is 'spacelike' in the sense of being spread out and in some sense existent as a whole in the way we intuitively imagine space to be. On this view, we're wrong to think of physical objects, including human beings, as 3D objects existing through time or subject to the flow of time. They're 4D objects with three spatial dimensions and one temporal dimension. As such they are in some sense 'always already' all there (Kant 1781–7: A346/B404).

This view may seem to support No Ownership of the Future, because one (earlier) temporal part of a 4D object can't be said to own another (later) temporal part in such a way that the latter can be said to be taken away from the former. And this is so even when the 4D object in question is a human being, i.e. something that can think explicitly about past and future, including its own. One might as well think that one section of a piece of a string (conceived of either in the normal 3D way or in a 4D way) can be said to own (or have as a part) another non-overlapping section.

However this may be, I take No Ownership of the Future to be independent of any particular theory of the nature of time. It may be that No Ownership of the Future follows directly from some view about the nature of time, such as 'presentism', the view (roughly) that only the present exists. It would be no bad thing if this were true, for many people believe that presentism is true. But I take it to hold good even if the past and/or the future are as real as the present, and even if time does pass in some sense incompatible with the 'block-universe' or four-dimensionalist conception of time.

5.8

If No Ownership of the Future is true, you can harm people directly in all sorts of ways, but you can't do so simply by bringing about their perfectly painless and

---

Note that on some views one ceases to exist—the window that is one's self shuts—if one becomes utterly different in character. On other views, Dainton's for example, the window can remain open, and remain truly *oneself*, however much one changes in respect of character and embodiment—even if one changes over time from being just like the Barry Dainton of 2015 to being just like Greta Garbo, or a *dreadnoughtus schrani*, or even the twenty-four-armed Anarch of Throg.

unforeseen death. By 'directly' I mean to put aside consequences of their death that they would dislike, such as other people's sorrow or the non-completion of the book they are writing. But even if I very much want to finish the book I'm writing (even if I very much want the book I am writing to be finished) I'm not harmed if I undergo instant annihilation before it's finished. I'm not a thing of a kind that can be harmed in this way. Nor am I harmed if other people suffer from my death; they are.

Most of us have various projects and desires and interests, some of which are very important to us, but we're not entities of such a kind that we're constituted by them or related to them in such a way that we're harmed if they're not completed or fulfilled specifically because we undergo instant annihilation. This at least, and once again, is the claim. To think otherwise, on the present view, is to make a natural but fundamental mistake about what people are, about what the being in time of a conscious being is.[8] The core fact is that you can't harm something that exists by bringing it about that it doesn't exist—and not just because it can't suffer if it doesn't exist. This seems to be easy for some to accept and hard for others to accept, but it's not as if it's true for some and not for others.[9]

One of the consequences of No Ownership of the Future—the idea that you can't harm someone by bringing about their painless and unforeseen death—may be active, attractively or not, in the common intuition that death (sudden death in a shoot out, for example) is a hopelessly inadequate punishment for someone guilty of great wickedness: 'Death is too good for him!' Certainly many people are mystified by the idea that death—by judicial execution, say—is the most severe punishment there is.[10]

5.9

As a young child I had great trouble sleeping, and I thought about death almost every night. I had no belief in an afterlife and an extraordinarily vivid conception of eternity. My sense of terror often took a visual form (if these were hypnagogic states, they were unusually prolonged). I would be alone in a boundless grey world, on a vast, featureless slope that was gradually growing steeper under me and that extended downwards for ever. I was having trouble holding my position. I was bound to begin sliding down.

It seemed completely plain to me then, although I was intensely afraid of death (both my own death and the death of the other members of my immediate family), that it didn't really matter when death occurred, given that it must come, and given the size of eternity—given that it would be for ever. But the child I was would have agreed that immortality could make a difference; and this is a view I rejected earlier in this paper. The child I was then would have agreed with Updike that it's 'the self as

---

[8] So it's not a mistake because you show the right attitude 'if you can meet with triumph and disaster / And treat those two impostors just the same' (Kipling 1895).

[9] This might, however, be thought to follow on Mark Johnston's intriguing view—see Johnston 2010: ch. 4.

[10] One doesn't have to approve of retributive punishment in order to think in this way.

window on the world that we can't bear to think of shutting' for ever (1989: 206), and with Dostoevsky that it's better to spend eternity in hell than to cease to exist.

5.10

—Suppose we read of a man who hears of his wife's death and decides in his distress to kill his three children and then himself. He puts the children to bed, fatally drugged. They go to bed happy, knowing nothing of their mother's death; then he kills himself. The grief we feel for the children has a special character. It is, at least in part, a grief felt for them because of the life they didn't have. We feel precisely that they've been deprived of something—indeed everything—although their death is entirely unfelt and unforeseen by them.

This is true. One feels extraordinary sorrow and dismay. I think though, that the feeling rests on a mistake. Those who are harmed by these deaths, grievously, are those left behind to mourn.

The mistake has its sources, perhaps, in the fact that we take the third-person point of view, not the first-person view, i.e. the view from inside the actual life of the child, where all is well. We're also subject to the common (and sometimes benign) Fallacy of Excessive Sympathy.[11] If we consider the children's point of view, if we consider their actual lives, nothing bad is to be found.[12] Suppose determinism is true (it's a common misapprehension that science gives us more reason to favour the view that determinism is false than the view that it's true). Then we may think that they lived out their full lives with nothing lost. The idea that they lost anything is seen to be an illusion.

I'm not appealing to Menander's claim that those whom the gods love die young, because I take it that this is too young. Nor am I following Solon's advice to count no person happy until they're dead, because I think he means that disaster can always strike one so long as one is alive. But there may be a connection here with the Epicurus–Lucretius position.

Jeff McMahan disagrees (in correspondence) with the claim that those who are harmed by death are those left behind to mourn. He thinks it implies 'a rather impoverished conception of mourning. Mourning typically has two dimensions: grief for the person who has died because of the misfortune he has suffered and distress at the gap that has been torn in one's own life. By claiming that the first dimension is irrational, you imply that rational mourning is wholly egoistic (except insofar as mourning involves sadness on behalf of other survivors who, like oneself, have lost something important in their lives)' (email, March 2002).

I quote this because I suspect that many will agree. I think it's mistaken. My best friend Simon Halliday was killed in 1975 when he was twenty-four. I feel about him as Montaigne felt about La Boétie. But my grief, which remains painfully powerful,

---

[11] Excessive sympathy is a complex phenomenon. It's almost invariably self-concerned in some way, albeit covertly.

[12] In another version of the story the parents act together, for whatever reason, and the children are not, as in the first version, saved from the sorrow of learning of their mother's death.

and surfaces in various ways, including, still, recurrent flashes of disbelief that he is dead, is for myself and for those who loved him, because I know he has suffered nothing in being dead.

I don't think that those who feel grief for a person who has died because they take him to have suffered a misfortune in dying are making a mistake relative to the notion of a person they're operating with. The mistake lies in the notion of a person they're operating with. It's a deep metaphysical-ethical mistake, on the present view, one that mostly lies hidden in everyday life but is exposed by the case under consideration. Grief felt for the person who has died seems like a natural expression of love, a natural expression whose absence would show failure of love.

Is this because love can collude with the false conception of what a person is—in a way for which we would not be inclined to take it to task? I don't think so. I think that love doesn't actually make this mistake. (I think, in fact, that it can't make this mistake.) I'd be unwilling to argue with anyone who disagreed, but if I were pressed further, I'd admit that I think that the view of mourning that is impoverished is the view that judges my view to be impoverished. It may have fine forms, but it runs a number of risks—of superficiality and sentimentality in the pejorative sense. On the present view, it fails in the end to take the reality of the other person seriously. It's a—strange—false—perhaps also moving—commodification of the existence of the other.

It's true that I can be sad that a person no longer exists quite independently of anything that I or others feel about her. In just the same way I can regret that a great picture no longer exists because it was destroyed in a fire. But this is not grief for the thing that has vanished because of the misfortune she or it has suffered.

5.11

—Suppose you know you're going to die in three days' time, before you can make peace with someone you love and are estranged from, or just before you can finally meet a child or parent you've never known. This is likely to cause you fierce unhappiness. It's true that it's not a case of completely unforeseen death (although we may suppose it will be painless). It seems none the less to show that it's not actually a mistake to think of the future experiences one is not going to have, but would have had if one had not been going to die in three days time, as a loss to oneself.

I agree about the force of the feeling. It's painfully expressed in Thomas Hardy's 1912–13 poems, which were written after his wife died unexpectedly at a time when they were estranged, destroying any chance of reconciliation. I think, though, that it's easy to be misled. The first thing to note is that your feeling will be essentially the same if you know that it's not you who is going to die in three days' time, but rather the person you want to meet—before you can reach him. This shows that the source of your unhappiness is not the idea that you're going to be deprived of some temporal part of your life. You may know, in this variation of the case, that you're predicted a long life. You may even know that one consequence of his death will be that you'll live longer than you would otherwise have lived.

Suppose you discover that you would have met him last year if only you'd turned right at the crossroads instead of left; now it's too late. The basic feeling is the same—the regret is felt for experiences not had—and the fact that the basic feeling is the same shows, I propose, that the feeling doesn't depend on one's thinking of one's own future as a possession in such a way that it makes sense to think that it can be taken away from one—although one may well also think in this way. In the original case of instant annihilation, wholly unforeseen and wholly unexperienced death, of course, there is no scope for regret.

When Gareth Evans was dying at the age of thirty-four he spoke of his intense regret that he wouldn't live to grow old with his wife. He thought of how beautiful she would be when she was fifty, and of how he wouldn't see this. My claim is only that regret of this kind—regret that one will not have certain experiences—doesn't depend on thinking of one's future as being some sort of possession that can be taken away from one (although one may well also think in this way). I believe that one would feel exactly the same regret if one knew that one was going to be completely cut off from the person one loves, irrevocably and for the rest of one's life, although neither of you were going to die; as in the case of Héloïse and Abelard.[13]

We can, then, regret that we will not have certain experiences, just as we can regret that we're missing certain experiences now, and missed certain experiences in the past. Quite generally, we can regret that something isn't happening to us, and that something didn't happen to us, just as we can regret that something won't happen to us. And our future death is indeed a powerful reason why certain things won't happen to us. What is certain is that human beings can suffer in many terrible ways. But none of them, I think, puts No Ownership of the Future in doubt. It doesn't follow, from the fact that people can suffer from the knowledge that they aren't going to experience, in their future life, something they dearly wish to experience, that they can be harmed by ceasing to exist—say in instant annihilation. Or so I propose.

That apart, I think I agree with Marcus Aurelius, who is almost as repetitious as I am, although he may well have metaphysical motivations that I lack:

Whether you live three thousand years or thirty thousand, remember that the only life you can lose is the one you are living now in the present. . . . In this sense the longest life and the shortest come to the same thing, for life in the present is the same for all. . . . One's loss is limited to that one fleeting instant; one cannot lose either the past or the future, for no one can take from one what one does not have. . . . So when the longest- and the shortest-lived among us die their loss is precisely equal, because the only life of which one can be deprived is life in the present, since this is all one has.   (*Notes to himself* II.14.)

A similar thought is expressed in Iris Murdoch's novel *Under the Net*:

Events stream past us like these crowds and the face of each is seen only for a minute. What is urgent is not urgent for ever but only ephemerally. All work and love, the search for wealth and fame, the search for truth, life itself, are made up of moments which pass and become nothing. Yet through this shaft of nothings we drive onward with that miraculous vitality that creates

---

[13] Space travel at near light speeds (or gravitational effects) can produce the same results in science fiction; a point recently dramatized in the film *Interstellar* (2014).

our precarious habitations in the past and the future. So we live; a spirit that broods and hovers over the continual death of time, the lost meaning, the unrecaptured moment, the unremembered face, until the final chop that ends all our moments and plunges that spirit back into the void from which it came. (1954: 275)

5.12

—If we have reason to assist Lucy's euthanasia in order to save her from torment in her final illness, then we must also have reason to prevent her instant annihilation if we know that she will otherwise have very good experiences in the days to come. So we must think that it is a good for her to continue to live and have certain experiences, even if we allow some sense in which her Future is not something that can be taken away from her. Surely instant annihilation is a harm, a harm *to her*, in this case? Or suppose that Louis is having wonderful experiences now, and we know that these will continue if he doesn't undergo instant annihilation. Suppose his instant annihilation is inevitable but that we can delay it. Surely we have a reason to delay it at least until the period of wonderful experience is over?

This is useful; it makes my position clearer to me. Perhaps it is simply Marcus Aurelius' position. The idea (again) is that there's a fundamental sense—an *ethically* fundamental sense, in the broad sense of 'ethical'—in which there is no entity to whom good is done by the delaying of instant annihilation. The fact that I find myself replying in this (by now predictable) way to this particular case may make it easier for you simply to dismiss my position. So be it. It remains for me to say that the reply arises naturally and irrepressibly—with the force of evident truth—for someone like me.

5.13

—When you were severely depressed you wanted not to continue to live. This is inconsistent with No Ownership of the Future, because any reason one has for thinking that one's future is not something that can be taken away from one is equally a reason for thinking that one's future is not something of which one can be relieved—not something one can be spared.

Is this an inconsistency? Perhaps I'm not emotionally or affectively neutral when it comes to the consideration of my future, in the way that rationality (which is sometimes useful) would seem to require. Or perhaps I am on the whole rational and consistent in my natural commitment to No Ownership of the Future, but become irrational in that respect when depressed. Vivid thoughts about extreme future suffering that occur outside depression don't produce the present wish not to continue to live—not even when they're thoughts about the extreme suffering of depression. So it seems that the effect occurs only when things are seen from inside the perspective of severe depression.

Would I feel the same if I suffered extreme and chronic pain but wasn't depressed? Perhaps. But when I consider this case I realize that what I wanted when I was depressed was simply for the present to stop, at any cost—with no thought at all for the future. It was not at all my future that concerned me; only and strictly my living present. The same may apply in the case of chronic extreme pain.

When I was severely depressed my Episodic or Transient nature seemed untouched. It seemed as clear as ever that I* wouldn't be there in the future. But this didn't help, because, again, it was the present moment that had to be escaped from at all costs.

Did my Episodicity (Transientism) also sometimes weaken in depression, so that when I considered the prospect of continuing experience of depression I did somehow feel that I* would be there in the future? Not at all; it was wholly a matter of the present. And yet perhaps I sometimes felt rather as I would have felt if I did think that I* would be there in the future—even though I didn't think that I* would be there in the future.[14]

5.14

In Larry Niven's science-fiction novel *Ringworld* there is a race of creatures, the Puppeteers, who can die as a result of accident but are otherwise naturally immortal (like Tolkien's Elves). Unsurprisingly, perhaps, they're fabulously cautious creatures, who have developed impenetrable hulls for spaceships. They raise the immortality question again. Would I feel the same as I do now if I were a Puppeteer?

Again I like to think so. I look forward to things—albeit in a faint way—but I'm not deprived of anything if I don't experience them because I die. I—what I am—is not deprived of anything. Am I deprived of them if I continue to live and they don't happen? In one natural sense, Yes of course. I may be disappointed when the time comes and they don't happen. I – I – I. This use of the term *I* is fine. There is, none the less, and once again, and finally, or so I think, a metaphysically fundamental use of the term *I* in thought or speech, given which the following is true: [1] there is no entity named by *I*, existing here and now, that can properly be said to be such that, if I die, it will not experience the thing I'm looking forward to. Nor is death crucial, given this fundamental sense of *I*. For [2] even if I live, there is no entity named by *I* existing here and now that will either experience or fail to experience the thing I'm now naturally looking forward to. I think, though, that one could hold [1] even if one didn't hold [2].[15]

5.15

Postscript: Rhys Southan asks (email, 2016) whether one of the ideas behind No Ownership of the Future is that you can't own something that you don't yet have, given that the future by definition is something you don't yet have. I didn't in fact intend anything like this, and see that the language of ownership may be misleading

---

[14] Although this is my experience, I have no reason to think that it's the same for others. Beike, Lampinen, and Behrend (2004) present evidence that (roughly) normally Diachronic people shrink into a smaller time frame—become more Episodic or Transient—when depressed. It would be interesting if it turned out that normally Transient people expand into a larger time frame—become more Diachronic—when depressed.

[15] I'd like to thank Roman Altshuler, Nicholas Dyson, Mark Johnston, Jeff McMahan, Michelle Montague, Ingmar Persson, Kenta Sekine, Rhys Southan, and Paul Woodruff, for (mostly) sceptical comments spread over many years. There is a revised version of this essay with the same title in Strawson 2018.

(perhaps one may say instead that one has no stake in the future). Suppose we assume [1] some sort of strong realism about the future, [2] that it is true of many entities present now that they (the very same entities) can be said to be there in the future [3] that it makes sense to think that some of these entities can be such that things that they were effectively guaranteed to have can be thought of as taken away from them if they don't get them—in such a way that they can be harmed by not getting them. Then the idea is that we (human subjects so far as their funda- mental ethical being is concerned) are not things of this kind—even though we may think we are.

6

'We live beyond … any tale that we happen to enact'

6.1 'Narrativity'

If one is *Narrative*, then—here's my first definition—one experiences or conceives of one's life, one's existence, oneself, in a narrative way, and in some manner lives in and through this conception. To be Narrative, as I will use the term, is to have a certain psychological characteristic.[1] It is in the first instance a natural disposition, even if it's open to cultivation. Narrativity, or the lack of it, is a natural dimension of human psychological difference, whatever the possible effects of training or cultural influence.

But what is it, exactly? What is it to experience oneself or one's life, or major parts of one's life, in a narrative way? This is a large question and I know of no clear answer. But there is widespread agreement that Narrativity exists. According to the neurologist Oliver Sacks, 'each of us constructs and lives a "narrative" … this narrative *is* us, our identities' (1985: 110). The psychologist Jerry Bruner holds that 'self is a perpetually rewritten story', and 'in the end, we *become* the autobiographical narratives by which we "tell about" our lives' (1994: 53, 1987: 15).[2] The philosopher Marya Schechtman claims that one 'creates [one's] identity by forming an autobiographical narrative—a story of [one's] life'.[3] Charles Taylor holds that 'we must inescapably understand our lives in narrative form' (1989: 52). 'We are all storytellers', according to Ruthellen Josselson, Amia Lieblich, and Dan McAdams, and 'we are the stories we tell' (2006: 3). David Velleman writes that 'we invent ourselves', in a paper called 'The Self as Narrator', adding that 'we really are the characters we invent' (2006: 206). According to Dan Dennett, we're all

virtuoso novelists, who find ourselves engaged in all sorts of behaviour, and we always try to put the best 'faces' on it we can. We try to make all of our material cohere into a single good story. And that story is our autobiography. The chief fictional character at the centre of that autobiography is one's self. (1988: 1029)

I think these quotations give the general idea. Most of them add the claim that one conceives of *oneself*—or *one's self*—in a narrative way to the claim that one

---

[1] I use an initial capital letter to mark the use of the adjective 'narrative' to refer to a psychological trait.
[2] Bruner (1990: 111–15) locates the rise of this view in the 1970s and 80s.
[3] 1996: 93. She modifies her view valuably in Schechtman 2007, and again in Schechtman 2014.

experiences *one's life* in a narrative way, and make no clear distinction between the two things. I have accordingly built this into the starting definition of Narrativity.

All these writers endorse what I call

(a)   the psychological Narrativity thesis

which states that *all normal people are Narrative*. All normal human beings conceive their lives, themselves, their existence, in a narrative way, and in some manner live in and through this conception. The psychological Narrativity thesis is an empirical, factual, descriptive thesis. This is how we are, it says, this is our nature.

Many also endorse a further thesis which embraces and extends the psychological Narrativity thesis. This is

(b)   the narrative self-constitution thesis

which states that *all normal people constitute their identity as persons or selves by virtue of being Narrative*—by conceiving their lives, their existence, in a narrative way, and living in and through this conception. One of the most prolific exponents of this thesis is Dan McAdams, who propounds what he calls the '*life-story theory of identity*' (2005: 95). '*Identity*', he says, '*is itself a life story*' (ibid. p. 99). Schechtman puts it as follows: 'we constitute ourselves as persons by forming a narrative self-conception according to which we experience and organize our lives' (2007: 162).

6.2 Are We All Narrative?

We have a major consensus. And it's arguable that there's a way of understanding the psychological Narrativity thesis, at least, in which it's trivially true. And if it's trivially true then of course I endorse it. Truth is always good, trivial or not. But I'm going to assume that it's meant to be non-trivially true, and consider the suggestion that it's false in any sense in which it's not trivially true. As I understand the psychological term 'Narrative', some of us aren't Narrative at all. Some of us don't naturally cast or construe our lives as a narrative or story of some sort, and we don't experience parts of our lives in this way either. Nor do we think of ourselves as opposed to our lives in a narrative way—whatever exactly this might be supposed to be. We may simply not be reflective about these things, or we may be like Bob Dylan:

I don't think I'm tangible to myself. I mean, I think one thing today and I think another thing tomorrow. I change during the course of a day. I wake and I'm one person, and when I go to sleep I know for certain I'm somebody else. I don't know who I am most of the time. It doesn't even matter to me.   (1997, interview in *Time*)

Or Samuel Hanagid a thousand years ago when he writes that

for my part, there is no difference at all between my own days which have gone by and the distant days of Noah about which I have heard. I have nothing in the world but the hour in which I am: it pauses for a moment, and then, like a cloud, moves on.

The Narrativity theorists admonish Dylan: 'Look, everyone is Narrative. Your "I'm one thing today, another thing tomorrow" thing is just part of your narrative about yourself.' And Bob Dylan has certainly told a lot of stories, when questioned about himself. But this, if anything, confirms the accuracy of his remark. As for the great Samuel Hanagid—spice merchant, warrior, poet, tax collector, grand vizier to the King of Granada—I think the Narrativity theorists should treat him with great care. At the very least, people vary greatly when it comes to the basic Narrative impulse. If you consider your friends for a while, I think you'll see how they differ in this respect.

The Narrativity theorists may concede that some people don't appear to be Narrative, but claim that they are really; it's just that they're doing it unconsciously or implicitly. The Narrativity theorists may back up their claim by instancing the deep human drive to make sense of things, find patterns and explanations at all costs, and, where necessary, 'confabulate' in the technical sense of experimental psychology: that is, make up, invent, patterns and explanations where there are none to be found.[4] Here again, though, we have to do with a central human 'individual difference', a psychological variable, a trait that is strong in some and weak in others. Keats congratulated Shakespeare on his 'Negative Capability', his capacity to rest in 'uncertainties, Mysteries, doubts, without any irritable reaching after fact & reason'—the sort of irritability that can easily lead to confabulation (1817: 193). I think some of us possess a good amount of negative capability when it comes to our attitude to ourselves and our own lives. Others could probably do with more of it. It may be sounder—closer to life—than the perilous reachings of narrative self-interpretation, let alone narrative self-constitution. We are perhaps, in certain ways, and to a deep degree, 'strangers to ourselves', in the words of the social psychologist Timothy Wilson (Wilson 2002). In many respects, it seems, we don't know what we're about. Perhaps we begin to know something about ourselves when we begin to appreciate this. Whether this is so or not, any large-scale project of self-constitution, narrative or not, is likely to involve a fantasy of control. It risks being violently Procrustean. 'If the hare has seven skins', as Nietzsche says, then 'the human being can shed seven times seventy skins and still not be able to say: "This is really you, this is no longer outer shell"' (1874: 129).

Nietzsche may be exaggerating, and I hear a voice—it is perhaps Marya Schechtman's voice—telling me that there are things that people mean by the expression 'narrative self-constitution' that I can't possibly wish to reject. That may be so. For the moment, if the Narrativity theorists insist that we're all really Narrative, I'll disagree vehemently, and again begin to wonder whether they're defining Narrativity in such a way that the psychological Narrativity thesis comes out as trivially true. When McAdams, Josselson, and Lieblich say that 'we are all storytellers . . . what is consciousness but an inner narration of experience?' (2006: 3), they seem to understand narration in a way that immediately lands them in triviality. It seems that to be conscious at all is to be in Kant's phrase 'always already' engaged in narrative (1781–7: A346/B404). So we're all Narrative, simply because we're all conscious (except for the zombies among us).

On another view, having and making plans already entails having a Narrative outlook and engaging in narrative self-constitution. In this case triviality threatens

---

[4] See e.g. Hirstein 2005.

again, for we all make some plans. Some have no long-term plans because they're feckless or shiftless, or, more positively, because they're highly spontaneous or happy-go-lucky, 'very improvident and cheerful', like the Flopsy Bunnies (Potter 1909: 1). Others make no long-term plans because they're desperately poor and are simply trying to survive from day to day. But we all make some plans. So we're back with triviality—and a continuing unclarity about what exactly the psychological Narrativity thesis and narrative self-constitution thesis amount to.

The unclarity derives from the key term in the definition of Narrativity: 'narrative'. What is to be done? Aristotle steps in with his usual reminder: don't attempt more precision than the subject matter admits. But the need for clarification remains. It doesn't help that most uses of the term 'narrative' in the humanities can be replaced without semantic loss by words like 'description', 'account', 'view', 'theory', 'explanation', 'understanding', 'theme', 'belief', 'concept', 'picture'.[5] Perhaps 95 per cent of all uses of 'narrative' are replaceable in this way, once we put literary theory aside, inside or outside the humanities.[6] Any description of anything whose existence involves change is now liable to be called a 'narrative'. And perhaps change isn't necessary—as in the case of the description of a painting.

This suggests a rule of engagement. Whenever anyone uses the word 'narrative', ask whether it can be replaced without semantic loss by one of the words listed above, or by some variant of the generic expression 'description or account of a temporally extended sequence of events'. If it can be replaced, let it be replaced. Then we'll be able to see more clearly what's left. If it's hard to say whether or not something is lost in the replacement, the burden of proof (proof that something has been lost) will fall on the user of the word 'narrative'. If we proceed in this way, we may be able to get more clarity into the debate. It will also help if we explicitly restrict attention to the use of the word 'narrative' in the ethical and psychological contexts that principally concern philosophers. We'll still need to make a direct assault on the question of the intended force of the word, but we'll have a much firmer base from which to start.

This, though, is a task for another time. Having marked the need for clarification, I'm going to rely on the characterization of narrative contained in the quotations I've already given, in opposing the psychological Narrativity thesis and the narrative self-constitution thesis, along with their ethical counterparts, which I haven't yet introduced.[7]

6.3 Difference

The key claim is simply that human beings differ. We differ dramatically in respect of Narrativity. There are the Dan Dennetts, on the one hand, spinning away, trying for whatever reason to make all of their life material 'cohere into a single good story', and the Bob Dylans, on the other, who are doing no such thing. There are people like Charles Taylor who hold that a 'basic condition of making sense of ourselves is that we grasp our lives in a *narrative*', and have an understanding of our lives 'as an unfolding story' (1989: 47, 52), and people like myself who find the idea of engaging

---

[5] 'Story' and 'tale' are not allowed.   [6] If you doubt this, take up some text and test it.
[7] For one recent helpful attempt, see Currie 2010: ch. 2. See also G. Strawson 2004.

in this sort of self-narrativizing activity profoundly alien, people who believe that they can get on quite well without it, whether or not they also believe that it risks being on a royal road to error. We differ in respect of Narrativity as much as Gerard Manley Hopkins and Iris Murdoch differ when it comes to their sense of themselves in the present moment. Hopkins speaks of his 'self-being',

my consciousness and feeling of myself, that taste of myself, of *I* and *me* above and in all things, which is more distinctive than the taste of ale or alum [or] the smell of walnutleaf or camphor, and is incommunicable by any means to another man.   (1880: 123)

Iris Murdoch's husband John Bayley reports that

Iris once told me that the question of identity had always puzzled her. She thought she herself hardly possessed such a thing, whatever it was. I said that she must know what it was like to be oneself, even to revel in the consciousness of oneself, as a secret and separate person.... She smiled, looked amused, uncomprehending.   (1998: 51–2)

Proponents of 'virtue ethics' tend to say that there is one right way to be. Aristotle claims that we should before all else possess the four 'cardinal' virtues of courage, temperance, 'practical wisdom', and justice. And these are surely all very good things to have. Even here, though, we need to recognize the fact and importance of human difference, the very different forms that human virtue can take given the vast field of human imperfection. There seem to be people whose virtues are forms of their failings. There are people whose gifts depend on their faults. There are people who inspire love and respect although they're rackety, partial, inconsistent, and comically faint-hearted (as opposed to temperate, just, practically wise, and courageous). There are on the one hand heroes and wise maidens with oil lamps, and, on the other hand, Don Quixotes, Fitzcarraldos, Shirley Maclaine figures, Mullah Nasruddins, Uncle Tobys, and Papagenos. There are people whose charm is inextricable from their rashness or naughtiness, people whose creative energies are constitutively linked to their cowardice or bad temper, people whose particular insight and humour depend on certain sorts of injustice and unfairness, people whose special capacities for generosity and great-heartedness are inseparable from their intemperance, hopelessly faulty people who have moral charm (a notion favoured by Isaiah Berlin)—moral charm which constitutively is bound up with their lack of practical wisdom. One must not be too quick or grand when one tries to generalize about the human condition—either about how it is or how it ought to be.

6.4 Two More Theses

Sacks, Bruner, McAdams, and many others endorse (a) the psychological Narrativity thesis and (b) the narrative self-constitution thesis. We're all Narrative, and we 'constitute ourselves as persons by forming a narrative self-conception according to which we experience and organize our lives' (Schechtman 2007: 162). 'Beginning in late adolescence and young adulthood',

we construct integrative narratives of the self that selectively recall the past and wishfully anticipate the future to provide our lives with some semblance of unity, purpose, and identity.

Personal identity is the internalized and evolving life story that each of us is working on as we move through our adult lives....I...do not really know who I am until I have a good understanding of my narrative identity.   (McAdams 2005: 287–8).

I find this bewildering. I certainly have an identity in the relevant sense, a psychological identity, and I certainly have a past, a history; even, if you like, a life story. But I'm blowed if I constituted my identity, or if my identity is my life story. I don't spend time constructing integrative narratives of myself or my self that selectively recall the past and wishfully anticipate the future to provide my life with some semblance of unity, purpose, and identity. When I read that this is a human universal, I think I must come from the planet Zog.

Some psychologists use the term 'identity' to refer not to how one fundamentally *is*, psychologically, but to how one *conceives* oneself to be—however misguided one is. Some also use the term 'self' in this way. On this view, one's self is just one's self-conception. One's identity, one's actual psychological identity, is how one conceives of oneself. This seems to me like saying that one's VW is a Rolls Royce (or conversely), because that's what one thinks it is. It also sounds rather alarming. But this, perhaps, is just a terminological matter; and since it seems that McAdams is using the term 'identity' in this special way, the disagreement between the two of us is considerably less than it seems. I can't, for example, object that his view seems to have the consequence that no one can ever be self-deceived.

Even so, disagreements remain—among them, the deep disagreement between those who think that one's self-conception is essentially some sort of narrative and those who don't. I'm also unsure what to make of McAdams's statement that 'I...do not really know who I am until I have a good understanding of my narrative identity.' The trouble is that the phrase 'know who I am' seems to me to connect inexorably to an 'objective' understanding of the word 'identity' to mean who I really am as a matter of deep psychological fact, opposed to the 'subjective' use of 'identity' to mean how I conceive myself to be. It seems all too painfully clear that I may have a very good understanding of my identity in the sense of my account of myself to myself, and not 'know who I am' at all. I may be clueless about myself, radically self-deceived as to my identity in the objective sense, and my cluelessness may consist precisely in my identity in the subjective sense, my McAdamian identity.[8]

But having noted this difficulty, and possible ground of misunderstanding, I'm going to put both aside for now. I'll continue to use 'identity' in the way I favour, as referring to who or what I am, fundamentally, considered as a person with a certain character, however much or little I know about the matter.[9] A person can of course

---

[8] The fact that someone has concocted the particular subjective or McAdamian identity that she has concocted is, no doubt, an important fact about her objective identity, but its falsity relative to her objective identity may be what is most revealing about it. 'Our fundamental tactic of self-protection, self-control,' according to Dennett, 'is...telling stories, and more particularly concocting and controlling the story we tell others—and ourselves—about who we are.... Our tales are spun, but for the most part we don't spin them; they spin us. Our human consciousness, and our narrative selfhood, is their product, not their source' (1991: 418).

[9] By 'person', in turn, I don't just mean the bare metaphysical category, insofar as this is thought of as something that can be considered independently of questions of personality. I don't just mean something that fits Locke's definition of a person, 'a thinking intelligent being that has reason and reflection, and can

be highly complex and inconsistent compatibly with there being a fact of the matter about how they are, fundamentally, considered as a person.

(a) and (b), the psychological Narrativity thesis and the narrative self-constitution thesis, are distinct. One can endorse (a), the view that we're all Narrative if normal, without in any way endorsing (b), the view that we (all normally) constitute our identity in that way. (a) is also independent from any other self-constitution view— any view according to which we constitute ourselves as persons in some way. Neither thesis has any evaluative implications; both are merely empirical and descriptive. But they both have evaluative or 'normative' forms. I call the normative version of the psychological Narrativity thesis

(c)   the ethical Narrativity thesis.

According to the ethical Narrativity thesis, one ought to have a Narrative outlook on one's life. One ought to think about oneself and one's existence in a narrative way and in some manner live in and through this conception. It's essential to a good life, essential to living well, essential, in fact, to true or full *personhood*.

We can illustrate this view by supposing that Socrates is right when he says that the unexamined life is not a full human life, not a life for a human being—right that we ought to be reflective about our lives in some way or other. I'm not sure that this is a universal human truth, in fact, but let's assume that it is ('in some way or other' may prove to be a fairly capacious dispensation). We may then take the ethical Narrativity thesis to be the thesis that we ought to reflect about our lives in a particular way: in the narrative way, in the narrative framework.

This view is widely held today, and it's usually part of the normative version of the narrative self-constitution thesis, which I'll call (somewhat heavily)

(d)   the *ethical narrative self-constitution thesis*.

According to this view, one's identity as a person or self ought to be constituted by (or perhaps in or through) one's narrative of one's life.[10]

Like (a) and (b), (c) and (d), the ethical Narrativity thesis and the more specific ethical narrative self-constitution thesis, are distinct. For one can endorse (c), the claim that one ought to be Narrative, without endorsing (d), the more specific claim that one ought to constitute one's identity in a narrative way. In practice, though, most of those who think that one ought to be Narrative seem to think that this is at least partly, if not wholly, because one ought to constitute one's identity in a narrative way.

We now have four connected theses: (a) a thesis about how we do normally think about ourselves and our lives; (c) a thesis about how we ought to do this (given that

consider it self as it self, the same thinking being in different times and places', not even when this famous part of his definition is put together with another no less essential part of it: an 'intelligent agent... capable of a law, and happiness, and misery' (Locke 1694: 2.27.9, 2.27.26). I mean (as is obvious in context) a person as just defined considered specifically as something that has a certain personality or character.

[10] Paul Ricoeur, for example, remarks that 'self-understanding is an interpretation' and holds that 'interpretation of the self... finds in narrative... a privileged form of mediation' (1990: 114 n).

Socrates is right that we ought to do it in some way or other); (b) a thesis about how our identity gets constituted; and (d) a thesis about how it ought to get constituted.

It may be said that the fundamental features of one's identity are what they are independently of anything one can do about them. There is, first and foremost, the matter of a person's position in the great state-space of core character traits, which once had four main parameters—sanguine, melancholy, phlegmatic, and choleric—and now has five, the 'Big Five', the bipolar categories Extraversion/Intraversion, Neuroticism/non-Neuroticism, Agreeableness/Disagreeableness, Conscientiousness/Irresponsibility, Openness/Closedness to Experience. Well, this is surely right (the point may deserve more attention from self-constitutionists). For the moment it's enough to note that one can ingest and savour this large dose of realism (highly restorative in a debate which sometimes runs wild) while continuing to endorse versions of the two self-constitution theses that have been modified to take account of this realism. The modified self-constitution theses remain highly substantive, although much more moderate than their original unrestricted versions, in focusing on self-constitution *insofar as there is anything we can do about ourselves and our identities.*[11]

6.5 Four Initial Positions

I want now to put aside the specific issue of self-constitution (theses (b) and (d)) for a while, and consider the four possible theoretical positions defined by acceptance or rejection of (a) and (c), the psychological Narrativity thesis and the ethical Narrativity thesis.[12]

First position. The descriptive psychological thesis is true but the ethical thesis is false. That is, we are indeed deeply Narrative in our thinking about ourselves, but it's not a good thing. It leads to self-deception, bad faith, inauthenticity, bullshit. This view is associated particularly with Jean-Paul Sartre, but we may also call the great (second-century) Stoic Marcus Aurelius as a witness.

Second position. The descriptive thesis is false, but the ethical thesis is true. It's not true that all normal people are naturally Narrative in their thinking about ourselves. But we should all be Narrative. We need to be, in order to live a good life. Bob Dylan needs to start narrativizing before it's too late. This is a common view today, and it also has respectable ancestry, e.g. in the person of (the first-century historian and philosopher) Plutarch.

Third position. Both theses are true: both the psychological Narrativity thesis, according to which all normal non-pathological human beings are naturally Narrative, and the ethical Narrativity thesis, according to which being Narrative is crucial to a good life. This seems to be the most popular view in the academy today, and indeed in the clinic, followed by the second view. It doesn't entail that everything is as it should be; it leaves plenty of room for the idea that many of us would profit from

---

[11] McAdams fully acknowledges the importance of the Big Five even as he chooses to use the word 'identity' in a different way; see e.g. McAdams 2005: 283–5.

[12] Here I draw on G. Strawson 2004.

being more Narrative than we are, and also, I take it, for the view that we can narrativize ourselves badly, and learn to do it better.[13]

Fourth position. The psychological Narrativity thesis and the ethical Narrativity thesis are both false. This is my view. I don't think it's true that there is only one general way in which (non-pathological) human beings think about themselves when they think about themselves in the larger, more overarching way that is at present in question—the Narrative way. And I don't think that there is only one good way for them to do so—the Narrative way. There are deeply non-Narrative people and there are good ways to live that are deeply non-Narrative. There are people who live well who are not only *not* naturally Narrative in temporal temperament, where this is something merely negative; there are people who live well who are naturally strongly *anti*-Narrative, where this is something positive in its own right. People like this not only lack any inclination to cast, conceive, construe, and conduct their lives (or parts of their lives) in a Narrative way; they also find it peculiarly hard to do. They're likely to stumble and stall in recounting events in their lives, and this is principally because they have a strong sense that something is being positively misrepresented, falsified, insofar as the events are being strung together in a narrative.

6.6 Two More Positions

With these four basic positions in place, we can return to the narrative self-constitution thesis, along with its normative version. The non-normative version, recall, says that your narrative of your own life constitutes your identity as a person or self. The normative version says that one's identity as a person or self ought to be constituted by one's narrative. The dominant view in the academy and the clinic, I think, is that both these theses are true. Proponents of this view hold a full house: we're naturally Narrative; we ought to be; we constitute our identity in this way; and we ought to. I'm at the opposite end. We're not all naturally Narrative; it's not clear that it is a good thing; we don't all constitute our identity in this way; nor ought we to. Perhaps Michael Jackson was destroyed by his belief in narrative self-constitution.

Who's right, and why does it matter? It matters both theoretically and practically. The psychological Narrativity thesis (according to which we're all Narrative) is an empirical claim whose truth or falsity is of great moment to anyone interested in human affairs. The ethical Narrativity thesis (we all ought to be Narrative) is a normative, evaluative claim, not a descriptive claim, but it also of course makes a claim to truth, an empirical claim, in fact, about what is actually good for people, and one reason why it matters is that if it isn't true then a considerable amount of damage may be being done—in psychotherapeutic contexts, for example—by people who think it is true. Therapy aside, and more generally, the ethical Narrativity thesis creates a problem inasmuch as non-Narrative people who are exposed to it may think there's something wrong with them and their lives when there isn't. Since I published

---

[13] It's natural to think that self-narrativizing must be bad when it's not true to the facts. Some, however, may claim that it can be good, both in general and in particular in therapy, even if it is inaccurate. Tom Dougherty has put it to me that this is true in the case of the philosopher Susan Brison, who had in her own words to 'remake her self' after she had been raped and left for dead (see Brison 2002).

'Against Narrativity' in 2004 I've heard from quite a number of people who have found the paper helpful for this reason.

One obvious possibility is that the Narrative life is right or best for some but not for others. It may be, for example, that naturally Narrative people ought to be Narrative—that this is a good way for them to lead their lives—while naturally non-Narrative people ought not. I'm certain that the Narrative life isn't good for everyone, and I'm interested in the polemical thesis that it isn't a particularly good way—or at least the best way—for anyone to live their lives. Perhaps it's essentially confining, essentially petty, excessively self-concerned, second-order, shopkeeperly. Perhaps the ethical Narrativity thesis is false for everyone, or almost everyone, because 'we live...beyond any tale that we happen to enact',[14] and the ethical Narrativity thesis seeks to confine us to our tales. When I first wrote about Narrativity I wanted to defend the non-Narrative or anti-Narrative temperament against what I took to be the prevailing orthodoxy, and I thought that the most important thing to do was to stress human difference and variety, as—so far—I've done again in this paper. Now I want to begin to go on the offensive against Narrativity. If the Narrativity thesis is the main thesis in town, we need the antithesis, the anti-thesis. (*Aufhebung* can wait.) I'm going to proceed in two stages.

6.7 Exetasis

Stage 1. I've allowed for the sake of argument that Socrates is right that we ought to think about or examine ourselves in a wide, general, life-assessing way. I've allowed that he's right that we ought to engage in what he called *exetasis*, or more accurately *auto-exetasis*—self-examination (I'm going to use the Greek word, because it's unfamiliar and to that extent theoretically unencumbered). Question: Does auto-exetasis, exetasis for short, essentially involve narrative, Narrativity? If I have to be exetatic, do I have to be Narrative? Is the Narrative way the best way, even if it's not the only way? I say No and No. Let me put down a clear marker straight away by saying that I don't think exetasis necessarily involves Narrativity even when it involves therapy that pays special attention to past life, especially early life.

Perhaps this shows that I understand the notion of narrative is a narrower way than others. So be it. I don't think that deriving therapeutic benefit from grasping and emotionally appreciating causal connections between one's early-life experiences and one's current travails need involve any sort of specifically or distinctively Narrative thinking—any more than learning that the scar on one's finger is due to an early fall. In most cases, I think therapy delivers a strikingly disparate clutch of insights, bits and pieces, elements of understanding (emotional understanding) that cast light severally on this and that. The insight-elements don't themselves make up a narrative sequence; nor is the way each one casts light individually a distinctively narrative matter. Truth in this area is mostly a matter of fragments and oddments, accurate exetasis is largely *bricolage*, smooth narrative is almost certainly fantasy (except, perhaps, for people who are obsessional in one way or another). I certainly don't

---

[14] Pritchett 1979: 47.

want to rule out the possibility that successful therapy or exetasis should in some cases have a narrative form. But if we measure therapeutic success partly by reference to getting at the truth, rather than just by reference to restoring or increasing everyday fitness for life,[15] then I think the possibility of achieving success with smooth narrative grows slimmer.[16]

No, say the narrativists, the facts are these. Almost all causal explanation of features of concrete reality—in this case, features of oneself, one's personality, one's present situation, and so on—involves identifying links between past and present. And when one's subject is oneself and one's life, all identification of links between past and present involves narrative. Granted, they say, this may not be true (or interestingly true) in the case of many explanations of features of oneself, medical and genetic explanations, for example, to do with eyesight and shoe size, but it is going to be true in the case of many of the most interesting character-related or more generally psychological explanations. This means that exetasis is bound to involve narrative as soon as it involves causal explanation, past–present linking. And it's bound to involve a considerable amount of highly substantive causal explanation if it is to get anywhere. So it must after all involve a considerable amount of highly substantive narrative.

In sum and in brief, we have an argument. Premiss [1]: Exetasis requires causal explanation, past–present linking. Premiss [2]: Causal explanation is necessarily narrative, when one's subject is oneself and one's life, and in particular one's ethical life, in the largest sense of that large word. Conclusion: exetasis is necessarily narrative.

The argument is valid, but I don't think it's sound. I reject both premisses. As for premiss [1], I don't think exetasis necessarily involves causal explanation; I think, with Proust, among others, that it often involves such simple things as discovering something about what really matters most to one (I'll come back to this). But although I don't think that exetasis necessarily involves causal explanation, I do think that it very often involves causal explanation. So I'm prepared to grant premiss [1] for the sake of argument. But not premiss [2]. I reject premiss [2]: causal explanation, psychologically significant causal explanation, isn't always narrative. It isn't 'always already' narrative, even when a life is in question. It can be, in an intuitive sense, non-Narrative. I can have no story of development, but capture an isolated key explanatory connection between past and present, an arc of contact that reaches above and is utterly independent of all the developmental, progression-involving details of my life.[17]

---

[15] Compare the notion of a 'functioning alcoholic'.

[16] If, as I assume, the goal of exetasis is understanding, then its goal is truth, because to understand something is to be right about it. So if successful therapy involves successful exetasis, it must involve the acquisition of truth. It may be said that therapy needn't care about truth (see e.g. note 13 above); it can help someone by giving them a good personal myth, because 'human kind cannot bear very much reality' (Eliot 1936). That may or may not be so. The present claim is only that therapy must aim at truth if it aims to make progress by exetasis rather than by some other means, whatever else it may usefully get up to.

[17] Note that the ethical Narrativity thesis becomes a truism if one grants both [1] and [2]. If exetasis aims at (ethical) self-understanding, and if self-understanding necessarily involves personality-related causal explanation, then, if personality-related causal explanation necessarily involves narrative, exetasis necessarily involves narrative.

6.8 'Le vrai moi'

Stage 2. So much (for the moment) for exetasis. Now for a frontal assault on the 'full house' view set out in §6.6. I haven't got this fully worked out, and I'm going to bring in a team of supporters. I can't write like Montaigne, but I can match him in appealing to others and moving from quotation to quotation. On my team I have, for a start, or so I believe, people like Proust, Emerson, Woolf, and at least one avatar of Nietzsche, who has, it seems as many avatars as the Hindu God Vishnu (at least one of which is on the other team). This initial list may sink some hearts, on the grounds that these people are just too sensitive, too highly strung, too transcenden-tal-intellectual—too hyper, in Amélie Rorty's phrase. But they're counterbalanced by the comparative bluntness of some of the other team members: the great short-story writer V. S. Pritchett, the source of my title, and the incomparable Chekhov, who inspired Pritchett's observation.

Kierkegaard has also been claimed by both sides in the Narrativity debate, but he starts well for me by saying that one shouldn't try 'to arrange oneself dramatically in [time or in] temporality' (1847: 252), for this sounds like a direct criticism of Narrativity, an exact rejection of the MacIntyre/Taylor project, and also, I think, the Ricoeur project, although Ricoeur's formulations seem gentler and more open than MacIntyre's or Taylor's. Kierkegaard's most famous remark on this subject runs as follows:

Philosophy is perfectly right in saying that life must be understood backwards. But then one forgets the other clause—that it must be lived forwards. The more one thinks through this clause, the more one concludes that life in temporality never becomes properly understand-able, simply because never at any time does one get perfect repose to take a stance: backwards.

(1843: 450)

This passage has probably been cited in support of the Narrative cause. It seems to me, though, that it rejects the idea that one should make use of a story of oneself in living forwards, i.e. in living—for there is no other way to live. Your narrative is something you work out, perhaps, if you want to, looking back, but you shouldn't let it dictate your stance to the future. Rather the contrary, when it comes to dictation. In another passage Kierkegaard says that we should live

like someone taking dictation, continually having his pen poised for what comes next, so that he does not presume meaninglessly to place a period before the meaning is complete or rebelliously throw away his pen.   (1847: 252)

This is, admittedly, in context, a counsel against despair, but it seems, more generally, a strongly anti-Narrativist injunction. I don't, however, want to rest anything on Kierkegaard's case, which is highly complex, particularly when it comes to the importance he accords to reflective recollection (as opposed to mere memory).[18]

Proust considers days when one finds oneself 'outside the regular tenor of life', 'en dehors du train courant de la vie' (1927: 227 (Fr. 496–7)), days when one is

---

[18] See e.g. Stokes 2008.

more inward. They're not days on which one finds oneself in a special position to 'appreciate what one has made of oneself'. They're days when one is simply more at home to what one just is, independently of any making, more at home to—or with, or in—'notre vrai moi', as Proust calls it (1927: 181, Fr. 451), the true me or true self, to which there is, on these days, some kind of reconnection, or better connection. One has been caught up in one's daily life in a way that has in some respect alienated one from oneself. Perhaps one has also been caught up in one's 'narrative' of one's life (one's view of one's own life) in a way that has alienated one from oneself. How could this be, the narrativists ask? Because we live beyond any tale that we happen to enact; and also, I propose, beyond any tale we tell ourselves about ourselves.

Proust gives great weight to what he calls 'involuntary memories', upsurgings of past episodes of extreme happiness. They teach you about yourself as nothing else can. They're rare and fundamental data. These data come from the past, to be sure. It doesn't follow that they have anything to do with narrative. On the contrary; they're isolated clues, *clés*, not clews you have to ravel up (narratively, temporally) to their source. They're complete in themselves in respect of their probative force. Proustian self-knowledge centrally involves things like this, suddenly realizing that one really loves something, something which is likely to seem wholly trivial from most points of view. Proust's greatest revelations come from the feel of a starched napkin, the sensation of uneven flagstones under his feet, hearing a spoon clink on glass, dipping a biscuit in tea. Such things are, perhaps, the fundamental clues to self, under all one's skins.

Of which there are at least 490, as Nietzsche says before he goes on to make the very point Proust is making. He, Nietzsche, is speaking of the dangers of self-examination, but he then says that

there is a means by which this absolutely crucial enquiry [into oneself] can be carried out. Let the young mind look back at its life with the question: what until now have you truly loved, what has entranced your spirit, what has governed it and at the same time made it happy?

(1874: 340 [trans. p. 129])

Again, this exetatic use of the past isn't specifically a matter of narrative. It's a leap outside narrative. Obviously in looking back one considers parts of one's actual life (one's actual history), but what one hopes to acquire is information about one's deep form, information about one's nature that is not constituted—perhaps not even partly constituted—by the events of one's actual life, let alone one's narrative of that life, information that may seem oddly trivial and thoroughly surprising.[19]

Emerson (deeply admired by Nietzsche) adds this, in his roaring essay on self-reliance:

What is the aboriginal Self...? The inquiry leads us to that source...which we call Spontaneity or Instinct...[or] Intuition. Every man discriminates between the voluntary acts of his mind,

---

[19] In *A la recherche du temps perdu* Proust speaks of being 'outside' time. His narrator's view is that we are, so far as everything that matters most about us is concerned, outside time, and a fortiori outside narrative. (What is perhaps most important about this, for Proust, is that it abolishes his fear of death; but that is another matter.)

and his involuntary perceptions, and knows that to his involuntary perceptions a perfect faith is due. He may err in the expression of them, but he knows that these things are so, like day and night, not to be disputed. All my wilful actions and acquisitions are but roving;—the idlest reverie, the faintest native emotion, command my curiosity and respect.   (1841: 269)

Here Emerson delivers a colossal blow against many who champion self-constitution by wilful choice and action, but this is only *en passant*. His principal message is that we're reliably accessible to ourselves only by intuition . . . we need to listen for ourselves . . . we are in Nietzsche's phrase 'pieces of fate' . . . we wander most blindly precisely when we try to regiment ourselves . . . things are not up to us . . . we ourselves are not up to us.

He takes the point to its fiercest conclusion:

Nothing is at last sacred but the integrity of your own mind. . . . I remember an answer which when quite young I was prompted to make a valued adviser, who was wont to importune me with the dear old doctrines of the church. On my saying, 'What have I to do with the sacredness of traditions, if I live wholly from within?' my friend suggested—'But these impulses may be from below, not from above.' I replied, 'They do not seem to me to be such; but if I am the Devil's child, I will live then from the Devil.' No law can be sacred to me but that of my nature. Good and bad are but names very readily transferable to that or this; the only right is what is after my constitution; the only wrong what is against it.   (ibid. pp. 261–2)

If this seems too much, remember that Emerson is betting on the basic goodness (or good-enoughness, in Winnicott's terms) of untainted human being.

Kant, by contrast, believed in radical evil, that is, a tendency to wrongdoing right at the root [*radix*] of human being. Kant's standards, though, were very high, and Emerson is at one with Kant in his paean to autonomy when he says that 'no law can be sacred to me but that of my nature'—even as he utterly rejects what Kant has in mind, and, as I read him, reverses the aspirations of those in the present day who seek autonomy in self-constitution.[20] Both Emerson and Kant agree with Nietzsche that 'you should become what you are' (Nietzsche 1882: §270).

—You can't fail to become what you are. It's tautological that you are at any stage of your life what you have thus far become.

Emerson's and Nietzsche's point is precisely that it's all too possible that you can fail to become what you are, and miss out on reality, 'that reality which we run a serious risk of dying without having known', according to Proust, 'and which is quite simply our life'.[21]

—No. Of all the things you could have quoted in support of your argument, this is the worst. For Proust's very next sentence reads as follows: 'True life, life finally uncovered and illuminated, hence the only life that is fully lived, is literature.'[22]

---

[20] He doesn't, of course, give reason the same place in our nature as Kant does (he replaces Kant's reason with Pascal's reasons of the heart).

[21] 1927: 204, French text p. 474; 'cette réalité que nous risquerions fort de mourir sans l'avoir connue, et qui est tout simplement notre vie'.

[22] 1927: 204, French text p. 474; 'la vraie vie, la vie enfin découverte et éclaircie, la seule vie par conséquent réellement vécue, c'est la littérature'.

What Proust means by this, though, is the polar opposite of what the narrativity theorists have in mind when they encourage us to be Narrative, to engage in narrative self-constitution. He means, very briefly, a certain high quality of apprehension of life and self that is free from the almost invincible distortions and blindnesses of habit, *le train-train*, and fundamentally independent of the actual course of your life—and a fortiori of any narrative account of it.

Proust might none the less be thought to believe in self-constitution. For he also says that 'we work away constantly trying to give our life its form'. But what happens when we do this, he says, is that 'in spite of ourselves we copy, as in a drawing, the traits of the person we are, not the person we would like to be'.[23] This is not really self-constitution, and even if it were it would not be distinctively narrative self-constitution. (It may be added that Proust seems here to have our public history and social persona principally in mind.)

That's enough Emerson, Nietzsche, and Proust. I'm sure we should get in touch with ourselves (although I'm not sure how this fits with projects of radical self-constitution). But doing so is often more a matter of luck than endeavour, and I'm now interested in a quieter point. For Mrs Ramsay, in Virginia Woolf's *To the Lighthouse*,

> it was a relief when they [the others] went to bed. For now she need not think about anybody. She could be herself, by herself. And that was what now she often felt the need of—to think; well not even to think. To be silent; to be alone. All the being and the doing, expansive, glittering, vocal, evaporated; and one shrunk, with a sense of solemnity, to being oneself, a wedge-shaped core of darkness, something invisible to others. Although she continued to knit, and sat upright, it was thus that she felt herself.   (1927: 72)

Here, I think, we have contact, contact with one's identity, the distinguished thing in both senses of the word (though not in Henry James's meaning). And it seems to be the negation, the pure negation, of narrative.[24]

Consider, also, Woolf's 'moments of being' (1939: 70, 73). Some Woolfian moments of being are good but relatively ordinary moments of life in which one is—manages to be—present in a way in which one is often not present.[25] Others are memories, not necessarily happy (they may be 'sledge-hammer' blows), that have Proustian force. These are, as it were, windows into one's essence, one's personal essence—something to whose existence I'm now happy to commit myself as a matter of basic psychological realism, without saying that we should go digging after it, or that it is unalterable, or that experience after early childhood can have no part in its constitution. Moments of being reveal something; something is made manifest.

---

[23] 1920–1: 184–5 (UK edn), 181 (US edn), French text p. 484; 'nous travaillons à tout moment à donner sa forme à notre vie, mais en copiant malgré nous comme un dessin les traits de la personne que nous sommes et non de celle qu'il nous serait agréable d'être'.

[24] For Woolf, this experience is strongly linked to experience of one's being as transcending one's existence as an individual human being. See e.g. Woolf 1939: 72; Woolf 1925: *passim*.

[25] Proust holds that one is for the most part completely closed down by habit, 'stupefying habit that hides almost the whole universe from us throughout our lives' (1925: 124: 'l'habitude abêtissante qui pendant tout le cours de notre vie nous cache à peu près tout l'univers').

—The metaphor of the window is not neutral, given the current debate. It's potentially question-begging: it presupposes a fixed place—a kind of shrine—into which one looks.

It needn't be taken so crudely.

—But these 'moments of being' are obviously part of one's 'narrative', in the sense of one's account of one's life.

This threatens to be question-begging in its turn. Or rather, it threatens to trivialize the claim that all normal people are Narrative. One can't be said to have a narrative of one's life, a narrative attitude to one's life, a narrative self-conception, simply because one has and remembers and treasures such moments. We all have histories, and nearly all of us have a reasonable number of memories of past events in our lives. This alone can't make it true to say that we are Narrative—short of trivializing the claim. And what distinguishes Woolf's moments of being, it seems to me, is their isolation from narrative. They are, certainly, actual events in her life, but that doesn't place them in a connected narrative. They're loci or manifestations of her fundamental form, or aspects of her fundamental form. Their power lies in their stillness, their self-sufficiency, their independence of the flow of life, their immunity to 'making'. They make me think of the stillness of a great portrait. There is a fundamental mode of human understanding in which to understand someone is like experiencing this stillness. The same goes, I propose, for understanding oneself. The correct image, in any case, and independently of the image of the portrait, is one of discovery, not creation or constitution.

Thoughts of this kind are no doubt familiar enough; the gathering conclusion is plain. (I'm moving rather fast at this point, with complete disregard for all the opportunities for counterquotation that I've created.) Theses (a)–(d) are all false. (a) and (b) are empirically false as descriptive theses. (c) and (d) are empirically false as normative theses. But suppose you are naturally Narrative: suppose you do naturally think of yourself and your life in a narrative way. Many don't do this, but suppose you do. So be it. That's one natural way of human being. But it seems to me that you should then be careful what else you do. For to *identify* oneself with one's narrative of oneself, to take one's narrative of oneself to *constitute one's identity*, is likely to be a desperately reductive (if not murderous) act—and for several reasons. Not only because we live beyond any tale that we happen to enact, but also because there are many respects in which we're not very good at knowing much about ourselves, or about why we do what we do. To all the broadly speaking Freudian evidence in support of this last claim we have to add all the situationist evidence from social psychology. Then we have to take full account of the non-Freudian notion of the 'adaptive unconscious' as expounded, for example, by Timothy Wilson in his book *Strangers to Ourselves*. The adaptive unconscious is the unconscious mind as acknowledged in cognitive science, a vast repertoire of mental processes that influence our judgments and decisions in ways inaccessible to conscious awareness. It turns out to do a great deal of the running of one's life, especially when things go well, sometimes with little regard for one's conscious elucubrations.[26]

---

[26] The connection with 'situationist' approaches is clear. See also Kahneman 2011.

Note that this doesn't mean that it isn't really one oneself who acts, when one acts. To think this is to make the great mistake, to identity oneself with the 'conscious self', which is, at best, the spindrift of your being. It just means that you're not generally au fait with what is going on in the way that you think. And the danger is that the more you identify with your explicit narrative of yourself, the less you're likely to know what is really going on. 'We do not deal much in fact when we are contemplating ourselves' (1902: 341), as Mark Twain observed. Some of us, do, perhaps, but most of us don't. 'It is all very well to be aware of your awareness', Lewis Thomas adds, 'even proud of it, but do not try to operate it. You are not up to the job' (1983: 141). The consequences for (b) and (d), the ethical Narrativity thesis and the ethical narrative self-constitution thesis are I think clear. I'm inclined to adapt William Blake's famous quatrain: 'Never seek to tell thy life, / Life that never told can be; / For the gentle wind doth move / Silently, invisibly.'

None of this is to say that one can't plan a life's work or pursue great projects. It's not to say that one can't try to be good, to become good. (For that, though, one need never look further than the present; to think of yourself as on a 'quest' is almost inevitably corrupting.) It simply raises doubts, grave doubts, in my opinion, about the value of being Narrative and about the goal of narrative self-constitution, or indeed any project that is explicitly conceived of as a project of self-constitution. It raises questions about the extent to which self-constitution is likely to be a form of self-abuse; about the extent to which the goal of autonomy is a form of enslavement. As Pritchett says in his essay about Chekhov's short stories, which surely inspired him, 'life is a fish that cannot be netted by mood or doctrine, but continually glides away between sun and shadow' (Pritchett 1979: 48).

6.9 Conclusion

I've tried to present an antithesis to the Narrativist thesis. There's a great deal more to say about all this, but this is as far as I've got at present.[27]

---

[27] I'm grateful to the British Academy and the Leverhulme Trust for a Research Fellowship (2009–10) which enabled me to write this paper.

7

The Unstoried Life

I want Death to find me planting my cabbages, neither worrying about it nor the unfinished gardening.

Michel de Montaigne (1563–92: 99)

7.1 Proem

'Each of us constructs and lives a "narrative"...this narrative *is* us, our identities.' 'Self is a perpetually rewritten story.' 'In the end, we *become* the autobiographical narratives by which we "tell about" our lives.' 'We are all storytellers, and we are the stories we tell.' 'We invent ourselves, but we really are the characters we invent.' A person 'creates his identity by forming an autobiographical narrative—a story of his life'. We're 'virtuoso novelists, who find ourselves engaged in all sorts of behaviour, and we always try to put the best "faces" on it we can. We try to make all of our material cohere into a single good story. And that story is our autobiography. The chief fictional character at the centre of that autobiography is one's self.' 'The story of a life continues to be refigured by all the truthful or fictive stories a subject tells about himself or herself. This refiguration makes this life itself a cloth woven of stories told.'[1]

According to these theorists—I'll call them the *narrativists*—life is life-writing. It's a narrative—autobiographical—activity. We story ourselves and we are our stories. There's a remarkably robust consensus about this claim, not only in the humanities but also in psychotherapy. It's standardly conjoined with the claim that such self-narration is a good thing, necessary for a full human life.[2] I think it's false—false that everyone stories themselves, false that it's always a good thing. These are not universal human truths, even when we confine our attention to human beings who count as psychologically normal, as I will here. They're not universal human truths even if they're true of some people, or even many, or most. Their proponents, the narrativists, are—at best—generalizing from their own case, in an all-too-human way.[3]

---

[1] Sacks 1985: 110, Bruner 1994: 53, Bruner 1987: 15, McAdams et al. 2006, Velleman 2005: 206, Schechtman 1996: 93, Dennett 1988: 1029, Ricoeur 1985: 246.

[2] Sartre, at least, disagrees on the second point, arguing in *La nausée* that self-storying, although inevitable, condemns us to inauthenticity—in effect, to absence from our own lives. Proust agrees, in *A la recherche du temps perdu*; see §7.4 below.

[3] I doubt that what they say is an accurate description even of themselves.

7.2 'Narrativity'

What exactly do the narrativists have in mind, when they say things of the sort just quoted? I haven't yet been able to find out. But it does seem that there are deeply *narrative* types among us, where to be narrative (here I offer a definition) is to be

naturally disposed to experience or conceive of one's life, one's existence in time, oneself, in a narrative way, as having the form of a story, or perhaps a collection of stories, and—in some manner—to live in and through this conception.

The popularity of the narrativist view is prima facie evidence that there are such people. But it's not decisive evidence, because human beings hold many views about themselves that have very little to do with reality; and many of us aren't narrative in this sense. 'Time travels in divers paces with divers persons',[4] and it also travels in divers guises. This paper offers dissenting testimony from many sources. Some of us are not just not naturally narrative. We're naturally— deeply—non-narrative. We're anti-narrative by fundamental constitution. It's not just that the deliverances of memory are, for us, hopelessly piecemeal and disordered, even when we're trying to remember a temporally extended sequence of events. The point is much more general. It concerns all parts of life, the 'great shambles of life', in Henry James's expression (1899: 198). This seems a much better characterization of the large-scale structure ($\approx$ structurelessness) of human existence as we find it.

Non-narratives are fully aware of life's biological temporal order (birth, infancy, childhood, adolescence, adulthood, prime of life, maturity, decline, old age, and death),[5] and its associated cultural temporal order and rites of passage (including, in these parts, acquisition of the right to drive, marry, drink, vote, adopt, retire, get a free bus pass). Even with all this knowledge of life structure they find themselves 'weltering through eternity' (Shelley 1818a: 198), even on the most ordinary mornings or under clear temporal duress (late for work), and not just (as in Shelley's lines) when thickly dreaming.

It makes no difference to non-narratives whether something has 'burst the spirit's sleep', i.e. caused them to wake up to life in a way that makes their past seem like sleepwalking (Bellow 1959: 312, echoing Shelley 1818b: 138). This Shelleyan experience is orthogonal (as philosophers say) to any experience of narrative coherence or narrative self-determination or 'self-authorship'. The two forms of experience appear to be 'doubly dissociable', in the terminology of experimental psychology: one can experience either in the absence of the other (or both together, or neither).

---

[4] *As You Like It* 3.2. Rosalind considers variations in the experienced pace of time that arise from temporary circumstances, but individual differences in temporal phenomenology run much deeper. In their book *The Time Paradox* (2008) Zimbardo and Boyd sort human beings into 'Pasts', 'Presents', and 'Futures' on the basis of their different temporal proclivities, and classify us further as 'past-negative' or 'past-positive', 'present-hedonistic' or 'present-fatalistic'. It's a familiar point that different cultures experience time very differently (see e.g. Levine 1998).

[5] A recent medical classification distinguishes between 'young-old' (65–74), 'old' (74–84), 'old-old' (85+).

7.3 'Self-authorship'

The experience of 'self-authorship'—the sense that one is engaging in self-determination in and through some process of 'life-writing' or narrative self-constitution—is one thing, mysterious to my kind. The existence of such a thing is another. Perhaps some people have the experience, or aspire to it; some seem to believe in the possibility of self-creation. 'The tendency to attribute control to self is a personality trait', as the psychologist Dan Wegner says, possessed by some and not others (2002: 202, citing Rotter 1966). There's an experimentally well-attested distinction between human beings who have what he calls the 'emotion of authorship' with respect to their thoughts, and those who, like myself, have no such emotion, and feel that their thoughts are things that just happen (Wegner 2002: 318, 325–6). This difference may run very deep, and it may track the difference between those who experience themselves as self-constituting and those who don't.

Whether it does or not, the *experience* of self-constituting self-authorship seems real enough. When it comes to the actual *existence* of self-authorship, however—the reality of some process of self-determination in or through life as life-writing—I'm sceptical. Mary McCarthy appears to speak for many when she says

> I suppose everyone continues to be interested in the quest for the self, but what you feel when you're older, I think, is that you really must make the self. It is absolutely useless to look for it, you won't find it, but it's possible in some sense to make it. I don't mean in the sense of making a mask, a Yeatsian mask. But you finally begin in some sense to make and choose the self you want. (1962: 313)

And this, I take it, is how she experiences things, and how—with an attractive degree of caution—she believes them to be. Germaine Greer is less nuanced. She thinks 'human beings have an inalienable right to invent themselves', and she presumably has experiences to match (*The Times*, 1 February 1986). I go with Emerson in 1837: 'we are carried by destiny along our life's course looking as grave and knowing as little as the infant who is carried in his wicker coach thro' the street' (1835–8: 392). We may be busy all day, intensely engaged in our work, but 'sleep lingers all our lifetime about our eyes, as night hovers all day in the boughs of the fir-tree. All things swim and glimmer. Our life is not so much threatened as our perception. Ghostlike we glide through nature, and should not know our place again.'[6] This is the price we pay for our mental complexity, a great difficulty in our condition, unknown to other animals, but a price that may be worth paying.

Emerson can be overpowering and for that reason unhelpful, even when he's right. And he uses the ever-tempting general 'we'—like the narrativists. Deep down, he says, we're all equally unknowing; he proposes a universal human truth. So it's not clear that one can use his words to try to distinguish one group of people from another—non-narratives from narratives, or (a different distinction) people who believe in life as life-writing from people who don't. And some naturally narrative types probably experience the pull of Emerson's remarks, even if others feel their lives

---

[6] 1844: 471; the last phrase echoes Psalm 103.

to be glimmer-free. So I'll put Emerson aside. The issue remains, the claim that all human life is life-writing, and that life-writing is not only a necessary task for any self-respecting human being, but also, at least in the best case, an exercise of autonomy—self-determination.

This view seems extraordinarily unappreciative of fate, but above all comic, like Einstein's moon—

If the moon, in the act of completing its eternal way around the earth, were gifted with self-consciousness, it would feel thoroughly convinced that it was traveling its way of its own accord on the strength of a resolution taken once and for all.... So would a Being, endowed with higher insight and more perfect intelligence, watching man and his doings, smile about man's illusion that he was acting according to his own free will   (1931)

—or the all-too-human monkey in *Journey to the West*, in which the Buddha challenges Monkey, aka The Great Sage, to get out of his (the Buddha's) right hand with a single somersault. Monkey, who knows he can cover thirty-six thousand miles in one somersault, accepts the challenge, jumps onto the Buddha's palm, performs a maximal somersault, and marks the distant place of his arrival by writing 'The Great Sage Equaling Heaven Was Here' and urinating—before returning to the Buddha's palm to claim his prize.

'I've got you, you piss-spirit of a monkey', roared the Buddha at him. 'You never left the palm of my hand.' 'You're wrong there', the Great Sage replied. 'I went to the farthest point of Heaven, where I saw five flesh-pink pillars topped by dark vapours. I left my mark there: do you dare come and see it with me?' 'There's no need to go. Just look down.' The Great Sage looked down with his fire eyes with golden pupils to see the words 'The Great Sage Equaling Heaven Was Here' written on the middle finger of the Buddha's right hand. The stink of monkey-piss rose from the fold at the bottom of the finger.   (Wu Cheng-en 1592: vol. 1. ch. 7)

If there is any defensible sense in which life is life-writing, I think it is—at best—'automatic writing'. One's life isn't 'a cloth woven of stories told', in Ricoeur's words, threaded with varying degrees of fiction. Never mind the fact that claims of this kind seem to insult those who have suffered greatly. Never mind the adamantine fact that one's life is simply one's life, something whose actual course is part of the history of the universe and 100 per cent non-fictional. For now it's enough to hold on to the point that Alasdair MacIntyre made right at the start of the current narrativist movement: 'we are never more (and sometimes much less) than the co-authors of our own narratives. Only in fantasy do we live what story we please' (1981: 199).

Every life comes with a thrilling stack of counterfactuals. You might so very easily never have met the person you love, or believe you love. And what are the chances of your coming into existence? There's a sense in which they're vanishingly small. Your parents might so very easily never have met, and their parents in turn, and their parents in turn. And if you hadn't gone to X because Y fell ill, you'd never have discovered Z. The irony is that these counterfactuals are great material for good stories, and easily give rise to a sense of wonder or providence. But the wonder has no justification, if only because spectacular counterfactuals hold true of one's life whatever happens. Consider X, amazed at his astonishing good fortune in meeting Y:

it might so easily never have happened. But if he hadn't met Y he might now be weeping with happiness at his good fortune in meeting Z.

7.4 'Life is not literature'

So I'm with Bill Blattner in his criticism of Alexander Nehamas's influential book *Life as Literature*: 'We are not texts. Our histories are not narratives. Life is not literature' (2000: 187). Somebody had to say it. You might think that Proust disagrees, and not only shows himself to be of a narrative disposition, but also sides theoretically with the narrativists, when he states that

real life, life at last uncovered and illuminated, the only life really lived, therefore, is literature—that life which, in a sense, lives at each moment in every person as much as in an artist.

(1913–27: 4.474)

But this would be a mistake, a perfect mistake, given the way in which Proust is using the word 'literature'. Proust's conception of how we can enter into our real life is complex, but one thing that is clear is that narrativity—a tendency to self-narration—constitutes one of the greatest obstacles to doing so. Literature as *la vraie vie*, literature in Proust's special sense of the word, is a matter of a certain rare state of self-awareness which is not generally much in one's control, and has absolutely nothing to do with narrativity. Roughly speaking, it's a state of absorbed, illuminated consciousness of what one most deeply loves. It's an awareness of an aspect of one's essence (a term one shouldn't hesitate to use) which is itself a participation in one's essence—something from which one is generally alienated. And this awareness is emphatically not a matter of narrative. It is, on the contrary, out of time. The unhappy truth of the human condition, according to Proust, is that we run a great risk of dying without ever knowing our real or true life in his sense ('cette réalité que nous risquerions fort de mourir sans avoir connue'). Our narrative tendencies are one of the principal reasons why this is so.

Keats says that 'A man's life of any worth is a continual allegory' (1819: 2.102). Suppose we allow this. Does it follow that he or she should know this, or try to work out what it is? I don't think so. The search might occlude—distort, destroy—its object. Suppose we further allow that allegories are narratives, so that (if Keats is right) lives of worth are always narratives. It certainly doesn't follow that anyone should be a narrative type, or that all worthy people are narrative types. 'Very few eyes can see the Mystery of his life', Keats continues, and I think he knows that this includes the worthy person in question.

7.5 'La vraie vie'

If Proust is right about life, 'real life' in his special normative sense of the term,[7] then it may be that non-narratives have a certain advantage—however small, and however

---

[7] One's real life in Proust's normative sense is not one's actual life as this is ordinarily understood. It's a matter of one's essence.

easily nullified by other encumbrances (it's a merely negative advantage—absence of a hindrance—not in itself a positive one). The narrativists, however, may refuse to admit the reality of non-narratives. 'Look, we're sure that you're sincere when you claim to be non-narrative, but really you're as narrative as the rest of us.'[8] In the last twenty years the philosopher Marya Schechtman has given increasingly sophisticated accounts of what it is to be narrative and to 'constitute one's identity' through self-narration. She now stresses the point that one's self-narration may be very largely implicit and unconscious, and that's an important concession, relative to the strong version of her original 'Narrative Self-Constitution View', according to which one must be in possession of a full and 'explicit narrative [of one's life] to develop fully as a person' (1996: 119). It's certainly an improvement on her original view, and it puts her in a position to say that people like myself may be narrative and just not know it or admit it.

In her most recent book, *Staying Alive*, she modifies her original thesis still further, but she still thinks that 'persons experience their lives as unified wholes' (2014: 100) in some way that goes far beyond their basic awareness of themselves as single finite biological individuals with a certain curriculum vitae. She still thinks that 'we constitute ourselves as persons...by developing and operating with a (mostly implicit) *autobiographical narrative* which acts as the lens through which we experience the world' (p. 101), and I still doubt that this is true. I doubt that it's a universal human condition—universal among people who count as normal. I doubt this even after she writes that '"having an autobiographical narrative" doesn't amount to consciously retelling one's life story always (or ever) to oneself or to anyone else' (p. 101). I don't think an 'autobiographical narrative' plays any significant role in how I experience the world, although I know that my present overall outlook and behaviour is deeply conditioned by my genetic inheritance and sociocultural place and time, including in particular my early upbringing, and also know, on a smaller scale, that my experience of this bus journey is affected both by the talk I've been having with A in Notting Hill and the fact that I'm on my way to meet B in Kentish Town.

I am, like Schechtman, a creature who can 'consider itself as itself, the same thinking thing, in different times and places', in Locke's famous definition of a person (1694: 2.27.9). I know what it's like when 'anticipated trouble already tempers present joy' (Schechtman 2014: 101). In spite of my poor memory, I have a perfectly respectable degree of knowledge of many of the events of my life. I don't live ecstatically in the present moment in any pathological or enlightened manner. But I do, with Updike and many others, 'have the persistent sensation, in my life..., that I am just beginning'.[9] Pessoa's 'heteronym' Alberto Caeiro is a strange man, but he captures an experience common to many (in some perhaps milder form) when he writes that 'I always feel as if I've just been born / Into an endlessly new world.'[10]

---

[8] 'That's precisely why Proust is so pessimistic', they may add.

[9] 1989: 239. Updike's testimony shows that this experience of life has nothing essentially to do with poor memory.

[10] 1914: 48. Pessoa's heteronyms are not noms de plume; see e.g. Zenith 2002.

Some will immediately understand this, others will be puzzled—and perhaps sceptical. The general lesson is the lesson of human difference.

In a rare interview Alice Munro speaks about her work:

there is this kind of exhaustion and bewilderment when you look at your work..... it's all in a way quite foreign—I mean, it's quite gone from you.... And all you really have left is the thing you're working on now. And so you're much more thinly clothed. You're like somebody out in a little shirt or something, which is just the work you're doing now and the strange identification with everything you've done before. And this probably is why I don't take any public role as a writer. Because I can't see myself doing that except as a gigantic fraud.

(*New Yorker*, 19 February 2001)

Here Munro is speaking specifically about writing, and (as I understand her) about her bewilderment at being identified with her previous work, but one's general relation to one's past can have a similar form. It can in any case be radically non-narrative and find its ideal representation in list form, as in Joe Brainard's *I Remember*, which contains over 1,000 'I remembers':

I remember when my father would say 'Keep your hands out from under the covers' as he said goodnight. But he said it in a nice way.
I remember when I thought that if you did anything bad, policemen would put you in jail.
I remember one very cold and black night on the beach with Frank O'Hara. He ran into the ocean naked and it scared me to death.
I remember lightning.
I remember wild red poppies in Italy.
I remember selling blood every three months on Second Avenue.

Or in Georges Perec's *Je me souviens*:

Je me souviens des photos de Brigitte Bardot nue dans *l'Express*.
Je me souviens de Ringo Starr et de Babara Bach dans un épouvantable film de Science-Fiction.
Je me souviens du Solarium au Val-André.
Je me souviens de la finale de la coupe du Monde de football à Munich en 1974, j'ai pleuré parce que les Pays-Bas de Johan Cryuiff avaient perdu...[11]

There's an echo of Munro's experience in Updike's complaint about biography:

the trouble with literary biographies, perhaps, is that they mainly testify to the long worldly corruption of a life, as documented deeds and days and disappointments pile up, and cannot convey the unearthly innocence that attends, in the perpetual present tense of living, the self that seems the real one.[12]

---

[11] Brainard 1970–3: 20; Perec 1978.
[12] *New Yorker*, 26 June 1995. Martin Amis (2015) has a more hopeful perspective in a review of a biography of Saul Bellow by Zachary Leader (who also wrote a biography of Kingsley Amis): 'You lose, let us say, a parent or a beloved mentor. Once the primary reactions, both universal and personal, begin to fade, you no longer see the reduced and simplified figure, compromised by time—and in Bellow's case encrusted with secondhand "narratives", platitudes, and approximations. You begin to see the whole being, in all its freshness and quiddity. That is what happens here.'

One may be suspicious of Updike, but one shouldn't think that those who feel that their pasts fall away are motivated by a desire to escape responsibility.[13]

According to Schechtman, 'the sense in which we have autobiographical narratives...is cashed out mostly in terms of the way in which an implicit understanding of the ongoing course of our lives influences our experience and deliberation' (2014: 101). And there's one natural reading of this claim given which it's obviously true. One is, say, in the second year of one's apprenticeship, and one knows this; one is coming up for promotion, or two years from retirement, or engaged to X, or about to move to Y, or four months pregnant or terminally ill, and one's knowledge of these facts is of course influencing one's experience and practical deliberation. One knows how old one is, one knows how long people usually live, and one knows how their powers decline after a certain age. But the obvious truth of Schechtman's claim understood in this basic way doesn't support the idea that it's also true in some—any—further sense. I don't think that it can be asserted in any stronger sense without flipping from true to false—false of many people, even if still true of some.

7.6 'A diachronically structured unit'

Schechtman concludes her discussion of narrativity in *Staying Alive* with a further concession:

> it seems more accurate and less liable to generate misunderstanding to give up the locution of 'narrative' in this context and to describe the type of unity that defines a person's identity not as a *narrative* unity but simply as the structural unity of a person's life.   (2014: 108)

It's the idea of a life as 'a diachronically structured unit' that 'is doing the real work' for her view (p. 108), and many things which form diachronically structured units are not narratives at all.

I think she's right to drop the word 'narrative', but what now comes to mind, given this reformulation, is the degree to which any sense of specifically diachronic structural unity seems to be lacking, for at least some human beings, in their experience of existence from moment to moment, day to day, month to month, year to year.

The lack may seem remarkable—hard to credit—given the profound diachronic/structural unity that does actually exist in any human life. A human being is a single-bodied creature whose constancies and continuities of character through adult life tend to be as powerful as his or her bodily constancies and continuities.[14] Many things conspire to underwrite a person's experience of the diachronic unity of their life; for we are, again, creatures who can and do explicitly 'consider [themselves] as [themselves]', in different times and places', in Locke's phrase. We're capable of 'mental time-travel', in Tulving's abbreviation of Locke (Tulving 1985: 5), and some of us do a lot of it (some biased to the future, others to the past). As far as the future is concerned, we all know that we will die. This is not a small matter. But none of these things support the narrativist thesis as usually expounded, the thesis

---

[13] See e.g. Strawson 2007.

[14] Putting aside genuine trauma (being 'born again' is a superficial change relative to one's deep structure).

that all human life is, in some sense, life-writing, and also ought to be. We can reduce the thesis to the thin claim that we have some sense of the unity of our life, and ought to. But I don't think it looks any better. The unity is there, no doubt, but it's not something one needs to be aware of. To think about it, to try to nurture it, is to risk fantasy and self-deception.

'No', you say. 'It's a necessary part of self-possession.' But what is it to be self-possessed? Does it involve 'self-authorship'? And does self-authorship involve self-editing? The claim that someone is very self-possessed can carry the suggestion that they're self-alienated, out of touch with their reality. Self-possession as self-alienation; it's a paradox of a familiar sort, but it captures a truth. 'It is all very well', as the great Lewis Thomas said, 'to be aware of your awareness, even proud of it, but do not try to operate it. You are not up to the job' (1983: 141). It's a familiar point in sports that self-control can depend on a kind of thoughtlessness.

7.7 'My name is Legion'

According to Dan McAdams, a leading narrativist among social psychologists:

beginning in late adolescence and young adulthood, we construct integrative narratives of the self that selectively recall the past and wishfully anticipate the future to provide our lives with some semblance of unity, purpose, and identity. Personal identity is the internalized and evolving life story that each of us is working on as we move through our adult lives.... I ... do not really know who I am until I have a good understanding of my narrative identity.
(2005: 287–8)

If this is true, we must worry not only about the non-Narratives—unless they are happy to lack personal identity—but also about the people described by Mary Midgley and Erik Erikson:

various selves.... make up our composite Self. There are constant and often shocklike transitions between these selves.... It takes, indeed, a healthy personality for the 'I' to be able to speak out of all these conditions in such a way that at any moment it can testify to a reasonably coherent Self.   (Erikson 1968: 217)

[Doctor Jekyll] was partly right: we are each not only one but also many.... Some of us have to hold a meeting every time we want to do something only slightly difficult, in order to find the self who is capable of undertaking it.... We spend a lot of time and ingenuity on developing ways of organizing the inner crowd, securing consent among it, and arranging for it to act as a whole. Literature shows that the condition is not rare.   (Midgley 1984: 123)

Erikson and Midgley suggest, astonishingly, that we're all like this, and many agree—presumably those who fit the pattern. This makes me grateful to Midgley when she adds that 'others, of course, obviously do not feel like this at all, hear such descriptions with amazement, and are inclined to regard those who give them as dotty'. At the same time, we shouldn't adopt a theory that puts these people's claim to be genuine persons in question. We don't want to shut out Paul Klee:

my self ... is a dramatic ensemble. Here a prophetic ancestor makes his appearance. Here a brutal hero shouts. Here an alcoholic *bon vivant* argues with a learned professor. Here a lyric muse, chronically love-struck, raises her eyes to heaven. Her papa steps forward, uttering pedantic protests. Here the indulgent uncle intercedes. Here the aunt babbles gossip. Here the maid giggles lasciviously. And I look upon it all with amazement, the sharpened pen in my hand. A pregnant mother wants to join the fun. 'Pshtt!' I cry, 'You don't belong here. You are divisible.' And she fades out ...   (1965: 177)

Or W. Somerset Maugham:

I recognize that I am made up of several persons and that the person that at the moment has the upper hand will inevitably give place to another. But which is the real one? All of them or none?   (1949: 21)

Or Philip Roth's Nathan Zuckerman, who is more or less intimately related to his author:

All I can tell you with certainty is that I, for one, have no self, and that I am unwilling or unable to perpetrate upon myself the joke of a self. ... What I have instead is a variety of imperson-ations I can do, and not only of myself—a troupe of players that I have internalised, a permanent company of actors that I can call upon when a self is required. ... I am a theater and nothing more than a theater.   (1986: 324)

What are these people to do, if the advocates of narrative unity are right? I think they should continue as they are. Their inner crowds can perhaps share some kind of rollicking self-narrative. But there seems to be no clear provision for them in the leading philosophies of personal unity of our time as propounded by (among others) Marya Schechtman, Harry Frankfurt, and Christine Korsgaard. I think F. Scott Fitzgerald is wrong when he says in his *Notebooks* that 'There never was a good biography of a good novelist. There couldn't be. He is too many people if he's any good' (1945: 159). But one can see what he has in mind.

7.8 'What little I remember'

There is, furthermore, a vast difference between people who regularly and actively remember their past, and people who almost never do. In his autobiography *What Little I Remember*, Otto Frisch writes 'I have always lived very much in the present, remembering only what seemed to be worth retelling' ... 'I have always, as I already said, lived in the here and now, and seen little of the wider views' (1979: ix, xi). I'm in the Frisch camp, on the whole, although I don't remember things in order to retell them. More generally, and putting aside pathological memory loss, I'm in the Montaigne camp, when it comes to specifically autobiographical memory: 'I can find hardly a trace of [memory] in myself; I doubt if there is any other memory in the world as grotesquely faulty as mine is!' Montaigne knows this can lead to misunderstanding. He is, for example, 'better at friendship than at anything else, yet the very words used to acknowledge that I have this affliction [poor memory] are taken to signify ingratitude; they judge my affection by my memory'—quite wrongly. 'However, I derive comfort from my infirmity.' Poor memory protects him from a disagreeable form of ambition, stops him babbling, and forces him to think through things for himself because he can't remember what others have said.

Another advantage, he says in his *Essays*, 'is that…I remember less any insults received'.[15]

To this we can add the point that poor memory and a non-Narrative disposition aren't hindrances when it comes to autobiography in the literal sense—actually writing things down about one's own life. Montaigne is the proof of this, for he is perhaps the greatest autobiographer, the greatest human self-recorder, in spite of the fact that

nothing is so foreign to my mode of writing than extended narration [*narration estendue*]. I have to break off so often from shortness of wind that neither the structure of my works nor their development is worth anything at all.   (1563–92: 120)

Montaigne writes the unstoried life—the only life that matters, I'm inclined to think. He has no 'side', in the colloquial English sense of this term. His honesty, although extreme, is devoid of exhibitionism or sentimentality (St Augustine and Rousseau compare unfavourably). He seeks self-knowledge in radically unpremeditated life-writing: 'I speak to my writing-paper exactly as I do the first person I meet' (1563–92: 891). He knows his memory is hopelessly untrustworthy, and he concludes that the fundamental lesson of self-knowledge is knowledge of self-ignorance.

7.9 'An ordinary mind'

Once one is on the lookout for comments on memory, one finds them everywhere. There is a constant discord of opinion. I think James Meek is accurate when he comments on Salter's novel *Light Years*:

Salter strips out the narrative transitions and explanations and contextualisations, the novelistic linkages that don't exist in our actual memories, to leave us with a set of remembered fragments, some bright, some ugly, some bafflingly trivial, that don't easily connect and can't be put together as a whole, except in the sense of chronology, and in the sense that they are all that remains.   (2013: 4)

Meek takes it that this is true of everyone, and it is perhaps the most common case. Salter in *Light Years* finds a matching disconnection in life itself: 'There is no complete life. There are only fragments. We are born to have nothing, to have it pour through our hands' (1975: 35). And this, again, is a common experience:

Examine for a moment an ordinary mind on an ordinary day. The mind receives a myriad impressions—trivial, fantastic, evanescent, or engraved with the sharpness of steel. From all sides they come, an incessant shower of innumerable atoms; as they fall, as they shape themselves into the life of Monday or Tuesday, the accent falls differently from of old; the moment of importance came not here but there; so that, if a writer were a free man and not a slave, if he could write what he chose, not what he must, if he could base his work upon his own

---

[15] 1563–92: 32–3. 'Since my memory is very short', he wrote to his father in 1563 after the death of Etienne de la Boétie, 'and was further disturbed by the confusion that my mind was to suffer from so heavy and important a loss, it is impossible that I have not forgotten many things that I would like to be known' (1562–92: 1276–7).

feeling and not upon convention, there would be no plot, no comedy, no tragedy, no love interest or catastrophe in the accepted style, and perhaps not a single button sewn on as the Bond Street tailors would have it. Life is not a series of gig lamps symmetrically arranged; life is a luminous halo, a semi-transparent envelope surrounding us from the beginning of consciousness to the end.... (Woolf 1925: 160)

It's hard to work out the full consequences of this passage from Virginia Woolf. What is certain is that there are rehearsers and composers among us, people who not only naturally story their recollections, but also their lives as they are happening. But when Sir Henry Taylor observes that 'an imaginative man is apt to see, in his life, the story of his life; and is thereby led to conduct himself in such a manner as to make a good story of it rather than a good life' (1836: 35) he's identifying a fault, a moral danger, a recipe for inauthenticity.[16] We should therefore worry if the narrativists are right, and such self-storying impulses are in fact universal.

Fortunately, they're not right. There are people who are wonderfully and movingly plodding and factual in their grasp of their pasts. It's an ancient view that people always remember their own pasts in a way that puts them in a good light, but there is solid evidence that it's far from universally true.[17]

7.10   The True Self?

In his poem 'Continuing to Live', Philip Larkin claims that 'in time, / We half-identify the blind impress / All our behavings bear' (2003: 94). The narrativists think that this is an essentially narrative matter, an essentially narrative construal of the form of our lives. But many of us don't get even as far as Larkinian half-identification, and we have at best bits and pieces, rather than a story. We're startled by Larkin's further claim that 'once you have walked the length of your mind, what / You command is clear as a lading-list', for we find, even in advanced age, that we still have no clear idea of what we command. I for one have no clear sense of who or what I am. This is not because I want to be like Montaigne, or because I've read Socrates on ignorance, or Nietzsche on skins—

How can man know himself? He is a dark and veiled thing; and whereas the hare has seven skins, the human being can shed seven times seventy skins and still not be able to say: 'This is really you, this is no longer outer shell'. (1874a: 340, 1874b: 174; translation modified)

I think of Simon Gray in his *Coda*, written when he knew himself to be dying of cancer:

the truth is that I don't really know even quite elementary things about myself, my wants and needs, until I've written them down or spoken them. (2008: 114)

---

[16] Cases in which the storying is done with perfect self-consciousness—'I was telling myself the story of our visit to the Hardys, & I began to compose it' (Woolf 1926: 102)—are not at issue.

[17] See e.g. Waggenaar 1994. See also the end of Tolstoy's story 'The Death of Ivan Illich'.

Gray is perhaps wise, given the continuation of the above passage from Nietzsche:

Besides, it is an agonizing, dangerous undertaking to dig down into yourself in this way, to force your way by the shortest route down the shaft of your own being. How easy it is to do damage to yourself that no doctor can heal. And moreover, why should it be necessary, since everything—our friendships and hatreds, the way we look, our handshakes, the things we remember and forget, our books, our handwriting—bears witness to our being?   (ibid. p. 340)

I can't, however, cut off this quotation here, because it continues in a way that raises a doubt about my position:

But there is a means by which this absolutely crucial enquiry can be carried out. Let the young soul look back upon its life and ask itself: what until now have you truly loved, what has drawn out your soul, what has commanded it and at the same time made it happy? Line up these objects of reverence before you, and perhaps by what they are and by their sequence, they will yield you a law, the fundamental law of your true self.   (ibid. p. 340)

'Perhaps by what they are...they will yield the fundamental law of your true self.' This claim is easy to endorse. It's Proust's greatest insight. Camus sees it too. But Nietzsche is more specific: 'perhaps by what they are *and by their sequence*, they will yield.... the fundamental law of your true self'. Here it seems I must either disagree with Nietzsche or concede something to the narrativists: the possible importance of grasping the sequence in progressing towards self-understanding.

I concede it. Consideration of the sequence—the 'narrative', if you like—may be important for some people in some cases. For most of us, however, I think self-knowledge comes best in bits and pieces. Nor does this concession yield anything to the sweeping view with which I began, the view—in Oliver Sacks's words—that all human life is life-writing, that 'each of us constructs and lives a "narrative", and that 'this narrative *is* us, our identities'.

8

Self-intimation

8.1 Introduction

In this paper I use the word 'experience'—the plural-lacking mass term—to refer to the phenomenological being or character or content of experiences or episodes of conscious awareness: to refer specifically and only to what experiences or episodes of conscious awareness are like, experientially. I use the plural-accepting count noun 'experience' to refer to experiences or episodes of conscious awareness considered as a whole, in a way that allows that these episodes may have non-experiential being in addition to experiential being.

I want to consider the nature of experience, and—as far as possible—I want to consider it without considering what experience is experience *of*. I say 'as far as possible' because there's something that experience is of in such an intimate way that one can't consider it without considering that something. This follows from the fact that all experiences have phenomenological content. Given that there's something they're like, experientially—otherwise they wouldn't be experiences—there's something they're correctly said to be *of*. Take any actual episode of experience *e* with any phenomenological content *F* (e.g. pins-and-needles experience). In having phenomenological content *F*, *e* is ipso facto—trivially, irreducibly—experience or awareness *of* phenomenological-content-type *F*. So in considering the phenomenological character of *e*, we *ipso facto* consider the phenomenological-content-type *F* that *e* is experience or awareness of. In this fundamental sense all experience is experience-of, awareness-of. Many have made the point, including Arnauld in 1683—

since it is clear that I am conscious, it is also clear that I am conscious of something, that is to say that I know and experience something, because consciousness is essentially like that ... it is impossible to be conscious without being conscious of something

—and Husserl in the 1900s—

every experience is 'consciousness' and consciousness is consciousness *of*.[1]

Prufer (1975) calls the essential ofness of experience the 'genitive of manifestation'. He contrasts it with the essential 'dative of manifestation'—the fact that every experience is necessarily experience *for* (given *to*) a subject.

---

[1] Arnauld 1683: 9–10, Husserl 1907–9: 291. See also Brentano 1874: 68. When I cite a work I give the date of first publication, or occasionally the date of composition, while the page reference is to the edition listed in the Bibliography. When quoting I mark the author's emphases by bold italics and my own by italics.

Some say that phenomenological-content-type *F* is an 'abstract entity', and that *e*, in having concrete phenomenological content of type *F*, is experience of this abstract entity, but there's no need to introduce abstract entities, in a way that makes some philosophers queasy, in order to secure the sense in which all experience or awareness is (necessarily and constitutively) *of* something simply because it (necessarily) has phenomenological content. Some prefer the 'adverbial' way of characterizing experience, and say that Lucy is 'experiencing redly', when she is having red-experience, rather than saying that she is having experience of red, but I understand the 'of' in such a way that these two forms of words say the same thing.

Is experience also always of something concrete or spatiotemporal (I'm assuming for argument that 'concrete' and 'spatiotemporal' are coextensional)? Opinions differ. One striking reason for thinking that experience is always experience of something concrete is that the phenomenological being of an experience, which is itself a concrete existent, something that actually occurs, is itself always one of the things the experience is of. This ancient view is the subject of this paper.[2] I could speak simply of experience throughout, but later I'll talk mostly of awareness, because the discussion flows more easily if one does. By 'awareness' (the mass term) I'll always mean 'conscious awareness' and I'll take 'awareness', like 'experience' (the mass term), to refer specifically and only to the phenomenological being of episodes of experience or conscious awareness.[3] I'll also use 'consciousness' from time to time, for what I mean by 'experience' or 'awareness' is the same as what many philosophers mean by 'consciousness'.

8.2 Real Realism about Experience

I'm an outright realist about experience or awareness, a *real* realist about experience, as I find myself saying when confronted with philosophers who claim to be realists about experience but are really no such thing (Dennett, for example). What is real realism about experience? Perhaps the best way to convey it is to say that it's to take experience—colour experience, say, or taste experience, or experience of pain, considered specifically in its phenomenological being[4]—to be exactly what one took it to be (knew it to be) simply in having it, before one did any philosophy; when one was six, for example. 'Considered specifically in its phenomenological being': children, like adults, standardly take colour as we experience it phenomenologically, 'colour-as-we-see-it' (Mackie 1976: 24), to be something that is itself out there in the world 'spread out on the surface of objects' (Malebranche c.1680–90: 6.68, characterizing Augustine's view); and this is a mistake. But this fact doesn't conflict with the fact

---

[2] I don't think there's any other good reason for thinking that experience is always of something concrete. For any phenomenological-content-type *F* (yellow-experience, horse-like-experience, etc.), sentient beings can possibly have *F*-type experience without there being anything in their universe that either (a) is *F* or (b) causes *F*-type experience in any creature by any normal sensory process, in such a way that it is for that reason itself naturally said to be *F*.

[3] It may be true to say of me when I'm dreamlessly asleep that I'm aware of the current financial crisis, but only conscious awareness has phenomenological character.

[4] 'Considered specifically in its phenomenological being' is redundant, given the opening definition of 'experience', but it does no harm.

that children have a fully competent grasp of what colour experience is considered specifically as experience, as they do also of pain, taste experience, smell experience, and so on. They know—for one thing—that objects that have a constant colour appear to be different colours in different lights, that their faces and the faces of their friends look a different colour under a neon light in a bathroom mirror. They make many experiments with experience, squeezing their eyeballs to see double, rubbing their closed eyes to 'see stars', blocking and unblocking their ears, spinning round until they're dizzy, then stopping to watch the world swirling, fully aware that it's their experience, not the world, that is swirling. They're fully competent with the general conception of experience that appreciation of these phenomena involves (the only conception of experience that concerns us at present), whether or not they can be said to possess this conception in any linguistically expressible form.

The word 'general' in the last sentence is important. When science informs us about the 'filling-in' that characterizes visual experience (for example), or 'change blindness', or 'inattentional blindness', or the complex and surprising mechanisms of taste experience, it reveals many ways in which the everyday view of experience can turn out to be very wrong.[5] For all that, a person's basic general understanding of what colour experience or pain experience is remains fully correct if it remains exactly the same as it was before he or she did any philosophy or science. To be a real realist about experience is to reject all views of the nature of experience or awareness that are in any way eliminativist or reductionist or deflationist relative to this ordinary, general, entirely correct, non-philosophical understanding of experience.[6]

8.3 The Simple View of Experience

For a long time, like most philosophers I know, I held a simple view of the nature of experience or awareness. What do I mean by 'simple'? Not easy to say. Obviously I don't mean the view that the content of experience or awareness is always qualitatively simple. It's usually highly complex, qualitatively speaking. (The overall content of experiences is highly complex even when one considers experiences in a wholly 'internalist' way, as here, i.e. just in respect of their phenomenological character.) It's also true that the existence of experience entails the existence of an experiencer, a someone-or-something that *has* that experience: the existence of experience involves at least the complexity or polarity that is involved in the existence of [a] experiencer and [b] what is experienced.[7] But this too is compatible with what

---

[5] See e.g. Grimes 1996, Simons and Levin 1997, Chun and Marois 2002, Pessoa and de Weerd 2003, B. Smith 2012; there are many other interesting cases.

[6] For further discussion see e.g. Strawson 2014. I don't use the word 'quale', because it has become another obscure battleground, but real realists qualify as 'qualia freaks' on any sensible understanding of the word. Real realists about experience like myself are also materialists, but they're *real* materialists, by which I mean *realistic* materialists, where the fundamental qualifying condition for being a realistic materialist is being a real realist about experience. (Many philosophers who call themselves 'materialists' or 'physicalists' fail to meet this condition.)

[7] I don't intend this claim about the essential 'dative' of manifestation in any sense that Buddhists would dispute (certainly the existence of an experience doesn't entail the existence of an experiencer that lasts

I have in mind in speaking of the simple view of experience or awareness. So is the complexity that is laid bare in a careful description of the character of time-consciousness—our moment-to-moment experience of time.[8] So is the extraordinary complexity of the neurophysiology of experience.

So what do I mean by 'simple'? I mean (at least) the view that the basic metaphysics of experience—experientiality considered just as such, independently of any of the details of its content in any particular case[9]—the basic how-things-are found in every case of experience without exception, however primitive—doesn't essentially involve any sort of *articulation* or *structure* of a sort which one might first try to characterize by saying that it involves some sort of loopedness or turned-on-itself-ness. A fortiori, the simple view rules out the idea that internal articulation or structure of this sort is a necessary condition of awareness being awareness at all.

8.4 Awareness of Awareness

This statement of the simple view is inadequate; I'll try to recast it later. For the moment, the key idea is that the simple view is incompatible with the idea that all experience or awareness has some sort of inner articulation or structure that can be characterized, at least initially, by saying that

(1)   all awareness involves awareness of that very awareness.

I think, however, that (1) is true; so I have to reject the simple view if it's incompatible with (1). I'm not sure (1) is incompatible with every view of awareness that has a reasonable claim to be called a simple view. This is part of what I want to try to find out.

Many philosophers agree that there's a fundamental sense in which all awareness involves awareness of awareness—awareness of that very awareness. But (1) doesn't sufficiently capture what's in question. 'Involves' is vague, and the words 'that very' do less than one might hope. As they stand, they don't rule out the idea that (1) is true because the existence of any episode of awareness A1 involves the existence of an ontologically distinct, 'higher-order' episode of awareness A2 which is awareness of A1.[10] It's plain that no such higher-order proposal can be the correct account of why (1) is true—if indeed it is—because it leads to an infinite regress, as Aristotle observed

longer than the experience). I think, furthermore, that there's a metaphysically primordial 'thin' way of taking the notion of an experiencer given which experience and experiencer are in the end the same thing—so that the seemingly irreducible ontological duality of experience and experiencer is not what it seems (see e.g. Strawson 2009: 345ff). I'm going to put this difficult idea aside here, however (it has distinguished supporters, including Kant, William James, Husserl, and also, I believe, Descartes: see e.g. §11.5, p. 218 below).

  [8] As famously analysed by Husserl, for example (Husserl 1907–09). See also Zahavi 1999: ch. 5, Dainton 2000, Lockwood 2005: ch. 17, Strawson 2009: Part 5.

  [9] And also, of course, of any account of what it consists in that is given in the languages of physics and neurophysiology.

  [10] (1) might also be said to be true if there were a necessarily existent omniscient entity—given the looseness of the word 'involves'; for then an episode of awareness couldn't possibly exist without awareness of it existing. But this is not what we're after.

(*De Anima* 425b15–17).[11] Nevertheless it seems worthwhile to replace (1) with something that explicitly excludes a higher-order reading and explicitly embraces a 'same-order' reading. This is easily done, for it seems that (1) is true because

(2)   all awareness involves awareness of itself.

This time-honoured proposal can seem both intuitive and paradoxical. My aim in this paper is to spread it out a little, descriptively, in a way that may make some who doubt it come to believe it.[12]

First, though, consider the cheerful proposal that the simplest and best way to express the claim that all awareness involves awareness of itself is simply to say that all awareness is—*awareness*, no less. All awareness is indeed—*awareness*! This statement has, as a tautology, the advantage of certain truth, but also, it will be said, the disadvantage of going nowhere. I think, though, that it can be used to express an important point, when made in the right way—with the right sort of emphasis. All awareness is *awareness*, no less. You just have to hear this right. All awareness is indeed, *awareness—with all that that entails*.

One thing that it may be said to entail is

(3)   for any episode of awareness A on the part of any subject S, the existence of A entails S's awareness of A.[13]

Obviously, you say. 'There's an ineliminable sense in which the existence of awareness A on the part of S entails S's awareness of A; a sense in which, if S isn't aware of A, then A isn't really an episode of awareness on the part of S at all. But this doesn't help, for to say that S is in this sense aware of its awareness A, awareness which has, let us suppose, content C, is really just to say in a cumbersome way that S is in a state of awareness that has content C, which is already given.'

Fine. In that case we're still in the safe haven of tautology—even if the claim takes a little thinking through, and even if we stumble slightly on the word 'of', which

---

[11] The restriction of attention to conscious awareness in §8.1 rules out all 'higher-order' theories of awareness or experience in which a conscious mental state is said to occur when one mental state S1 that is not intrinsically conscious becomes a conscious state by becoming the object of another mental state S2 that is also not intrinsically conscious. See, paradigmatically, Rosenthal 1986: there's no infinite regress on Rosenthal's theory, because the higher-order state S2 that is said to render the first-order state S1 conscious by taking S1 as its object is not itself conscious in a way that would require it to be itself the object of a further higher-order state. I'm not going to consider this view (although I fully agree with Rosenthal that 'there is a strong intuitive sense that the consciousness of mental states is somehow reflexive or self-referential' (1986: 345)), because I reject the idea that experience (real experience) could ever arise from one non-experiential state taking another non-experiential state as its object.

[12] Note also the formally possible case—which seems to count as a same-order case—in which (1) is true because there are in any case of awareness two ontologically distinct episodes of awareness which involve awareness of each other.

[13] Remember that by awareness I always mean *conscious* awareness. So the claim in full is that in the case of any episode of conscious awareness A on the part of any subject S, the existence of conscious awareness A entails conscious awareness, on the part of S, of conscious awareness A. It can make perfectly good sense to talk of unconscious awareness; the flexibility of the word 'conscious' seems to allow us to say that one can in fact be conscious of something of which one has no conscious awareness. One can also be said to be conscious of something *x* (subliminally) although one has no idea that this is so (so that one even might talk of unconscious consciousness of *x*). But none of these things are in question here.

may seem to overarticulate things, and to introduce the idea of intentionality in a puzzling way.

There's also a formulation that makes no explicit reference to the subject of awareness in the way that (3) does. This is (2), already noted: all awareness involves awareness of itself. Almost all those who have discussed this question have moved between formulations that explicitly mention the subject and formulations that don't. I take it that both are valid, and ultimately come to the same thing (independently of the position recorded in note 7).

'No. An experience or episode of awareness can never itself be aware of anything, neither itself nor anything else; only a subject of experience can ever be aware of anything.'

There's no real difficulty here. An experience is an experienc*ing*, it's a necessarily subject-involving thing. An episode of awareness is an episode of *awareness*, a being-aware of something.

8.5 Epistemology and Ontology

All awareness is a matter for epistemology, so reflexivity of awareness is a matter for epistemology. But reflexivity is also, of course, an ontological matter, and it seems that the reflexivity indicated in (2) may be necessary for the existence of the thing it characterizes: awareness. I suspect that awareness may be unique in this respect, *sui generis*, unique in being 'looped' on itself in this way (there is still a question about whether the loop metaphor is a good one).

To say that awareness is *sui generis* is not to say that it's rare. There's a massive quantity of awareness on this planet, by any remotely realistic accounting. One possibility is that awareness is the most commonplace thing in the universe: it may be that being looped on itself in this way—a property which seems to make awareness stand out as *sui generis* relative to our ordinary scheme of things—is what it takes for anything concrete to exist at all. I think Kant may have suspected this,[14] and perhaps also Leibniz, and perhaps also Schopenhauer and Nietzsche and James—among others. Or at least, they may have suspected that all *Sein* is, at bottom, *Fürsichsein*. I'm beginning to suspect this myself.

This view is a form of panpsychism, and some philosophers will dismiss it for that reason. But no one who has any genuine feeling for physics—and reality—thinks that

[14] 'For every substance, including even a simple element of matter, must after all have some kind of inner activity as the ground of its producing an external effect, and that in spite of the fact that I cannot specify in what that inner activity consists. ... Leibniz said that this inner ground of all its external relations and their changes was a power of representation [consciousness, experience]. This thought, which was not developed by Leibniz, was greeted with laughter by later philosophers. They would, however, have been better advised to have first considered the question whether a substance, such as a simple part of matter, would be possible in the complete absence of any inner state. And if they had, perhaps, been unwilling to rule out such an inner state, then it would have been incumbent on them to invent some other possible inner state as an alternative to that of representations and the activities dependent on representations. Anybody can see for himself that if a faculty of obscure representations is attributed even to the simple, elementary particles of matter, it does not follow that matter itself has a faculty of representation, for many substances of this kind, connected together into a whole, can after all never constitute a unified thinking entity' (Kant 1766: 315).

panpsychism is too far out to be true, whatever they think of this particular version of it.[15] Awareness is in any case, and without doubt, the most important thing in the universe, and the present question is this: if all awareness involves awareness of awareness, how and why is this so? I'm going to start again.

8.6 Aristotle and Others

'If we are aware', Aristotle says in the *Nicomachean Ethics*, 'we are aware that we are, and if we think, that we think.'[16] Dignāga, Dharmakīrti, Śaṅkara, Śāntarakṣita, Citsukha, Descartes, La Forge, Arnauld, Locke, probably Hume, Reid, Brentano, Husserl, Sartre, Gurwitsch, Merleau-Ponty, and many others agree.[17] They all agree that all awareness (consciousness, experience) somehow or other involves awareness of that awareness. The details of their views diverge and excite scholarly disagreement. The expression 'somehow or other involves' is loose, as remarked, and needs tightening or replacement. But the shared starting claim, to repeat it, is that

(1)   all awareness involves awareness of that very awareness.

Is this true? There's a way of taking the second of the three occurrences of 'awareness' in (1) which makes it seems false. It can seem natural to say that we're often not aware of our awareness—not only when we're watching an exciting movie but also in most of daily life. Aristotle notes this, in effect, when he says that

knowledge and perception and opinion and understanding always have something else as their object, and themselves only by the way.   (*Metaphysics* 12.9.1074b35–6)

Certainly we're rarely in a state of awareness that involves a state of awareness taking a state of awareness as an express object of reflective attention. This, however, is compatible with the view that there is always some sort of awareness of awareness in any case of awareness, and necessarily so. Focused, 'thetic', *reflective* attention to awareness apprehended as such isn't what's in question. Reflective attention to awareness is always a matter of introspection, and introspection (as I understand the term) is essentially retrospective—however short the time-lag.[18] The awareness of awareness that appears to be essential to the very existence of awareness isn't retrospective or introspective in any way. What's in question is a kind of *reflexive* awareness of awareness that must be there, on the current view, if there is to be any

[15] See e.g. Eddington 1928, Nagel 1979, Sprigge 1983, Strawson 2006, 2012.
[16] *NE* 9.9.1170a29–b1. One shouldn't make too much of the explicitly propositional formulation 'perceive *that* we perceive' in Aristotle. (The same goes for Locke—see §8.12 below, p. 150.)
[17] Including those who follow Ibn Sina (Avicenna) in the Islamic tradition. Among the Indian philosophers Dignāga, Dharmakīrti, and Śāntarakṣita are Buddhists (Dignāga's and Dharmakīrti's exposition of the view is closely tied in with their representationalism), Śaṅkara and Citsukha are Advaitins. Among more recent exponents let me mention Frank, Frankfurt, Henrich, Kriegel and Williford, D. W. Smith, Thompson, and Zahavi (Kriegel and Williford are unusual in this company in that they seem to wish (in Kriegel and Williford 2006) to give a reductive account of consciousness, i.e. an account of phenomenal consciousness in non-phenomenal terms, whereas all the other thinkers are—I take it—real realists about experience). For some striking further examples, see Heller-Roazen 2007.
[18] In Ch. 10 below I argue that one can in certain very special conditions be immediately aware of one's own present awareness in a fully express, fully thetic manner, without time-lag.

awareness at all, however primitive.[19] The reflexive awareness of awareness must be there in the simplest entity of which it is true that it has conscious experience.

8.7 Variations

Perhaps the word 'awareness' works on our intuitions in an unhelpful way. Suppose we replace 'awareness' by 'consciousness' to get

(1a)   all consciousness involves consciousness of that very consciousness.

Some think (1a) sounds less plausible than (1), but I can't hear this difference. Some stumble on the word 'of', in a way to which Sartre was interestingly sensitive (see §8.17 below, p. 161 n. 65), but the 'of' occurs in (1) just as it does in (1a), so it can't be the reason why (1a) sounds less plausible than (1)—if it does.

Suppose we replace 'consciousness' by 'conscious experience', and then shorten 'conscious experience' to 'experience'—taking it to be true by definition, as before, that all experience is conscious experience. (1) becomes

(1b)   all experience involves experience of that very experience.

I think this formulation can sound less plausible than the two that precede it, because many of our ways of taking the word 'experience' (and again the word 'of') push us towards the way of taking (1) that I noted when considering someone who is watching an exciting film, i.e. the way in which (1) seems false. Even so, (1b) may be helpful in a way that becomes apparent when we modify it to

(1c)   all experiencing involves experiencing of that very experiencing,

which, with its verbal noun, may seem somewhat more acceptable than (1b), then drop the 'of', to get

(1d)   all experiencing involves experiencing that very experiencing,

and then listen for the sense in which (1d) is necessarily true (it doesn't of course involve any doubling of experience).

Necessary truth. Does that signal tautology? Why worry about that, given the 'paradox of analysis' (according to which all correct conceptual analyses are tautologies)? Perhaps awareness or experience or consciousness, considered as an object of theoretical enquiry, has the following property: we can grasp a fundamental fact about its nature by comprehending a tautology about it in such a way that the tautology makes an impact on us. A lot of philosophy consists in getting used to ways of putting things, and I think the transitions from (1) to (1d) can be useful. The way we take the word 'of' is, again, of considerable importance. Many are initially inclined to hear the 'of' as indicating inspectorial—spectatorial—distance, explicit reflective attention of a sort that makes (1) seem dubious or false. But one needn't hear it in this way.

[19] Here I follow many who use *reflexive* for the same-order relation and *reflective* for the explicit higher-order relation.

I take (1d) to be strictly equivalent to (1c), given the reading of (1c) according to which (1c) is true (i.e. putting aside the exciting movie objection), and welcome the respect in which the necessary and seemingly tautological truth of (1d) reverberates back through (1c) and (1b) into (1a) and (1). What it comes to, in the end, and again, is that consciousness is—consciousness, no less. Awareness is—awareness. What's special about it, what these successive verbal formulations try to express, is that it is in some sense 'self-illumined' or 'self-luminous' (*svaprakāśa*), in the old Indian expression, or 'self-aware', or perhaps 'auto-cognizing' (*svasaṃvedana*). One might say, with Ryle, that it's 'phosphorescent', adopting his word while cancelling his mocking tone (1949: 159), or 'self-intimating' (ibid. 158)—intrinsically self-presenting. This is what we're trying to get at, and do I think succeed in getting at, when we say such things as that (1) all awareness involves awareness of that very awareness—even if we remain with a sense that something still needs to be understood. This is how I will use the term 'self-intimation'.

8.8 'Involves'

'Involves' as it occurs in (1) is an accommodating word; it leaves open several answers to the question why (1) is true, if indeed it is. One *prima facie* possible answer is that (1) is true because the intrinsic nature of awareness is such that it's an absolutely inevitable, necessary *causal consequence* or *requirement* of its existing at a given time t that awareness of it also exist at t. But this causal suggestion (which might be thought to overstretch the meaning of 'involve') reawakens the threat of infinite regress. To posit a causal relation between x and y is to suggest that x and y are ontologically distinct, even if there's a dependence relation between them, and as soon as the episodes of awareness mentioned in (1) are supposed to be ontologically distinct, we're off on the regress. Aristotle saw this immediately, as did many of the Indian philosophers.[20]

Might each episode of awareness somehow involve two distinct 'moments', each incorporating awareness of the other in some sort of strange closed causal loop? I don't know. I'm attracted by the idea that awareness may be 'self-sprung' in some fundamental way ('sprung' in the sense that a mattress is said to be sprung), but causal language doesn't seem appropriate for trying to express what self-sprungness might be—even if we allow that cause and effect may be simultaneous. Certainly no causal hypothesis can be a serious contender if it allows for the possibility that there could be any sort of temporal delay between the coming into existence of awareness and the coming into existence of awareness of that very awareness. We may take it to be built into (1) that the second-mentioned awareness of the first-mentioned awareness is awareness on the part of the same subject of experience as the first-mentioned awareness, and we can make this an explicit part of the causal suggestion as follows: the intrinsic nature of awareness is such that it's a necessary causal consequence or

---

[20] See e.g. Aristotle, *De Anima* 425b12–25, and (on Aristotle) Caston 2002. For an excellent introduction to the Indian view, see Dreyfus and Thompson 2007. See also Mackenzie 2007, Dreyfus 2010, Ram-Prasad 2010.

requirement of its existing at *t* that awareness of it, on the part of the same subject of experience, also exist at *t*. But the causal suggestion still seems wholly unpromising.

8.9 'Comports'

A second answer to the question is that (1) is true because (2) is, because all awareness involves awareness of itself. Or rather—dropping the overaccommodating word 'involves'—because

(4)   all awareness *comports* awareness of itself;

where 'comport' expresses the idea that (1) is true because anything that is correctly identified as an episode of awareness somehow contains awareness of itself wholly within itself.[21] On this view, all awareness is intrinsically or essentially 'self-intimating'. (This makes indexing to a particular time and subject unnecessary.) On the Indian front Śāntarakṣita and the Advaitins Śaṅkara and Citsukha, hold (4) explicitly, as do Dignāga and Dharmakīrti, although they're not thinking of awareness in the same way as Śaṅkara and Citsukha.[22]

Brentano has something very like (4) in mind when he writes, of experience of sound, that

inner experience seems to prove undeniably that the presentation of the sound is connected with the presentation of the presentation of the sound in such a peculiarly intimate way that [the] existence [of the latter] constitutes an intrinsic prerequisite for the existence of [the former].[23]

In other words, the existence of the presentation of the presentation of the sound constitutes an intrinsic (non-temporal) prerequisite for the existence of the presentation of the sound. The idea can seem difficult, but I think that we have to make sense of it, and that (1) may now be finally put aside in favour of (4). All awareness comports awareness of itself. This is the Self-Intimation thesis—*Self-Intimation*, for short.

The core meaning of 'to intimate' is to make known,[24] and the sense of 'know' in question here is the fundamental sense given which it is correct to say that when it comes to knowing what experience of pain (say) is like, *the having is the knowing*. This is knowledge in the sense of direct acquaintance. Using the impersonal idiom

---

[21] This use of 'comport'—to *carry with(in)*—is inspired by the French *comporter*.

[22] See §8.13 below. According to Citsukha, 'self-luminosity' is 'the fitness to be immediately known without being an object of any cognition' (*Tattvapradīpika*, 13th century, quoted in Gupta 2003: 101). One difficulty with assessing Dignāga's and Dharmakīrti's view about self-intimation is that it's entangled with their representationalism ('representationalism' in the standard but recently obscured Lockean—essentially indirect-realist—sense of the term), and their tendency towards some form of idealism, in ways that threaten to confuse the issue. See Thompson 2010 for an explicit separation of these issues. Note that the Nyāya school vigorously opposes the same-order view, insisting that a conscious act becomes conscious only by becoming an object of another act of consciousness.

[23] 1874: 98. I've inserted 'latter' and 'former' to clarify Brentano's phrasing, which is as it stands ambiguous (thanks to Peter Simons for advice). I assume that Brentano takes this to be Aristotle's view, according to which 'perceiving that we perceive is integral to the original perceiving' (Caston 2002: 769).

[24] *OED*; meanings for the adjective include 'inmost, most inward, intrinsic'.

noted in §8.3, one might say that for something to be self-intimating is for it to be something that is in occurring known to itself in the direct-acquaintance sense. 'Consciousness cognizes itself in cognizing its object', as Siderits puts it when characterizing Dignāga's view (2010: 318).

One might alternatively call this the Phosphorescence thesis—*Phosphorescence*, for short—although I'm going to question the metaphors of light. It's an essentially same-order account, rather than a higher-order account, of why (1) is true—of why all awareness involves awareness of awareness.[25] There does seem to be something disturbingly paradoxical about it, as remarked, if only because it seems that the awareness must somehow be already all there in order to be taken as object of awareness in the way that is necessary for it to be awareness at all. That seems to be the implication of the quotation from Brentano. The 'already all there' surely can't be quite right.[26]

8.10 Reflexivity

Consider some possibly analogous cases, such as the thought *this very thought is puzzling*.[27] I think this quite often, as a test thought, when thinking about philosophical issues. It's a real thought when I think it, and it's true when I think it. There's no logical or metaphysical difficulty in my thinking it, although it has to be about itself in order to exist at all. It's being about itself is straightforwardly essential to, and constitutive of, its existence. One might think that a thought has to exist already in order to be there to be available to be thought about, and one might think that the thought *this very thought is puzzling* is impossible, because it can't exist already in order to be available to be thought about, because its being thought about is part of what constitutes its existence. But such a thought is perfectly possible.

It's arguable, in a similar vein, that being aware that you're entering into a contract is a necessary condition of doing so, a necessary constitutive condition of actually entering into a contract.[28] But then the thing you have to be aware of to enter into a contract can't actually pre-exist the awareness that makes it true that it exists. So how do you manage to be aware of it? But you do; there's no practical problem here, hence no theoretical problem. Consider also the suggestion that when it comes to radical free will of the sort that could ground ultimate moral responsibility, believing that you're radically free (experiencing yourself as radically free) is a necessary constitutive condition of actually being radically free.[29] If this seems too recherché, imagine a lottery in which the necessary and sufficient conditions of winning a prize are (a) having a ticket with a prime number and (b) believing you're a winner. In this case

---

[25] There's also a respect in which all awareness involves the subject of that awareness's being aware of itself, but I won't develop this point here (see §10.4 below, pp. 193, 195–6).

[26] 'Indian philosophers generally accept a principle of irreflexivity, to the effect that an entity cannot operate on itself. Even the most skilled acrobat, it is said, cannot stand on their own shoulders' (Siderits 2010: 321).

[27] Here I draw on Strawson 1986.

[28] This is not true in law, in fact.

[29] This can be true even if such radical free will is impossible—even if there are no sufficient conditions of radical freedom.

believing you're a winner is a constitutive condition of being a winner. A lottery of this sort could be staged.[30]

What should we make of these cases? Do they help? I'm not sure. Some of them depend on the existence of conventions in a way that seems to make them unhelpful or not very interesting. But the thought *this very thought is puzzling* doesn't seem like that at all. I'll come back to it, after recasting one of the reasons why Self-Intimation can seem so surprising (not to say implausible) when one first encounters it.

8.11 Flatness

There's a natural conception of experience—the simple conception first character-ized in §8.3—according to which it is, in a fundamental respect, 'flat', dimensionally flat, essentially metaphysically single-leveled, fundamentally non-reflexive, non-loopy—however rich and imbricated its contents and modalities. Put aside normal complex adult human experience for a minute. Consider the blissfully thoughtless experience of yellow, either on one's own part or on the part of a new born baby.[31] Here the flatness seems manifest. Nor does greatly enriching the sensory content seem to change the fundamental flatness—the quality of experience that one might express by saying that there is a sense in which everything that is experienced, however multimodal, is on a single experiential plane, the only experiential plane there is, which is, quite simply, the plane or 'field' of experience.

At the very least, it seems unclear that one has to introduce any reference to *reflexivity* into one's account of the fundamental nature of awareness. Awareness seems something just given, given with its intrinsic glow, independently of any notion of reflexivity. The claim that any adequate account of awareness must advert to reflexivity seems to threaten to obscure—falsify—the essential planeness of every-day awareness. It seems that there must be some way in which the intrinsic nature of awareness can be fully characterized or specified independently of the fact that (4) is true, if indeed it is: completely independently of the fact (if it is a fact) that all awareness comports awareness of that very awareness.

I don't, however, think we can do without (4). So we have to find a way of reconciling the flatness intuition (whatever the best name for it) with the seemingly essential reflexivity of experience.

8.12 Witnesses

Before attempting let me quote some other expressions of Self-Intimation. Among present-day analytic philosophers, Alvin Goldman writes that:

---

[30] There are, in sum, cases of belief that seem to contravene what one might call the principle of independence, according to which one's belief that p is true is justified only if sufficient conditions of the truth of p obtain independently of the fact that one believes that p.

[31] I'm assuming that an experience of a particular shade of colour can be said to be phenomenologically simple in spite of the complexity it involves in having (necessarily) a particular brightness, saturation, and hue.

In the process of thinking about x there is already an implicit awareness that one is thinking about x. There is no need for reflection here, for taking a step back from thinking about x in order to examine it and see if it is a case of thinking about x. When we are thinking about x, the mind is focused on x, not on our thinking of x. Nevertheless, the process of thinking about x carries with it a *nonreflective self-awareness*.   (1970: 95–6; my emphasis)

Doubts may be raised about the notion of implicit awareness, but the general idea is clear, and Harry Frankfurt puts it well, using the word 'consciousness', when he asks what it

would ... be like to be conscious of something without being aware of this consciousness? It would mean having an experience with no awareness whatever of its occurrence. This would be, precisely, a case of unconscious experience.[32] [This] does not mean that consciousness is invariably dual in the sense that every instance of it involves both a primary awareness and another instance of consciousness which is somehow distinct and separable from the first and which has the first as its object. That would threaten an intolerably infinite proliferation of instances of consciousness. Rather, the ... consciousness [of consciousness] in question is a sort of *immanent reflexivity* by virtue of which every instance of being conscious grasps not only that of which it is an awareness but also the awareness of it. It is like a source of light which, in addition to illuminating whatever other things fall within its scope, renders itself visible as well.
(1987: 161–2)

The last sentence is carefully put, and runs close to Ryle's description of the view when he says that mental processes are thought to be

phosphorescent, like tropical sea-water, which makes itself visible by the light which it itself emits.   (1949: 159)

It's arguable that these formulations show up an inadequacy in the metaphor of self-luminosity, and indeed all metaphors of light.[33] The flame of a candle (say) doesn't illuminate itself in the way in which it illuminates anything else. It is in that sense not self-luminous; it's merely luminous.[34] What happens if we carry this point back to the target of the metaphor, and say that experience or awareness is not strictly self-luminous, but merely luminous? The word 'luminous' may still seem appropriate, insofar as both light and awareness may be said to disclose things (although light only discloses things given the presence of awareness); but it loses the aspect of reflexivity marked by the prefix 'self-' and preserved in 'self-intimating'. The metaphor of light falls short because light isn't turned on itself in anything like the required way. I suspect that only consciousness or experience can have this property. The point

[32] Frankfurt intends this to be a contradiction in terms.

[33] Ryle writes that 'the metaphor of "light" seemed peculiarly appropriate, since Galilean science dealt so largely with the optically discovered world. "Consciousness" was imported to play in the mental world the part played by light in the mechanical world. In this metaphorical sense, the contents of the mental world were thought of as being self-luminous or refulgent' (ibid. p. 159). This is completely off beam: the metaphor of light is natural quite independently of Galileo, and ancient, as the Indian literature shows.

[34] 'Light, which is the discoverer of all visible objects, discovers itself at the same time' (Reid 1785: 1.481 (§6.5)).

may then be better marked by the word 'self-intimation'; for intimation is an essentially mental (indeed cognitive) phenomenon.[35]

Staying in the West, and moving back in time, consider Descartes in 1641. On one of the many occasions when he is stressing the point that he uses the term 'thinking' as an entirely general word for all forms of awareness, including sensation, he says that it applies

to all that exists within us in such a way that we are *immediately* aware of it. Thus all the operations of the will, intellect, imagination, and senses are thoughts/thinkings.

(1641: 2.113; my emphasis)

Elsewhere he says that

when I will or fear something, I *simultaneously* perceive that I will or fear

and that

it is certain that we cannot will anything without *thereby* perceiving that we are willing it. And.... this perception is *really one and the same thing* as the volition.[36]

This last quotation provides unusually powerful support for the view that Descartes holds that all episodes of awareness comport awareness of that very awareness, given that he's prepared to affirm the identity of the willing and the perception outright even as he notes that it is strictly speaking incompatible with his view that perception is passive and willing active. The point is that the perception or awareness of itself is entirely built into the willing, as it is to every conscious episode.[37]

The use of the term 'conscious' is fluid in the seventeenth century, and Descartes sometimes uses '*conscius*' and '*conscientia*' to mean specifically higher-order reflection. But he also and no less clearly equates consciousness with first-order awareness, as when he says (replying to Hobbes) that 'understanding, willing, imagining, having sensory perceptions... all fall under the *common concept* of *thought or perception or consciousness*' (1641: 2.124; my emphasis), and overall it seems that he's best thought of as a same-order theorist—a Self-intimationist—about experience, i.e. about consciousness in the present-day general sense of the term, i.e. about 'thinking' (*cogitatio*) in his sense.[38]

---

[35] How does the ancient luminosity metaphor fit with Williamson's use of 'luminous', according to which a condition is luminous if and only if 'whenever it obtains (and one is in a position to wonder whether it does), one is in a position to know that it obtains' (2002: 13). Self-Intimation draws on the fundamental respect in which knowledge doesn't essentially involve any discursive or conceptual articulation of anything, and marks the respect in which all conscious states are 'luminous' by Williamson's definition. Williamson, operating with a restricted, intellectualist understanding of 'know', reaches the conclusion that 'for virtually no mental state S is the condition that one is in S luminous' (ibid.: 14).

[36] 1641: 2.113, 1641: 2.127, 1648: 1.335–6; my emphases. 'By the term "thought" I understand everything which we are conscious of as happening within us, insofar as we have consciousness of it' (1644: 1.195 *Principles* 1.9).

[37] Thiel 2011: 48 takes the opposite view, citing Barth 2011.

[38] Thiel has an excellent discussion of this (2011: 43–8). Descartes also writes that 'the initial episode of awareness [*cogitatio*] by means of which we become aware of something does not differ from the second episode of awareness by means of which we become aware that we were aware of it, any more than this second episode of awareness differs from the third episode of awareness by means of which we become

La Forge, a doctor and close follower of Descartes, writes in 1666 that

the nature of experience (thought) consists in that consciousness, awareness [*tesmoinage*] and inner feeling by which the mind is aware of everything it undergoes, and in general of everything which takes place immediately in it, at the same time as it acts or is acted on. I say 'immediately' so that you know that *this awareness and inner feeling is not distinct from the action or being acted on*, and that it is the action and being acted on themselves that apprise the mind of what is taking place in it; and so that you do not confuse this inner feeling with the reflection that we sometimes bring to bear on our [mental] actions, which is not found in all our experiences because it is only one type of experience. So too, I said 'at the same time as it acts or is acted on' so that you would not think that when a particular mental action on the part of the mind is over (i.e. when its experience changes) it has to remember having so acted, and having been aware of doing so.[39]

Arnauld is clearer, perhaps, and briefer, when—using 'think' and 'perceive' in the standard Cartesian way to mean experience or awareness or consciousness in general—he writes in 1683 that:

thought or perception is essentially reflective on itself, or, as it is said more aptly in Latin, *est sui conscia* [is conscious of itself].[40]

There is here no higher-order operation. This is the same-order view of awareness of awareness. In the next paragraph Arnauld calls same-order awareness of awareness 'réflexion virtuelle', and contrasts it with the 'réflexion expresse' of higher-order awareness of awareness, which occurs when we examine one experience by making it the explicit object of another.

Using 'think' and 'perceive' in the same broad way, Locke in 1689 puts it by saying that

it is altogether as intelligible to say that a body is extended without parts, as that anything thinks without being conscious of it... *thinking consists in being conscious that one thinks* ... [just as] hunger consists in that very sensation.   (1689–1700: 2.1.19, my emphasis)

Locke's illustration in terms of hunger is very clear, and scotches the view that he favoured a higher-order account of experience. The sense in which 'thinking [or experiencing] consists in being conscious that one thinks [or experiences]' is, he says, the same as the sense in which 'hunger consists in that very sensation'.[41] To experience is of course *to experience, to be aware of*, one's experiencing. As always,

aware that we were aware that we were aware' (1641: 2.382), but this, placed in context, doesn't itself support the view that Descartes is a same-order theorist (see Thiel 2011: 47; I wrongly cite it as support in Strawson 2009: 346).

[39]   1666: 54–5; my emphasis, translating 'pensée' by 'experience'. A more literal translation of the end of the passage is 'so that you would not think that when the mind is not acting any more—that is, when its experience has changed—it has to remember having acted, and having been aware of doing so'. Here La Forge may have Burman in mind.

[40]   1683: 71; again, this is the broad Cartesian use of 'thought' and 'perception' to mean experience in general, all conscious goings on.

[41]   For discussion see Thiel (2011: 109–18); also Weinberg 2008, Coventry and Kriegel 2008.

the claim can be heard in such a way that it seems false. But it can also be heard in such a way that it can be seen to be necessarily true.

It may then be thought trivial. It may for all that be effective in conveying the lit-up nature of experience. Henry Grove is very clear when he writes in 1718 (using 'thought' in the standard general way) that 'thought is an operation that *involves in it* a consciousness of itself' (1718: 187), and Reid concurs in an unpublished note 'I know nothing that is meant by consciousness of… present perceptions but the perceiving that we perceive them. I cannot imagine there is anything more in perceiving that I perceive a star than in perceiving a star simply; otherwise there might be perceptions of perceptions in infinitum' (1748: 317).[42]

Some think this is trivial in the sense in which it's trivial that to dance is to dance a dance, but the case isn't the same. When I'm dancing, I'm not dancing dancing; but when I'm experiencing, I am experiencing experiencing. In a variant on a passage already quoted, Brentano writes:

In the same mental phenomenon in which the sound is present to our minds we simultaneously apprehend the mental phenomenon itself. What is more, we apprehend it in accordance with its dual nature insofar as it has the sound as content within it, and insofar as it has itself as content at the same time.[43]

According to Husserl, in a remark already quoted,

---

[42] It seems pretty clear that Hume is also a same-order theorist. He distinguishes between reflection and consciousness, using 'reflexion' to denote an intentionally directed higher-order operation of taking one's perceptions as objects of attention in a way that contrasts strongly with his use of 'consciousness' when he writes that our 'perceptions… are *immediately* present to us by consciousness' (*Treatise* 1.4.2.47/212). He also says that '*all* actions and sensations of the mind are known to us by consciousness' (*Treatise* 190/ 1.4.2.7), a claim which immediately triggers the fatal infinite-regress objection—which was well-known then as now—if understood in a higher-order manner. Again, he holds that '*consciousness* never deceives' (*Enquiry* 7.13/66), whereas 'it is remarkable concerning the operations of the mind, that, though most intimately present to us [by consciousness], yet, whenever they become the object of *reflexion*, they seem involved in obscurity' (*Enquiry* 1.13/13). It may be said that this last quotation doesn't settle the matter, because Hume may be distinguishing 'reflexion', as an intentionally undertaken higher-order inspection of one's perceptions, from consciousness as a completely automatic but nevertheless still higher-order awareness of one's perceptions. Once again, though, the obviousness of the infinite-regress objection to the higher-order interpretation of 'all actions and sensations of the mind are known to us by consciousness' favours attributing to Hume the same-order view that is found also in Locke. Garrett agrees, proposing that by 'consciousness' Hume 'generally means an immediate awareness involved in *having* a perception, *not* some further idea *of* that perception' (2009: 440); but some uncertainty remains. For a helpful discussion, see Thiel 2011: 403–6.

[43] Brentano 1874: 98. In saying that we apprehend it 'in accordance with its dual nature' I take it that he doesn't mean that we apprehend that it has a dual nature in any cognitive fashion. The passage continues: 'We can say that the sound is the *primary object* of the *act* of hearing, and that the act of hearing itself is the *secondary object*', and some, following Husserl, have objected to Brentano's use of the word 'object' on the ground that to say that something *x* is an 'object' (whether primary or secondary) of a mental episode or operation is to commit oneself to the view that the subject takes up an intentional attitude to *x* of a sort that requires some sort of express or explicit focusing on *x* (for a good summary account of this position, see Zahavi 2006). There is, however, no compelling reason to think that the word 'object' has this implication for Brentano (who sometimes uses the word 'object' as equivalent to 'content', *Inhalt*), or that his use of the phrase 'secondary object' is designed to do anything more than make the point Aristotle makes in the *Metaphysics*, quoted in §8.6, p. 142 above.

every experience is 'consciousness' and consciousness is consciousness *of*. . . . But every experience is itself experienced [*erlebt*], and to that extent also 'conscious' [*bewußt*].[44]

Sartre puts the point by saying that

consciousness is conscious of itself, that is, the fundamental mode of existence of consciousness is to be consciousness of itself   (1936–7: 4);

we ought not to consider this consciousness (of) itself as a new consciousness, but as *the only mode of existence which is possible for a consciousness of something*. . .; what can properly be called subjectivity is consciousness (of) consciousness.   (1943: lxi[28])[45]

Gurwitsch concurs:

consciousness. . . . is consciousness of an object on the one hand and an inner awareness of itself on the other hand. Being confronted with an object, I am at once conscious of this object and aware of my being conscious of it. . . . In simply dealing with the object I am aware of this very dealing.   (1941: 330)

One's awareness is almost invariably focused on the world, or at least on something other than itself (e.g. a philosophical thesis such as this one), but it is always also awareness of itself.

There are many more interesting and apposite expressions of the same-order view that awareness is self-intimating or phosphorescent. Ryle uses the term 'phosphorescent' with disparaging intent, as remarked, but I'm inclined to take it over in a positive spirit, in spite of the difficulties with the metaphors of light—I'm a Phosphorescentist!—along with his description of what it involves:

mental processes are conscious, not in the sense that we do or could report on them *post mortem*, [i.e. after they have occurred] but in the sense that their intimations of their own occurrences are properties of those occurrences and so are not posterior to them.   (1949: 160)

Here we have a number of good expressions of the view. But it still seems puzzling. It's puzzled people for at least 2,500 years.[46]

---

[44] 1907–9: 291. Husserl also holds that all experience always involves a self-appearance, a '*Für-sich-selbst-erscheinens*' (1923–4: 189; cf. 412).

[45] Again: 'every conscious existence exists as consciousness of existing. We understand now why the first consciousness of consciousness is not positional [i.e. doesn't involve any sort of cognitive operation of taking something—itself—as object of consciousness]; it is because *it is one with the consciousness of which it is consciousness*. At one stroke it determines itself as consciousness of perception and as perception. The necessity of syntax has compelled us hitherto to speak of the "non-positional consciousness of self". But we can no longer use this expression in which the "*of itself*" still evokes the idea of [positional] knowledge. (Henceforth we shall put the "*of*" inside parentheses to show that it merely satisfies a grammatical requirement.)' (1943: liv; my emphasis).

[46] It has always been a central topic in the Phenomenological tradition in philosophy, although hardly visible in the recent analytic tradition. For good surveys, see e.g. Zahavi 1999, 2005. In the Indian tradition, much of the discussion centres round the 'Memory Argument' (one can't remember what one didn't experience, so one can't remember a past experience unless one is at the time one has the experience not only aware of the object but also of the experiencing of the object; so all experiences must be reflexively self-aware). For a helpful recent discussion which defends the argument against the charge of begging the question, see Thompson 2010, also Siderits 2010: 321–3.

8.13 Pure Awareness?

—It's all very well to say that the case for Phosphorescence is overwhelming. How can you be sure that it isn't going to encounter some hidden but insuperable logical or metaphysical objection? And how are you going to reconcile the fact that (4) is true—(4) with its suggestion of looped complexity—with our powerful sense of the respect in which awareness is (at least in some cases) an essentially simple or flat or non-looped phenomenon? The loop just doesn't show up in the phenomenology.

I agree. And when we consider the question, it's helpful to stick to a basic case of awareness of the sort already introduced, something phenomenologically very simple, blissfully thoughtless yellow-experience, conscious experience of or as of an expanse of bright yellow, or of or as of a single pure note played by a flute. For if Self-Intimation is true, it must hold for these cases as for all others. We don't need to consider anything more complex than this, although we can also consider more complicated conscious states if we want.

Do we also need to consider something *less* complex? The question arises because Advaitins like Śaṅkara and Citsukha hold that consciousness or awareness can be directly self-aware without having any ordinary everyday content at all. They hold, in fact, that there's a sense in which consciousness or awareness, considered in itself and just as such, never has any such content.[47] On this view, although all everyday contentful mental states can perfectly well be said to be particular positive qualitative determinations or modes of consciousness, consciousness itself is distinct from any and all ordinarily contentful mental states, and devoid—empty—of any such content. In itself, it's just an 'arena of presence', in Mark Johnston's phrase (Johnston 2010: 139–41).

Having noted this use of 'content', I'm going to continue to use the word in the familiar way according to which consciousness always and necessarily has content simply because it's always and necessarily *of* something. This is not to deny the possibility that consciousness can be entirely empty of all ordinary everyday content. This is something one may achieve in meditation. In such a case there is still consciousness or awareness. The arena happens now to be empty of ordinary content, but it still exists and is still 'live' (one mustn't be misled by the metaphor of the arena to think that it could exist and not be 'live'; the arena is constituted by live awareness). It still possesses the property of self-intimation because it possesses this property essentially, hence even when devoid of any ordinary content.[48]

On this view, then, the 'empty' case, in which consciousness has no ordinary everyday content, but is still self-intimating, is the limiting or minimal case of

[47] See e.g. Ram-Prasad 2010. As I understand him, Sartre agrees (see e.g. Sartre 1943). Berkeley may also agree when he says that 'the Substance of Spirit we do not know it not being knowable. It being purus Actus'—having in itself no positive qualitative content (1707–10: §701). G. E. Moore also agrees, it seems, in his well known paper 'The Refutation of Idealism', when he claims that the 'consciousness' that is a constitutive 'element' of 'sensation' is, although entirely 'diaphanous', nonetheless fully real (Moore 1903: 450). This remark of Moore's is usually hopelessly misunderstood; but not by William James, who published his equally well known paper 'Does Consciousness Exist?' a year later (1904) specifically to challenge Moore's conception of consciousness. (James certainly did not question the existence of consciousness as we ordinarily understand it today.)

[48] Fasching speaks suggestively of the 'self-presence of presence', the 'self-presence of experiencing itself' (2008: 474, 464).

content.[49] Should we allow it? I think so. It's not easy to get into a state of awareness empty of any everyday content, a state of 'pure awareness' or 'pure consciousness experience', but it seems it can be done. There must still be a sense in which there's something it is like to be in this state, on the present view, if it's to count as a state of experience or awareness or consciousness at all. For, once again, all experience or awareness or consciousness is necessarily experience or awareness or consciousness *of* something in the sense of having some experiential character; but there's no content of any standard sort.[50]

Having noted this case, I'm going to focus on more substantive everyday examples of basic awareness. As I understand it, Śaṅkara and Citsukha remain onside even after we restrict attention to awareness with everyday content—even if they take self-intimation to be most properly a property of consciousness itself, and even if some of their advocates consider the self-intimation of consciousness itself to be somehow independent of the awareness of awareness that appears to be essential to conscious experience of any everyday content (an unhelpful view, I think, whether or not it's endorsed by any Advaitin). They remain onside inasmuch as they agree that conscious mental states that are contentful in the everyday way are immediately and automatically manifest to awareness by virtue of the general, essentially self-intimating character of awareness.[51]

8.14 The Structure of Consciousness?

So we have for consideration an intuitively phenomenologically simple case of ordinary awareness—uniform, uninflected yellow-experience. We approach it with

---

[49] Although Sartre holds that consciousness in itself has no content, he also holds that it can't exist without being of something, and, in particular, something that is transcendent with respect to it—the 'transcendent object': 'consciousness is consciousness *of* something. This means that transcendence [being about something other than itself] is a constitutive structure of consciousness; that is, that consciousness arises [necessarily] bearing on a being *which is not itself*' (1943: lxi; my emphasis; the standard translation by Hazel Barnes translates 'portée sur'—bearing on—incorrectly as 'supported by'). This in effect is Moore's 'refutation of idealism'.

[50] See e.g. Albahari 2009, who calls pure consciousness experience 'witness-consciousness'. If experiential what-it-is-likeness ceases entirely, then consciousness ceases, on the present view.

[51] Phrases like 'pure consciousness experience' used to make my heart sink. I doubted people's claim to have experienced such a thing, and tended to lose confidence in their claims even if I found them sympathetic. I now think that a form of pure consciousness experience is relatively easy to attain, if only fleetingly, quite independently of any spiritual benefit (see §10.7 below, pp. 202–3), so now my heart sinks when I think of those whose hearts sink when they read something like this because they think it's not intellectually respectable. It seems hard to deny that philosophers who are seriously interested in the nature of mind ought to try meditation (e.g. Carrington's *Clinically Standardized Meditation*). It's arguable that it ought to be part of undergraduate philosophy of mind courses. This may seem burdensome, but no one who claims to take an empirical approach to the mind can dismiss it, for it's a piece of wholly empirical research that can only be undertaken by each person individually. Rosch puts the point well: 'Some years ago I was questioned by a visiting Tibetan monk about how psychology was studied in the West. Carefully I tried to delineate our fields of psychology—cognition with its subareas such as attention and memory, personality psychology, developmental, and so on. He looked puzzled. I attempted to explain what we meant by empirical method. He seemed even more puzzled. I talked about operational definitions and described some psychological experiments. Suddenly his look of intensely interested bewilderment turned to one of insight: "Aha! So you are saying that in America people teach and write about psychology who have no meditation practice?" "Yes, of course", I answered. "But then how can they know anything!" and then, giving me a piercing look, he asked, "Do you think that's ethical?"' (Rosch 1997: 185).

two divergent attitudes: on the one hand, the intuition of the essentially 'flat' or unlooped nature of the phenomenological being of experience considered just as such (i.e. just in respect of its phenomenological character); on the other hand, the proposal that experience is in fact, in some sense that still remains to be elucidated, an essentially reflexive—somehow looped or self-sprung—phenomenon, as much in the present phenomenologically simple case of experience as in any other. Against the intuition of flatness comes the thought that *reflexivity* is essentially a *relation*, and that all genuine *relationality* essentially involves *structure*; so that all genuine concrete relationality of the sort that concerns us at present, given that we're dealing with actual spatiotemporally located episodes of awareness, concretely existing phenomena, must therefore involve real concrete *metaphysical articulation*.

This thought returns us to the terms—structure, articulation—in which the problem was initially posed in §8.3. How should we proceed?[52] It may first be questioned whether the supposed self-intimation of awareness is really a relation at all. As I understand it, the leading position among those in the Phenomenological tradition is that the awareness of awareness that interests us is not truly or genuinely relational. There's general agreement that it's correctly described as a matter of *reflexivity* of awareness, and it is as such said to be 'pre-reflective', 'immediate', 'immanent', 'implicit', 'non-positional', 'non-objectifying', 'non-conceptual', and 'non-propositional'.[53] But it's also said to be irrational, and hence to be sharply distinct from *reflective* self-awareness, which is, in being reflective, essentially mediated, explicit, objectifying, thematizing, positional, conceptual, relational. In *reflective* awareness, as opposed to immediate *reflexive* awareness, a state of awareness takes another state of awareness as its object of attention.

I think all can agree on this characterization of reflective self-awareness, and on the distinctness of such reflective self-awareness from the seemingly immediate reflexivity of awareness that concerns us now. I accept all but one of the adjectives Phenomenologists use to describe the non-reflective or pre-reflective way in which awareness of awareness appears to be a necessary feature of awareness. I don't, however, see why one should give up the relationality claim. For reflexivity is surely a matter of relationality, and essentially so; relationality which is, furthermore, and surely, and simply in being relationality, a kind of structure, an articulation of reality. How can genuine reflexivity not be genuine relationality?

8.15 Relationality

Well, how tight can relationality get while remaining genuine relationality? Reflexive relations can be intensely intimate, because they're relations that things have to themselves. So the answer seems to be 'very tight indeed'. After all, identity,

---

[52] We do well, I think, to adopt an event/process ontology for concrete reality, and conceive of the phenomenological being of experience as (quite literally) a kind of stuff, process stuff; but we don't need this idea in order to experience the conflict between the simple and non-simple views.

[53] It's a feature of all awareness whatever, and is therefore found in the simplest creatures that have experience.

self-identity, is a relation—a reflexive relation. Clearly, nothing relational could be more intimate than the relation of self-identity that everything has to itself; so perhaps self-identity is a good model for the reflexivity of experience or awareness or consciousness. Perhaps consciousness is/comports consciousness of itself rather as a thing is identical with itself.

One may, however, doubt this. The more one thinks, the more it seems unclear how self-identity could be a good model for anything other than itself. In fact one may reasonably wonder whether self-identity is really a relation at all. It is certainly a relation formally or logically speaking, but it also holds trivially, it's trivially true of everything, and one may feel that it leaves a lot to be desired, metaphysically, as a relation. It seems metaphysically epiphenomenal, as it were—empty.

In some lights its claim to relationality seems wholly metaphysically respectable. 'It's just a patent metaphysical fact that everything is identical with itself.' Here self-identity seems to be not only a fully and unproblematically concrete metaphysical relation, but also the most fundamental metaphysical relation. In other lights one may wonder whether one's intuitions haven't been buzzed by philosophy. Perhaps one is mistaking something that undoubtedly qualifies as a true proposition, a valid structure in discursive thought (A = A, as the German Idealists used to say), for a real metaphysical something—a real relation, a real piece of structure in reality—that isn't really any such thing.

This doubt about whether self-identity is real relationality may now look potentially helpful. The relation of self-identity is, certainly, reflexive, but here it seems we may have a case of genuine, indisputable *reflexivity* without any concrete structural *relationality*. And at one point that was what we thought we wanted, when we thought about the self-intimation of experience: relationality that is fully formally respectable, holding true of real concrete phenomena in the world, but without involving any concrete relationality in the sense that requires structure or articulation. Perhaps self-identity is after all a good analogy or metaphor for self-intimation—the essential reflexivity of consciousness.

But now new doubts arise. The relation of self-identity may seem too inert, as a relation. The reflexivity of self-intimation may seem by contrast something dynamic, live. It seems as if the reflexivity of awareness is part of what actualizes awareness from moment to moment. It's not only essential to awareness, as self-identity is essential to all things, but is in some sense the inner motor of its being the particular, *sui generis* occurrent phenomenon it is.

But perhaps this idea of actualization goes too far. Perhaps we should stick with the idea that the reflexivity of self-intimation is intrinsic to awareness, essential to it, but not part of its 'mechanism' in any sense. But then again it seems that it is rightly thought of as part of its dynamic essence—of what its actualization always and necessarily involves.

Perhaps one can recover self-identity as the fundamental model for self-intimation by imagining a dynamic version of self-identity. Perhaps one can model self-intimation as a circle, conceived of as a dynamic entity. On this view, the immediate awareness of awareness or self-intimation that is essential to all awareness bears some resemblance to a circle revolving round its own centre, whose motion is invisible, so that it appears simply as a circle.

Perhaps that doesn't help. Another consideration arises. We may have escaped the threat of infinite regress, in preferring a same-order account to a higher-order account, but perhaps there's a threat, not of an infinite regress, but of an infinite whirl, as awareness goes about the business of being awareness of itself, where the 'itself' in question already comports awareness of itself, which already comports awareness of itself.

I don't, however, think this is a serious worry. It is, perhaps, a mirage, generated by the irreducibly discursively structured, analytically divisive, subject-predicate, hard-relation forms of our language. The reply, in terms of the image of the circle, is that the circle is, although a dynamic entity, just a single circle. It doesn't whirl in an infinitely regressive way.[54]

'This is just another image. None of this really helps. Why not hold to the simple or naïve view of experience or experiential what-it-is-likeness, according to which it's just there, patent, and patently what it is, in no way complex or folded on itself in the way you suggest? Consider again the simplicity of a present experience of, say, greenness. It's just there. This is bedrock.'

As before, I don't want to disturb anything in this intuition, in insisting that there's some sort of metaphysical complexity in awareness or experience. When we reflect on the statement that all awareness comports awareness of that very awareness I think we see that it's true, once we've completely overcome any tendency to misunderstand it as a report of some sort of intentionally targeted reflective taking of awareness as object of awareness. But the immediate intuition of the simple character of experience isn't undermined. The metaphysical complexity of self-intimational reflexivity is part of what the existence of this phenomenological simplicity consists in, but the phenomenological simplicity is not other than it seems in seeming simple.

Is there then real relationality? Yes, if only because it's true, literally and forever inescapably true, to say that all awareness comports awareness *of* itself. The 'of' is quite correct, and it is automatically and irreducibly relational. By the same token, there's real intentionality there, in the crucial, maximally inclusive, Brentano–Montague sense of intentionality, which certainly doesn't require any ontic distinct-ness of intentional state and intentional object, nor any sort of 'objectifying' or 'thematic' or 'positional' attentional focus.[55] The *of* is real, and real ofness of this kind (aboutness, if you like) is certainly sufficient for intentionality, for it's simply what intentionality is. So too it's essentially relational. All intentionality is irreducibly relational, even if something is of or about itself.[56]

---

[54] To the challenge that Self-Intimation posits or gives rise to a vicious circle, Sartre replies that 'there is no circle, or if you like, it is the very nature of consciousness to exist "in a circle"' (1943: 20/liii).

[55] Brentano 1874, Montague 2009: 497–502.

[56] All phenomenological content is intentional for the reason given in §8.1: whatever its phenomenological-content-type, it is automatically and necessarily experience *of* that phenomenological-content type. Note that this simple point, coupled with the point that there is cognitive phenomenological content as well as sense-feeling phenomenological content, is all one needs in order to deal with all cases of thought and experience that have led people to talk so alarmingly and unnecessarily (if sometimes delightfully) of 'non-existent objects' and to say, *obviously falsely*, that we can think about non-existent objects.

Again there may seem to be a sense in which the relationality isn't genuinely, articulatedly relational. Again the 'of' may begin to seem misleading, even if not actually incorrect, in the way pointed up by Sartre. ('If experience is really going to get into a genuine concrete relation with itself, it's going to have to distance itself from itself in such a way that it'll never be able to get back to being the unified, simply given phenomenon it plainly is.') But why? Perhaps we need to revisit the question whether we can make some sense of the notion of 'irrelational relationality'. Once again we have the model of self-identity, the relation or pseudo-relation of being identical with itself that everything has to itself. But once again self-identity seems unhelpful, inasmuch as it is in some sense a merely logical relation, trivially true of everything.

8.16 *Puzzling*

The self-intimation relation is supposed to have the following five properties. It's a non-logical (non-trivial), concrete, essentially one-term, reflexive, and somehow dynamically real—temporally live—relation. With what can we compare it?

If I'm thinking about myself then I stand in the thinking-about-self relation to myself, and it fulfils all these requirements: it's a non-logical relation, non-trivial, concrete, one-term, reflexive, and it's dynamically real in the sense that it's occurring in time. But this isn't an adequate model of what we want, because (fortunately) my thinking about myself isn't essential to my being. We need a genuine, concrete, reflexive, one-term, etc. relation which also has the property that its obtaining is an essential feature of the existence of the thing with respect to which it obtains. Once again the relation of self-identity suggests itself. Once again, though, it doesn't seem to be an essential feature of the existence of what stands in it in a way that helps us understand self-intimation.

It's not hard to find something better. Consider again *this very thought is puzzling*—I'll call it *Puzzling* for short. *Puzzling* is a real thought when I think it, and it is as remarked true when I think it. It's a real concrete thing, a concrete, clockable occurrence, which is unequivocally about itself. It's a clear case of non-trivial, concrete, reflexive, one-term relationality, non-trivial concrete *self*-relationality, and its being about itself in the way that it is is essential not only to its being the particular thought it is (having the particular content it has), but also (and therefore) to its existing at all. The reflexivity isn't just a matter of linguistic reflexivity, linguistic self-referentiality. It's a temporally live reflexive relation that an occurrent thought stands in to itself. It's also a property that the thought taken as a whole seems to have to itself taken as a whole, and this matches the sense that self-intimation is a property that experience considered at a given moment must have to itself taken as a whole at that moment, simply in order to be what it is.[57] *Puzzling* is, admittedly, itself an awareness-involving phenomenon, a conscious experiential phenomenon.[58] It's an

---

[57] One shouldn't think there's any conflict between the Self-intimation thesis and the fact that experience can be dim, peripheral, and so on.

[58] Some will say that conscious thoughts aren't or needn't be experiential phenomena. For the point that this can't be so, see Montague 2014. Could *Puzzling* be a non-conscious but none the less occurrent

instance of the very phenomenon we're trying to model and so understand. But that need not prevent it from being potentially elucidatory of, or at least demystificatory of, the property we want to attribute to experience or awareness or consciousness in general. It wouldn't be surprising if any good example of the required kind was itself a case of experience (awareness, consciousness), for experience (awareness, consciousness) may very well be *sui generis* in this respect (I'm sure it is). It may be the only possible case of non-trivial, one-term, essential, fully concretely real, live reflexivity.

Puzzling plainly has complex structure, and it may now be said that there has to be complex structure or articulation of the sort found in *Puzzling* for there to be genuine reflexivity. In which case *Puzzling* can't be truly elucidatory or demystificatory of the supposed reflexivity of self-intimation, which must be present even in the simplest possible case of experience.[59] One can, though, put *Puzzling* aside, and consider a simpler case. One can simply think *This*—understanding (experiencing) this *This* to refer to itself, i.e. to the mental act of thinking *This*. If you doubt it, try it. When there's reflexivity, there must indeed and of course be the structure that is definitionally essential to any reflexivity (the looping on itself). But with this *This* we have, perhaps, an illustration of the required kind of reflexivity that has no further structure. It may be said again that self-referentiality is a familiar feature of linguistic constructions, but isn't helpful, because linguistic constructions are in themselves static and abstract, not in any way dynamic. But we're concerned here with thoughts, actual occurrent episodes of thought like *This*, not abstract linguistic constructions.

One reason why the self-intimation of awareness continues to seem paradoxical is—to repeat—that it seems that the awareness must be already all there in order to be taken as an object of awareness in the way that is according to the self-intimation thesis necessary for it to be awareness at all. It seems this can't be right. It can't be the right description, even if it's groping after the right fact. I don't, however, have any remedy for this discomfort, except the following—which may seem worse than the discomfort it aims to assuage.

Perhaps there is no radical or absolute non-relationality in reality (and not because everything is identical with itself—that's a merely logical topping on things). Perhaps relationality—intrinsic relationality—is quite generally constitutive of being, not for any of the reasons that may be standardly cited in support of 'relational metaphysics', but simply because self-loopedness or 'self-sprungness' is essentially constitutive of the existence of the very things that are the leading candidates for being the basic, intrinsic, non-relational items that enter into all the larger relations that we generally discern in reality.[60]

This seems a murky idea; but perhaps it's a thing's being turned on itself or being self-sprung that gets it into being at all. (One might say that all concrete existence is energy, and that 'self-sprung' is an apt characterization of what concretely existing energy is.) 'Gets it into being' is a bad metaphor, however, for how can we suppose

---

thought? I think not, because non-conscious phenomena can't strictly speaking be said to have determinate content. But this point needs argument (see Strawson 2008), and isn't important here.

[59] Sam Coleman put this point to me.

[60] If experience is *sui generis* in being self-looped or self-sprung in this way, an argument for panpsychism begins here.

that there was a time when being was not, and that it (!) then turned on itself and so came to be—as if something that didn't exist at all could do anything like that? Being may be self-sprung in some way, where being self-sprung is an essentially self-relational but also fully internal matter, but it can't get back behind itself in order to lever itself into existence.[61] The puzzle remains—the puzzle about how awareness can somehow be there already in order to be taken (by itself) as object of awareness in the way that (then?) constitutes it (?) as awareness in the first place.

'Yes, and this is a waste of time, because all real relationality is *essentially extrinsic*. In all cases of real relationality, i.e. putting aside pseudo-relations like the self-identity relation, there is a relatum—there are relata—relative to which any relation is something extrinsic. This, in fact, is why the subject of awareness can never take itself as it is in the present moment of awareness as object of awareness—any more than the eye can see itself.'

I'm not sure that it's true that the subject of awareness can never take itself as it is in the present moment of awareness as object of awareness.[62] And perhaps this last idea about the necessary extrinsicness of relationality is just a deep bias or error of discursive thought—of the necessarily discursive form of human thought. Perhaps human thought has as a basic unexamined category—a basic metaphysical building block—the idea of *a perfectly unrelated thing*. It takes this idea as the epitome of existence itself, and then supposes that any relationality has to add in some way to the postulated perfectly unrelated thing. But perhaps the idea of the perfectly unrelated thing is already fundamentally wrong (Nāgārjuna and the Mādhyamikas agree). Does the thought *this very thought is puzzling* have to loop out or away from itself in any way at all in order to then return on itself, in order to be about itself in the way that it is? I don't see that it does. There can be real, concrete relationality without extrinsicality. If we think of lines as dynamically real, it seems again that the intrinsic non-trivial (non-logical) self-relationality of awareness may be depicted by a circle. It has the self-relationality of a circle, a dynamic circle.[63] Perhaps the minimum existent is at least the circle, not the point, or the closed figure, the loop, not the line. But the spatial character of these metaphors may not in the end be helpful.

8.17 Relationality Again

Discussing Henrich and Frank, Zahavi writes that they

acknowledge that pre-reflective, irrelational self-awareness is characterized by a certain internal differentiation and complexity; they never offer a more detailed analysis of this complex structure. That is, when it comes to a positive description of the structure of original pre-reflective self-awareness they are remarkably silent, either claiming in turn that it is unanalysable, or that the unity of its complex structure is incomprehensible. This is hardly satisfactory.   (2007: 281)

---

[61] Serious cosmologists sometimes say things that sound as if they think that being can somehow lever itself into existence, but they usually turn out to mean something far less dramatic. See e.g. Krauss 2012.

[62] This is the subject of Ch. 10 below.

[63] Williford 2006 attempts to model the self-representational structure of consciousness mathematically.

Zahavi wants members of the 'Heidelberg school' to say more about the relation between experience and subject of experience, and the temporality of experience. And no doubt they should. Still, analysis comes to an end, and we shouldn't be surprised to come across a respect in which the metaphysics of experience is mysterious to us, given our cognitive capacities, even while we recognize the unshakable, fundamental general respect in which we know what experience is just in having it. When we think hard and clearly about awareness we may come to see, with Aristotle and many others, that we say something true when we say that all awareness comports awareness of itself.[64] This expression of this feature of reality, couched as it is in necessarily discursively articulated thought or language, can seem paradoxical. But the reality it describes, and says something true about, is entirely unparadoxical, and indeed fundamentally simple in character. It is just: experience (awareness, consciousness), the reality you know—and know as it is in itself, in a fundamental respect, and know right now, in its phenomenological unloopedness—simply in having experience.

All awareness comports awareness of itself. I don't think we need to be coy about this, linguistically or otherwise. We can allow that the '*of*' is fully metaphysically correct, rather than an unhappy grammatical obligation. We can insist that there is something irreducibly internally *relational* about the self-intimation of experience or awareness, even as we allow that it's an entirely pre-reflective phenomenon, acknowledge the simple (essentially non-loopy) phenomenological character that experience or awareness has for us as we have it, and stress that this phenomenological character is itself part of the ultimate nature of reality that is known as it is in itself (because the having is the knowing). So too we can say without flinching that awareness is its own *object*, even as it also has some other object, and even though it is not its own object in any express or 'thematic' fashion.[65] So too we can say that awareness is—essentially—fully *intentional* with respect to itself, even though it isn't in any sense thematically directed at itself. And we can say that awareness takes itself as part of its own *content*; we can allow that this is one acceptable way to express what its self-intimation or 'phosphorescence' consists in. We can in other words reject all those characterizations of the self-awareness of awareness that insist that it is essentially irrelational or non-intentional, and can't in any sense be its own object or take itself as its own content, while properly acknowledging the puzzlement that drives these suggestions.

---

[64] There is a fine exposition of Aristotle's position in Caston 2002 (see especially §5, pp. 768–73).

[65] Sartre denies that consciousness is its own object in order to reserve the word 'object' for things other than consciousness of which consciousness is conscious (things 'transcendent' with respect to or essentially over and above consciousness—see note 49). Accordingly, he brackets the word 'of' in the statement that consciousness is consciousness of itself, in order to reserve it for the relation in which consciousness stands to such transcendent objects. But these choices, however understandable (they're deeply embedded in Sartre's account of consciousness as nothingness; see e.g. Rowlands 2011), are ultimately terminological. So long as we're clear about what is at issue I believe we can retain the full-blown 'of', and (with Brentano) the heavy seeming word 'object', in the statement of Self-Intimation.

8.18 Is Self-intimation Perception?

The puzzlement may renew itself—finally—when we introduce the notion of *representation* or *presentation*.[66] Once it's allowed that an episode of experience or awareness A1 is genuinely intentional with respect to itself, then it must surely be allowed that it represents or presents itself.[67] Again this may seem troubling. It doesn't really introduce any new element (*Puzzling* remains a clear example of how this sort of thing is possible), but the sense of trouble may be exacerbated by asking whether we must now also allow that the self-intimation of A1 is a case of perception, albeit a special one. Can a mental representation really be a *perception* of itself—even if it's also a perception of something else? Or can it be a (re)presentation of itself but not a perception of itself?

Again I'm inclined to be terminologically liberal. I think that the self-intimation of A1 can be allowed to count as a case of perception—conscious perception—although this may be felt to weaken my case. For the following rough line of thought seems applicable. [1] If something x is a certain way in one's environment, and one experiences x in some way, registering how it is (at least to some degree) in some essentially partly phenomenological mode of representation, then this is a case of conscious perception.[68] [2] If the self-intimation of experience or awareness is in general as I've claimed it to be, then the self-intimation of A1 must surely be allowed to fulfil this sufficient condition of being a case of perception—even if the self-intimation of A1 is at the same time essential to the very existence of A1 in the way that we still can't claim to fully understand. This bumps up against the principle that a thing has to exist in order to be represented, or perceived, in such a way that its being represented or perceived can't be essential to what it is for it to exist. But this is just one more expression of the intuitive difficulty we've encountered several times. And again I think we shouldn't be too quick or confident in our judgement. For insofar as there's a real philosophical problem about consciousness (as opposed to the non-problem of how the existence of consciousness is compatible with what physics reveals about the world), it lies here. (It is, perhaps, the mystery of concrete being in general.) The claim that the representing is somehow mysteriously partly essential to the very existence of what is represented doesn't in itself bring into question the proposal that we have to do with a case of perception, even if the claim is problematic in itself.[69]

---

[66] Here I assume that 'representation', as standardly used in philosophy of mind, is best taken to be synonymous with 'presentation' (the 're-' of 'representation' shouldn't be thought to imply any repetition of presentation).

[67] 'Whatever else a conscious state represents, it always also represents itself'; the subjective character of an episode of experience or awareness 'consists in its representing itself in a certain suitable way' (Kriegel 2009: 13, 2).

[68] One may reasonably speak of unconscious perception, but all experience or awareness is conscious by definition, hence phenomenological by definition (there is cognitive phenomenology as well as sense-feeling phenomenology).

[69] Note that the suggestion that the self-intimation of experience or awareness is a form of perception appears to raise the possibility that perception of something isn't necessarily a causal matter, even if it's necessarily a matter of representation. This, though, adds nothing new to the difficulty already posed by self-intimation. It may not be any more paradoxical than the fact that we can convey the nature of our

It may finally be denied that one can make proper sense of the notion of a modality of perception and (re)presentation without allowing for the possibility of misperception and mis(re)presentation in that modality. But if the reasons for allowing that self-intimation is a matter of perception or (re)presentation are good, then we must give up this principle, if only in this one case.[70]

8.19 Conclusion

I'll conclude with a statement of what I think we need to do, rather than a statement of what I've established (the latter might be rather thin). [1] We need to preserve the simple view of experience in some form, because experience as defined in §8.1 really is unlayered or non-loopy, phenomenologically speaking. It follows that it really is non-loopy metaphysically speaking, in one fundamental respect, because there's a fundamental respect in which it is in itself something wholly phenomenological, and, hence, in which its whole metaphysical being is its phenomenological being.

[2] When we bring experience before the tribunal of discursive, analytical thought, I think we must accept that it has a valid description as structurally complex—that the relational idioms and notions are appropriate. I think this is the best we can do. Experience is self-intimating; it's reflexive on itself, self-intentional, genuinely 'of' itself, self-representing, even self-perceiving in the accommodating sense of 'perception' just defended. It's not wrong to say that it's part of its own content, or that it is its own object—given an acceptably relaxed use of the word 'object'. This is part of what it is for it to be what it is truly represented to be in the simple view of experience just characterized.

[3] To say that the language of structure and relation is needed, or is the best we can do, when we try to analyse the nature of experience in discursive thought, isn't to say that it's fully adequate to its object—experience, the glow of experience. I think we need to acknowledge the inadequacy, and accept that it lies in the nature of discursive thought.

This conclusion may be galling, initially, but it's hardly unprecedented. Consider how discursive thought bounces between the intolerable bare-propertyless-substrate view of objects and the intolerable mere-bundle-of-properties view of objects. There is, however, a solution to the ancient object-property difficulty—a full *philosophical* solution. It's enough to hold or look at any ordinary object and think about it, the propertied thing, until one simply sees that there's no real metaphysical problem, that the apparent problem—a seemingly inevitable product of discursive thought when it thinks about objects and their properties—simply doesn't exist. With luck, this will

---

direct acquaintance with the experiential 'what-it's-like' of our experience by saying that 'the having is the knowing'.

[70] Zahavi thinks this account 'glosses over the difference between one-level representationalism [of the kind expounded in e.g. Kriegel 2009] and a truly pre-reflective account of self-consciousness' (private communication), but I take myself to agree with Zahavi, although we disagree in our terminology. The present claim is precisely that relationality, intentionality, and representation (self-relationality, self-intentionality, self-representation) are all there in fully pre-reflective self-intimation. They don't require cognitive articulation or distancing.

only take a few seconds. We can adapt Ramsey's famous remark, replacing 'language' with 'discursive thought': 'The whole theory of particulars and universals is due to mistaking for a fundamental characteristic of reality what is merely a characteristic of discursive thought' (1925: 23).

I think something similar holds in the case of the self-intimation or phosphorescence of experience. Reflecting on experience in the living flow of experience, one sees that no metaphysical problem stems from the fact that all awareness comports awareness of itself. One might say that it's enough to grasp the tautology that all awareness is indeed, awareness, with all that that entails. This is of no use to anyone who doubts it, but it's true.[71]

---

[71] Thanks to François Récanati, Dan Zahavi, and the pugnacious anonymous referees of this paper for some very useful comments.

9

Fundamental Singleness
How to Turn the Second Paralogism into a Valid Argument

9.1 Introduction

One's experience—one's overall or total field of experience—is *complex* at any given time, but there's also a fundamental sense in which it's *unified* at any given time. One of the many reasons why philosophers have posited an entity called 'the self' has been to furnish themselves with something that might possibly help to explain the unity of the experiential complex at a given time. Something, it seems, must tie or bind the complex or manifold of experience into a unified whole, somehow constitute it as a unified whole. The self is posited as that which either performs this operation or is at least the locus of this unity—something that is ontologically additional to the elements of the complex.

In this case the aim is to explain the *synchronic* unity of experience. Many also appeal to the idea of the self when giving an account of the *diachronic* unity of experience. It seems to me, though, that Hume, Kant, James, and others have fatally undermined the idea that we need to postulate a single persisting metaphysical entity called 'the self' in order to explain the phenomena of the diachronic unity of experience (I'm not entirely sure what these phenomena are meant to be). So I'm going to restrict my attention to the synchronic case. By 'synchronic', though, I don't mean a durationless instant, because there can be no experience at a durationless instant. I mean experience during a short temporal interval which I'll call the 'living moment of experience', taking this term to cover such things as the time in which the grasping of a thought occurs.[1]

I'm going to argue that the self exists, and that there's a very close relation between the self and the (synchronic) unity of experience. I'm also going to argue that selves themselves are unities of a very striking kind, and that they may qualify for the title 'object' in fundamental metaphysics—if any entities do. But I'm not going to give them any *explanatory* work to do, as far as the phenomenon of the (synchronic) unity of experience is concerned. And I'm going to talk about subjects of experience rather than selves.

---

[1] More strictly, I take the living moment of experience to be a very short period of time, as short as the shortest period of time in which experience can be said to be going on at all, and therefore much shorter than the so-called 'specious present', which probably has a maximum extent of around a third of a second. I follow Dainton in this estimate (2000: 171) although he may since have lowered it.

This shouldn't lead me astray, for if selves exist, then they're certainly subjects of experience; in which case anything I establish about subjects will also hold true of selves. That said, I'm going to focus on a restricted notion of the subject that will lead some—perhaps most—to deny that what I think of as subjects are what they think of as selves.

9.2 Experience

I start from the point that consciousness—conscious experience or as I will simply say *experience*—exists:

[1]   experience exists (is real).

This is obvious, but I'll list it as an assumption. By 'experience' (mass term) I mean the experiential-qualitative character or experiential 'what-it's-likeness' of experiences (count noun), where this experiential-qualitative character is considered just as such, hence wholly independently of anything else that may be supposed to be part of what experiences consist of when they're considered as a whole, and (more generally) wholly independently of anything else that may be supposed to have to exist when experiences exist. The relevant conception of experience—experiential content—is therefore wholly 'internalist', in present-day terms.[2] Simple examples are enough by way of illustration—pain, the 'what-it's-likeness' of seeing the colour red, tasting bananas, itching, finding something funny. Some (e.g. functionalists) claim to be realists about experience when they are really no such thing. So let me be clear that I'm a real realist about experience. What is it to be a real realist about experience? It's to take the what-it's-like of colour experience or taste experience or pain experience to be what one took it to be—knew it to be—quite unreflectively, before one did any philosophy, e.g. when one was five.[3] However many new and surprising facts real realists about experience learn from scientists—facts about the neurophysiology of experience, say, or the 'filling-in' that characterizes visual experience, or 'change blindness', or 'inattentional blindness'[4]—their basic grasp of what colour experience or pain experience (etc.) is remains exactly the same as it was *before they did any philosophy*. It remains, in other words, correct, grounded in the fact that to have experience at all is already to know what experience is, however little one reflects about it. When it comes to experience, 'the having is the knowing'. It's knowledge 'by acquaintance'. To taste pineapple, in Locke's old example, is sufficient, as well as necessary, for knowing what it's like to taste pineapple.[5]

This way of saying what I mean by 'experience', and hence by 'realist about experience', guarantees that anyone who claims not to know what I mean is being

---

[2]   I take 'what-it's-likeness' to cover the total character of our experience, everything that the Phenomenologists take as their object of study, and to be as much cognitive as sensory.

[3]   One doesn't need to attribute a general conception of experience to five-year olds to make the point, but one shouldn't underestimate five-year-olds—or think that they can't make a distinction between the character of their experience and what it is experience of.

[4]   See e.g. Pessoa and De Weerd 2003, Simons and Levin 1997, Chun and Marois 2002.

[5]   I put aside the point that different people may have different taste-experiences in tasting pineapple.

disingenuous. The last paragraph wouldn't be necessary if philosophers like Dennett hadn't reversified—looking-glassed—the term 'consciousness' or 'experience'.[6]

It follows from [1] that

[4]   subjects exist

or that at least one subject of experience exists, because it's a necessary truth that

[2]   [experience → subject]:

'an experience is impossible without an experiencer' (Frege 1918: 27). It's 'an obvious conceptual truth that an experiencing is necessarily an experiencing by a subject of experience, and involves that subject as intimately as a branch-bending involves a branch' (Shoemaker 1986: 10). In other words: there can't be experience without a subject of experience, because

[3]   experience is necessarily experience *for*.

Spelled out a little: experience is a matter of experiential 'what-it-is-likeness', and experiential what-it-is-likeness is necessarily what-it-is-likeness *for* someone or something. Whatever the metaphysical nature or category of this experiencing something, its real existence can't be denied. This point is secure even if individual-substance-suggesting noun phrases like 'an experiencer' or 'a subject of experience' are somehow misleading.[7]

I take [3] to be a sufficient answer to those who seek to deny [2] (to claim that there can be experience without a subject), for no one can sensibly deny [3], the essential for-someone-or-something-ness of experience, and I understand the notion of the subject of experience in such a way that to say [2] that experience entails a subject of experience is simply to express [3] in a different way. One could put the point paradoxically by saying that if *per impossibile* there could be pain-experience without a subject of experience, mere experience without an experiencer, contrary to [2], then there'd be no point in stopping it, because no one would be suffering.[8]

Another way to put the point is to say that

[5]   [subjectivity → subject].

It's worth stating this explicitly because some like to deny [5], claiming precisely that although there obviously can't be experience without subjectivity

[6]   [experience → subjec*tivity*]

still there can be subjectivity without a subject—so that [2] isn't true after all.

---

[6] To looking-glass or reversify a term is to define it in such a way that whatever one means by it, it excludes what the term means.

[7] Descartes makes the point in his Second Meditation (1641: 18).

[8] 'Of course there'd be a point: the universe would be a better place, other things being equal, if there were fewer pain sensations. Pains are intrinsically bad, even without owners.' Reply: Pains without owners, pains without someone-or-something pained—call them 'pains*'—are pains without pain! Pains* are impossible (apart from not being intrinsically bad).

I sympathize with the impulse behind this claim, but what it shows, I think, is that those who endorse it are making certain metaphysical assumption about what subjects are that I'm not making. They are, perhaps, thinking that subjects must be things that persist for an appreciable length of time, or substances, in some traditional, heavy sense of the word 'substance'. My notion of what a subject is involves no such metaphysical commitments.[9] In fact it's no more metaphysically committed than their notion of subjectivity. It rests on no more than [3]. One can indicate its maximally noncommittal metaphysical nature by saying that it has the consequence that [5] is necessarily true given that [3] is, so that [2] is secure. Given what I understand by 'subject', subjectivity entails a subject.

9.3 Materialism ('Um-ism')

I'm going to restrict attention to concrete phenomena like chairs, pains, and electrons, as opposed to abstract phenomena like the idea of justice or the number 2.[10] In fact I'm going to assume the truth of *concretism* for the purposes of this paper:

[7]   [real → concrete].

By 'concrete phenomena' I mean phenomena that are actually located somewhere in the universe. I take it for the purposes of argument that all location is at least temporal, if not also spatiotemporal—while noting that we may be very wrong about the nature of such location.[11] Immaterial souls, then, should they exist, are 100 per cent concrete, as are the vaguest fleeting feelings. They may seem flimsy compared with a bullet, but that has nothing to do with metaphysical concreteness.

I'm also going to assume that stuff monism and in particular materialism is true, i.e. that all concrete phenomena are constituted of the same stuff—physical stuff:

[8]   [concrete → physical][12]

which with [7] entails

[9]   [real → physical].

The converse of [8], i.e.

---

[9] Again I follow Descartes in his Second Meditation. All he claims to know at this stage of his argument is that he is *something*, a really existing phenomenon, whatever its ontological category.

[10] I'm using 'phenomenon' as a general term for any sort of existent or candidate existent, suppressing its old meaning of 'appearance'.

[11] I take 'temporal' and 'spatiotemporal' to be referring terms that pick out and refer to an objectively real dimensionality (the actual dimensionality of the concrete real). They refer to it however wrong we are about its nature.

[12] [8] on its own amounts to materialism, given the way the term 'materialism' is standardly used in the philosophy of mind (to rule out things like immaterial souls), but materialism can also be understood in a stronger sense which incorporates [7], the assumption that all real phenomena are concrete phenomena. Some, of course, reject [7], holding that there are 'abstract objects', numbers for example, that are part of reality in every sense in which concrete physical objects are ('abstract' and 'concrete' are defined as mutually exclusive and exhaustive opposites).

[10]   [physical → concrete]

is obviously true, and [8] and [10] sum to

[11]   [concrete ↔ physical]

from which I'll take it to follow that

[12]   [concrete object ↔ physical object].

In this discussion, then, one can always replace 'concrete' by 'physical', and conversely. [1] and [9] entail

[13]   [experience → physical],

and I'm not just a materialist. I'm also, given [1], a 'real' materialist, a realistic materialist, a philosophically serious materialist, i.e. a materialist who is fully realist about the existence of (conscious) experience. Real materialism holds that experience—the concretely existing phenomenon of 'what-it's-likeness' considered just as such and so wholly independently of anything else—is wholly physical, although physics has no resources for characterizing its nature so considered.[13]

Having declared my materialism, let me stress that I take 'material' and 'physical' to be *natural-kind* terms, and that natural-kind terms are paradigmatic examples of terms that succeed in referring to what they're introduced to refer to even though we who introduce and use them may be very wrong about the nature of what they refer to. There's no less reason for us to take 'material' and 'physical' to be natural-kind terms than there is for us to take terms like 'gold' and 'tiger' to be natural-kind terms. But although almost all present-day philosophers take 'gold' and 'tiger' to be natural-kind terms, very few do so in the case of 'physical' or 'material'.

One reason for this, perhaps, is that we find it hard to take 'temporal' and 'spatiotemporal' to be natural-kind terms, in the way endorsed above; and one thing then leads to another. Another source of resistance may be this: to take 'physical' to be a natural-kind term that certainly refers to the reality that physics concerns itself with, but leaves it open that we may be very wrong about fundamental aspects of the nature of this reality, is to allow that the ultimate nature of the thing that physics is about, the physical as denoted by the natural-kind term 'physical', may possibly be irreducibly mental or experiential in character: not only in part, as I've already proposed, but even perhaps as a whole. Eddington and Russell are among those who suppose that the physical (natural-kind-term use) is or may be wholly mental or experiential in character. I'm inclined to agree with them, if only for reasons of theoretical parsimony. Few, however, can stomach this consequence of taking 'physical' as a natural-kind term. They insist on supposing that it retains a descriptive force that goes beyond anything warranted by physics. (In particular, they suppose that 'physical' entails 'non-experiential'.)

This is certainly understandable. To take 'physical' to be a natural-kind term amounts in effect to taking it to be equivalent to the neutral term 'real and concrete', so that the difference between materialism and mentalism or idealism, say, can no longer be

<hr>

[13] See e.g. Strawson 2003a.

expressed. Common terminology is further offended when it's pointed out—by Eddington, Russell, and R. W. Sellars among others—that physics only ever characterizes the structural, mathematically representable nature of the physical, and that we can know the non-structural or non-mathematically-characterizable nature of the physical only in being directly acquainted with the character of our experience (the having is the knowing). I continue to call myself a materialist in order to stress the point that my view is [i] a view about the actual nature of the concrete reality that physics deals with and [ii] a view that allows for the possibility that—indeed takes it that—physics has got a great deal right about the (ultimate) nature of reality. I have, however, no real hope that this natural-kind term use of the term 'physical' is going to catch on. It's going to continue to be judged to be eccentric; even, perhaps, a misuse of the word. To counter this, I could introduce 'um' as a synonym for the natural-kind term use of 'physical'. I'm an um-ist (an *Ur*-materialist). But I'll continue to use the term 'physical' for the most part, because the materialist or um-ist claim that matters most at present is simply the claim that experience is wholly a matter of brain activity, and until the word 'um' is widely used (surely it will not be long), the fact that I take physics and neurophysiology to have got a very great deal right about the brain is better kept in focus by using the word 'physical' than the word 'um'.

So far, perhaps, so good. But I've spoken of objects, and said that I'm going to argue that subjects of experience are objects—

[20] [subject (of experience) → object]

—so I need to say what an object (or 'individual substance') is. This is a very big, very general and very difficult question in metaphysics. I think we need to renounce tables and chairs as paradigm cases of objects in order to approach it.

9.4 Object [1]

The first thing to say, I think, is that whatever an object is, it is a certain sort of *unity*

[14] [object → unity (of some sort)]

and if it's a concrete object then it is—I take it—a certain sort of concrete unity

[15] [concrete object → concrete unity]

and if it's a physical object, as it is if materialism is true, then it is—I take it—a certain sort of physical unity

[16] [physical object → physical unity].

Since I'm restricting my attention to the concrete, and hence the physical (given materialism), I'll regularly drop the words 'concrete' and 'physical' from now on.

What kind of unity is in question? If anything is going to qualify as an object in fundamental metaphysics, by which I mean (at least) metaphysics that gives no special weight to the ordinary categories of thought, then it must—I propose—be a *strong* unity

[17]   [object → strong unity]

in a sense I'll try to illustrate.

I think, in fact, that strong unity is not only necessary but also sufficient for objecthood

[18]   [strong unity → object]

which sums with [17] to give

[19]   [strong unity ↔ object]

—the view that unity, of a certain sort which remains to be specified, is the sole and sufficient criterion of objecthood.

I'll go on to claim that subjects of experience qualify as strong unities, and that there are in fact no better candidates for the title 'strong unity' than subjects of experience

*[20]   [subject → strong unity].[14]

I've given [20] an asterisk to mark the fact that it's something I want to try to explain or argue for, i.e. not something I'm [a] taking to be evident, or [b] taking to be true by definition, or [c] assuming without significant discussion, or [d] claiming to be able to derive from things in categories [a]–[c]. I can derive

[21]   [subject → object]

from *[20] if I can make a sufficient case for [18].

Clearly I need to say more about the notion of a strong unity. Before that, though, I should say more about what I mean by 'subject of experience'.

9.5 Subject

There are various different conceptions of what a subject of experience is. I'll consider three and focus on one. There is, first,

[C1]   the *thick* conception according to which human beings and other animals considered as a whole are subjects of experience.

Secondly, there is

[C2]   the *traditional inner* conception of the subject according to which a subject of experience properly or strictly speaking is some sort of persisting inner locus of consciousness, an inner someone, an inner mental presence.[15]

Both [C1] and [C2] build in the natural assumption that a subject of experience may and standardly does continue to exist even when it's not having any experience. For whether you think that human subjects of experience are whole human beings, or

---

[14] Note that Cartesian souls are unbeatable examples of concrete strong unities, even though they're ruled out by materialism.

[15] As a materialist I understand 'inner' literally, in a straightforwardly spatial sense.

whether you think they're inner loci of consciousness, you're likely to allow that they can continue to exist during periods of complete experiencelessness, e.g. periods of dreamless sleep.

In this respect [C1] and [C2] contrast with a third conception of the subject

[C3]   the *thin* conception of the subject according to which a subject of experience is an inner thing of some sort that exists if *and only if* experience exists of which it is the subject.

The thin conception of the subject stands opposed to both [C1] and [C2] precisely because they both assume something that [C3] rules out: the idea that a subject of experience can be said to exist in the absence of experience. As a materialist (um-ist) I take it that the goings on that wholly constitute the existence and experience of a thin subject consist entirely of activity in the brain.[16] A thin subject, I take it, is a certain sort of neural 'synergy', a neural synergy that is literally (spatiotemporally) part of the neural synergy that is an occurrence of experience—experience which is of course necessarily-subject-of-experience-involving experience.[17]

I face a problem of exposition, because most are so accustomed to [C1] and [C2], and to the idea that [C1] and [C2] exhaust the options, that they can't take [C3] seriously. And yet [C3] simply makes a place for a natural use of the term 'subject' according to which it's a necessary truth, no less, that there can't actually be a *subject of experience*, at any given time, unless some *experience* exists for it to be a *subject of*, at that time, i.e.

[22]   [subject of experience → experience]

which couples with [2] to give

[23]   [experience ↔ subject of experience].

Given the thin conception of the subject, there can no more be a subject without an experience than there can be a surface without extension. The thin conception requires that the subject be *live*, as it were, in order to exist at all. On this conception, there is no dispositional use of the expression 'subject of experience'.

I think it's very important to have the thin or live conception of the subject available and in play in metaphysics, and from now on I'm only going to consider the thin notion when arguing for the exemplary unity of the subject. If you think the thin conception of the subject or self is eccentric, bear in mind that it's endorsed by Descartes, Leibniz, Kant, Fichte, Nozick, and many others. At one point Kant writes, strikingly, that 'the thinking or the existence of the thought and the existence of my own self are one and the same' (1772: 75). Hume invokes thin subjects when characterizing the notion of the subject of experience that is philosophically legitimate given his strict empiricist principles (i.e. when expounding the 'bundle' theory of

---

[16] This claim isn't 'reductive' or experience-denying in any way, given real materialism. One might rather call it 'adductive'. It doesn't claim that experience is anything less than what we ordinarily conceive it to be, but rather that the brain is much more than what many people ordinarily conceive it to be.

[17] Elsewhere I consider the suggestion that the subject synergy is not just part of the experience synergy, but identical with it (see e.g. Strawson 2003b and §§13.2-3 below, pp. 254-5).

the self): 'when my perceptions [experiences] are remov'd for any time, as by sound sleep', he writes, 'so long am I insensible of *myself*, and may truly be said not to exist'.[18] Sprigge writes that 'each of us, as we are at any one moment, is most essentially a momentary centre of experience or state of consciousness with the duration of the specious present' (Sprigge 2006: 474).

To focus on the thin conception of the subject is not to reject the thick and traditional inner conceptions. The three conceptions can coexist. The current dominance of the thick and traditional inner conceptions does however make it important to stress that thin subjects certainly exist as defined—whatever the best view of their ultimate ontological category. They certainly exist because experience certainly exists, and to speak of a thin subject is just to speak in a certain way of a feature of reality that certainly exists given that experience exists ([2]). In fact it's to speak of a feature of reality that's an essential *part* of what it is for experience to exist. One can put the point by saying that experience necessarily involves experienc*ing* (experience just is experiencing) and the existence of a thin subject is guaranteed by the fact that there's experiencing.

I suspect that human processes of experience are as a matter of empirical fact constantly interrupted, and that thin subjects are consequently short-lived in the human case. But ephemerality isn't an essential part of their definition. To believe that experience is unbroken throughout any period of wakefulness in a normal human being is to leave room for the view that thin subjects can last at least as long as human beings can stay awake. To believe that experience never ceases in a normal human being, from the first moment of experiential quickening to its final extinction, is to leave room for the view that thin subjects can last a lifetime. If we use the word 'inner' loosely to mean something like 'not identical with/not the same thing as the human being considered as a whole', and allow it to cover immaterial souls, then a Cartesian immaterial soul qualifies as a thin subject, and we make room for the view that thin subjects can last for ever.

9.6 Object [2]

So much for the notion of a thin subject; back now to objects. I've proposed that there are no better candidates for being concrete objects than subjects, by which I now mean thin subjects. But are there any concrete objects? Is there any place for the notion of a concrete object or substance in fundamental metaphysics—in which I include physics?[19]

Some say No, e.g. proponents of radical 'structural realism' like the philosophers of science Ladyman, Ross, Spurrett and Collier in their recent book *Every Thing Must Go*. I take it that the idea is also rejected in Whitehead's 'process philosophy'. It's an old idea, at least as old as Nāgārjuna's *Fundamental Verses on the Middle Way*,

---

[18] 1739–40: 1.4.6.3/252. Contrary to widespread belief, Hume never claims that there's no subject or self at all when there's experience. The point is sufficiently established by the quotation, but it would be no less clear without it. See further Ch. 13.

[19] See also Schaffer 2010. I take 'substance' to be a general term for a fundamental existent that has no connection to its etymological meaning of 'standing under'.

written about 1800 years ago. I am nevertheless going to take it to be a truth of fundamental metaphysics that

[24]   there is at least one object

or substance, and hence that the concept of an object or substance does have legitimate application in fundamental metaphysics.

Is it also true that the concept of an object or substance has plural application in fundamental metaphysics? This is a considerably more difficult question. I'm attracted by Spinoza's 'thing-monism', his view that there is, properly speaking, only one object or substance.[20] For the purposes of argument, however, I'm going to assume that there are many. In particular, I'm going to make the 'smallist' assumption that there is a plurality of fundamental physical entities (leptons and quarks, say, or 'fields', 'loops', 'field quanta', ...) or as I will say 'ultimates'

[25]   there is a plurality of ultimates

and that they can qualify as strong unities if any things do

[26]   [ultimate → strong unity]

and that they can therefore (given [19]) qualify as objects if any things do, and in spite of the phenomena of entanglement,

[27]   [ultimate → object];

from which it follows that

[28]   there is a plurality of objects.[21]

I don't think [28] is obvious, when it comes to fundamental metaphysics, at least not if it is considered independently of the view that

[29]   there is a plurality of subjects

—which might be held to be obvious (although it too has been questioned), and which, with [20], entails [28].[22] The truth or otherwise of [28] is a serious question in

---

[20] The universe, or, in his terms, 'God or nature'. Parmenides agrees. It's arguable that Descartes holds that there is strictly speaking only one physical object or substance, even as he takes it that there is a plurality of non-physical concrete objects or substances—souls. There's also considerable support for the thing-monist view in current physics and cosmology. One recent version of thing-monism has it that spacetime itself is best thought of as a concrete object, a substance (not a mere dimensionality, as it were), and indeed as the only object there is. On this view, the fundamental entities currently recognized—leptons and quarks—are not strictly speaking fundamental and are to be 'explained as various modes of vibration of tiny one-dimensional rips in spacetime known as strings' (Weinberg 1997: 20). Particles also fail to qualify as fundamental entities in quantum field theory. Others hold that the wave function (understood in an ontological manner) is the only concrete existent. See also Horgan and Potrč 2008, Strawson 2009, Schaffer 2009.

[21] For 'smallism' see e.g. Wilson 2004, Coleman 2006.

[22] [20] depends on [18] and [19], for which some sort of case still has to be made. Note that [28] can be argued for quite independently of any theory about ultimates.

metaphysics, as indeed is the question whether there are any objects at all. I am, however, going to assume [28] for argument.

9.7 Interim Summary

I now have to do three things. I have to try to explain further what I mean by saying [17] that objects are strong unities

[17]   [object → strong unity]

and equally what I have in mind in saying that all strong unities are objects

[18]   [strong unity → object].

Then I have to show that (thin) subjects are strong unities

*[20]   [subject → strong unity].

This will allow me to conclude that all (thin) subjects are objects

[21]   [subject → object].

Might it be true not only that all (thin) subjects are objects but also that all (genuine, strong-unity) objects are subjects

[30]   [object → subject]?

With Leibniz, I suspect that [30] is also true, at least in our universe, and hence, given [20], that

[31]   [subject ↔ object]

is also true in our universe. This, though, is a form of panpsychism—something for another time. One possibility at this point is to rest the idea of an object and present the argument just in terms of the idea of a (strong) unity—an idea which is perhaps clearer than, and no doubt more fundamental than, the idea of an object. I'll continue to use 'object', but one can if one wishes read 'object' as 'strong unity', at the cost of putting up with a few tautologies ('all objects are strong unities').

9.8 Object [3]

The question is now this. What are the best candidates for being concrete objects, given that we want to retain the category *object* (or *individual substance*) in our fundamental ontology or metaphysics, and are committed to the view that there's more than one concrete object?

I'm going to take it in a conventional materialist way that every candidate for being an object is either an ultimate or is made up of some number of ultimates in a certain physical relation.[23] A physical object, then, is either a single ultimate or a plurality of

---

[23] I take it that 'virtual' ultimates (virtual particles) and 'anti-matter' ultimates (anti-matter particles) are also objects, given that there is a plurality of objects at all.

ultimates in a certain relation. Given that all single ultimates are physical objects, the remaining question is which pluralities of ultimates—if any—are physical objects? What should be our criterion?[24]

As before, the first and most certain thing to say about a physical object is that it is at least, and first and foremost, and essentially, some kind of unity or singularity. So the question is: given that ultimates themselves constitute unities of the right kind, which pluralities of ultimates do?

The phrase 'some kind of unity' is as vague as it is crucial, and some philosophers—the *subjectivists*—think that there are no metaphysical facts of the matter about which phenomena are objects and which aren't. On their view, whenever we judge something to be an object we implicitly or explicitly endorse an ultimately subjective principle of counting or individuation relative to which the phenomenon *counts as* a (single) object. I'll put this by saying that we endorse an ultimately subjective *principle of objectual unity*.

Can this be right? Many judgements of objecthood—many principles of objectual unity—are so natural for us that the idea they are in any sense subjective seems preposterous (nearly all of us think that cups, marbles, meerkats, jellyfish, fingers, houses, planets, and molecules are individual objects, and there are clear pragmatic and evolutionary reasons why this is so). The subjectivists, however, are unimpressed. It doesn't follow from the fact that some judgements of objecthood are very natural for human beings, they say, that those judgements are correct, or record metaphysical facts. If we were neutrino-sized, they say, our natural judgement about a stone might be that it was a mere collection of things, not itself a single object in any interesting sense.

It seems odd at first to think that merely subjective principles of objectual unity underlie our judgements that chairs and stones are objects, but it becomes increasingly natural as one moves away from such central cases. Although nearly everyone thinks a chair is a single object, not everyone does.[25] Although many think cities, newspapers, galaxies, and blenders (assembled from parts) can correctly be said to be single things, quite a few do not. Although some think a body of gas is an object, many do not.

At the other extreme, very few think that three spoons—one in Hong Kong, one in Athens, and one in Birmingham—constitute a single thing. But some philosophers believe that the three spoons have as good a claim to be considered an individual object as anything else: according to one form of 'universalism', any plurality of ultimates in the universe, however scattered, counts as a single object in every sense in which a table does. A lepton in your amygdala, a quark in my left hand, and the ultimates that make up the rings of Saturn jointly constitute a single object just as surely as your pen or pet duck. No plurality of ultimates has a better claim to be an object than any other.

---

[24] This is van Inwagen's 'Special Composition' question (van Inwagen 1990).

[25] van Inwagen does not, in *Material Beings*, and his reasons are of considerable interest. The same goes for Nāgārjuna (*c.*150). Richard Feynman also thinks that things like chairs are really pretty inferior candidates for being objects, when one gets metaphysically serious.

On the face of it, universalism is a wholly *objectivist* theory of objects. It endorses a principle of objectual unity that delivers a clear principle of counting. It tells you that if there are n ultimates in the universe then there are exactly (2^n-1) objects in the universe. But it also has a highly subjectivist or 'post-modern' aura. It tells you that anything goes and everybody wins, that there's no real issue about whether any particular plurality of ultimates is an object or not. It's arguable, accordingly, that genuinely objectivist positions emerge clearly only when more specific and limited principles of objectual unity are endorsed, e.g. by common sense, which rules in favour of tables and chairs and against the three spoons, or by Spinoza, who holds that there is only one thing or substance, the universe ('God or Nature'), or by van Inwagen, who argues forcefully that only individual ultimates and living beings—and not, say, tables and chairs—qualify as physical objects in fundamental metaphysics.[26]

I'm going to take it that there are at the very least various grades and types of physical unity, and that some candidates for objecthood have, objectively, a much better claim than others—given that we've committed ourselves to working with the notion of an object in our basic metaphysics. I think a human being has a better claim than your lepton + my quark + the rings of Saturn or the three spoons, given this commitment. There are vast numbers of merely 'conventional' unities or objects (to use Buddhist terminology) that are not of central concern in fundamental metaphysics, but there are also perhaps, certain irreducibly real objective unities, or objects.[27]

9.9 Fundamental Singleness

With this in place, consider the following suggestion. As one advances in genuine physicalism, or um-ism, deepening one's intuitive grasp of the idea that *experiential, mental* phenomena are physical phenomena in every sense in which non-experiential, non-mental phenomena are,[28] one of the things that becomes apparent is this: when it comes to deciding which phenomena in the universe count as objects and which do not, there are no good grounds for thinking that *non-experiential, non-mental criteria or principles of unity*—of the sort that we use to pick out a dog or a chair—are more valid than mental or experiential criteria or principles of unity. It's arguable, in fact, that there is no more indisputable unity in nature, and therefore no more indisputable physical unity or singularity, and therefore no better candidate for the title 'physical object', than the unity that we come upon when we consider the phenomenon of the (thin) subject of experience as it exists in the living moment of experience, experiencing seeing books and chairs and seeing them as such, say, or consciously comprehending the thought that water is wet—an event that necessarily involves the concretely occurring thought-elements WATER and WET forming a true unity of some sort, a unity without which the thought *water is wet* can't be said to

---

[26] For van Inwagen, as for Aristotle (see e.g. *Metaphysics* Z 7.1032a19, 8.1034a4), animals are the paradigm substances. I am not sure what they would make of the fact that 90 per cent of the cells in one's body are microbial cells.

[27] For further discussion see e.g. van Inwagen 1990.

[28] Assuming that there are any non-experiential phenomena (it's a fundamental feature of real materialism that 'physical' doesn't entail 'non-experiential').

have occurred at all.[29] I can think of no better candidates in concrete reality for what I'm calling 'strong' unity, unity that is not only [17] necessary for genuine objecthood (if there is such a thing) but also—I am going to propose—[19] sufficient. As far as I can see, the only serious (and mutually excluding) competitors for equal first place are

(a)   the universe,

to be identified, perhaps, with spacetime (or the wave function ontologically understood) considered as a substance, and, lagging somewhat behind,

(b)   individual ultimates

—if indeed there are any. Between these two extremes, and given the absolute centrality of unity or singularity considerations when it comes to determining objecthood, it's arguable that subjects of experience as just characterized are the best qualified plurality-of-ultimates-involving candidates there are for the status of physical objects.

The idea, then, is to show that subjects are strong unities and therefore objects. The subjects I have in mind are 'thin' subjects as they exist in the living moment of experience. Some may think that thin subjects in the living moment of experience are intolerably odd candidates for being objects. The strength of their candidacy follows from the idea that strong-unity considerations are paramount when it comes to establishing claims to objecthood in fundamental metaphysics. 'No entity without identity', as Quine used to say: no object without 'identity conditions', 'criteria of identity'; and no concrete object, presumably, or at least no spatiotemporal object, without synchronic and diachronic identity conditions. In the synchronic case, one needs to be able to draw a line round the object—here a thin subject—in thought in such a way as to be able to say, at a given moment t_1, 'Here's one thin subject, and here's another'. In the diachronic case, considering thin subjects as things that may last longer than the living moment of experience, and restricting our attention to single brains for simplicity, we presumably need to be able to draw a line round them in such a way as to be able to say 'This is one thin subject, existing from time t_1 to time t_2, and this, now, is another different one, existing from t_2 to t_3, or from t_3 to t_4.'

I say 'presumably' because I'm not sure that we do have to be able to give an account of the diachronic identity conditions of something, even in principle, in order to have reason to say that that something is an object or substance (always assuming that we want to retain the categories of object and substance in our metaphysics). I'm not sure what I would say to someone who insisted that I could no longer claim to be dealing with the notions of object and substance at all, in abandoning the requirement of specifiable diachronic-identity conditions, but I'm going to put this question aside and restrict attention to the synchronic case.[30]

---

[29] There's no implication here that the subject of experience is or must be thought of as an agent that brings about the binding or seizing; see §9.1 above.

[30] See Strawson 2009: 403. Note that to claim that there are no better candidates for the title 'physical object' than the unities we come upon when we consider subjects of experience in the living moment of experience isn't to claim that we come upon living-moment-of-experience-sized objects. If time is dense

Consider, then, an experiencing subject at a given moment. Consider the totality of its experience at that moment, its 'total experiential field', the total content[31] of its experiential field at a given moment. Ask whether it could fail to be experientially single or unified in being what it is.

To ask the question is to see the fundamental sense in which the answer is No. The total experiential field involves many things—rich interoceptive (somatosensory) and exteroceptive sensation, mood-and-affect-tone, deep conceptual animation, and so on. It has, standardly, a particular focus, and more or less dim peripheral areas, and it is, overall, extraordinarily complex in content. But it is for all that a unity, and essentially so. It is fundamentally unified, utterly indivisible, as the particular concrete phenomenon it is, simply in being, indeed, a total experiential field; or, equivalently, simply in being *the* content of the experience of a single subject at that moment.[32] The unity or singleness of the (thin) subject of the total experiential field in the living moment of experience and the unity or singleness of the total experiential field are aspects of the same thing. They're necessarily dependent on each other even if they aren't the same thing.

I think, in fact, that there's only a conceptual distinction between them, not a real distinction, in Descartes's sense. For neither can conceivably exist without the other. In which case there's no dependence relation of a sort that requires two really (really) distinct entities.

The present point, however, is independent of any dramatic metaphysical claim about the ultimate metaphysical identity of the unity of the (thin-subject) experiencer and the unity of the experiential field (the experiential content, the experience). It's simply the point—the simple point—that *a* field, a single field, entails *a* subject, a single subject, and conversely. If you bring a single thin subject into existence at t_1, then you necessarily bring a single, unified experiential field into existence at t_1, and conversely. The singleness of the (thin) subject at t_1 entails, and is essentially constitutive of, the singleness of its total experiential field at t_1. So too, the singleness

and periods of experience are continuous, then living moments of experience are theoretical abstractions from a continuum, not genuinely discrete entities. In this case the qualifying phrase 'considered in the living moment of experience' doesn't chop the subject at the boundaries of the living moment of experience (which don't exist) to deliver a distinct living-moment-of-experience-sized object. (The objects in question must be theoretical abstractions if time is dense, because although they're countable in the mathematical sense—countably infinite—and although 'countable' suggests 'discrete', no concrete infinity of things can exist in any finite period of time. To think that there could be a concrete infinity in a finite period of time is, in effect, to think that a concrete infinity is or could be finite.) It's an empirical question how long thin subjects last, and there's no good reason to suppose that the analytical cut that thought makes in considering the subject in the living moment of experience corresponds to a real division in nature. Questions about the temporal extent of objects must in other words be a matter of natural fact, and can't depend on what we can intelligibly isolate as objects of thought. If time is real but is not a continuum, consisting of discrete 'chronons', as some suspect, then living moments of experience may be chronon-sized, and there are other ways in which things could turn out to be relatively straightforward—if, for example, experience-constituting activity in the brain comes in discrete pulses, 40 a second, say. (I can't see that the 'temporal parts' of the analytic metaphysicians are of any interest in this connection.)

[31] Content is understood in an internalist way, or phenomenologically, as before.

[32] There's no need to rule out the possibility that there can be more than one total experiential field in a human being at a given time. If there can, the present point about necessary singleness will apply to each one individually (Strawson 2009: §§2.19–2.20).

of the total experiential field at t_1 entails the singleness of its subject at t_1.[33] For the material that is experienced is necessarily experienced in a single or unified experiential perspective.[34] The point is a 'logical' one, as 'trivial' as it is important.

I'll call it *Fundamental Singleness*. It applies to all necessarily-subject-of-experience-involving experiential-field unities, whatever their duration, and to all possible subjects of experience, however primitive. To this extent it's independent of Kant's much higher-level claim that when we consider ourselves as subjects we must necessarily apprehend ourselves as single; his claim (in the Paralogisms section of the *Critique of Pure Reason*, which I'll call 'the Paralogisms') that 'the proposition *I am simple* [i.e. single] must be regarded as a direct expression of apperception'.[35] For one thing, his claim is about expressly self-conscious creatures like ourselves, whereas the present Fundamental Singleness claim doesn't depend on the subject's having any sort of express experience of itself as subject, let alone any such experience of itself as single considered specifically as subject. If worms have experience, their experience has Fundamental Singleness, at any given time, and not just by being very simple. So does the chaotic experience of schizophrenics, considered at any given moment.

There's another respect in which Fundamental Singleness is more basic than the claims about unity for which Kant is famous. What is in question is a necessary unity of experience or experiential field that we can know to exist before we've had any distinctively Kantian thoughts about the 'necessary unity of consciousness' or 'necessary synthesis of the manifold'.[36] It is, in other words, a necessary unity of experience that we can know to exist before we come to any aspect of the unity of experience that we can know to exist because it's a necessary condition of the possibility of other relatively complicated things that we know to exist—e.g. articulated thoughts like *grass is green*; or experiences that involve 'co-consciousness' in being at once and indissolubly both visual and olfactory and auditory; or what Kant calls 'experience', by which he means what some now call 'objective experience', i.e. experience that has, for the experiencer, the character of being experience of a world of objects existing independently of the experiencer. What is in question is a still more basic necessary unity of experience or experiential field we know to exist not by running any kind of

---

[33] The former is also arguably essentially constitutive of the latter—in which case the asymmetry of the 'X constitutes Y' relation lapses, and simple identity is indicated—but I won't press the point. Elsewhere (Strawson 2009: 410) I consider the idea that the experiential content *c* of the experience of the subject *s* is related to *s* 'in such a way that its being is at least partly constitutive of the being of *s*. On this view *c* is, as it were, the body or flesh of *s*, without which *s*... cannot exist and is nothing. *s*, we feel, cannot simply be the same as *c*, but *s* is nothing without *c*—not just utterly empty, but non-existent.'

[34] Anything that is experientially there in any sense at all is automatically part of the unity—just as any paint intentionally added to a painting by the painter is automatically part of the picture.

[35] *Critique of Pure Reason* 1781–7: A355 (henceforth *Critique*). If one moves to a notion of apperception (i.e. an entity's awareness of its own mental being) that allows apperception to entities that lack anything like full or express self-consciousness, then the two claims may—perhaps—come together again; but even then there is a natural way of taking the notion of apperception given which the present point holds completely independently of any questions about apperception.

[36] '...the necessary unity of consciousness, and therefore also of the synthesis of the manifold' (*Critique* A109; this is the only occurrence in the *Critique* of the phrase 'necessary unity of consciousness').

transcendental argument of this kind but simply by considering what it is for a subject to be having any experience at all—by considering what it is for there to be an experiential point of view at all.[37]

I think, then, that the Fundamental Singleness point is secure, and it gives me the strong unities I need. But I'm now going to call Kant in support.[38]

9.10 Kant on Fundamental Singleness

In the 'Transcendental Deduction' and 'Paralogisms' sections of the *Critique of Pure Reason* Kant discusses experiential unities that are the thinking of thoughts in the narrower, cognitive, non-Cartesian sense, particular events of proposition-comprehension, e.g. judgements. We can, I propose, discern—or at least extract—the following unity argument.[39] We know, to begin, that

(1)   particular thoughts exist.

We also know that

(2)   such thoughts must have distinguishable elements, or at least a certain complexity, in order to be genuine thoughts at all, discursively articulated thoughts like grass is green.

We also know that

(3)   these distinguishable elements, or this complexity, must form a unity, the (mental) unity that is the phenomenon of the comprehension of the proposition by a subject, if there is to be a genuine thought at all.

On the present materialist (um-ist) view

(4)   such unities are wholly physical unities, in being mental unities, although they may not present as intuitively unitary entities when non-experientially considered (e.g. when examined by neurologists).[40]

We know, then, that there are actually existing physical entities that concretely realize a certain sort of unity. This (interim) conclusion is not very exciting, because the same can be said of cars or bananas.[41] The further point is that the concrete unity in question is a unity of an extremely strong sort. It's the 'logical unity of every thought' (A398). Cars and bananas can lose car parts or banana parts and retain their identity as the cars or bananas they are, so long as we're reasonably relaxed about the identity

---

[37] Note that I take it as given that things just are a certain way for one, experientially, at any given moment of experience, and that it is entirely determinate how they are, even if—even though—we cannot specify in exhaustive detail how they are (see Strawson 2008: 77–8).

[38] See also William James (1890: 276–8, 371), who argues for the 'indecomposable unity of every pulse of thought'.

[39] The main argument occurs in Kant's Transcendental Analytic in his *Critique of Pure Reason*, but can be easily integrated with his discussion of the 'I' or self in the Paralogisms section of the Transcendental Dialectic in the *Critique*, and I move freely between the two.

[40] See Kant *Critique* A355.   [41] As Darragh Byrne pointed out in discussion.

conditions of things. A thought, by contrast, can't lose any thought-part and retain its identity as the particular thought it is. The same goes for a total experiential field. Every part is as essential as every other part just in being, indeed, a part. They are indivisible (and in that sense simple) unities.

If we accept this, we can infer that

(5)   there are actually existing physical entities—thoughts—that concretely realize a certain sort of very strong, 'logical' unity.

What is this unity? It's the unity specified in (3), nothing more; the unity that must exist if a thought is to occur at all. It is, on the one hand, a very ordinary everyday thing, but it is also, on the other hand, something completely exceptional, because it's an absolute, concretely existing unity.

There's a further reason why it's exceptional. If we ask generally what logical or absolute unity or indivisibility might be, a first thought is that it involves perfect simplicity. On this view, if something is an absolute unity, then

[U] it has no true description that furnishes any sense in which it can be said to involve complexity, or parts.

The proposed absolute or logical unity of a thought such as *grass is green* is not like this, however, for

[¬U] it has a true fundamental description that displays it to have a certain sort of complexity

(the same goes, presumably, for almost any total experiential field). If this is right, then even if [U] is sufficient for absolute unity or indivisibility, it isn't necessary. One might call absolute unities/indivisibilities which fail to satisfy [U] 'complex absolute unities', and one might then wonder whether there can be such things. I am at present supposing that there are many of them, however mysterious they may seem considered under this description, but one might also suppose that there's only one—the universe. This, though, raises the question of the one and the many, which I don't want to consider. (The best answer to the question, perhaps, given discursive thought's limited capacity to represent the nature of reality, is that it is true that there is only one thing and true that there are many things.)

The heart of Kant's notion of logical unity is in any case simple. It's the Fundamental Singleness point, adjusted to the particular case of thought. If a thought is had, if a proposition is genuinely entertained, then it's necessarily had or entertained by a single subject. In Kant's words,

(6)   the 'logical unity of every thought' is inseparable from the 'absolute...logical unity of the subject' of the thought (A356).

And it's not only true that concretely occurring thoughts realize a certain sort of unsurpassable concrete unity. It's equally true that

(7)   the (thin) subjects of thoughts—concretely realize a certain sort of 'absolute... logical' unity.

As Kant observes:

that ... the I in every act of thought is *one*, and cannot be resolved into a plurality of subjects, ... is something that lies already in the concept of thought, and is therefore an analytic proposition. (B407)

I think these two unities are in fact and at bottom the same unity, and take it, again, that Kant agrees, in a passage already quoted, when he says that 'the thinking or the existence of the thought and the existence of my own self are one and the same'. But this is a further, difficult idea. For the moment we may take it that when we have to do with these actual concrete logical or absolute unities we have to do with unities of an absolute or unsurpassable sort, unities that must count as strong unities on any account of what strong unity is.

So in knowing that such thoughts really, concretely exist, as I take it we do, and in knowing that any thought must have a certain sort of absolute unity if it is to exist at all (even though there's also a respect in which it must involve difference and complexity), we know—to put it in terms that may seem provocative to some Kantians, but shouldn't seem so to Kant, so long as he grants that thoughts really concretely exist—that there exist entities that are genuine, *concrete, metaphysical* unities or indivisibilities of an unsurpassable sort. (Obviously one needs to drop 'physical' and use 'concrete' in order to state the point in a way Kant can accept.)

The same degree of unity exists in the case of multimodally complex sensory experiences, and a parallel argument can be constructed for the necessary singleness of the subject of any such experience.[42] The same degree of unity also exists in the case of experiences that are absolutely simple in content, of course—if such experiences, sensory or otherwise, are possible.[43] The only difference is that in this case, as opposed to the case of a (necessarily complex) thought, we lack the vivid illustration of the force of the unity that derives from the respect in which there is absolute unity in spite of complexity.[44]

Here, then, or so I propose, we move validly (i.e. without paralogism) from a 'logical' or 'logico-phenomenological' point to a substantive metaphysical conclusion. There may be neurological or cognitive-science accounts of what's going on that find astonishing complexity in these cases, many disparate and discrete events. None of this matters as long as there's a genuine, concrete *experiential* unity—i.e. the having of a thought, the actual occurrence of a thought. For, crucially, this unity is itself a concretely existing metaphysical unity or indivisibility of an unsurpassable sort, the unity of the concrete event of the genuine entertaining of a thought.

---

[42] Kant's intellectualism may suffice to explain any privileging of thoughts over sensory experiences, but it's also important (a) that he regularly uses 'thought' in the wide Cartesian sense to mean 'experience' and (b) that he explicitly allows for the possibility that there could be thought without sensory experience, i.e. 'intellectual intuition'.

[43] We might allow a sense in which a pure note is simple although it involves pitch, timbre, and loudness, and there seems no reason in principle why a sensory state-space could not be strictly one-dimensional.

[44] There are cases in which it's natural to say that someone has had or has entertained a thought, but in which what we mean by 'a thought' is such that having or entertaining it involves more than one unity of the sort I have in mind at present.

The phrase 'experiential unity' mustn't be misunderstood. There is as already remarked no requirement that the subject have any express experience of itself or its thought as a unity. The requirement is only that it have a genuine thought—that a genuine thought occur. This is the experiential unity in question, which is itself an unsurpassable, concrete metaphysical unity. And in fact any experience will do.

It may be granted that Kant is committed to the existence of thoughts and judgements, by his moral views if by nothing else, but objected that he can't and won't claim to know that these existent thoughts are metaphysically unsurpassable unities, if only on the grounds that they have an irreducibly temporal character, so far as we know anything about them, and so can't be known by us as they are in themselves, but only insofar as they appear to us. Against this we may bring Kant's own claim that they—and their subjects—involve 'absolute' unity. I think that Kant would—must—on this ground be prepared to agree that they're unsurpassable unities that we can know to exist and to be such. My present aim, though, is to make a proposal, not to attempt detailed Kantian exegesis.

—I really don't think you can expect Kant's blessing. What about the passage in which Kant speaks of the 'merely logical qualitative unity of self-consciousness in thought in general, which has to be present whether the subject be composite or not' (B413)? His point here is precisely that there may be no real substantial metaphysical unity at all although there may be and indeed must be this 'qualitative unity'.[45]

Kant has a very specific ad hominem purpose in the Paralogisms. His aim is to stop the [simple/single → indivisible → immaterial → incorruptible → immortal] chain of metaphysical argument that was popular in his time.[46] In this traditional sense of 'metaphysical' Kant's claim is indeed, quite unequivocally, that we have no good grounds for believing that there's a real metaphysical singularity or simplicity or unity. This is his correct objection to the use that the Cartesian 'rational psychologists' aimed to make of Fundamental Singleness (it's not original to him). The present proposal, though, is that there's another wider sense of 'metaphysical' that Kant not only can but seemingly must allow, which yields a real, known metaphysical unity after all,[47] and doesn't disrupt his argument against the rational psychologists. In this way we legitimize the Second Paralogism argument by removing the equivocation on the word 'subject' that renders it paralogistic: the subject that is knowably single is also knowably a metaphysically real concretely existing entity.

The proposal depends as before simply on the claim that Kant agrees that thoughts—experiences, judgements—really, concretely exist (I avoid the explicitly

---

[45] Compare, also, the use of 'qualitative' in the Transcendental Deduction, *Critique* B114.

[46] 'Everyone must admit that the assertion of the simple nature of the soul is of value only insofar as I can thereby distinguish this subject from all matter, and so can exempt it from the dissolution to which matter is always liable. This is indeed, strictly speaking, the only use for which the above proposition is intended' (*Critique* A356; my emphasis). There is a respect in which we may 'allow full objective validity' to the 'proposition... everything which thinks is a simple substance' (A357), but 'we still cannot make the least use of this proposition in regard to the question of [the mind or soul's] dissimilarity from or relation to matter' in such a way as to hope to establish immateriality and thence incorruptibility and immortality.

[47] It's known that it exists, and that it's a unity, whatever the sense in which its nature remains unknown.

temporal word 'occur'); that they are indeed metaphysically real. It goes from there to the point that he must then agree that the unity that their existence essentially involves must truly exist and be real, a genuine metaphysical unity of some sort, although it licenses absolutely no conclusions about immortality and so forth.

9.11 Two Objections

It may be objected that the unities in question (unity of subject, unity of thought or experience) are 'merely functional' unities, but it's not clear what this 'merely' means, when applied to concretely actualized entities (a concretely existing total experiential field and a concretely existing subject for whom that field is an experiential field). In particular, it's not clear that it detracts in any way from these unities' claim to be true metaphysical unities. Even if we can find a sense in which they're 'merely' functional unities, this won't touch the fact that they're concretely existing unities, genuine metaphysical unities. And by the time we've revised and processualized the notions of object and substance in the way we have to if they're to retain any place in fundamental metaphysics, and stripped them of their claim to stand in fundamental ontological contrast with attributes or properties (see e.g. Strawson 2009: 304–17), we'll be in no position to hold on to any view that has the consequence that these unsurpassable thought unities or experience unities, these thinker unities and experiencer unities, have less claim to be objects or substances than paradigmatic examples of ultimates (or indeed good old fashioned immaterial minds).

We may as materialists suppose that the existence of these unsurpassable mental unities involves the existence of a large number of neurons (and a fortiori ultimates) acting in concert. In this case we may say that it essentially involves a plurality of 'different substances acting together', to use Kant's general formulation in his discussion of the Second Paralogism (A353). Kant is right that we can't ground any claims about the non-materiality and hence possible simplicity or indivisibility and hence incorruptibility and hence immortality of the soul on the knowable existence of these 'absolute' concrete unities of subject and experiential field.[48] This, again, is the line of thought he demolishes in his discussion of the Paralogisms. This demolition is, however, wholly compatible with, and, crucially, derives its principal force from, the fact that we can know that these fundamental and unsurpassable unities exist. We can know they exist even though they're of no use in establishing the existence of a persisting immaterial subject. It's Kant himself, as remarked, who makes it most vivid that the fact that 'the I in every act of thought is one...lies already in the very concept of thought'. He's prepared to *'allow full objective validity'* to the *'proposition... everything which thinks is a simple substance'*, at least for the sake of argument, for his point is that even if we do this 'we still cannot make *the least use* of this proposition in regard to the question of [the mind or soul's] dissimilarity from or relation to matter' in such a way as to hope to establish immateriality and thence incorruptibility and immortality (A357; my emphasis).

---

[48] Kant does take his arguments in the Paralogisms to show that materialists can't give an adequate explanation of the existence of the subject, given its 'logical' simplicity property. But the immaterialists or 'rationalists' are no better off. See e.g. *Critique* B417–18n., 419–20.

We can know the necessary singleness or simplicity of the subject of experience in the having of experience, but to know this is not to have 'knowledge of the simple nature of the self as subject, such as might enable us to distinguish it from matter, as from a composite being' (A360). So much for the 'merely functional unity' objection.

It may now be objected that Fundamental Singleness is a 'merely experiential unity' and so not a real metaphysical unity. In one version, the objection is that the claim that the total experiential field of an experience is itself something that is a true metaphysical unity is unwarranted, because this unity is really only an appearance—because it's only from a certain point of view that the total experiential field presents as unified. In a second version the objection is aimed directly at the (thin) subject of the experience, the objection being that the unsurpassable unity of thin subject, too, is, somehow, 'merely experiential' or 'subjective', and so not ultimately real.

There's a lot to say to this, but the basic reply is simple: what's 'merely' about this unity? It's true that the unity of the total experiential field of an experience is essentially, and if you like 'merely', an *internal experiential* or *IE* unity, whatever else it is or isn't. It's true that it's a unity considered just in respect of its internal experiential character, a unity considered from the point of view of its subject, a unity that is in fact constituted as such by the existence of the point of view of its subject (however unreflective the subject is, however little explicit apprehension it has of the fact that the unity in question is a unity). It's true that there is a crucial sense in which its fundamental-unity characteristic is wholly a matter of its experiential being (when we consider the existence of the experience non-experientially, and from the smallist point of view, we find millions of ultimates in a certain complex state of interaction). All this is true. But it's no less true that it's an objective, ground-floor metaphysical fact that subjective experience exists and that it has the character it does. That is: the experiential fact that one of these IE unities exists is itself an objective, ground-floor metaphysical fact, a fact about the world. It's a fact that stands as a fact from a perspective external to the perspective internal to the IE unity.

The reason why we're right to judge an IE unity to be a fully metaphysically real unity when considering it *externally*, from the outside, objective point of view, is indeed nothing other than the fact that it is indeed a strong *internal* experiential unity. But there's nothing odd about the sense in which subjective phenomena can be objective facts. This is part of any minimally sensible realism about the subjective. All that's added here is the slightly more specific point that the existence of an IE unity that consists of the experiencing of a total experiential field by an experiencing subject at a given moment is itself an objectively existing real unity (experience is real!), both in its single-subject aspect and in its single total-experiential-field aspect (which may at bottom be the same thing). The statement that this unity exists and is wholly metaphysically real holds true outside the perspective of the subject in question, although the unity in question consists wholly of the phenomenon of the existence of that subject having that experience, with the content that it has, at the time in question. The qualification one then (again) needs to enter is that there need be no distinctive experience of unity on the part of the subject of the IE unity, inasmuch as the necessary unity in question is simply the fact already mentioned: the trivial fact that any subject necessarily experiences all the material it experiences at any given time in a single experiential perspective. (Some Phenomenologists may hold that there must in every case, however lowly, be some sort of experience of unity experienced as such. I think I can agree to this, in any sense in which it is true, without disturbing the point of this qualification.)

9.12 Conclusion

One can dispute all sorts of details, but the Fundamental Singleness point and Kantian points remain secure. The unity of the thin subject and the experiential unity of its experience are two aspects of the same unity. There is, as remarked at the beginning, no explanatory relation between them. The unity in question is by hypothesis a concrete unity, and I've argued that it is an exemplary strong unity, an unsurpassable example of a unity:

[20]   [subject → strong unity].

Given, then, that strong unity is the fundamental—and sufficient—criterion of objecthood, i.e.

[18]   [strong unity → object],

it follows that

[21]   [subject → object]

—that concretely existing subjects of experience, which we know to exist, are objects in the fullest metaphysical sense. More moderately, I've argued that there are no better candidates in nature for the title 'strong unity'—at least until we give up the struggle to maintain that there is a plurality of objects, and revert to the lovely Spinozan position that there is only one, 'Nature', i.e. the Universe. If there are any objects at all, then subjects are objects. In fact they're the best examples of strong unities that we have. Any metaphysics that has trouble with this point needs an overhaul.

10

Radical Self-awareness

10.1 Experience

I want to consider the claim that the subject cannot in the present moment of awareness take itself as it is in the present moment of awareness as the object of its awareness—where by 'awareness' I always mean 'conscious awareness'. In the first two sections I'll set out some assumptions.[1]

First, I assume that physicalism is true. By 'physicalism' I mean *realistic* physicalism, which I call 'real physicalism'. Real physicalism is wholly realist about the *experiential qualitative character* or *experiential what-it's-likeness* of our conscious mental goings on, and accordingly takes this to be a wholly physical phenomenon (I'll call this experiential qualitative character 'experience', for short). When real physicalists say that experience—colour-experience, pain-experience—is wholly physical, they're not saying that it's somehow less than we know it to be in having it. That wouldn't be real physicalism, realistic physicalism, because it would involve the denial of something that obviously exists. Rather, they're saying that 'the physical' must be something more than it's ordinarily supposed to be, given that it's ordinarily supposed to be something entirely non-experiential. It must be something more than it's ordinarily supposed to be because experience (what-it's-likeness considered specifically as such) is itself wholly physical.

Experience is necessarily experience-*for*—experience for someone or something. I intend this claim only in the sense in which it's necessarily true, without commitment to any particular account of the metaphysical nature of the someone-or-something. To claim that experience is necessarily experience-for, necessarily experience-for-someone-or-something, is to claim that it's necessarily experience on the part of a subject of experience. Again I intend this only in the sense in which it's a necessary truth, and certainly without any commitment to the idea that subjects of experience are persisting things.

Some say one can't infer the existence of a subject of experience from the existence of experience, only the existence of subjectivity. But I understand the notion of the subject in a maximally ontologically non-committal way—in such a way that the presence of subjectivity is already sufficient for the presence of a subject, so that 'there is subjectivity, but there isn't a subject' can't possibly be true (compare §9.2).

Consider pain, a regrettably familiar case of experience. It is, essentially, a feeling, and a feeling is just that, a *feeling*, i.e. a feel-*ing*, a being-felt; and a feel-*ing*

---

[1] §§10.5–8 of this paper develop ideas in §§3.10 above and Strawson 2009: 176–81.

or being-felt can't possibly exist without there being a feel-*er*. Again I'm only interested in the sense in which this is a necessary truth. The noun 'feeler' doesn't import any metaphysical commitment additional to the noun 'feeling'. It simply draws one's attention to the full import of 'feeling'. The sense in which it's necessarily true that there's a feeling and hence a feeler of pain if there is pain is the sense in which it's necessarily true that there's a subject of experience if there is experience and, hence, subjectivity. These truths are available prior to any particular metaphysics of object or property or substance or accident or process or event or state. Descartes is very clear about this in his *Second Meditation*.

Some like to claim that there can be subjectivity or experience without a subject. That's why it's important to bring out the full import of the notion of subjectivity or experience by stressing the fundamental sense in which it can't exist without a subject. But there's a no less important point in the other direction. If (as I claim) all you need to know, in order to know that there is a subject, is that there is subjectivity or experience, then you can't build more into the notion of a subject than you can know to exist if subjectivity or experience exists.

I think, in fact, that the whole object/property distinction is metaphysically superficial, in the sense that there is at bottom no 'real distinction', in something like Descartes's sense, between the being of an object, considered at a given time, and the being of that object's propertiedness, i.e. its whole actual concrete qualitative being at that time, i.e. everything in which its being the particular way it is at that time consists. But that is a difficult issue for another time.[2]

10.2 The Thin Subject

I am going to take this unchallengeable, ontologically non-committal notion of the subject of experience in a minimal or 'thin' way. By 'subject', then, I don't mean the whole organism (the whole human being, in our case). I mean the subject considered specifically as something 'inner', something mental, the 'self', if you like, the inner 'locus' of consciousness considered just as such.

One relatively minimal way to think of this inner subject or self is as some complex persisting neural structure or process.[3] One could conceivably survive as such a subject if all that was left of one was one's head (or even something less). Another still more minimal way to think of it is this. Consider the neural activity that is the existence of your current experience right now. Imagine that this neural activity somehow exists on its own—nothing else exists. In this case a subject of experience exists. It must exist, because experience exists. This last claim is not the epistemological claim that we can know that a subject exists because we know that experience exists, although this is true. It's the metaphysical claim that whatever constitutes the existence of your experience must already suffice to constitute the existence of a

---

[2] I take this view—that an object is identical to its instantiation of its properties—to be distinct from the traditional 'bundle view' of objects; see e.g. Strawson 2008c, and references there to Descartes, Nietzsche, Ramsey, and others.

[3] Or else, perhaps, as a subject in Dainton's sense, 'a collection of experiential powers', a subject-constituting 'C-system' (Dainton 2008: 252).

subject of experience. Otherwise it couldn't suffice to constitute the existence of your experience, which it does by hypothesis.

The conception of the subject as a persisting neural structure or process is probably the most common physicalist conception of the inner subject, but I prefer the more minimal 'thin' conception of the subject. There's no incompatibility between these two conceptions. They're just two possible ways of thinking of parts of reality that can be truly said to constitute or contain a subject of experience (a third way of doing this is to think of a subject of experience as a whole animal). According to the thin conception the presence of experience is not only sufficient for the existence of the subject but also necessary: no experience, no subject of experience. So there's a new subject of experience every time there's a break in experience, and there's no subject of experience when one is dreamlessly asleep. We already have it as a necessary truth that

[existence of experience → existence of subject of experience].

Now we add the converse

[existence of subject of experience → existence of experience].

This is the thin subject. According to the present proposal, this isn't just a way of isolating an aspect of the subject, where the subject proper must be supposed to be the whole human being, or a persisting neural structure, or some such. Rather, when we consider the subject as defined by the thin conception of the subject we have to do with something that is, whatever its metaphysical category, at least as good or solid a candidate for qualifying as an entity, a thing, an object (even a substance, if you like) as the whole human being, or a persisting brain structure.

This is not to say that reality contains anything that actually makes the grade as a thing or object or substance. The Buddhist doctrine of 'dependent origination' suggests that in the final analysis nothing makes the grade. An alternative view is that only one thing does—the universe. On this view, Parmenides and a number of leading present-day cosmologists are right. There's really only one A-Grade thing or object or substance—the universe. (Nietzsche and Spinoza agree that nothing smaller will do.)

That's one important view. The present claim is neutral on this issue. It's simply the claim that thin subjects are as good, as candidates for 'thinghood', as anything else. In fact I think they're better candidates than a persisting brain structure, or any ordinary physical object, and indeed any supposed fundamental particle, but I won't pursue this idea here.[4] I mention it to try to counter the natural thought that thin subjects are somehow not real things or entities, and are in this respect ontologically worse off than persisting brain-structures, for example. This view isn't sustainable, when metaphysics gets serious, and stops spending its time pursuing the project of trying to square ordinary language and ordinary thought categories with reality.[5]

---

[4] I support it in Strawson 2009: 294–320, 379–88.
[5] All debates about the relation between a statue and the lump of clay (for example) are projects of this kind.

That said, most of the claims I'm going to make will apply to the persisting-brain-structure subject as well as to the thin subject. The difference between these two conceptions of the inner subject isn't really at issue when it comes to the main present aim, which is to consider the ancient claim that the subject can't in the present moment of awareness take itself as it is in the present moment of awareness as the object of its awareness. The thin subject is my favourite candidate for the title 'self', if we're going to talk of selves at all, but I'm open to thinking of the self as a persisting brain system of some sort, and this issue—the issue between those who agree with me about this and those who feel that any candidate for the title 'self' must be something more enduring—can be put aside for the purposes of this paper.

I'm going to use various numbers and letters to set things out, and apologize to those who don't like this sort of thing. I hope that my approach to the issues I discuss may contrast helpfully with some Indian approaches.[6]

10.3 Present-moment Self-awareness

Some claim that the subject can no more take itself as the object of its awareness than the eye can see itself, or, putting aside the word 'taking', that

(i) the subject can no more be the object of its awareness than the eye can see itself.

Some make the more restricted claim that the subject cannot in the present moment of awareness take itself as it is in the present moment of awareness as the object of its awareness; or, putting aside 'taking' again,

(ii) the subject in the present moment of awareness cannot be the object of its awareness in the present moment of awareness,

and is in this sense, in Ryle's memorable phrase, forever and 'systematically elusive' to itself (1949: 186).

(i) and (ii) express an ancient view, as already remarked. I think it's mistaken in both forms. A quick if unimportant point against (i) is that subjects that persist for appreciable periods of time can have themselves as object of awareness, in the fullest sense, when they remember themselves experiencing something yesterday, or a moment ago. Against that, it may be said that it's part of the meaning of the word 'aware', used as it is here to denote a state of conscious experience, that 'awareness of x' can refer only to apprehension of x as it is in the present moment, *modulo* whatever time lapse is integral to the mode of awareness in question (visual, auditory, inner self-awareness).

However this may be, I'm going to concentrate on (ii), the case of present-moment awareness, and argue that there are two distinct ways in which

---

[6] Approaches of the sort canvassed in the book in which this paper originally appeared (*Self, No Self: Perspectives from Analytical, Phenomenological, and Indian Traditions*, edited by Siderits, Thompson, and Zahavi, 2010).

[1]   the subject of awareness can be aware of itself as it is in the present moment of awareness.

First, less controversially, and in line with Phenomenological orthodoxy, I'll argue that the subject can be present-moment aware of itself in a *non-thetic* way, where to be aware of something *x* in a non-thetic way is to be aware of *x* although one isn't specifically attending to *x*. Secondly, less familiarly, I'll argue that subjects of experience can also (if exceptionally) be present-moment-aware of themselves in a *thetic* or attentive way.[7] I take this second claim to be a direct challenge to the ancient view, which seems to rely on the idea that the reason why the subject can never truly grasp itself as it is in the present moment of awareness is that it must in so doing take (have) itself as a thetic object of thought in some way that means that the thing that it is taking (that it has) as object can't really be the very same thing that is doing the taking, i.e. itself as it is in the present moment of awareness.

I'm going to use 'present-moment' rather than 'immediate', at least for now, because 'immediate' also carries the non-temporal sense 'not mediated'. Temporal immediacy may imply non-mediatedness, but I want to leave this question open.

I'll begin by considering a popular source of support for the non-thetic case which licenses a much stronger claim than [1]. On this view

[2]   the subject of awareness is *always* aware of itself as it is in the present moment of awareness

whenever it's aware in any way at all.[8] We can rephrase this as

[2]   Present-Moment Self-awareness is Universal

and rephrase its weaker sibling as

[1]   Present-Moment Self-awareness is Possible.

Taking 'self-awareness^{PM}' to stand for 'present-moment self-awareness', we can call [2] the Universal Self-Awareness^{PM} thesis, *Universal Self-Awareness^{PM}* for short, and we can call [1] the Possible Self-Awareness thesis, *Possible Self-Awareness^{PM}* for short.

According to [2], it isn't possible for a subject to be aware of anything without being present-moment-aware of itself. This is true of every subject of awareness, however lowly. If sea snails have any sort of awareness, then they're necessarily aware of themselves in the present moment of awareness. I take [2] to be endorsed by many in the Phenomenological tradition. Husserl, for example, writes that 'to be a subject is to be in the mode of being aware of oneself' (Husserl 1921–8: 151; see also Zahavi 2006).

As it stands, the ancient view rejects both [1] and [2], both Possible Self-Awareness^{PM} and Universal Self-Awareness^{PM}, in both their non-thetic and thetic

---

[7] I use 'thetic' in the Sartrean way to mean simply 'in the focus of attention' rather than in the Husserlian way, insofar as the latter implies belief.

[8] The thin notion of the subject makes the words 'whenever it's aware in any way at all' redundant; but the thin notion is of course at odds with the standard dispositional use of 'subject of awareness', which allows that a subject of awareness (whole human being, persisting brain structure, whatever) can exist in a state of dreamless sleep.

versions.[9] I'm going to start by putting the case for non-thetic Universal Self-Awareness[PM] and thetic Possible Self-Awareness[PM], beginning with the former. Since non-thetic Universal Self-Awareness[PM] entails non-thetic Possible Self-Awareness[PM], only thetic Universal Self-Awareness[PM] will be unsupported—as it should be.

It may be objected that it's best to stop now, because it's obvious that Universal Self-Awareness[PM] and Possible Self-Awareness[PM] can't be true, simply because the neuronal processes that constitute awareness (at least in our own case) take time: there's an inevitable time-lag that rules out all present-moment self-awareness. I'll leave this objection until later. It may turn out that rejecting Universal Self-Awareness[PM] and Possible Self-Awareness[PM] for this reason is like holding that we never experience pain as it is in the present moment—even if the two cases seem at first disanalogous.

10.4 The 'AOI' Thesis (All Awareness Comports Awareness of Itself)

Why should anyone assert [2], Universal Self-Awareness[PM]? I'm going to assume the truth of the following two general principles:

[3]   awareness is (necessarily) a property of a subject of awareness,

which has already been argued for (and is in any case evident, given that it is legitimate to talk of properties at all), and

[4]   awareness of a property of x is *ipso facto* awareness of x.[10]

[3] and [4] entail

[5]   any awareness, A1, of any awareness, A2, entails awareness of the subject of A2

and we can get [2], i.e. Universal Self-Awareness[PM], from [5] if we add the thesis that

[6]   all awareness involves awareness of awareness,

or rather

[7]   all awareness involves awareness of that very awareness,

or rather (the key premiss), more specifically,

[8]   all awareness involves awareness of itself.

[8] is in fact the only defensible version of [7], as Aristotle pointed out.[11] It's the only defensible version of [7] given the threat of an infinite regress of awarenesses of

---

[9] 'As it stands': as far as I know the ancient view isn't really concerned with the non-thetic versions.

[10] I take it that [3] and [4] say something true even if there is in the final metaphysical analysis no fundamental (categorial) ontological division corresponding to the distinction between object and property. I'm assuming that x is a concrete object and taking [4] to mean that one is aware of the concrete instantiation of the property.

[11] See Aristotle *De Anima* 3.2. 425b12–17; as remarked, I'm using 'awareness' to mean 'conscious awareness', although there are contexts in which it makes sense to speak of unconscious awareness. For an

awarenesses that [7] is still subject to as it stands, given a sufficiently relaxed reading of 'involves' which allows that [7] may be true even if the awareness of awareness that any state of awareness involves may consist in the existence of a distinct state of awareness that takes the initial awareness as its object.

I'll call [8] the AOI thesis, 'AOI' for 'awareness of itself', *AOI* for short. The claim is, then, that [8], i.e. AOI, together with the two principles [3] and [4], entails

[2]   Universal Self-Awareness^{PM}.

More briefly: [8] = AOI and [5] entail [2] Universal Self-Awareness^{PM}. The argument isn't formally valid as it stands, but the idea is clear.

It may be allowed that [8] is true, that all awareness involves awareness of itself, but doubted that

[9]   all awareness is or involves *present-moment* awareness of itself

on the grounds that there is always a time-lag, or an episode of what Ryle calls 'swift retrospective heed' (1949: 153). But it seems that this is not possible, if [9] is true at all, because the last moment in any episode of awareness couldn't in this case involve awareness of itself (all streams of awareness would have to last for ever).

The substantive premiss is in any case AOI. The question is, why believe AOI? Why—to strengthen it slightly—believe

all awareness essentially involves awareness of itself,

or again, more heavily,

[10]   all awareness essentially, constitutively, and intrinsically involves awareness of itself

('intrinsically' and 'constitutively' aim to block the possibility, arguably left open by 'involves', and noted above, that AOI can still be said to be true in the case in which the awareness A1 of the awareness A2 is something ontologically separate from A2), or, more lightly, to the same effect,

all awareness is at least in part awareness of that very awareness,

or, to rephrase again,

[11]   all awareness comports awareness of that very awareness

(where the word 'comport' signals that the awareness of awareness in question is essentially part of the initial awareness), or, reintroducing the subject of awareness,

[12]   all awareness on the part of any subject comports awareness, on the part of that same subject, of that very awareness

or again, reintroducing multiply redundant explicit reference to the present moment,

[13]   all awareness on the part of any subject at any moment comports awareness, at that moment, on the part of that same subject, of that very awareness at that very moment,

excellent recent discussion of these questions in the context of Indian philosophy, see e.g. Mackenzie 2007. Note that [7] and [8] make no explicit reference to the present moment.

or, shortening the last formulation to what I hereby designate as the canonical version of AOI,

[14]   all awareness comports awareness of itself?[12]

Good question, about which there is a lot to say. I think AOI is initially difficult, but compelling on reflection. It's endorsed by many, including Aristotle, La Forge, Arnauld, Locke, Brentano, Husserl, Sartre, and most thinkers in the Phenomenological tradition.[13] All of them insist that the awareness of awareness that is held to be partly constitutive of all awareness mustn't be thought of as involving some 'higher-order' mental apprehension, A1, say, bearing on an ontically distinct, separate, 'lower-order' mental apprehension A2 (for this triggers an infinite regress). The relevant awareness of awareness is, rather, an intrinsic feature of any episode of awareness considered independently of any other, given which it is correct to say that [14] = AOI is true.[14]

One might say that [14] = AOI can be re-expressed by talking of

[15]   the self-awareness of awareness

but [15] is paradoxical, at least initially, in a way that [14] isn't, because it seems clear that awareness is necessarily a property of a subject of awareness (as [14] still allows, given the word 'comport'), and can't properly—or indeed possibly—be said to be a property of awareness itself. That said, I think that [15] is an acceptable way of putting things. First, it's an acceptable shorthand for [12]: all awareness on the part of any subject comports awareness, on the part of that same subject, of that very awareness. Secondly, and more strongly, the fact that all awareness is, necessarily, awareness on the part of a *subject* of awareness—the fact that reference to a subject must enter into any fully articulated description of what is going on when there is awareness—does not in any way undercut the truth of [15], according to which it is a constitutive feature of the phenomenon of awareness itself that it comports awareness of itself. Thirdly (a much stronger and more difficult point), I think that there is a metaphysically fundamental conception of the subject given which

[16]   the subject of awareness (that which wholly constitutes the existence of the subject of awareness) isn't ontically distinct from the awareness of which it is the subject

or in other words

[17]   the subject of awareness is identical with its awareness.

---

[12] One can rewrite [14] as [14a] *all awareness comports self-awareness* so long as one is clear that the occurrence of 'self-' in 'self-awareness' is merely reflexive, so that [14a] means exactly the same as [14], and doesn't imply any awareness of something rightly called a 'self'.

[13] See e.g. the quotations from Sartre in Ch. 8, pp. 152, 157n. Compare a note by Reid: 'I cannot imagine there is anything more in perceiving that I perceive a star than in perceiving a star simply; otherwise there might be perceptions of perceptions in infinitum' (1748: 317).

[14] Descartes appears to endorse AOI when he writes: 'we cannot have any thought of which we are not aware at the very moment when it is in us' (1641: 2.171), but his position is not fully clear, and disputed. See Thiel 2011: 43–9.

I'll call [17] the Subject of Awareness/Awareness Identity thesis or *Subject=Awareness* thesis, for short.[15] It's a difficult idea, as noted, and it can only hope to be true given the fundamental thin conception of the subject set out §10.2 (as opposed to the whole-organism way of conceiving of the subject, or the persisting brain-system way). That said, it's endorsed at some point by Descartes, Spinoza, Kant, Nietzsche, and James, among others, in the Western tradition,[16] and if one accepts it, as I do, then [15], the further proposed version of AOI, can also be understood to be fully equivalent to [2] = Universal Self-Awareness[PM]. That is,

[18]   [[AOI & Subject=Awareness] → Universal Self-Awareness[PM]].

If Subject=Awareness is too strong for you even as one possible conception of the subject among others, then you may be able to accept the weaker claim (already formulated in §10.4) that

[19]   [[AOI & [3] & [4]] → Universal Self-Awareness[PM]].

If you think principles [3] and [4] are trivially true, you can shorten this to

[20]   [AOI → Universal Self-Awareness[PM]].

In any case, all I've done, in moving from [8] to [14] ± [15], is re-express AOI in a number of different ways. One might also say that all I've done is re-express Universal Self-Awareness[PM] in a number of different ways. The AOI thesis is focused on the nature of awareness, whereas Universal Self-Awareness[PM] is more focused on the self or subject, but they're very closely connected.

Arnauld puts AOI well when he writes that 'thought or perception is essentially reflective on itself, or, as it is said more aptly in Latin, *est sui conscia*', is conscious of itself.[17] In endorsing the AOI thesis, as he does here, he also endorses Universal Self-Awareness[PM], given that he follows Descartes in accepting the Subject=Awareness thesis.

Ryle also puts it well, although with disparaging intent, when he speaks of the idea that consciousness is 'self-intimating' in some constitutive way, or 'self-luminous', or 'phosphorescent' (1949: 158–9; see also 162–3, 178). Frankfurt is also helpful in the following passage (already quoted in §8.12, p. 148), although parts of it are potentially misleading:

what would it be like to be conscious of something without being aware of this consciousness? It would mean having an experience with no awareness whatever of its occurrence. This would

---

[15] I argue for Subject=Awareness in Strawson 2003b, revised in Strawson 2009: pp. 345–9, 405–19. It entails the 'thin' conception of the subject while making an even stronger claim about the relation between the subject and its experience.

[16] In his famous letter to Herz, Kant writes that 'the thinking or the existence of the thought and the existence of my own self are one and the same' (1772: 75). Although Descartes and Spinoza often write as if the subject is ontically distinct from its states of experience or awareness, they're committed to the view that the concrete being of a substance (considered at any given time) is not ontically distinct from the concrete being of its attributes at that time (whatever modes of the attributes are currently instantiated).

[17] 1683: 71; he uses 'thought or perception' to cover all conscious mental goings on.

be, precisely, a case of unconscious experience. It appears, then, that being conscious is identical with self-consciousness. Consciousness *is* self-consciousness. The claim that waking consciousness is self-consciousness does not mean that consciousness is invariably dual in the sense that every instance of it involves both a primary awareness and another instance of consciousness which is somehow distinct and separable from the first and which has the first as its object. That would threaten an intolerably infinite proliferation of instances of conscious-ness. Rather, the self-consciousness in question is a sort of *immanent reflexivity* by virtue of which every instance of being conscious grasps not only that of which it is an awareness but also the awareness of it. It is like a source of light which, in addition to illuminating whatever other things fall within its scope, renders itself visible as well (1987: 162).[18]

The claims that are most likely to mislead in Frankfurt's passage are

[a]   consciousness   *is* self-consciousness

and the immediately preceding

[b]   being conscious is identical with self-consciousness,

but [a] doesn't I think say more than [14], the AOI thesis that all awareness comports awareness of itself, and [b], which may presumably be adjusted to (or at least entails) *being conscious is identical with being self-conscious*, may be understood to be the same as [2], Universal Self-Awareness[PM], the key thesis that the subject of awareness is always present-moment-aware of itself. The—in my opinion correct—suggestion is (once again) that Universal Self-Awareness[PM] falls out of the AOI thesis as a necessary consequence of it, given principles [3] and [4] in §10.4 above. If one also accepts [17], the Subject = Awareness thesis, the ultimate identity of the subject and its awareness, then [a] and [b] come to the same thing.

10.5 Ground of the AOI Thesis

There's a lot to say about the metaphysical grounding of AOI. I take the central metaphysical question to be the following. Given that AOI is true—given that all awareness (necessarily) comports awareness of itself—why is this so? There seem to be two main options.

[21]   Option 1: AOI is true because it's a necessary *consequence* of the intrinsic nature of awareness; and this intrinsic nature can none the less be specified independently of AOI in such a way that we can see why AOI is true.

[22]   Option 2: The fact that AOI is true is *constitutive* of the intrinsic nature of awareness in such a way that that intrinsic nature can't be specified independently of the fact that AOI is true.

Locke endorses the second view, when he writes that 'thinking consists in being conscious that one thinks... [just as] hunger consists in that very sensation.

---

[18]   On the claim that consciousness is self-consciousness, compare again the quotations from Sartre in ch. 8. Among Indian philosophers, Dignāga, Dharmakīrti, Śaṅkara, and others regularly use the trope of the light that illuminates itself. See e.g. Dreyfus (2010: 120) and Ram-Prasad (2010: 234).

(1689–1700: 2.1.19; he uses 'thinking' in the broad Cartesian sense to cover all experiential goings on). Arnauld's position in the quoted passage is perhaps compatible with [21], although it is most naturally taken as [22]. The same goes, I think, for the quotation from Descartes in note 14.

These are questions for another time. My present aim is simply to lay out the way in which the non-thetic version of Possible Self-Awareness[PM], i.e.

[1]   the subject can be aware of itself as it is in the present moment of awareness

taken in its strong universal form, i.e. as Universal Self-Awareness[PM]

[2]   the subject is always aware of itself as it is in the present moment of awareness

is seen to follow from a substantive thesis, the AOI thesis, which I've put through a series of formulations, beginning with

[6]   all awareness involves awareness of awareness,

passing through

[13]   all awareness on the part of any subject at any moment, comports awareness, at that moment, on the part of that same subject, of that very awareness at that very moment,

and ending with

[14]   all awareness comports awareness of itself.

The move made here, from the claim that the subject is necessarily aware of its awareness to the claim that it is necessarily aware of itself, is guaranteed given [3] and [4] (sc. [5]). AOI itself may still need defence, and even when its truth is granted questions about its fundamental metaphysics will remain. But these are matters for another occasion.

10.6 Non-thetic Present-Moment Self-Awareness

Does the plausibility of Universal Self-Awareness[PM] depend essentially on AOI? I'm not sure, and I'm now going to consider some other ways of expressing non-thetic present-moment awareness of self. According to Louis Sass:

the most fundamental sense of selfhood involves the experience of self not as an object of awareness but, in some crucial respects, as an unseen point of origin for action, experience, and thought.... What William James called ... the 'central nucleus of the Self' is not, in fact, experienced as an entity in the focus of our awareness, but, rather, as a kind of medium of awareness, source of activity, or general directedness towards the world.   (1998: 562)

Bernard Lonergan remarks that

objects are present by being attended to, but subjects are present [to themselves] as subjects, not by being attended to, but by attending. As the parade of objects marches by, spectators do not have to slip into the parade to be present to themselves.   (1967: 226).

In Samuel Alexander's words:

in knowing the object I know myself, not in the sense that I contemplate myself, for I do not do so, but in the sense that I live through this experience of myself. (1924: 1.xiv)

Arthur Deikman makes the same point:

we know the internal observer not by observing it but by *being* it...knowing by being that which is known is...different from perceptual knowledge.[19]

This is knowledge 'by acquaintance'. There's a narrow, philosophically popular, independent-justification-stressing conception of knowledge that makes it hard for some to see this is really knowledge, but the claim doesn't really need defence. Rather the reverse: this particular case of knowledge, self-knowledge in non-thetic Self-Awareness, shows the inadequacy of the narrow conception of knowledge. The general point is backed up, most formidably, by the fact that knowledge of this kind must lie behind all knowledge of the narrower justification-involving sort, as a condition of its possibility. This is because it's a necessary truth that all justification of knowledge claims is relative to something already taken as given.

Certainly the eye can't see itself (unless there is a mirror). The knife can't cut itself (unless it is very flexible), and the fingertip can't touch itself. The idea that the subject of experience can't have itself as it is in the present moment as the object of its thought—the idea that 'my today's self', in Ryle's words, 'perpetually slips out of any hold of it that I try to take' (1949: 187)—has many metaphorical expressions. Laycock says that it is part of 'perennial Buddhist wisdom' (1998: 142), and so it is, considered as a truth about the limitations of a certain particular sort of thetic, object-posing self-apprehension. But it is, so taken, fully compatible with the claim that there's another non-thetic form of occurrent self-apprehension in which the subject can be directly aware of itself in the present moment, for example in the way just indicated by Lonergan, Sass, Alexander, and Deikman. Dignāga and Dharmakīrti also hold that a cognition cognizes itself, and is in the present terms non-thetically aware of itself, although they don't in this context distinguish explicitly between thetic and non-thetic awareness.[20]

Does it follow, from the fact that this form of occurrent present-moment self-awareness is *non-thetic*, that it isn't *explicit* in any way? Is it some sort of *implicit* awareness? No; there's a key sense in which the implicit/explicit distinction lacks application when 'awareness' is used to refer to occurrent conscious experience, as here. 'Awareness' also has a dispositional use, as when we say of someone who is dreamlessly asleep that she's aware of your intentions, and this can make it seem natural to contrast implicit awareness with explicit awareness, just as we contrast

---

[19] 1996: 355. Plainly 'knowing by being that which is known', or rather, perhaps, knowing (oneself) by being that which is knowing, does not require knowing everything there is to know about that which is known. On a standard physicalist view, one may grant that that which is known, in this sort of self-presence of mind, has non-experiential being whose nature is not then known at all.

[20] See e.g. Dreyfus 2010. On the terms of the thin conception of the subject and the Subject=Awareness thesis, then, Dignāga and Dharmakīrti can also be said to agree that the subject can be non-thetically aware of itself.

implicit with explicit understanding, and implicit with explicit belief. The implicit/ explicit distinction applies naturally enough in the dispositional realm, as when we say of a dreamless sleeper that she explicitly believes or understands or is aware that *p*, given that she has actually consciously entertained and assented to the thought that *p* at some time, or that she implicitly believes or understands or is aware that *q*, given (say) that she would assent to *q* but hasn't ever actually consciously thought or realized that *q*.

The fact remains that there's no such thing as implicit awareness, given that 'aware- ness' is currently being used to mean only occurrent, conscious awareness. Anything that is really part of or 'in' occurrent conscious awareness must actually be on display (as it were) in the overall 'field of awareness'—even if it's also correctly classified as non- thetic.[21] So non-thetic occurrent awareness can't be said to be implicit occurrent awareness; it's simply awareness of content that isn't in the focus of attention, or rather, more simply, isn't *in attention*.[22] We can also call it background awareness, perhaps, for background awareness isn't 'implicit' awareness either, any more than dim or peripheral awareness is. It's just in the background, or dim—but really there.

Another way to put the point is to say that all occurrent awareness is *ipso facto* and *eo ipso* explicit awareness just in being, indeed, awareness, occurrent awareness, genuinely given in awareness, part of the actual content of experience that is experienced by the subject. This is, admittedly, a non-standard use of 'explicit', inasmuch as it allows that explicit awareness can be very dim, but one can use the word 'express' (favoured by Arnauld) to do most of the work usually done by 'explicit', and the basic distinction is in any case clear: it's the undeniably real if soft-bordered distinction between express, foreground, attentive, thetic awareness, on the one hand, and more or less dim, peripheral, non-attentive, background, non- thetic awareness on the other.[23]

The distinction can be refined. Self-awareness of the sort described by Sass, Lonergan, and Deikman can be said to be in the foreground, even though it isn't thetic: it can be (is) a centrally structuring part of experience, in such a way that it's plausibly classified as a foreground *aspect* of experience, even though there's also a clear respect in which it normally passes unnoticed, being entirely non-thetic. In the penultimate paragraph I said that we can equate 'non-thetic' with 'background'. I'm now inclined to overrule this by introducing a wider notion of foreground, and claiming that

experiential elements may be constitutive of the nature of the foreground while not being thetic.

---

[21] This is not to say that one couldn't give sense to a notion of implicit awareness.

[22] 'In attention' is often better than 'in the focus of attention', because the notion of focus seems to contain the foreground/background distinction and to exclude the possibility that there may be nothing more to one's experience, when one is attending, than what is in attention.

[23] One can even talk of unconscious occurrent awareness when considering things like blindsight; see e.g. Rosenthal 2005. Note that although 'peripheral awareness' has a good use in describing visual experience, and perhaps experience in other sensory modalities, the spatial metaphor is potentially misleading when giving a general characterization of elements of awareness that are out of (the focus of) attention.

At this point we have five distinct expressions. The terminology is threatening to go out of control. But the idea should be discernible to a sympathetic eye. On the present terms [i] all awareness is indeed *explicit* in the weak sense, since this now simply means is that it is genuine awareness, genuinely given in awareness. [ii] Some explicit awareness is *background*, and not at all thetic or express. [iii] Some explicit awareness is *foreground*, but still not *thetic* or *express*. [iv] Some foreground awareness is in addition *thetic* or *express*.

These matters need careful treatment (a careful terminology). I won't say much more here, except to note a parallel with the case of the qualitative character of the sensation of blue when one looks at the sky. There's a clear respect in which the qualitative character of one's sensation of blue is in the foreground of experience—it floods one's experience—as one looks at the blue sky. But it is at the same time wholly 'diaphanous', in the sense that one sees 'through' it, as it were, in seeing the blue sky, and it is in that sense wholly non-thetic: it is not, that is, in the focus of attention conceptualized specifically as a sensation.[24] This being so, I'm tempted to split 'express' from 'thetic', just as I split 'foreground' from 'thetic', and to say that the awareness of the sensation of blue is express (and indeed foreground) but not thetic. I'll return to this idea in §§10.9–10.10 below.

I think these distinctions capture real differences, and need careful further work. Experience is an extraordinarily complex part of reality. This is one dimension of its complexity.

10.7 Thetic Present-Moment Self-Awareness

The form of present-moment self-awareness described by Sass and others is plainly non-thetic. This means that it isn't in conflict with the ancient eye objection, if the eye objection can be expressed as the claim that the subject of experience can't take itself as it is in the present moment of experience as the thetic object of its attention. As already remarked, I think that present-moment (no time lag) self-awareness can also be fully thetic, so that the eye objection is false even in that formulation, and I will now try to say why.

—This is too vague—and you haven't answered the 'systematic elusiveness' objection. You may think *I'm now thinking a puzzling thought*, or *I'm looking down on India*, or just *Here I am*, in an attempt to apprehend yourself as mental self or subject or thinker in the present moment, but in entertaining these contents you necessarily fail to apprehend the thing that is doing the apprehending—the entertainer of the content, the thinker of the thought, i.e. yourself considered as the mental subject at that moment. Ryle is right: any mental performance 'can be the concern of a higher-order performance'—one can think about any thought that one has—but it 'cannot be the concern of itself' (1949: 188–9). When one thinks an I-thought, this performance 'is not dealt with in the operation which it itself is. Even if the person is, for special speculative purposes, momentarily concentrating on the Problem of the Self, he has failed and

---

[24] This use of 'diaphanous' to characterize sensation is not the same as Moore's famous use to characterize 'bare' consciousness (1903: 450). See e.g. Van Cleve (2005). The place to start, when considering these questions, is with Reid 1785: 193–6 (§2.16); see also Montague 2009: 501–2.

knows that he has failed to catch more than the flying coat-tails of that which he was pursuing. His quarry was the hunter' (1949: 187). William James, whom you favour, quotes Comte's statement of the same point, and agrees with him that 'no subjective state, whilst present, is its own object; its object is always something else'.   (1890: 1.190)

It's arguable, though, that to think *this very thought is puzzling,* or *I'm now thinking a puzzling thought,* is precisely to engage in a performance that is concerned with itself; in which case a certain kind of seemingly immediate self-presence of mind is possible even in an intentional, designedly self-reflexive, and wholly cognitive act—a point quite independent of considerations of the sort adduced by Lonergan, Sass, Alexander, Deikman and many others. On this view, it's *only when one tries to apprehend expressly that one has succeeded* that one triggers the regressive step. Nor is it clear that hunters can't catch the quarry when the quarry is themselves. A detective with partial amnesia, sitting in her chair and reasoning hard, may identify herself as the person who committed the crime she is investigating. Wandering in the dark, I may get increasingly precise readings regarding the location of my quarry from a Global Positioning System, programme my noiseless grabber robot to move to the correct spot, press the Grab button—and get grabbed.[25]

It may be said that concentration on cognitively articulated thoughts like *I'm now thinking a puzzling thought* or *Here I am* can't deliver what is required, or provide a compelling practical route to appreciation of the point that it's possible to have express awareness of oneself apprehended specifically as the mental subject of experience in the present moment of experience. I agree. The best route to this point is much more direct. It doesn't involve any such discursively articulated representations, although it does require being in some sort of meditative condition. Then it's simply a matter of coming to awareness of oneself as a mental presence (or perhaps simply as: mental presence) in a certain sort of alert but essentially unpointed, global way. The case is not like the eye that can't see itself, or the fingertip that can't touch itself. These old images are weak. A mind is rather more than an eye or a finger. If Ryle had perhaps spent a little more time on disciplined, unprejudiced mental self-examination, or had tried meditation—even if only briefly, and in an entirely amateur and unsupervised, Senior Common Room sort of way—he might have found that it's really not very difficult—although it's certainly not easy—for the subject of experience to be aware in the present moment of itself-in-the-present-moment. It's a matter of first focusing on the given fact of consciousness and then—letting go in a certain way. As far as the level of difficulty is concerned, it's like maintaining one's balance on a parallel bar or a wire in a let-go manner that is relatively but not extremely hard to attain. One can easily lose one's balance—one can fall out of the state in question—but one can also keep it, and improve with practice.[26]

The attainment of such self-awareness, for brief periods in the unpractised (and the incompetent, such as myself), appears to be a state that has no particular content

---

[25] There is also the case of Winnie the Pooh, Piglet, and the Heffalump (Milne 1928).

[26] One such method is Patricia Carrington's Clinically Standardized Meditation (1998).

beyond the content that it has insofar as it's correctly described as awareness or consciousness of the awareness or consciousness that it itself is, awareness that includes in itself awareness that it is awareness of the awareness that it itself is, but doesn't do so in a way that involves any sort of experience of propositional articulatedness, or anything thetic in the standard, apparently necessarily cognitive-distance-involving, object-of-attention-posing sense of the word 'thetic' (a word whose sense I am now aiming to expand in a certain way).[27] The route to the self-awareness I have in mind involves a preparatory focusing on the fact of consciousness that stops the ordinary flow of content. It isn't just a matter of meditative awareness of breathing, say, or of whatever is passing in the mind, although these practices may precede and facilitate the same result. It's consciousness that is consciousness of the consciousness that it itself is and that includes consciousness that it is consciousness of the consciousness that it itself is.

It may be a form or development of what people have in mind when they speak of 'pure consciousness experience'. This is something that I take to be routinely achieved relatively early in standard meditative practice, although it is in such cases only ever fleeting; something about whose reality, precise character and (relative) ease of attainment there's a pretty robust consensus. So characterized, I take it that it amounts to something less than what I'm after—*thetic* self-awareness[PM], thetic present-moment self-awareness. For although this pure consciousness experience may be said to be consciousness that is consciousness of the consciousness that it itself is, and that doesn't include any other content, I don't think that it need comport consciousness *that* it is consciousness of the consciousness that it itself is. If so, it's something less than the phenomenon I'm trying to capture.

Another thing pure consciousness experience and thetic present-moment self-awareness have in common is that they standardly involve an experience of 'selflessness', an experience it's natural to express by saying that it seems that there is just subjectivity, rather than a subject (although there is still—necessarily—a subject in the metaphysically non-committal sense of this paper, because all experience is necessarily experience-*for*, and although a subject in this basic sense of the term may still be said to be experienced).[28] This is true, and potentially misleading. One mustn't be misled by the fact that thetic self-awareness[PM] involves a sense of selflessness, or by the fact that it is natural to characterize it by using the impersonal mass terms 'awareness' and 'consciousness', into thinking that it isn't after all a genuine case of the phenomenon whose reality I'm trying to establish: thetic awareness on the part of the subject of experience of itself in the present moment of experience.

---

[27] It may be what Karme Chagme is describing here: 'when it [awareness] stares at itself, with this observation there is a vividness in which nothing is seen. This awareness is direct, naked, vivid, unestablished, empty, limpid luminosity, unique, non-dual clarity and emptiness. It is not permanent, but unestablished. It is not nihilistic but radiantly vivid. It is not one, but manifoldly aware and clear. It is not manifold but indivisibly of one taste. It is none other than this very self-awareness' (Karma Chagme c.1660: 108, quoted by Dreyfus 2010: 121–2). See further Forman 1998, Shear 1998; see also Parfit 1998b.

[28] Such experience doesn't involve any experience of self in the negative ethical sense.

The proposal, then, is that

[23]   the subject of awareness can be fully thetically aware of itself as it is in the present moment of awareness

which earns the laborious title

[23]   the Possible Thetic Present-Moment Self-Awareness thesis

—*Possible Thetic Self-Awareness*[PM], for short. It claims that thetic present-moment self-awareness is possible. It incorporates the idea that the neural time lag objection mentioned at the end of §10.3 doesn't apply.

10.8 Doubts about Thetic Present-Moment Self-Awareness

Can the claim that present-moment self-awareness can be fully thetic be maintained? It certainly seems right to say that the awareness of oneself can in this case be fully *express*, no less express than any awareness of anything is when one's awareness of it is thetic—even though there is in this case no sort of distancing posing or positing or positioning of oneself for inspection of the sort that may seem to be built into the meaning of the word 'thetic'. I think, in fact, that it can equally well be said to be *thetic*, taking the core meaning of 'thetic' to be just: genuinely fully in attention, and rejecting the idea that such attention requires cognitive or discursive articulation or construction of such a kind that the subject is bound to present to itself in a posed or staged or set-up way given which it can't be said to be aware of itself as it is at that moment. On this point I think Ryle and a host of others are simply wrong. Their model of awareness is too rigid, insofar as it pushes the subject—the 'now-subject', one might say—into being necessarily cut off from its (attempted) object—itself. It simply hasn't been shown that there's an insuperable difficulty in the matter of present-moment or immediate (im-mediate) self-awareness—in apprehending the subject 'live'. This is certainly something special, but it seems that I can engage in it with no flying coat-tails time-lag. The eye can't see itself, but the I—the subject—isn't much like an eye.

If we take the word 'thetic' to entail some kind of structured operation of positing or positioning of an object of attention, a focusing that typically requires some sort of effortful maintenance, some sort of intellectual upkeep, then we may do best to distinguish 'thetic' from 'express' and fall back to 'express', leaving 'thetic' to denote an essentially time-lagged, distancing, cognitively articulated operation. On this understanding of 'thetic', present-moment self-awareness of the sort I have in mind can still be said to be foreground and express, but can't strictly speaking be said to be thetic. My inclination, however, is to resist this move, on the ground that an adequate and therefore broad understanding of *cognition* needs to allow for—acknowledge—the genuinely cognitive nature of this present-moment self-awareness. We need perhaps to try to wean our understanding of 'thetic' away from too narrow a conception of what cognition is, to allow that one can achieve a fully thetic state of awareness by a certain sort of letting go, and so assert Possible Thetic Self-Awareness[PM] outright. I'm prepared to retreat to

[24]   the subject of awareness can be fully *expressly* aware of itself as it is in the present moment of awareness

i.e.

[24]   the Possible Express Present-Moment Self-Awareness thesis (*Possible Express Self-awareness*[PM]),

if the word 'thetic' is judged to be irretrievably out of bounds. In the rest of this paper, though, I'm going to continue to defend the possibility of thetic self-awareness[PM]. I'm going to take the word 'thetic' to connect principally and primordially to the idea of attention, attentiveness, full attention, and attempt to cultivate a sense of how attention (and cognition) can have forms that don't involve anything like discursively structured operations of positing or positioning things as objects of attention.

10.9 Defence of the Possibility of Thetic Present-Moment Self-Awareness

The core objection to the idea that thetic self-awareness[PM] is possible is that thetic awareness is necessarily a *mediated* form of awareness, where this means not only that there is necessarily a time lag, but also that one inevitably has to do with a *presentation* of the phenomenon one is aware of which is not the phenomenon itself. Here we come up against some very general questions about knowledge, and I'll limit myself to a few remarks.

'Cognitive' means 'of or pertaining to . . . knowing'. It follows immediately that the standard distinction between cognition and emotion is illegitimate, because our emotions, however fallible, are one of our key sources of knowledge of how things are. Putting that aside, the claim is that we need when thinking about cognition to acknowledge the reality as knowledge or cognition—knowledge or cognition in the fullest sense—of knowledge by direct acquaintance. This is how I know the nature of the pain that I feel now. Such knowledge by direct acquaintance is, one might say, perfect. (Knowledge of a priori truths can be no less perfect.) There's a crucial aspect of reality, one's experience (the experiential-qualitative character or what-it's-likeness of one's experiences) that one knows as it is in itself, simply because 'the having is the knowing', and in such a way that there is no time lag (see §1.1, p. 3). One can of course be wrong about it in many ways as soon as it falls into the past, and when one reports on it. But this point is wholly compatible with the truth of the claim that the having is the knowing.

—Suppose I accept this as an example of knowledge or cognition by direct acquaintance, if only for the sake of argument. It isn't going to be enough to illustrate what's supposed to be going on in thetic self-awareness[PM]. There are at least two objections.

[a] The notion of direct acquaintance may seem clear enough when we consider sensory or feeling (sense/feeling) aspects of experience, but the direct acquaintance is standardly *non-thetic* in these cases, however express it is—however much it is in the overall experiential foreground. So it provides no model for *thetic* direct acquaintance.

[b] You've given us a proposed case of direct acquaintance for *sense/feeling* aspects of experience, but thetic self-awareness^PM—if it exists at all—is presumably some kind of *non-sense/feeling* or *cognitive* direct acquaintance with oneself as subject; in which case, presumably, it has no experiential-qualitative feeling aspect at all. Even if you could come up with a model of thetic direct acquaintance in the sense/feeling case (which you haven't yet done), it wouldn't help with the case you're aiming at, which is a case of the non-sense/feeling direct acquaintance of the subject with itself.

My first reply is that I reject the equation of experiential-qualitative phenomena with sense/feeling phenomena. This is because there is, in addition to sense/feeling phenomenology, sense/feeling experience, cognitive phenomenology, cognitive experience. Our experience has cognitive experiential-qualitative character in every sense in which it has sense/feeling experiential-qualitative character. I've argued for this in other places and will take it for granted here.[29] There is, furthermore, a fundamental sense in which *all* experience as currently defined, i.e. all what-it's-likeness, is a matter of direct acquaintance, be it sense/feeling or cognitive. So far, then, there's no reason to think that the idea of cognitive-experiential direct acquaintance is any more problematic than the idea of sense/feeling direct acquaintance. Some may find the idea of direct acquaintance with 'cognitive what-it's-likeness' alarming, but it's backed by a point parallel to the point about knowledge made in §10.6 (p. 199): if there is any kind of cognitive experience at all, this kind of direct acquaintance must exist as a condition of its possibility.[30]

Secondly: I agree that the direct present-moment acquaintance involved in sense/feeling experience is standardly non-thetic. Sense/feeling experience is a huge part of our overall experience, e.g. when we perceive things, but we very rarely focus on it considered as such.[31] So it's unclear how we can work a passage from the understanding of direct acquaintance given to us by non-thetic sense/feeling cases to the possibility of thetic self-awareness^PM, a subject's direct thetic present-moment acquaintance with itself, assuming that this involves some essentially non-sense/feeling and hence cognitive element, some cognitive apprehension of self.

Let me try to take an intermediate step. My having-is-the-knowing direct acquaintance with my headache is usually non-thetic, even when I'm painfully aware of it, so that it's in the overall experiential foreground. I find, though, that I can bring it about that I have it as thetic object of attention and *also* have having-is-the-knowing direct acquaintance with it. At the least, I can bring the pain sensation to (thetic) attention, and then, having done so, fall at the same time into experiencing it in the direct way in which I ordinarily take myself to experience objects in the world. And because what I am experiencing in this case is in fact my own sensation, this way of experiencing it can be having-is-the-knowing direct acquaintance.

---

[29] See e.g. Strawson 1994: 5–13, Strawson 2011b. For the purposes of argument I take 'sense/feeling' and 'cognitive', broadly understood as above, to be mutually exclusive and jointly exhaustive of the field of experience.

[30] I believe there is a connection here with Searle's notion of the Background. See Searle 1983.

[31] This is the truth in the 'transparency thesis', which is often inflated into a larger and false thesis.

This 'falling' is another relatively delicate operation, relative to ordinary everyday full-on thetic attention. For in everyday, full-on thetic attention, I take it, the fact that the object of attention is being taken as object of attention is itself part of what is being given in the overall character of the experience. But it is—I propose—precisely this aspect of everyday full-on thetic attention that can lapse, leaving the pain *in full attention* without there being any awareness of oneself as taking it as object of attention. When this happens, the fact that the object of attention is being taken as object of attention is no longer part of what is given in the overall character of the experience. Only the pain is. This can also occur more naturally, without being engineered for purposes of empirical philosophical research, as it is here. It can happen in cases when one passes from willed thetic concentration on something to a state of absorption in it, artistic or otherwise.

One can do the same with the sensation of blue that one has when one looks at the blue sky. One can take the sensation of blue as thetic object of attention even as one continues to look at the sky.[32] When one does this in a standard way, as a philosophical exercise of the sort prescribed by Reid, one's awareness of the sensation of blue will comport some sort of awareness of the fact that the sensation of blue is being taken as object of attention. But one can also go beyond this, I propose, into a state of direct thetic having-is-the-knowing acquaintance, a state of holding the sensation of blue in full attention in which one's experience ceases to have, as any part of its content, the content *subject-attending-to-something*.[33]

If this is right, we now have a model of thetic direct acquaintance in the sense/feeling cases, and it's not clear why we should suppose that some huge further gulf must appear when we turn from such cases—pain, or blue-experience—to the case of the subject. In fact, if the Subject=Awareness thesis is correct, as I think it is, then direct thetic acquaintance with pain or blue-experience is already direct thetic acquaintance with the subject. Relative to such cases, the special, alert, unpointed way of coming to awareness of oneself as a mental presence (or as mental presence) described in §10.8 is special only in that it doesn't involve any particular content like pain or blue-experience, and is therefore a candidate for the title 'pure consciousness experience'.[34]

---

[32] It's not easy—a fact that has led some influential philosophers to deny that it is possible. It requires practice, as Reid pointed out: 'it is indeed difficult, at first, to disjoin things in our attention which have always been conjoined, and to make that an object of reflection which never was before, but some pains and practice will overcome this difficulty in those who have got into the habit of reflecting on the operations of their own minds' (1785: 196). See also James: when we consider perception, we see 'how inveterate is our habit of not attending to sensations as subjective facts, but of simply using them as stepping-stones to pass over to the recognition of the realities whose presence they reveal' (1890: 1.231).

[33] This isn't possible in Reid's model of attention to sensation, in fact, in which attention can only be paid to sensation that is—however fractionally—already past. See Yaffe 2009.

[34] It's still pretty special. Hume gives a correct (if widely misunderstood—see Ch. 13 below) report of the results of ordinary reflective mental self-examination when he denies that he ever has any such experience: 'when I enter most intimately into what I call *myself*, I always stumble on some particular perception or other....I never can catch *myself* at any time without a perception, and never can observe any thing but the perception' (1739/40: 1.4.6.3/252).

—Even if you've now secured a case of thetic present-moment direct acquaintance, you've done it only for the sense/feeling case. You still need to show how there can be *non*-sense/feeling present-moment direct acquaintance.

Well, again it's not clear that we need to build a bridge from the proposed cases of direct and thetic present-moment acquaintance with sense/feeling content in order to understand, or at least acknowledge the possibility or reality of, thetic self-awareness[PM]: direct, present-moment acquaintance of the subject with itself. Thetic self-awareness[PM] must presumably be a non-sense/feeling matter, hence a cognitive matter, in some sense of cognitive; at least in part. But we already have it that there is such a thing as cognitive experience (it pervades every moment of our lives), and there is as observed a fundamental sense in which it's essentially constitutive of something's being experiential content at all that its subject or haver is in a relation of direct acquaintance with it—whether it be sense/feeling content or cognitive-experiential content.[35]

I've claimed that thetic self-awareness[PM] must be an essentially non-sense/feeling matter, at least in part, but I'm not sure quite what this amounts to, if only because currently standard classifications of what one may call the *experiential modalities* are extremely crude. Many assume that all experiential modalities are sensory or sense/feeling modalities; they exclude the idea that there are cognitive experiential modalities from the start. And even those who admit that there is a distinctively cognitive experiential modality may wish to exclude the idea that there may be a *non-propositional* or *non-discursive* experiential modality which is none the less a non-sense/feeling experiential modality, and indeed a genuinely cognitive experiential modality. They're also likely to assume that the division between sense/feeling content and cognitive experiential content is absolute, as I have done for purposes of argument (without committing myself to the view that either can occur wholly without the other).

These are difficult issues, about which I feel unsure. I do, however, feel sure about the possibility of thetic self-awareness[PM], the possibility of having direct thetic (in the wider sense) awareness of oneself as subject as one is in the present moment of awareness. And I'm strongly inclined to think that this is, precisely, a non-propositional, non-discursive form of awareness which is none the less properly said to be a matter of cognition.

10.10 Can the Subject Know its Nature as it is in Itself?

In the last section I shifted from talking about present-moment *awareness* to talking about present-moment *direct acquaintance* without explicitly acknowledging that this is a substantive move. As it stands, Possible Thetic Self-awareness[PM] doesn't in speaking of awareness make any claim about *knowledge of the nature* of the subject as it is in itself, still less about complete knowledge of the nature of the subject as it is in itself, of a sort that may seem built into the idea of direct acquaintance. And this, so

---

[35] Cognitive-experiential content is content wholly internalistically understood. It's what you have wholly in common with your philosophical Twins, whether they're on Twin Earth, or in a vat, or have just popped miraculously into existence. See Strawson 2008c: 294–5, 2011b.

far, may seem agreeable, because the picture of the subject as some kind of active principle lying behind all its experience, in such a way that one can't know its essential nature, even if one can be present-moment-aware of it as existing, remains beguiling. And given that it's beguiling, it seems good that it should be, so far, compatible with Thetic Possible Self-awareness[PM].

I think, though, that Possible Thetic Self-Awareness[PM] must accept its responsibilities; it must square up and take on the burden of implying that the subject have at least some acquaintance with itself as it is in itself. Supporters of Possible Thetic Self-Awareness[PM] like myself should in other words accept that any argument that as-it-is-in-itself self-awareness is impossible is an argument against Possible Thetic Self-Awareness[PM].

The first thing to do, perhaps, is to ask why the picture of the subject as some kind of active principle lying behind all its experience is beguiling. Part of the explanation is that the metaphysics of subject and predicate forces itself on us almost irresistibly, demanding that we distinguish between the subject of awareness and its various states of awareness in a way that I believe we must ultimately reject (quite independently of any commitment to the Subject=Awareness thesis), and opening the way to the idea that we are at best aware of its states and so not of itself as it is in itself.[36] More respectably, our sceptical instincts are active, as they should always be, and they too invite us to acknowledge that we could perhaps be present-moment-aware of something and yet not know anything of its essential nature. They then suggest that absolutely all awareness of anything, other than the what-it's-likeness of experience, is *mediated* by a *representation* of that thing. So if the subject is aware of anything other than the what-it's-likeness of experience, then even if that other thing is itself, itself considered specifically as subject, still there is an affecting relation, albeit a self-affecting relation. The Kantian conclusion is then triggered: 'nothing which emerges from *any* affecting relation can count as knowledge or awareness of the affecting thing as it is in itself'.[37]

Kant famously takes the subject itself to be for this reason unknowable by itself as it is in itself, to be knowable only as it appears to itself (if only because it can only be encountered in the spatiotemporal—in particular temporal—form of sensibility).[38] The present suggestion is precisely that this isn't so—that it's possible to be aware of the subject of awareness in an immediate but none the less express and indeed thetic (in-full-attention) way that is parallel, at least in respect of immediacy, to the immediate (im-mediate) awareness we have of experiential what-it's-likeness. Usually, representation/mediation gets in the way, leaving us with 'mere appearance'; but not in this case. On this view Fichte's principal objection to Kant, which he expressed by saying that the subject can apprehend itself as subject in 'intellectual intuition', is quite correct, even if he has quite different reasons for it.[39]

---

[36] On this, and the dubiousness of the 'so', see e.g. Strawson 2008c.

[37] P. F. Strawson (1966: 238), summarizing Kant. See also Langton 1998.

[38] Consider for example his remark that 'I do not know myself through being conscious of myself as experiencing/thinking, but only when I am conscious of the intuition of myself as determined with respect to the function of experiencing/thinking' (1781/7: B406).

[39] Fichte 1794–1802. The notion of 'intellectual intuition' is precisely an attempt to characterize a kind of knowledge-of-*x*-involving *relation* with *x* that does not involve being *affected* by *x* in a way that inevitably limits one to knowledge of an *appearance* of *x*. Note that if one goes into a state of thetic

Here, then, I boost the thesis that thetic self-awareness[PM] is possible into being committed to the thesis that present-moment self-awareness is and must involve some sort of awareness of the nature of the subject as it is in itself, a step I'm happy to take for other Cartesian-Kantian-Jamesian reasons (the Subject=Awareness thesis, the ultimate identity of subject and experience, experiencer and experiencing). Note, as a final reflection, that phrases like 'the subject's awareness of itself considered specifically as subject' can be taken in a stronger and a weaker sense. The stronger sense takes 'as subject' to mean that the subject's awareness of itself involves its bringing itself under the concept SUBJECT. The weaker sense requires only that what the subject is in fact concerned with is itself insofar as it is a subject, and allows that it may not in being so concerned be deploying anything recognizable as a concept of itself as subject. Here I have the weaker sense in mind. It allows for the idea, which seems necessary, that although all ordinary adult human beings possess the concept SUBJECT, it simply lapses—is not deployed in any way—in immediate thetic self-awareness. It also allows that children may be capable of immediate thetic self-awareness prior to possessing anything that can be dignified by the name 'concept'.[40]

10.11 Conclusion

I've proposed that the mental subject can be immediately relationally aware of itself, both in the non-thetic, everyday Sass-Lonergan-Deikman way, and also, exceptionally, in the express, thetic 'pure consciousness experience' way.[41] Evidence? Each must acquire it for himself or herself *in foro interno*. This doesn't mean it isn't empirical; it's wholly empirical. It does mean that it isn't publicly checkable, and it will always be possible for someone to object that the experience of truly present self-awareness is an illusion produced—say—by Rylean flashes of 'swift retrospective heed' (1949: 153). I think, though, that this notion of heed has the flying coat-tails error built into it, and there is another larger mistake that can I think be decisively blocked.

Suppose that it's in the nature of all naturally evolved forms of experience/consciousness that they are in the usual course of things incessantly and seemingly constitutively in the service of the perceptual and agentive survival needs of organisms. It doesn't follow that this is essential to the nature of consciousness, that experience/consciousness must be defined in terms of adaptive function or perceptual content, even in part. The notion of pure consciousness experience is incompatible with any such conception of the nature of experience, but it's certainly not in

---

self-awareness[PM], one's awareness is bound to be genuinely awareness of oneself, the subject that one is—by the nature of the case.

[40] Is one present-moment aware of oneself as being *oneself*, in immediate thetic self-awareness? One might think 'Yes, but in some non-conceptual way', or 'No, inasmuch as nothing that really qualifies as a sense of individuality remains.'

[41] According to Fasching, Indian soteriological traditions such as Advaita Vedānta and Sāṃkhya-Yoga equate this with realization of the 'self'—'which is nothing other than becoming aware of experiential presence (consciousness) as such' (Fasching 2010: 207).

tension with naturalism, properly understood, or with anything in the theory of evolution by natural selection.[42]

This is another topic that needs separate discussion. Here I simply want to note that even if experience isn't a primordial property of the universe,[43] and even if it came on the scene relatively late, there's no good reason—in fact it doesn't even make sense—to think that it first came on the scene because it had survival value. Natural selection needs something to work on and can only work on what it finds. Experience/consciousness had to exist before it could be exploited and shaped, just as non-experiential matter did. The task of giving an evolutionary explanation of the existence of consciousness is exactly like the task of giving an evolutionary explanation of the existence of matter: there is no such task. Natural selection moulds the phenomena of experience it finds in nature into highly specific adaptive forms in exactly the same general way as the way in which it moulds the phenomena of non-experiential matter into highly specific adaptive forms.[44] The evolution by natural selection of various very finely developed and specialized forms of experience (visual, olfactory, etc.) is no more surprising than the evolution by natural selection of various finely developed and specialized types of bodily organization.[45] Even if (even though) evolved forms of experience have come to be what they are because they have certain kinds of content that give them survival value, kinds of content which are (therefore) essentially other than whatever content is involved in pure consciousness experience, it doesn't follow that pure consciousness experience is some sort of illusion. On the contrary: evolution gives us an explanation of how anything other than pure consciousness ever came to exist. Pure consciousness experience as we can know it may become possible only after millions of years of EEE-practical forms of consciousness, but it may for all that be uniquely revelatory of the fundamental nature of experience.[46]

---

[42] Naturalism, by which I mean real naturalism, acknowledges experience or consciousness as the most certainly known natural fact.

[43] I think it must be; see e.g. Strawson 2006a.

[44] It may be that everything physical is experiential in some way, but I'll put this point aside.

[45] To speak of such forms of consciousness is not to reject the possibility that functional equivalents of, e.g., visual and auditory experience could exist in the complete absence of consciousness.

[46] My thanks to Mark Siderits for his very helpful comments.

11

I and *I*

Immunity to Error through Misidentification of the Subject

11.1

In this paper I consider and defend, where necessary, the following partly overlapping claims.

[1] All genuine uses of *I* are immune to error through misidentification of their referent.

[2] One always refers to oneself when one uses *I*.

[3] No genuine use of *I* can possibly fail to refer.

[4] One always intends to refer to oneself, when one uses *I* normally or sincerely.

[5] *I* doesn't always refer to the same thing, or kind of thing, even in the thought or speech of a single person (!)

[6] To be (fully) self-conscious is to be able to think of oneself *as oneself* (definition of self-consciousness).

[7] If I'm thinking about something specifically as *myself*, I can't fail to be thinking of myself.

[8] I can't fail to know that I'm thinking of myself when I'm thinking of myself as myself.

[9] A genuine understanding use of *I* always involves the subject grasping itself as itself, whatever else it does or doesn't involve.

[10] If it's true that I take myself to be thinking about myself, then I am thinking about myself.

11.2

Louis MacNeice reckoned a human being to be

> ...a dance of midges,
> Gold glass in the sunlight,
> Prattle of water, palaver
> Of starlings in a disused
> Chimney...

> ...a flutter of pages,
> Leaves in the Sibyl's cave,

Shadow changing from dawn to twilight,
Murmuration of corn in the wind...,[1]

and there are many respects in which we don't know who or what we are. John Updike writes that our names 'are used for convenience by others but figure marginally in our own minds, which know ourselves as an entity too vast and vague to name'.[2]

This is a very accurate remark. There is, nevertheless, a rock-bottom sense in which

[1]   all genuine uses of 'I', 'me', 'my', 'mine', and 'myself' are immune to error through misidentification of their referent.

The same goes for all genuine occurrences in thought of the concept or thought-element I (ME, MY, MINE, MYSELF), and in expounding the point I'll use *I* in italics to cover both 'I' and I (similarly for *me, my, mine, myself*) and move freely between the cases of thought and speech. I'll use 'term' to cover both words and thought-elements.

Let me rephrase [1] in terms of *I*, using an expression of Sydney Shoemaker's:

[1′]   all genuine uses of *I* are 'immune to error through misidentification relative to the first-person pronoun' *I*.[3]

This is true in at least the following sense:

[2]   one always refers to oneself when one uses *I*

and it follows from [2] that

[3]   no (genuine) use of *I* can possibly fail to refer.

It's also true that

[4]   one always intends to refer to oneself, when one uses *I* (normally or sincerely).

One always intends to refer to oneself, when one uses *I* normally or sincerely, whatever *else* one intends to do, and whatever else may be going on. This has been wrongly doubted, for reasons discussed in §11.6.

Ludwig Wittgenstein makes a well-known distinction between the use of *I* 'as object' as opposed to its use 'as subject'.[4] I don't, however, think that he really picks out two different uses of *I*, let alone a use of *I* that is well named 'the use "as object"'. I don't think there's really any such thing as the use of *I* 'as object'. That said, I agree with what some philosophers have had in mind when they've said that there is such a thing. I'm not making any radically new suggestion on this question; I just think that the point hasn't been well put.

[1] From 'Plant and phantom' (1941: 170). The poem takes its title from a line in the prologue to Nietzsche's *Also Sprach Zarathustra*: 'even the wisest among you is only a jarring and hybrid of plant and phantom' (1883–5: 170).
[2] 2000: 76. Compare Woolf 1931, *passim*.
[3] Shoemaker 1968: 556. This picks up on the discussion in P. F. Strawson 1966: 164–6.
[4] See Wittgenstein 1933–5: 65–9, Moore 1959: 306–10.

To deny the existence of the use of *I* 'as object' is not to say that *I* is univocal, and I'm going to argue, with Locke, that there's a key sense in which it isn't univocal—a key sense in which

[5]   *I* doesn't always refer to the same thing, or kind of thing, even in the thought or speech of a single person.[5]

I won't, however, give up the claim—to vary [2]—that

[2′]   *I* always refers to its user, the subject of experience who speaks or thinks.

It's seemingly paradoxical to combine [5], the claim that *I* doesn't always refer to the same thing (in a single person's use), with [2′], the claim that *I* always and necessarily refers to its user, and is therefore [1] entirely immune to error through misidentification of its referent. How can *I* refer to two or more distinct things, and still refer always and necessarily and only to the subject of experience that produces it? Answer: there's a certain sort of nesting relation which makes this possible. So I'll argue in §11.4.

The next four sections (§§11.2–5) defend [5]. The last three (§§11.6–8) focus on well-known questions about 'immunity to error', or 'IEM'. Those who wish can now go straight to §11.6 (one can reject or remain agnostic about [5] while accepting all the other numbered claims in this paper).

11.3

If one is going to argue that *I* is absolutely immune to error through misidentification of its referent, it is sensible to establish what *I* refers to. I'll approach the issue through some considerations about the notion of the self.

I'm a human being, and when I say or think *I* (*me, my, mine, myself*), I surely refer to myself, the human being that I am, whom I'll call 'GS'. I am GS, then, and the 'am' in 'I am GS' is, most surely, the 'am' of identity:

[i]   I = GS.

Suppose, though, that there's such a thing as the self. Then when I say or think *I*, I surely speak or think as the self that I am, whom I'll call 'S'; and in referring to myself by using *I*, I refer to the self that I am. I am S, and the 'am' is again the 'am' of identity:

[ii]   I = S.

All this seems sound enough. But it follows, by the logic of identity, that the self that I am is just (just is) the human being that I am:

[iii]   S = GS.

So the self that I am is just the human being that I am. Selves, more generally, are just human beings (I'll restrict attention to the human case.)

---

[5] See Locke 1694: 2.27.20, Strawson 1999a: 131.

To say this, though, is as much as to say that there aren't really any such things as selves. For if there is such a thing as the self, it surely can't be the same thing as the human being. Admittedly one can't prevent philosophers from stipulating that the term 'self' is synonymous with the term 'human being'. But this then makes use of the term 'self' unnecessary and misleading. For the fundamental idea behind the use of the term 'self' is and always has been that the self—if there is such a thing—is something that is distinct from, in the sense of not being identical with, the whole human being.[6]

I'm going to take it, accordingly, that if the term 'self' refers at all, it doesn't refer to the same thing as the term 'human being'. If, then, S exists, [iii] is false,

$$S \neq GS$$

and this is not because I'm special: the same goes *mutatis mutandis* for all human beings.

There now appear to be two choices. Either I'm not a human being, because I'm a self, or I'm not a self, because I'm a human being. But I'm certainly a human being, so it looks as if I have a firm negative answer to the grand old metaphysical question 'Is there such a thing as the self?' It turns out to be an easy question. The supposition that there is such a thing as the self leads to a contradiction.

Metaphysics is not so easy. One can't resolve the problem of the self by attending to a few simple facts about language.[7] I think, in fact, that the best answer to the question whether selves exist is Yes—even when one has ruled, as I have, that selves, if they exist, can't be identified with human beings considered as a whole. I think good and important sense can be given to the claim that there is such a thing as the self distinct from the human being considered as a whole.

In this paper I'll simply assume that this is so, for purposes of argument.[8] I'll also assume that materialism (physicalism) is true, and that selves and human beings stand in a straightforward spatiotemporal part–whole relation (the 'inner self' is literally inner). Finally, I'll assume with Nozick that 'the self has a particular character, that of an entity'—I'll assume that it is (to use a purposefully vague word) a *thing* of some sort.[9] This will help me to animate the discussion of immunity to error in what is I believe a useful way.

---

[6] Olson thinks it best to identify the self with the whole human being. He agrees with the Benedictine monk Léger–Marie Deschamps, who protests in 1761 that 'le *moi* [self] est le tout de mon corps, et quand je dis, par exemple, que j'ai telle sensation, je ne dis rien sinon que mon tout, que l'ensemble de mes parties, qui est moi, a telle sensation.... Vouloir que le mot *moi* exprime autre chose que le tout de notre corps, quand il s'agit de nous comme hommes, c'est vouloir une absurdité'. ('The I or self is the whole of my body, and when I say, for example, that I have a certain sensation, all I say is that the whole which I am—the totality of my parts, which is myself—has a certain sensation. To want the word "I" to denote anything other than the whole of our body, when we're concerned with ourselves as human beings, is to want something absurd' (2.381)).

[7] For the view that one can, see e.g. Kenny 1988, 1989.

[8] I argue for the view in Strawson 2009, 2010.

[9] Nozick 1989: 148. Selves, if they exist, are subjects of experience, they can be in some experiential state or other. They sufficiently qualify as 'things' for this reason alone, inasmuch as properties and states, and events or processes as ordinarily understood, can't be said to be in experiential states. That said, I think these standard metaphysical categories are ultimately superficial, and (connectedly) take the claim that the self is a thing of some sort to be compatible with Fichte's striking claim that the self is a *Tathandlung*, a 'deed-activity' (1794–1802: 97).

11.4

I'm a human being, then, and I take it that I'm also a self. I take it, in fact, that I = GS and I = S. I don't, however, think that the self that I am is the human being that I am: I deny GS = S.

How can I do this? I don't reject the logic of the identity relation. That would be silly. I reject the assumption that *I* is univocal in the thought or speech of any given individual. I've assumed that there is such a thing as the self distinct from the human being considered as a whole, and this opens the way to the possibility that the reference of *I* standardly shifts between these two different things in my thought and speech and in the thought and speech of others. Certainly *I* is sometimes used with the intention to refer to a human being considered as a whole, and sometimes with the intention to refer to a self, and these are two things which have quite different identity conditions, one being a part of the other.[10]

Obviously this fact about our referential intentions doesn't guarantee that selves exist (some people believe themselves to be immaterial souls). It's simply a fact about how *I* is used. If it turns out that the best thing to say about selves is that there aren't any, then the best thing to say about *I* may be that it is univocal after all—that the apparent doubleness of reference of *I* is an echo in thought and language of a metaphysical illusion. On this view, *I* isn't in fact used to refer to selves as distinct from human beings, even when its users intend to be making some such reference, expressly or not, and believe they're doing so. The truth is rather that the semantic intentions of *I*-users incorporate a mistake about how things are, in all such cases.

I think, however, that we do at different times successfully use *I* to refer to different things, to human beings considered as a whole and to selves. Sometimes, I think, uses of *I* can be taken either way. Sometimes they can be taken to refer to both things at once. It's all pretty relaxed.

Some think that the univocity of *I*, and the fact that it refers to a human being considered as a whole when it occurs in a human being's thought or speech, can be established a priori from considerations about the essentially public nature of language, which are assumed to have implications for the essential nature of thought. From this they argue to the non-existence of selves considered as distinct from human beings considered as a whole. This is a Wittgensteinian or perhaps rather 'Wittgensteinian' version of the view that the grand old metaphysical question is easily answered, which I've already rejected.[11]

So suppose we take it that *I* is not univocal. 'What then am I?', as Descartes once asked (1641: 18)? Am I two different things, I^H ('H' for human being) and I^S ('s' for self), at a given time? This seems an intolerable conclusion—logically and metaphysically intolerable. In fact, though, it's simply a reflection (an accurate reflection) of how *I*

---

[10] 'How can it not be univocal in my use if it always and without fail refers to me, i.e. to *the same thing*?' Precisely because '*me*', i.e. '*I*', is not univocal. More accommodatingly: there's a complication, which I'll come to, in the notion of 'the same thing'.

[11] For a more detailed response to this proposal, see §§4.2–3 above. A different argument for the view that the self is to be identified with the whole human being develops the idea that the only legitimate conception of the self is the 'EEE' conception of it (see §3.4 above) as essentially environmentally embedded, embodied, 'ecological', and 'enactive' (and even, perhaps, 'extended' in the sense of Chalmers and Clark 1998). This argument is also unsuccessful in my view.

works. It refers to two different things at different times in the thought and speech of beings like ourselves. Its referential reach varies, so that it refers to more or less, according to occasion of use. John Locke, who uses the words 'self' and 'person' interchangeably in his discussion of personal identity, notices this phenomenon, in effect (though his purposes are somewhat different), when he writes that 'we must here take notice what the word "I" is applied to; which, in this case, is the man [human being] only. And the same man being presumed to be the same [self or] person, "I" is easily here supposed'—quite wrongly, in his view—'to stand also for the same [self or] person' (1694: 2.27.20).

11.5

The referring term *I* is often contrasted with the referring terms *here* and *now*, which can also vary in their referential reach. But the reference of *I* doesn't expand and contract in a continuous fashion, like that of *now* and *here* (*here* may refer to this room, this town, this country, this planet,...). Instead, I propose, it moves between two fixed positions. A referring expression like *the castle* provides a better illustration of how *I* functions than *now* and *here*. For *I*, like *the castle*, and unlike *now* and *here*, is ordinarily taken to refer to a thing of some sort, whether it's taken to refer to the whole human being or the self. Sometimes *the castle* may be used to refer to the castle proper, sometimes it may be used to refer to the ensemble of the castle and the grounds and associated buildings located within its perimeter wall. (Compare 'I'm going to the castle' used by someone twenty miles away and by someone inside the grounds.) Similarly, when I think and talk about myself, my reference may extend to the whole human being that I am, or it may extend only to the self that I take myself to be, however the self I take myself to be is best or correctly conceived in fundamental metaphysics.

Intention alone can't determine reference—a man may intend to refer to himself as the immaterial soul he believes himself to be although it doesn't exist; or he may say, madly but sincerely, 'I am Nefertiti', or 'I am this *ficus benjaminus*'. Intention can nevertheless be determinative of the reference of the use or occurrence of a term (word or thought-element) when there is more than one real possibility about what the term refers to, as there is in the case of the term *bank*, for example, and also, I propose, in the case of *I*.[12]

Most think that selves persist for long periods of time, perhaps for life—if, that is, they exist at all. This seems a reasonable position, and most who seek to combine it with materialism are likely to identify the self with some complex persisting structure or set of structures in the brain: whichever structure or set of structures supports and realizes what one might call the *self-phenomena*, e.g. the consciousness and personality of a human being. I'll call this putative persisting entity the 'brain-system self'.[13] Crucially, it allows that the self or subject of experience may exist when there is no experience going on, e.g. when one is dreamlessly asleep.

---

[12] Rory Madden helped me to clarify this point.

[13] See e.g. Flanagan 2003. See also Nagel 1986. A bloody way to get a fix on this idea is to imagine radical surgery which leaves one with only a head, but still fully present, however uncomfortably, as a subject of experience.

With William James, Fichte, Kant in 1772, Husserl, many Buddhists, and also, I think, Descartes, and also, perhaps, Nozick (and many others), I prefer a different view. I believe that the 'thin' or 'live' conception of the subject of experience, according to which

no *subject of experience* exists unless *experience* exists for it to be the *subject of*

is of fundamental metaphysical importance, when it comes to questions about the self. On this view, a subject of experience cannot be said to exist, strictly speaking, when there is no experience going on. A subject of experience is something that is essentially experientially live, something that exists only in the act or activity of experience.[14]

Kant goes further, at one point, identifying the self/subject of experience with its experience, claiming that 'the thinking or the existence of the thought and the existence of my own self are one and the same' (1772: 75). With James, and, as I understand him, Descartes (and also Spinoza, and perhaps also Leibniz), I also favour this extreme identity view.[15] But one needn't go this far when recognizing the validity of the thin conception of the subject of experience, or endorsing the view that the best candidate for the title 'the self' is the subject of experience as it is present and alive in the living moment of experience—an entity which may be very short-lived, and cannot in any case survive any gaps in the human process of consciousness.

On the materialist view, the self so conceived is identical with a pattern or 'synergy' of neural activity, possibly short-lived. I'll call it 'the synergy self'. It joins up with the brain-system self and the whole human being to constitute a nested triplet of intended or actual candidates for the referent of *I* in the thought or speech of an individual human being, as represented in Figure 11.1.[16] And if *ātman*[17] is *brahman*, in some nesting sense that allows that *ātman* is none the less a distinct object from *brahman*, there may be not three, but four candidates for the reference of *I* (so also, perhaps, if Spinoza is right about the metaphysics of reality).[18] Nor do I see any

[14] Fichte writes that 'the I exists only in so far as it is conscious of itself. ... The *self posits itself*, and by virtue of this mere self-assertion it *exists*; and conversely, the self *exists* and *posits* its own existence by virtue of merely existing' (1794–1802: 97). Nozick writes that 'it is reflexive self-consciousness that constitutes ... the self' (1989: 14); 'there is no preexisting I; rather the I is delineated, is synthesized around the reflexive act. An entity is synthesized around the reflexive act and it is the "I" of that act ... the self which is reflexively referred to is synthesized in that very act of reflexive self-reference ... an entity coagulates' (Nozick 1981: 87, 91, 88). Husserl writes that 'my consciousness of myself and I myself are, concretely considered, identical. To be a subject is to be in the mode of being aware of oneself' (c.1922: 151). These claims provide powerful grounds (to put it mildly) for asserting *I*'s immunity to error through misidentification relative to *I*, but the immunity thesis doesn't need anything as powerful as this to secure it, and these claims differ in various ways from the claim in the text that no subject of experience exists unless experience exists for it to be the subject of.

[15] James proposes that 'the thoughts themselves are the thinkers' (1892: 191). Descartes holds [i] that 'the attributes [of a substance], when considered collectively, are indeed identical with the substance', and [ii] that the only attribute of mind (apart from general attributes common to all concrete things, i.e. existence and duration) is thinking = contentful consciousness (1648: 15; for some further discussion, see Strawson 2017).

[16] Adapted from Strawson 2009: 336.

[17] *ātman* in the sense of that which appears to be an individual subject of experience in the case of each human being.

[18] It's also true that you are *brahman*, if *brahman* exists. So you're the same subject as I am, if *brahman* exists. But that's not a *reductio*. For if it's true that there's one mind, then it's true that you and I are the same subject. On such questions see e.g. Johnston 2010.

The referential behaviour of *I*

1 = a–d whole human being
2 = a–c persisting mental self traditionally conceived = 'brain-system self', on the materialist
   view
3 = a–b synergy self, self of the living moment of experience

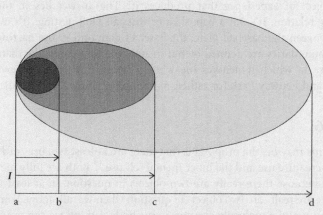

Figure 11.1 The referential behaviour of *I*

First view. If the actual reference of *I* ever shifts from 1, the whole human being (if we do ever succeed in referring to ourselves as an inner mental subject rather than as a whole human being) then it shifts to 2, the persisting inner self. The *intended* reference of *I* is certainly to a persisting inner self, when it is not to the whole human being, and this is also its *actual* reference (note that an intended reference can be completely unreflective). If materialism is true, the reference is in fact to a brain-system, the 'brain-system self'. If on the other hand we have immaterial souls, the reference is to an immaterial soul—the 'immaterial self'. Either way we never intend to refer to 3, and we never do so in fact.

Second view. There is in fact no such thing as 2, the *persisting* inner self (there are complex theoretical reasons for thinking that there's no such genuine object of reference). So although one intends to refer to such a thing, when thinking of oneself as a self, what one actually refers to, at any given time, *and insofar as one succeeds in referring to a self at all*, is 3, the 'thin' subject, the inner subject of experience as it is present and alive in the living moment of experience—because it's the only available candidate. It follows that one has many false beliefs about the thing one actually refers to. One believes, for example, that it is a persisting thing that continues to exist even when one is in a dreamless sleep (*nb* a 'bundle' theory of the persisting self won't help, because a series or bundle of selves isn't a real persisting self at all).

What about the *completely unreflective intended* reference, i.e. the thing one unthinkingly takes oneself to be referring to when one says 'I'? Again, it seems that the unreflectively intended reference is either to 1, the whole human being, or to 2, a persisting inner self as traditionally conceived. Some (including committed materialists) feel it is more often, or virtually always, or always, or at least most fundamentally, to 2; others think the same about 1. Some, though, think of the inner self as 3, and it's arguable that many people sometimes naturally 'speak out of' the self of the present moment—in which case the unthinkingly intended reference is to 3. (Compare Nozick: 'The self which is reflexively referred to is synthesized in that very act of reflexive self-reference' (1981: 91).) Even in this case, though, the unthinkingly intended reference is almost always also to something considered as persisting, however vaguely.

reason why *I* can't indicate more than one position in any actual use or occurrence in thought or speech. It's arguable that it often does so, in fact, given the extreme fluency—lability—of our semantic intentions for *I*. They can flicker between two positions, or comport both at the same time, or be indeterminate with respect to them.

How can an individual's use of *I* possibly refer to two or more distinct things, either successively or simultaneously, and still refer always and necessarily and only to the subject of experience that produces it? The answer lies in the nature of the nesting relation. It's not a babushka or Russian Doll nesting. It's more like the relation between the baseball plate, the baseball diamond in the narrower sense in which its boundaries are defined by but include the four bases, the diamond in the larger sense in which it denotes the whole playing field (perhaps excluding foul territory), and Fenway Park (or rather, in my preferred case, Citi Field).

11.6

However this may be, the proposal is that there are at least two uses of *I* 'as subject', the whole-creature use and the inner mental self use.[19] Both are fully metaphysically legitimate, because there really are two objects in question, in at least the sense in which there are really are two objects in question when we talk about Tom and Tom's hand, or Tom and a molecule of water in his body. I think we can acknowledge, as materialists, and without any reference to *façons de parler*, that an outright truth can be expressed by the claim (so deeply backed by intuition) that I'm not the same thing as my living body considered as a whole: we can acknowledge that there are cases in which what we mean by *I* is not the same thing as the whole human being. At the same time, we can insist that an outright truth is expressed by the claim that I'm a human being. There's no sound argument from the nature of the word or thought-element *I* to the conclusion that this commits us to saying that two things with different identity conditions are in fact the same thing.[20]

This distinction between the two uses of *I* will seem immediately plausible to non-philosophers, but philosophers may doubt its propriety as a way of representing what is the case even if they accept it as an accurate report of how we sometimes think and talk.

—I'm not going to accept any such thing. Even if *I* is used with the semantic intention of referring only to the putative 'self' (your 'I^S') its referential force automatically flows on out to encompass the whole human being (your 'I^{Hu}'). This is a non-negotiable fact about the essentially public, essentially intersubjective phenomenon of language. It overrides any alleged facts about variations in semantic intention. In fact I'm tempted to say that such a semantic intention isn't

---

[19] Compare Johnston, who defends a distinction 'between two sorts of *de se* thought, a merely indexical thought directed to the person or human being that I am, and a truly subjective thought, as it were directed to the self that I am' (2010: 180; see also pp. 192–4).

[20] We're already prepared for this point if we allow that dualism, although false, isn't incoherent. For when dualists say 'I'm distinct from my body', they manage to refer by the use of 'I' and to say something true, if dualism is true; and they can still use 'I' to refer to the whole human being in statements that say something true about the speaker or thinker.

really possible, because the possible content of thought is a function of the possible content of language conceived as an essentially public institution with essentially public objects of reference.

This is the argument from language I rejected in §§11.2 and 11.3. And what matters more, now, is the claim that I^S and I^H are different things, at least as different as the castle and the castle proper, which stand, no doubt, in a standard spatiotemporal part–whole relation.

—This can't work. If you distinguish I^S and I^H then you must in the case of any proper name like 'Louis' also distinguish $Louis^S$ and $Louis^H$, and this shows up the fundamental implausibility of the proposal, because Louis is Louis is $Louis^H$. Period.

It's true that what goes for 'I' goes for 'Louis', but all that follows is that a truth can be expressed both by saying that Louis is $Louis^H$ and by saying that Louis is $Louis^S$, even though $Louis^H$ and $Louis^S$ are different objects (I've already rejected the objection from the transitivity of the identity relation). I agree with you, in fact, that Louis is $Louis^H$, insofar as the name 'Louis' is assumed to refer to an object with relatively long-term diachronic continuity, because I favour the synergy self as the best candidate for being the self, and am correspondingly disinclined to say that there's any other object (such as a traditional inner self) that can be rightly called 'Louis' and that has long-term diachronic continuity. For the moment, though, I'm leaving in play the popular view that $Louis^S$ may reasonably be thought of as something that has long-term continuity, the traditional inner (non-thin) view of $Louis^S$ as something that persists through periods of experiencelessness. On this view, the claim that $Louis^H$ and $Louis^S$ are two different objects is as straightforward (at least in one respect) as the claim that Tom's hand isn't the same object as Tom, although the case of Tom and his hand differs from the case of $Louis^H$ and $Louis^S$ in that '$Louis^H$' and '$Louis^S$' both refer to Louis considered as a subject of experience whereas 'Tom' and 'Tom's hand' don't both refer to Tom considered as a subject of experience.[21]

My claim is somewhat more complicated, not only because I believe that thin subjects are always short-lived in the human case, but also because I take it that there aren't any thin subjects at all in Louis when he isn't conscious. But we can put this idea aside for the moment.[22]

—This account of things has the consequence that when Louis says or thinks *I am F*, *I am F* is said or thought twice, both by $Louis^H$ and $Louis^S$. This is hopelessly implausible.

This is a version of the 'too many minds' argument deployed by 'animalists' in the personal identity debate, against the view that persons are simply identical with their bodies (see e.g. Olson 1997, Shoemaker 1999b). I agree that this would be an unacceptable consequence, but it has no force here, because of the nesting relation described at the end of §11.4.

---

[21] Note a sense in which to pick out Tom is to pick out Tom's hand, and equally a sense in which to pick out Tom's (undetached) hand is to pick out Tom.

[22] One can distinguish $Louis^S$ from $Louis^H$ at any time when Louis is conscious, on my view, just as one can distinguish Tom and Tom's hand; but when Louis isn't conscious there is nothing—no object—that is $Louis^S$ ($Louis^S$ is more like a goose pimple than a hand).

—Suppose I produce a long sentence, lasting half a minute or so, and in which I use the word 'I' several times. Am I to suppose that it has a different reference each time?

Not insofar as you take your 'I' to refer to you considered as a whole human being. If, however, you take it to refer to you considered specifically as a self or inner mental presence, and if traditional persisting selves are unavailable as bona fide objects—if, as I propose, selves are short-lived thin subjects insofar as they exist at all—then this is indeed what you must suppose.[23] You don't have to worry about this view of mine, or believe it, but this succession of thin subjects is, I suggest, the reality that underlies any experience of being a persisting inner self—any experience, in the case in question, of being the same self throughout the having of the thought.   ·

—But who, or what, actually speaks or thinks when Louis says or thinks *I*?

Louis does. The reference of *I* is fluid in his thought and talk in the way just described. We move naturally between conceiving of ourselves primarily as a human being and primarily as some sort of inner subject. Sometimes we mean to refer to the one, sometimes to the other, sometimes our semantic intention hovers between both, sometimes it embraces both.

—The reference to semantic intention isn't going to work, because you think that inner subjects are thin, like **3** in your diagram: 'synergy subjects'. But human beings certainly don't conceive of themselves as thin subjects when they conceive of themselves as inner subjects; they conceive of themselves as 'traditional' persisting inner subjects, like **2** in your diagram. So they never refer to thin subjects, so far as their semantic intentions go. And I don't think you do either, in daily life. I think you face the question Merian put to Hume: 'What is the meaning in your mind and your mouth of these personal pronouns which you cannot prevent yourself from continually using, and without which you would not know either to think or to express your thoughts, *me*, *I*, *we*, etc?'[24]

I've already granted that most (not all) people think of themselves as traditional persisting inner subjects like **2**, when they think of themselves as inner subjects, but my reply to your previous question stands. If in the end the best thing to say is that there's no such thing (object) as the persisting inner subject, then we obviously fail to refer to any such object when we think of ourselves as things (objects) that are inner subjects. I think that the actual reference of *I*, when we take ourselves to be referring to the persisting inner self, is to **3** or a series of **3**s, but if I'm wrong, if **2** can qualify as a subject of experience, then 'I' can refer to it. What is certain, in any and every case, is that my use of 'I' can't refer to something that isn't the subject of experience that I am (i.e. there is really no use of *I* 'as object'; a point still to be argued).

What about the *completely unreflective intended* reference of *I*, i.e. the thing one completely unthinkingly takes oneself to be referring to when one says or thinks *I*? Again, it seems that the unreflectively intended reference of *I* is either to **1**, the whole human being, or to **2**, a persisting inner self as traditionally conceived. When

---

[23] Unless you can treat 'I' as a loose way of referring to a single set or bundle of such selves. I say 'loose' because *I* must presumably refer to a subject of experience, and sets can't be subjects of experience.

[24] Merian 1793: 190. For a reply on Hume's behalf, see Strawson 2011a (§2.1).

I sample the views of philosophers and non-philosophers, I find that some feel that the intended reference of *I* is more often, or virtually always, or most fundamentally, to 2, while others think that it's more often, virtually always, or most fundamentally, to 1. There are also a few who think that 2 is really just a matter of 3; and it's arguable, independently of this last fact, that many people sometimes naturally 'speak out of' the self of the present moment—in which case the unthinkingly intended reference is to 3 (or a series of 3s). This is compatible with their automatically relying on *I* to stretch to refer to 1 (or 2) to cope with anything in what they say that implies the past and future existence of the person they're talking about—themselves. (Obviously, when one is talking to others, one has their conception of oneself as something persisting in mind, although it may be much less salient when one is alone and thinking.)

On a somewhat different tack, note that just as one may say that the actual reference of my use of *I* is *always* to whatever I actually am, so too my intended reference is or at least may always be to what I actually am, whatever I am, and whatever I think I am; because there's a fundamental standing respect in which I intend to refer to myself whatever I am—whatever I *think* I am! So if I'm an immaterial soul, then that's what I refer to, and intend to refer to—even if I'm a committed materialist. For one thing, again, is certain: I always intend to refer to myself, whatever I am, when I (sincerely) say or think *I*. And I'm far from clueless, when it comes to the question of what I am, even if I'm wrong to be a materialist, or wrong to believe in immaterial souls; I'm far from clueless even when I've suspended all metaphysical commitments as far as possible. For one thing I know is that I'm a subject of experience. And every ordinary adult human being has a very good general grasp of what a subject of experience is just in being one and being self-conscious, whatever else they may or may not know about the matter.

In sum: I am this thin subject speaking now, now, now, now. And I am this human being speaking now. And if you believe in the persisting inner self, you can say I'm this persisting inner self speaking now. And if you think Spinoza is right, you can allow a sense in which I'm the universe speaking now. In all cases, the use of 'I' refers to the subject who uses it, in speech or thought. Don't say there are 'too many minds'. There's one thought episode, one subject. The 'too many minds' objection is without any force. But there's also a sense in which 'I' is non-univocal, a sense in which—I claim—it means different things in different contexts.

How much will I mind, if you insist that I give up the claim that 'I' is not univocal? Leibniz's Law will take a hit, because the thin subject has different properties from the human being, as does the brain-system self. But the truth in the idea that 'I' in my use can denote GS the human being, and can also denote the self that I am, and can also denote both at once, will perhaps find attractive new expression. If you press me on the point, though, I'll probably collapse inwards (if Spinoza is wrong, and *brahman* isn't real): for metaphysical reasons I can't go into here (see Strawson 2009), I'll say that the subject *sensu strictissimo* is the momentary thin subject as it is present and alive in the living moment of experience, and that persisting brain structures and whole human beings are rightly called subjects of experiences only by natural extension: only because they are things that can be the locus of subjects *sensu strictissimo*.

If on the other hand Spinoza is right, I may collapse outwards, and say that the subject *sensu strictissimo* is the universe as it is present and alive in the living moment of experience. If time isn't real, or rather doesn't 'flow' in the way presentists suppose, strike the words 'as it is present and alive in the living moment of experience' (unless they can still be given a respectable meaning in the true theory of time). On the mindedness of the universe: I'm a strict atheist, and an out and out naturalist with respect to the whole of concrete reality, but I'm a serious or *real* naturalist, i.e. someone who takes the existence of conscious experience as the fundamental given natural fact, and (as such) I don't think there's much doubt that the most parsimonious and hard-nosed form of naturalism—which I'm still happy to call 'materialism'—is panpsychist in some form.[25] On the oneness of the universe: there seems to be a lot of agreement in present-day cosmology that there is a fundamental and non-trivial sense in which the universe is a single thing. None of this matters, however, to the issue that is central at present.

11.7

I've argued that

[5]   there is an important sense in which *I* is not univocal

although

[2´]   *I* always refers to the subject who says or thinks it,

in such a way that

[1]   *I* is immune to error through misidentification of its referent

or equivalently (in Shoemaker's terms)

[1´]   all genuine uses of *I* are 'immune to error through misidentification relative to the first-person pronoun' *I*.

I want now to marshal reasons for affirming [1]/[1´]. But let me first put in place and endorse the standard definition of full self-consciousness, by which I mean express or explicit self-consciousness of the sort possessed by every ordinary adult human being (and indeed any human being more than two years old).[26]

According to the definition

[6]   to be (fully) self-conscious is to be able to think of oneself *as oneself.*

Full stop. If I'm fully self-conscious, I can think of myself *specifically as myself,* and not (say) just as the oldest person on Facebook called 'Ataraxia Smith', or the person most worried about water shortages, or the sad-eyed person I can see in this foggy

---

[25] For a sketch, see Strawson 2006. Many scoff at panpsychism, unaware of their resemblance to flatearthers. Recent candidates for philosophy jobs have been warned not to reveal the fact that they take panpsychism seriously.

[26] I say 'full' self-consciousness to allow for lesser forms of self-consciousness, such as the self-consciousness that a dog shows when it removes its paw thoughtfully from the path of an steadily oncoming projectile; or the self-consciousness that Phenomenologists attribute to every sentient creature on the ground that all awareness comports awareness of that very awareness and, hence, awareness of the thing that has the property of possessing that very awareness. For lesser forms of self-consciousness see e.g. Zahavi 2006: ch. 1, Damasio 1999: 125–6, 236–43.

Versailles mirror. It's a familiar point that this is a way of thinking about oneself that is unlike any other.[27] I can think about the oldest person on Facebook called 'Ataraxia Smith', or the person most worried about water shortages, or the sad-eyed person in the mirror, and be thinking of myself, and not know that I'm thinking of myself, and believe I'm not thinking of myself. So too, and conversely, I can think of the three individuals correctly identified by these descriptions, and think that I'm thinking of myself, and be wrong. But

[7] if I'm thinking about something specifically as *myself*, I can't fail to be thinking of myself.

This would be true even if it weren't also true that

[8] I can't fail to know that I'm thinking of myself when I'm thinking of myself as myself

although [8] is also true. (Any doubts about [8] should be dissolved in the next section.)

There's widespread agreement about the correctness of the definition of self-consciousness just given, and many also agree with [7]. Many also agree that thinking of oneself in the special way that is distinctive and definitive of full self-consciousness is essential to—essentially informs—any genuine understanding use of *I*. They agree that

[9] a genuine understanding use of *I* always involves the subject grasping itself as itself, whatever else it does or doesn't involve[28]

—even if it *also* involves thinking of something else as the referent of *I* (for a case of this, see the next section). And if [9] is true, then, together with [7], it secures [1]/[1']. In which case we're done. But some, perhaps, may doubt [9], and it's worth rehearsing the point with a few examples.

11.8

Consider a being for whom all the appearances are that it is thinking about itself.[29] That is, all the appearances *for it* are that it is thinking about itself. We can take this as our starting point. But, given this starting point, the end point is secure. For there is no possibility that any being can be wrong about who or what it's thinking about when all the appearances, for it, are that it's thinking about itself.

More briefly: consider a being of whom it is true to say that it takes itself to be thinking about itself (I take it that this 'taking' can be very unreflective). Then there is no possibility that it can be wrong about who or what it's thinking about.

---

[27] See e.g. Castañeda 1966, Perry 1979. It is sometimes called '*de se*' thought, following Lewis 1979.

[28] Grasping oneself as oneself in the distinctive fully self-conscious way is essential to any genuine understanding use of *I*, but the converse is not true. This is another familiar point: I don't have to use *I* to think/speak of myself when thinking/speaking of myself as myself. I don't have to speak a language that has a first-person pronoun. I can use my proper name to refer to myself whenever I think of myself as myself in the distinctive fully self-conscious way. We can nevertheless pick out the relevant way of thinking of myself by reference to the notion of a genuine understanding use of *I*.

[29] This section and the next expand on Strawson 1999b: 329–31.

[10]   If it's true that I take myself to be thinking about myself, then I am thinking about myself.[30]

This is the fundamental anchor of the fact that one can't possibly miss one's target, when one thinks in terms of *I* (i.e. in a fully self-conscious manner); the fundamental respect in which any *I*-thought that one has is necessarily about oneself and is absolutely immune both to reference failure and to 'error through misidentification of the subject' of the thought, even if it involves a major error of some kind. No doubt the logico-grammatical reference rule for 'I'—that it always refers to whoever produces it—secures the impossibility of error just as well. The fundamental phenomenon is none the less psychological. It's simply a matter of *what it is genuinely to think of oneself as oneself*—which one always does when one genuinely (meaningly) thinks or says *I*.

Suppose (to take a couple of odd but standard philosophical examples) that you see an arm painted blue in a mirror in a crowded room, believe wrongly that it's your own arm, and think *I have a blue arm*. This is a typical example of the use of *I* that Wittgenstein called the use 'as object'. Or suppose you have a false 'quasi-memory', i.e. an apparent memory of a past experience that derives directly (by some peculiar mechanism) from someone else's past experience,[31] and think *I fell in the river* or *I was sad*. In all such cases you're wrong about who has the property, but you're not wrong, and can't be wrong, in your (criterionless) latching onto or identification of yourself. Confusion has arisen from the phrase 'immune to error through misidentification of the subject', largely, perhaps, because 'identification' has two uses. One is related to the notion of simply identifying or latching onto something, possibly in a criterionless way. The other is related to the notion of identifying something *with* (or *as*) something (else).

Consider again your thought *I have a blue arm* or *I was sad*. It's false, and it makes sense to say that it's false not because the predicate-term fails to match the right property in the world, but because the subject-term fails to match the right object in the world (something really does have the property in question; an error has been made about what it is). It doesn't, however, follow that there has been any misiden-tification of the subject of the thought. For you certainly intend to refer to yourself with *I*, and you know this, and you certainly (inevitably) succeed: here there is no possible misidentification of the subject of the thought. When it comes to genuine use of *I*, there is no possible error that consists in my missing myself as referent.

But now there seems to be a puzzle. If we're allowing that the predicate-term matches the right property in the world, and also insisting that there is a fundamental sense in which there has been no misidentification of the subject of the thought, how can the thought be false? The answer, plainly, is that the thought can be false because although you do (necessarily) intend to refer to yourself by means of your genuine use of *I*, in this case as in every case, and although you succeed in doing so, it seems plausible to say that you *also* intend to refer to *the person with the blue arm* by means of *I*. It's this phenomenon that lies behind the idea that there is such a thing as the use

---

[30] Note that one doesn't have to write 'If it's true that I take myself to be thinking about myself *as myself*, then . . .'.

[31] Shoemaker (1970) coined the term 'quasi-memory' for a phenomenon Locke discusses in 2.27.13 of his *Essay*.

of *I* 'as object', and it is, of course, the source of the error in your thought. Your error is the (mis)identification of yourself *with* the person with the blue arm.

Your use of *I* refers, as always, only to you. Your error lies in the fact that in thinking the thought *I have a blue arm* you mistakenly think, of yourself, that you have the property 'am (identical with) the man with the blue arm'. The completely unshiftable sense in which there is no misidentification of self, of the referent of *I*, remains completely unshifted, but there is indeed a major misidentification-*with*, a misidentification of self/*I* with something that is not self/*I*. Given this misidentification-*with*, we can intelligibly say that there is a sense in which the error in the thought stems not from the descriptive import of the predicate term, but from the referential import of the subject-term. But there is also a fundamental sense in which this isn't really so. Or rather: although there is a sense in which the error in the thought stems from the referential import of the subject-term, this is not because the use of the subject-term involves *an error of reference*. On the contrary: the source of the error in the judgement lies in the fact that there isn't (and can't be) any error at all in the referential import of the subject-term. *I* inevitably refers to you—and is inevitably intended by you to refer to you, given that it is a genuine use of *I*. So insofar as we allow a sense in which the error in the thought stems from the referential import of the subject-term, we may allow a *sense* in which the falsity of the thought stems from 'error through misidentification relative to' *I*. But Shoemaker's careful phrase 'relative to' is well chosen, and this somewhat quixotic sense in which there is 'error through misidentification relative to' *I* doesn't touch the fundamental respect in which there is no error of misidentification in the use of *I*. There is no failure to 'hit' oneself referentially, nor any possibility of such a failure— whatever else may (also) be going on.

In fact, and again, any sense in which there is error through misidentification relative to *I* depends essentially and precisely on the fundamental sense in which there is and can be no error. It depends precisely on the fact that your *I*-thoughts are *always* about yourself, whatever else they may be about, and are in that fundamental respect absolutely immune to error through misidentification of the subject. *I* never referentially hits the wrong thing, even if its occurrence is prompted by my wrongly thinking I see myself in the mirror. One might say (again) that all my uses of 'I' are always backed by a *general* intention to refer to myself whatever I am, even if I'm sometimes also thinking of myself specifically as a whole human being or as an inner self, or as some person or entity that I am not, e.g. the person in the mirror, or an immaterial soul.

We can put this by saying that your use of *I* inevitably refers to you, given your intention in using it, given the fact that it is a genuine use of *I*, even if your overall intention in using it *also* underwrites the claim it *also* refers to the person with the blue arm (this is the point of the clause 'whatever else it does or doesn't involve' in claim [9]). The thought *I have a blue arm* doesn't involve a use of *I* 'as object'. It doesn't involve a partial use 'as object'. It doesn't involve a secondary use 'as object', in addition to a primary core use 'as subject'. It's wholly a use 'as subject'— the only use there is! The thought is false because you don't have a blue arm. What's special about the case is simply this: that we can reasonably allow that part of your intention in using *I*, in this case, is to refer to the person with the blue arm, someone who is in fact not you. But we can allow this only because you have misidentified that person as (with) *yourself*. There remains as always, a fundamental sense in which your intention can only be to refer only to yourself. In this case you're still thinking of yourself as yourself, and referring to yourself considered as yourself, and making a wholly 'subject' use of *I*. We have to go via the fact that you intend only to refer to yourself, in a wholly 'subject use' way, to make sense of the fact that there is also a sense in which you can be said to intend (on the basis of your misidentification of yourself with that person) to refer to the person with the blue arm by your use of *I*.

11.9

I'll conclude with a further comment on the point that if there is an apparent *I*-thought, then there is a real *I*-thought, which can't fail to refer; the point that [10] if the subject takes itself to be thinking about itself, then it is in fact doing so.

Gareth Evans questions this in his book *The Varieties of Reference*. Developing his argument, he writes:

It seems possible to envisage organisms whose control centre is outside the body, and connected to it by communication links.... An organism of this kind could have an Idea of itself like our own, but if it did it would be unable to cope with the situation that would arise when the control centre survived the destruction of the body it controlled. Thinking like us, the subject would of course have to regard itself as somewhere, but in this case it would not make any sense to identify a particular place in the world it thought of as *here*. The place occupied by the control centre is certainly not the subject's *here*; and even if we counterfactually suppose the control centre re-equipped with a body, there is no particular place where that body would have to be. Because its 'here' picks out no place, there is no bit of matter, no persisting thing, which the subject's Idea of itself permits us to regard as what it identifies as itself. Here, then, we have a very clear situation in which a subject of thought could not think of itself as 'I'; its 'I'—its habitual mode of thought about itself—is simply inadequate for this situation.[32]

Evans thinks that this sort of inadequacy can also afflict us in more ordinary situations: 'our ordinary thoughts about ourselves are liable to many different kinds of failings, and...the Cartesian assumption that such thoughts are always guaranteed to have an object cannot be sustained' (p. 249).

It seems to me, however, that Evans, with characteristic honesty and insight, provides the best objection to his own view, and that the above passage makes it vivid that *I* succeeds in hitting its mark—the I, the subject of experience that indubitably exists, whatever its ultimate nature, if an apparent *I*-thought occurs—even when there is 'no bit of matter' or other 'persisting thing' that it can identify as itself. It shows that a subject's apparent thoughts about itself—its apparent *I*-thoughts, thoughts that lack nothing, so far as the subject is concerned, when it comes to their *seeming* to be *I*-thoughts—always have an object. And in fact they always have the object they're thought to have, however many false beliefs the subject has about its own nature.

---

[32]   pp. 254–5. Compare Platner (1772: §193): 'we are conscious of ourselves, that is of our existence, if we know the spatial, temporal and other relations of our condition. If we do not know where we are and when we are, then we are not conscious of ourselves.'

Even if it could somehow be shown that such thoughts don't always have an object, it would still be true that they can have an object in situations in which Evans denies that they can, for a more direct objection to Evans's case runs as follows. Suppose the subject thinks 'I'm in big trouble, wherever I am', or 'I don't know where I am, or how much of me is left intact, but I'm in big trouble, wherever I am, and however much of me is left.' In this case there seems to be no good reason to think that 'the control centre', which I assume to be the locus of the subject's consciousness, 'is certainly not the subject's *here*'.

Evans considers another case in which one has a false memory, an apparent memory of perceiving a certain past event *e* that in fact derives directly from someone else's perception of that event (it is therefore a 'quasi-memory'). One thinks, in the present, *I perceived e*, or *I perceived e in 1990*; but in fact it was Louis, not oneself, who perceived *e*. Evans claims that one's *I*-thought *I perceived e* has no object in this case, because one is bringing 'both present-tense... and past-tense... information to bear upon [one's current] self-conscious reflections, and there is no one thing from which both kinds of information derive'. He compares this to a case in which one is looking at one cup and feeling another, and falsely supposes that there is just one cup, and thinks 'this cup is well made' (pp. 249–50).

The case of the cups is a good one in its own right, but I think it's unhelpful in this context, for, once again, the occurrence of *I* in the thought that *I perceived e* (or, generally, *I was F*) is guaranteed a reference. It unfailingly cleaves to one thing, oneself, present at the time of the thought. It refers to oneself thought of as a thing that exists now and that existed in the past. It's false precisely because one did not perceive *e* in the past. It isn't a thought that involves any confusion about who or what the subject of the thought is, even though it involves a mistake.

Evans further claims that 'it is of the essence of an "I"-Idea that it effects an identification that spans past and present' (p. 246), but it's hard to see why this might be thought to be a general truth, for it's hard to see why there could not be a self-conscious being that had no significant sense or conception of the past at all.[33] And even if the claim is granted, it doesn't provide grounds for an objection to the view that one's apparent *I*-thought has an object, in the case in question, and has, indeed, the object one takes it to have. Even if it is of the essence of an *I*-Idea to effect an identification that spans past and present, it remains true that one's quasi-memory concerns only oneself—oneself present now and thought of, if only implicitly, as temporally extended and as existing both now and in 1990. This fundamental fact effortlessly trumps any facts about the actual source of the information carried in the quasi-memory.[34,35]

---

[33] On this point see e.g. Strawson 2009: 199–204.

[34] I believe that Evans goes wrong because he is, like a number of other philosophers in Oxford at that time, overimpressed by P. F. Strawson's ultimately unsuccessful neo-Kantian argument that self-consciousness requires a sense of oneself as tracing a continuous route through an ordered (spatial or quasi-spatial) world (Strawson 1966).

[35] Many thanks to Rory Madden and Simon Prosser for their comments.

12

'The secrets of all hearts'
Locke on Personal Identity

12.1 Introduction

Many people think that John Locke's account of personal identity is inconsistent and circular. In fact it's neither of these things—Locke has been massively misunderstood. The blame for the misunderstanding falls principally on two otherwise admirable bishops—Berkeley and Butler—and an otherwise admirable doctor of divinity—Thomas Reid.[1] Their influence has been such that almost no one since their time has had a chance to read what Locke wrote without prejudice. Catherine Cockburn fully understood Locke's view in 1702, in her *Defence of the Essay of Human Understanding Written by Mr. Locke*, and another bishop—Bishop Law—put Berkeley and Butler right in 1769, when he was Master of Peterhouse, Cambridge, and Knightbridge Professor of Philosophy, in his *Defence of Mr. Locke's Opinion Concerning Personal Identity*. But no one paid any lasting attention.

The root cause of the misunderstanding, perhaps, has been the tendency to read the term 'person' in Locke's *Essay* as if it were simply a sortal term like 'human being' or 'thinking thing', a term for a standard temporal continuant. This approach is bound to lead to error because it fails to take proper account of Locke's use of 'person' as what he calls a 'forensic' term (*Essay* 2.27.26; in what follows I will refer to paragraphs of Book 2 Chapter 27 simply by their paragraph numbers, e.g. §26).

Many have acknowledged the importance of the forensic use, but they've continued to suppose that Locke's principal aim is to provide criteria of diachronic identity for persons considered simply as persisting subjects of experience, and so considered independently of forensic matters. They have thought that Locke is trying to answer the following canonical question about personal identity: [i] consider a subject of experience at time t_1 (2000, say) who is a person as we ordinarily understand this term—call this person 'P_1'. [ii] Consider a subject of experience at a later time t_2 (2015, say) who is a person as we ordinarily understand this term—call this person 'P_2'. Question: What has to be the case for it to be true that P_1 at (time) t_1 is the same as person P_2 at (time) t_2, the same persisting subject of experience?

Locke isn't interested in this question—not as it is ordinarily understood. He takes the notion of a persisting subject of experience or locus of consciousness for granted in his discussion of personal identity, and answers four other questions:

---

[1] The most well-known formulations of the inconsistency objection are Berkeley 1732 and Reid 1785. The circularity objection is standardly attributed to Butler 1736. It was, however, stated by Sergeant in 1697, and Sergeant adapted it from a debate between South and Sherlock that was well known in Butler's time, in which South (1693) made it validly against Sherlock (1690). See Thiel 1998: 875–7, 898. Garrett (2003) also argues that both objections fail.

[A] what does a subject of experience that qualifies as a person consist of, ontologically speaking, considered at any given time?

[B] what mental capacities must a subject of experience have in order to qualify as a person?

[C] what sorts of changes of substantial composition can a subject of experience that qualifies as a person undergo while continuing to exist?

[D] which actions is a subject of experience who qualifies as a person responsible for at any given time?

These are the questions he sets himself to answer and does answer—as I will now try to show. (For [A] see in particular §12.9, for [B] §12.10, for [C] and [D] §12.12.)

12.2 'Subject of Experience'

Let me establish an uncommitted term that allows one to refer neutrally to *the kind of thing that Locke is concerned with when he raises the question of its personal identity* (the aim is to avoid begging or obscuring any relevant questions and triggering irrelevant questions). The term must be neither *soul* nor *man* nor *person*, all of which Locke famously distinguishes from each other (§7). Nor can it be any of the terms he uses interchangeably with *soul*, i.e. *immaterial substance* (§14), *(immaterial) spirit* (§14, 15), *immaterial being* (§14), *individual immaterial substance* (§23), *immaterial thinking thing* (§23); nor any of the terms he uses interchangeably with *man*, i.e. *rational animal* (§8, parrots being *sub judice*) and *(human) animal* (§§6, 8). Nor can it be any of the terms Locke uses when he wishes to put aside the question of whether 'that which is conscious in us' (§25) is material or immaterial—terms like *intellectual substance* (§13) and *thinking substance* (§13, §23). These terms also fail to be neutral in the required way, if only because they introduce the notion of substance, for one of the things that Locke aims to question is precisely whether a person is or must be supposed to be a substance.

The same goes for *conscious thinking thing* (§17), 'that *thinking thing* that is in us' (§27), *thinking being* (§25), *intelligent being* (§25), and other such terms. For *thing* and *being*, here, are essentially the same as *substance*. Nor is *self* a sufficiently neutral choice, for Locke treats *self* as synonymous with *person*.[2] There are, among all his unhelpfully numerous terms, some that could perhaps serve as the uncommitted term. One possibility is *intelligent agent* (§26), or *individual agent* (§13), but at certain points problems arise even with *agent*.[3] Locke's use of 'consciousness' as a count noun in §23—'could we suppose two distinct incommunicable consciousnesses acting the same body, the one constantly by day, the other by night'—might serve the purpose. It is, in a sense, exactly what we want, and it's Locke's own use. It would, however, be confusing to use 'consciousness' in this way in this paper, in addition to using it in the more standard way as a non-count noun.

---

[2] Thiel uses *self* as the uncommitted term, in effect, and successfully makes the key points about Locke in this way, but the term is not ideal given that Locke uses it interchangeably with *person* in 2.27.

[3] '*The mind*' is another candidate term, given Locke's use of it (see e.g. §§13, 23), but this choice would cause other unclarities. As for *rational being*, it is identified with *person* in §9 and with *thinking being* in §8.

I propose therefore to introduce my own term: *subject of experience*. The entity that Locke is concerned with, when he raises the question of what its personal identity consists in, is a subject of experience. Not any kind of subject of experience, such as an elephant or a dog or a fox (2.1.19, 2.11.7), but a subject of experience whose mental capacities are such that it qualifies as a person (§§9, 26). Subjects of experience of any species can be persons, so long as they possess the requisite capacities, but Locke's principal concern is unsurprisingly with ourselves, human persons, human subjects of experience considered either at a particular time in life or on the Day of Judgement. This is where he starts from—the given fact of complex, self-conscious, diachronically persisting personalitied subjects of experience like ourselves who are born, live, and die (but who may, he crucially argues, conceivably survive switches of body and soul), who act, who are capable of pleasure and pain, happiness and misery, and who are on Locke's view eventually resurrected. In asking about the *personal identity* of such subjects of experience, Locke's focus is always on the forensic issue of what they're (morally and legally) responsible for. His question is about their personal identity in the sense of their moral or legal identity, their overall standing, at any given particular time, when it comes to the question of moral and legal responsibility at that time.

12.3 'Person'

The word 'person' has a double use and has perhaps always done so. In its most common use, today as in the seventeenth century, it denotes a human being considered as a whole: a *person₁* as I will say. But a less common use, henceforth *person₂*, is no less available to us, no less natural and no less readily understood. This is the use that allows one to say of a human being 'She isn't the same person any more' or 'He's become a completely different person'. When Henry James writes of one of his early novels 'I think of...the masterpiece in question...as the work of quite another person than myself...a rich...relation, say, who.... suffers me still to claim a shy fourth cousinship' (1915: 562–3) he knows perfectly well that he's the same human being (person₁) as the author of that book. It's just that he doesn't feel he's the same person₂ as the author of that book and we all know what he means—even though the notion of a person₂ is somewhat vague. Here James is using the word 'person' in the familiar way that allows one to distinguish the person or self that one is from the human being that one is considered as a whole.

The person₂ use of 'person' is plainly connected to the notion of personality, and we ordinarily think of personality as a property of a creature, not as a thing of any sort; and yet when we use 'person' to mean a person₂ we do still think of it as denoting a thing or entity of some sort—a subject of experience, a 'self'. We don't think that we're using the word just as a way of talking about personality, where personality is a mere property of a person₁. Much of the difficulty of exposition of Locke's view lies in a similar fact about his use of 'person'.

A Lockean person—a *Person*, as I'll say, using an initial capital letter to mark Locke's special use of the term (except when quoting Locke or others)—is certainly not a person₁, i.e. (or e.g.) a human being. A (Lockean) Person isn't a person$_2$ either, as ordinarily conceived (i.e. an instance of the kind of thing that Henry James takes himself to be in 1915 when he says that he's a different person from the person who wrote his early novel). Locke's use of 'person' does share certain features with the person$_2$ use. It shares [i] the person$_2$ use's fundamental connection with the property-denoting notion of personality (or rather, in Locke's case, the property-denoting notion of one's overall moral personality or standing). But it also shares with the person$_2$ use [ii] the person$_2$ use's property of being naturally taken to denote a thing of some sort, i.e. not merely a property, but rather something that is naturally thought of as a temporal continuant, however vague its temporal boundaries. And the trouble is that [i] and [ii] pull in different directions. Lockean Personal identity is not simply a matter of the diachronic identity of a temporal continuant, in spite of the [ii]-affinity. To take proper account of the [i]-affinity is to see that there's a key sense in which one's overall moral personality or being changes all the time, on Locke's view, simply insofar as one engages in new actions and experiences. Thus a person—a Lockean person, a subject of experience who is a Person—is different every day and indeed every moment, on Locke's view, so far as its *Personal identity* or *Personhood* is concerned. And this is of course not so given the standard person$_1$ use or the standard person$_2$ use of 'person' according to which a person's personal identity remains unchanged through time.

12.4 ' "Person" a Forensic Term'

Plainly there is scope for confusion. I hope things will become clearer in what follows. One can put the point by saying that there's a sense in which 'person' is indeed a property term, a term for a *moral quality*, in Locke's text, in spite of its natural use as a thing term. Throughout the seventeenth century, as Thiel observes:

'person' most commonly referred to an individual human being: it was simply a term for the individual human self, as it is today. But in some philosophical discussions 'person' referred to a particular aspect, quality, or function of the individual human being.   (1998: 868–9)

This second use of the word derives from Roman law, in which '*persona*', which originally meant 'mask', refers 'to the individual human being specifically insofar as he or she stands in a relationship to legal matters' (ibid.).

J. L. Mackie generally reads Locke well, and he's right when he says that Locke's theory 'is...hardly a theory of personal identity at all, but might be better described as a theory of action appropriation'. This, after all, is exactly what Locke says himself. But Mackie then goes on to claim that 'Locke seems to be forgetting that "person" is not only "a forensic term", appropriating actions and their merit, but also the noun corresponding to all the personal pronouns', i.e. a thing term (1976: 183). But Locke isn't forgetting this. He's chosen to use the word 'person' in a less common but time-honoured way which, for all that it is forensic, can still correspond to the personal pronouns. He's well aware that his use of 'person' is non-standard. He says so himself: 'Person, *as I take it*'—'Person', *as I am taking the word*—'is a forensic term' (§26).

12.5 The Field of Responsibility and the Field of Concernment

'Person ... is a forensic term appropriating actions and their merit' (§26). It applies to subjects of experience who are 'intelligent agents' (§26), i.e. subjects of experience whose mental capacities are such that they qualify as Persons by Locke's definition. Consider S, a subject of experience who is suitably complex and so qualifies as a Person. Given the forensic sense of 'person' the question of *what S's Personal identity consists in* considered at some particular time is simply the question of what S is morally or legally responsible for at that time.[4] This is the force of 'forensic'. One could put the point by saying that the question of which or what Person S is is a question about S's overall *field* of responsibility at that time.

A little more accurately, one could say that it is a question about S's overall field of *concern* or *concernment* at that time. The adjustment is needed because one's field of concernment is wider than one's field of responsibility. One's field of concernment contains everything that one is intimately involved in in such a way that it can be a source of one's 'pleasure or pain; i.e. happiness or misery; beyond which we have no concernment' (4.11.8). It therefore extends beyond matters of specifically moral or legal concern—to one's mind and body and toothache. One's field of responsibility falls wholly within one's field of concernment because what one is responsible for has vast consequences for one's happiness or misery both here on earth and on and after the Day of Judgement, but one's field of responsibility is not coextensive with one's field of concernment because many pains and pleasures have nothing to do with responsibility.

What is the extent of a person's concernment? As we ordinarily understand concern, one can be concerned for or in or about many things: one's family, one's possessions, one's business concerns, the fate of the world, the baggage retrieval system at Heathrow. In his *Essay*, however, Locke focuses on a much narrower notion of concernment which I'll mark with a capital letter—*Concernment*. He makes the scope of Concernment clear by tying it tightly to consciousness in his special sense of 'consciousness' which I'll also flag with a capital letter—*Consciousness*—except when it appears in quotations. He holds that Consciousness entails Concernment: 'concern for happiness [is] the *unavoidable concomitant* of consciousness' (§26); 'self is that conscious thinking thing ... which is sensible or conscious of pleasure and pain, capable of happiness or misery, and *so* is concerned for itself, *as far as that consciousness extends, and no farther*' (§17).

12.6 'Consciousness'

To understand the precise scope of Concernment, we have to know exactly what Consciousness is. Fortunately the matter is straightforward: to be Conscious of *x* is to experience *x in a certain immediate kind of way*—whether *x* be one's actions and

---

[4] It may (somewhat confusingly) be rephrased as the question of *which Person S is* considered at some particular time, or (slightly less confusingly) as the question of which *forensic* Person S is at some particular time.

experiences, one's mind, or one's body. One's awareness or consciousness of one's present actions and experiences is the paradigm case of such immediacy (for illustrative quotations, §12.11 below, p. 244). It's the immediacy of the way in which we experience our own pains, to take a familiar example. Our present-day use of the word 'conscious' allows that we can be said to be conscious of other creatures' experiences but we don't think that we are or can be conscious of others' experiences in the immediate kind of way in which we are conscious of our own.

One may say that to be Conscious of x is to experience x *as one's own* in a certain immediate kind of way, but one does then run the risk of being misunderstood. To avoid misunderstanding one needs to stress that this kind of experiencing something as one's own is found in all sentient beings; it doesn't require any sort of express self-consciousness of the sort characteristic of human beings, any sort of explicit conceptual representation of x as one's own, although it does standardly involve this in the special case of a Person, since a Person is a fully self-conscious creature that 'can consider itself [specifically] as itself' (§9).[5]

This is what Locke means by 'consciousness'. It's not an elaboration or variation of what he means. To be Conscious of x is to experience x in a certain immediate kind of way. It is in fact the way in which a subject of experience S can experience an action or experience or mind or body only if it is in fact S's own action or experience or mind or body.

We can now ask why Consciousness of x entails Concernment about (or in or for) x. The answer is simple. Locke takes it, reasonably enough, that one is necessarily concerned for oneself. One is necessarily concerned for what is one's own in the narrow sense of being part of oneself, the Person one is; where this crucially includes, on his view, one's actions and experiences in addition to one's substantial realization (material or otherwise).

In taking it that the converse is also true, i.e. that Concernment entails Consciousness (see the last three words of the last section), Locke makes it clear that he's focusing on a notion of concernment—Concernment—which is narrow in precisely the following sense. One's Concernment (one's capital-C Concernment) extends *only to whatever one experiences (as one's own) in a certain immediate kind of way*. That is, it extends only to whatever one is Conscious of in his sense of 'conscious'. That is, it extends only to oneself, the Person one is, where 'the Person one is' includes one's actions and experiences—since this notion of Person is a forensic notion—in addition to one's current substantial realization, material or otherwise.[6]

---

[5] Grice agrees: consciousness 'for Locke means " consciousness of ... as one's own"' (1941: 341).

[6] For a qualification see Strawson 2014: 38–9. The general notion of concern or concernment is taken as given, and the scope of the special restricted notion—capital 'C' Concernment—is fixed by reference to Consciousness. The effect of the restriction is clear: whatever one's wider concerns, one is only *Concerned* for oneself. Locke had already tied concernment tightly to the notion of Personal identity in the first edition of the *Essay*: 'if we take wholly away all consciousness of our actions and sensations, especially of pleasure and pain, and the *concernment* that accompanies it, it will be hard to know wherein to place personal identity' (2.1.11). He has it always in mind that one's eternal fate subsequent to the Day of Judgement must always be one's greatest Concern(ment).

12.7 The Field of Consciousness

The notion of experiencing something as one's own is crucial when it comes to the forensic consequences of Consciousness for subjects of experience who are Persons. Briefly (and to anticipate) if you genuinely no longer experience something as your own in the required immediate kind of way then you're no longer Conscious of it. It follows that you're no longer genuinely Concerned in it. It follows in turn that it's no longer part of your Personal identity, i.e. your forensic identity. It follows in turn that you are no longer properly held responsible for it.

One is of course (lower-case) concerned for one's family members or possessions, on Locke's view, but one is not (upper-case) Concerned for them. One's field of Concernment is restricted to oneself—so that it is at any given time identical with one's field of Consciousness at that time, which, to repeat, includes one's body[7] in addition to one's mind and one's actions and experiences. See Figure 12.1.

Lockean Consciousness isn't memory, contrary to what so many commentators have supposed, although memory can certainly involve Consciousness. If one still feels immediately 'personally involved' in or with one's past actions and experiences in remembering them, if one feels about them rather as one does about one's present actions and experiences, which are the paradigm cases of what one is Conscious of, then one is still Conscious of them. But memory as such—even autobiographical memory—needn't involve any Concernment. Nor therefore need it involve any Consciousness—any experiencing of what is remembered as one's own in the immediate kind of way that Locke has in mind in talking of Consciousness. I'll return to this in §12.11.

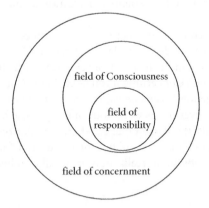

Figure 12.1 The fields of responsibility, Consciousness and concernment[8]

---

[7] This may be doubted, for it implies that Locke is dramatically extending the then standard notion of consciousness, which restricted consciousness to knowledge of one's own mental goings on. See further the passages quoted in note 30 below. See also Strawson 2014: 31–2, 39 n.

[8] If one capitalizes the word concernment in the diagram, so that it represents Lockean Concernment, the outer circle shrinks on Locke's view to become identical to the field of Consciousness circle.

Nor need being Conscious of one's experiences—experiencing them as one's own—involve any sort of explicit second-order apprehension of them as one's own, any more than experiencing one's mind or body as one's own does. In the case of one's present experiences, which are always and paradigmatically Conscious, it never involves this. It's just a matter of what it is like to have the experiences, a matter of their 'immediate givenness'. Locke makes this plain when he says that Consciousness is

inseparable from thinking, and as it seems to me essential to it: it being impossible for any one to perceive, without perceiving, that he does perceive. When we see, hear, smell, taste, feel, meditate, or will anything, we know that we do so. Thus it is always as to our present sensations and perceptions.   (§9)

This passage is enough to settle the point that Consciousness is not an explicit second-order matter, in Locke's view. If one thing is certain it is that Locke—that most sensible of philosophers—doesn't think that we spend our whole lives having explicit second-order thoughts about all our first-order experiences.[9]

We can vary the characterization of Consciousness by using the expression 'from the inside'.[10] Subject of experience S's field of Consciousness is identical with S's *field of from-the-inside givenness*. If, however, it is allowed that past events can be given from-the-inside in memory in a way that is empty of affect or personal 'identificatory involvement' (Concernment), then we will need to say rather that S's field of Consciousness, in Locke's sense of 'consciousness', is identical with S's *field of morally-affectively-concerned from-the-inside givenness*. This is a pretty barbarous expression so I won't use it again. The point is that Locke has in effect built moral-affective Concernment into Consciousness: (Lockean) Consciousness is essentially accompanied by Concernment: 'self' or Person, he says, 'is that conscious thinking thing... which is sensible or conscious of pleasure and pain, capable of happiness or misery, and *so is concerned for itself, as far as that consciousness extends*'.

12.8 The Reach of Consciousness

One's field of from-the-inside givenness, one's field of Consciousness, isn't just a matter of whatever one is now aware of in occurrent thought or sensation or memory. It also, and crucially, has a dispositional aspect. In addition to containing all the experiences one is having now, together with any past experiences one is at present explicitly recalling, it contains all of those past experiences, and in particular actions, that one *can* remember from the inside.

---

[9] Locke uses 'thought' in the Cartesian sense to cover all conscious mental goings on, as this passage shows (see also §12.10 below, p. 242); I'll use the word 'experience' instead. Note also that Locke takes 'action' to cover mental goings on as well as larger-scale bodily actions (it covers anything that is morally assessable).

[10] Coined, as far I know, by Sydney Shoemaker (1970). The difference between remembering something from the inside and remembering it only from the outside is the difference between *remembering falling* out of the boat, the water rushing up to meet you, and so on (memory from the inside) and *remembering that you fell* out of the boat, something that might be all that you have left in the way of memory of the event, and something that someone other than you might equally well remember (memory from the outside).

How far into the past does this 'can' reach? The brief answer is that Locke takes it to reach beyond what one can now bring back to mind unaided (and perhaps also beyond what one can remember when suitably prompted or shocked) to all of those past actions that one is Conscious of in one's conscience or heart (§22). What one is Conscious of in one's heart may not be fully known or accessible to one now but on the Day of Judgement 'the secrets of all hearts will be laid open' (§§22, 26). On that alarming day you'll recall things that you are in fact still morally-affectively involved in, in such a way as to be properly held responsible for them, even if they've slipped beyond recall in your ordinary everyday life.[11]

One's Consciousness doesn't reach back to early childhood, though—if only because of the phenomenon of 'childhood amnesia'. Nor does it reach back to most of the actions of childhood. On one natural reading of Locke it needn't reach back to these actions even if they're remembered, because one can remember one's past actions while no longer experiencing them as one's own in the required immediate way, and while no longer feeling morally-affectively Concerned about (or in) them. Nor does it reach back to the bulk of one's past life. When Locke imagines a 'spirit wholly stripped of all its memory or consciousness of past actions, as we find our minds always are of a great part of ours', he indicates the sense in which *most of one's past actions are not actions of the Person one is now.*[12]

One way to express the tension between Locke's use of 'person' and 'personal identity' and our use is to say that on Locke's view *same person* doesn't entail *same personal identity*; whereas on our view it does. On Locke's view one is the same person throughout life in the sense of being the same mentally complex and morally responsible persisting subject of experience, although one's (forensic) personal identity changes all the time.

Thomas Reid tells the story of a young boy who becomes an officer who is Conscious of something the boy did, and then a general who is Conscious something the officer did but has wholly forgotten—and is no longer Conscious of—what the young boy did.[13] Following Berkeley in the insensitivity of his reading of Locke, Reid objects that on Locke's account of personal identity

(i) the general is the same person as the young officer, because he's Conscious of some experience had by the young officer,

(ii) the young officer is the same person as the boy, because he's Conscious of some experience had by the boy,

while

---

[11] Can one be responsible for a past action that one remembers *that* one did, although one no long remembers doing it *from the inside*? It may be thought that Locke can't allow this, because he says that Consciousness of a past action requires being able to 'repeat the idea of [the] past action with the same consciousness [one] had of it at first' (§10), which requires rich 'from-the-insideness'. To this extent his theory seems to give a wrong result, for one can feel responsible for an action that one knows one did although one no longer has any memory of doing it from the inside. One can accommodate the case by arguing that the mere fact that one still feels responsible for it shows that one is still Concerned in it, Conscious of it, in the required way.

[12] §25. It's not helpful to take this simply as a huge understatement on Locke's part, i.e. as the claim that we are not at any given time *occurrently* Conscious of a great part of most of our past actions.

[13] I'm putting aside the point that Reid wrongly takes Locke to mean 'memory' by 'consciousness'.

(iii) the general is not the same person as the boy, because he's not Conscious of the experience of the boy.

Reid's objection is that the conjunction of (i), (ii), and (iii) contradicts the principle of the transitivity of identity and that Locke's theory is therefore inconsistent.

The conjunction of (i), (ii), and (iii) does contradict the principle of the transitivity of identity but this isn't an objection to Locke's account of personal identity. It's a perfect illustration of its fundamental and forensic point—the plausible idea (it's plausible relative to the story of the Day of Judgement) that human beings won't on the Day of Judgement be responsible for all the things they've done in their lives but only for those that they're still genuinely Conscious of—still genuinely morally-affectively Concerned in, implicated in. What they'll be responsible for will in practice be a bundle of actions dating from many different periods of their lives.

Butler misses Locke's point as spectacularly as Berkeley and Reid. In speaking of Locke's 'wonderful mistake' he makes a wonderful mistake. Ignoring Locke's explicit statement that he's using 'person' specifically as a forensic term, and Locke's definition of Consciousness in terms that have nothing to do with memory, Butler takes Locke to mean memory by the word 'consciousness' and writes as follows:

to say, that [consciousness] makes personal identity, or is necessary to our being the same persons, is to say, that a person has not existed a single moment, nor done one action, but what he can remember; indeed none but what he reflects upon. And one should really think it self-evident, that consciousness of personal identity presupposes, and therefore cannot constitute, personal identity; any more than knowledge, in any other case, can constitute truth, which it presupposes. (1736: 440–1)

One should really think it self-evident that this isn't any sort of objection to Locke's theory. It's a statement of its central point. As a subject of experience you have a lifetime of actions and experiences behind you—most of which you've completely forgotten. The ones that are part of your Personal identity, i.e. the ones that constitute your forensic identity, i.e. the ones that *constitute the Person you are*, considered as a moral being, a forensic entity, are simply those which you're still Conscious of, hence still Concerned in: those that you still experience as your own in the crucial moral-affective way.

It's worth stressing that the Lockean question of Personal identity is always a question raised about a subject of experience S *considered at a particular time*. The particular time at which the question is raised (now, say, or on the Day of Judgement) is crucial because S's Personal identity or Personhood is differently constituted every day, on Locke's view. This follows immediately from the fact that S's field of Consciousness, and in particular the overall field of things S is responsible for, changes each day and indeed every moment. This is so for no other reason than that S has done more things a day later. But it may also be so for other reasons. S may for example have ceased to be Conscious of certain things that S was Conscious of yesterday.[14]

---

[14] In Strawson 2014 I raise the question of how *repentance* can change one's field of responsibility. Note that Butler's addition of 'indeed none but what he reflects upon' is particularly stupid.

12.9 Locke's Definition of 'Person' 1

Although Berkeley, Butler, and Reid are largely to blame for the misunderstanding of Locke, 'marvellously mistaken', as Law observes (1769: 21), Locke isn't blameless. Part of the misunderstanding stems from the fact that he offers a definition of 'person' that is independent of his definition of it as a forensic term. I'll now consider this definition, and offer a general statement of what Locke takes a Person to be.

I'm an individual agent, a thinking being, a persisting human subject of experience, very much as I think I am. All good. But what am I insofar as I am a Person—according to Locke? This still doesn't seem clear.

The first answer we can give is terminological: the *Person* that I am is the *self* that I am: 'Person, as I take it, is the name for this self. Wherever a man finds what he calls himself, there, I think, another may say is the same person' (§26). This is one of many places where the terms are equated.

The second answer is more substantive. It's the answer to the first of the four questions listed in §12.1 above, question [A]: what does a subject of experience that qualifies as a Person consist of, ontologically speaking, considered at any given time? The answer is that the self or Person that I now am—the individual, persisting, morally accountable subject of experience that I am—considered at any given particular time *t*, consists, literally consists, of the following things. First

[1] my living body at *t*

for as Locke says 'any part of our bodies vitally united to that, which is conscious in us, makes a part of our selves' (§25); all the particles of our bodies

whilst vitally united to this same thinking conscious self, so that we feel when they are touched, and are affected by, and conscious of good or harm that happens to them, are a part of our selves: i.e. of our thinking conscious self. Thus the limbs of his body are to everyone a part of him self: he sympathizes and is concerned for them.   (§11)[15]

What else is part of the Person I am? Well, if I have an immaterial soul—which may be doubted, as Locke observes—then the person that I am at *t* consists also of

[2] my soul at *t*

the immaterial soul-substance in which my thinking goes on; for 'any substance [now] vitally united to the present thinking being, is a part of that very same self which now is' (§25), be it material or immaterial.

That [1] and also [2] are literally part of the self or person I am at *t* (assuming that materialism is false and that [2] is therefore to be included) is explicitly stated by Locke. The third and for many purposes central component consists of everything else (everything other than [1] and [2]) of which I am Conscious at *t*, i.e.

---

[15] Note that Locke is using 'ourselves' ('our selves') in a sense directly related to his use of the word 'self', not in some more indeterminate or generic way. To quote more fully from §25: 'Thus any part of our bodies, vitally united to that, which is conscious in us, makes a part of our selves: but upon separation from the vital union, by which that consciousness is communicated, that, which a moment since was part of our *selves*, is now no more so, than a part of another man's self is a part of me: and 'tis not impossible, but in a little time may become a real part of another person' (§25).

[3] all the experiences (thoughts and actions, past and present) of the individual-persisting-subject-of-experience that I am of which I am now occurrently or dispositionally Conscious at t.[16]

Consciousness of the past is thus a fine-grained matter, in Locke's view. For I may still be Conscious of one thing I did on my birthday twenty years ago and not be Conscious of a thousand other things I did on that day, things I've completely forgotten and am no longer 'Concerned in' in any way.[17] In that case they're no longer any part of the Person I am, for it is only 'that with which the consciousness of this present thinking thing can [now] join itself' that 'makes the same person, and is one self with it'. The present thinking being that I am

attributes to itself, and owns all the actions of that thing, as its own, as far as that consciousness reaches, and no farther;[18]

if there be any *part* of [an immaterial substance's] existence, which I cannot upon recollection join with that present consciousness, whereby I am now myself, it is *in that part of its existence no more myself*, than any other immaterial being. For *whatsoever any substance has thought or done, which I cannot recollect, and by my consciousness make my own thought and action*, it will no more belong to me, whether [or not] a part of me thought or did it, than if it had been thought or done by any other immaterial being anywhere existing.[19]

So when Locke says that Consciousness of one of Nestor's actions would make one 'the same person with Nestor' he doesn't mean that one would be the same person as Nestor with respect to all Nestor's actions. In the case imagined one's Consciousness doesn't reach any further into Nestor than that one single action, 'that part of [Nestor's] existence', and one is the same person as Nestor only so far as that action is concerned.[20]

This, then, is a Person ontologically considered, a person in Locke's special sense of the word. This is the answer to question [A]. A Person is a [1] ± [2] + [3].[21] This is the ontological core. Now we need to answer question [B]: what mental capacities

---

[16] When Locke says that 'anything united to the…present thinking being…by a consciousness of former actions, makes also a part of the *same* self, which is the same both then and now' (§25) the scope of 'anything' is only 'former actions'. It's not as if the material particles that made you up ten years ago when you performed a certain action of which you are now conscious are (thereby) still part of the person you are now.

[17] It's even more fine-grained than Parfitian psychological connectedness, which also picks and chooses. See §12.13 below.

[18] §17. In full the passage reads 'that with which the *consciousness* of this present thinking thing can join itself, makes the same person, and is one self with it, and with nothing else; and so attributes to itself, and owns all the actions of that thing, as its own, as far as that consciousness reaches, and no farther'. It may help understanding to remove the last two commas: the present thinking being acknowledges 'all the actions of that thing as its own as far as [its] consciousness reaches and no further'. It acknowledges the actions of that thing as its own *only* as far as its present consciousness reaches them.

[19] §24. Locke is here focusing on the case of an immaterial substance, but the point is for him quite general. Note how the 'and' in this passage distinguishes memory and Consciousness.

[20] §14. Here I disagree with Garrett (2003). Note that even if one were supposed to connect with the whole forensic Person that Nestor was at the time he performed the action in question one would surely not connect forensically with any actions that he had at that time not yet performed.

[21] Locke takes an orthodox Christian position in holding that we can't be said to exist as persons unless we're embodied. Like almost everyone else at the time, he agrees with Boethius that a person consists

must a subject of experience have in order to qualify as a person? We need to list the defining characteristics of Personhood, the properties that distinguish Persons from other subjects of experience that have bodies and experiences and act (and even perhaps have immaterial souls), but aren't Persons.

12.10 Locke's Definition of 'Person' 2

The first thing to record is that Persons are essentially

[i]   capable of a law, and happiness, and misery (§26)

where to say that something is 'capable of a law' is to say that it is capable of grasping the import of a law in such a way that it can understand itself to be subject to it *and can thereby be subject to it*. Given that this is an essential part of Locke's definition of 'person' as a forensic term, it's regrettable that it occurs several pages after his famous more narrowly cognitive-functional definition of 'person' in §9 according to which a Person is

a thinking intelligent being, that has reason and reflection, and can consider itself as itself, the same thinking thing, in different times and places; which it does only by that consciousness, which is inseparable from thinking, and as it seems to me essential to it . . .   (§9)

The trouble is (and Locke must take some of the blame) that this part of his definition tends to be cited in isolation from the point that a Person is also essentially 'capable of a law, and happiness, and misery' (§26) and the intimately connected point that 'person' is for Locke an essentially 'forensic' term (§26).

Regrettable—but there it is. What does the cognitive-functional definition say? It's very clear. Capacities for

[ii]   thought (experience)

[iii]   intelligence

[iv]   reason

and

[v]   reflection

are essential preconditions of being a Person.[22] But they're not sufficient, nor are they the central focus of the definition. The crucial further cognitive-capacity condition is a Person's

[vi]   capacity to consider itself as itself, the same thinking thing in different times and places

essentially of 'soul and body, not soul and body separately' (Boethius *c*.510: 11). A disembodied soul would not be a person. See Thiel 1998: 870.

[22] In Strawson 2014 (pp. 62–4) I argue that Locke specifies four separate conditions by the words 'thinking' (used in the wide Cartesian sense—see note 8), 'intelligent', 'reason', and 'reflection'. There is no redundancy.

'which it does only by that consciousness which is inseparable from thinking, and, as it seems to me, essential to it'. This condition fits tightly with the requirement of being 'capable of a law', for on Locke's view one can reward and punish intelligent beings for what they've done because and only because they possess this cognitive capacity, which keeps them in touch with their past actions, and makes it possible for them to be aware that these actions are their own.[23] To see this, imagine a thinking, intelligent, reasoning, reflecting being that is 'capable of a law' (it can act out of morally good or bad intentions in the moment of action) but has no memory of its past at all. It makes no moral sense to punish or reward it for its past actions (we can assume punishment and reward have no practically beneficial effect on future behaviour either). It has no personal identity in Locke's sense—given that personal identity is an essentially diachronic notion.

There's a further and connected problem that arises from restricting one's attention to the famous part of Locke's definition in §9. The famous part specifies Consciousness in a merely cognitive way that makes no explicit mention of the essential connection between Consciousness and Concernment (Concernment is mentioned two paragraphs later in §11). To see this imagine an utterly emotion-lacking subject of experience that fully satisfies the famous part of the definition. It is a cognitively highly sophisticated, fully memory-equipped subject of experience that qualifies as Conscious inasmuch as it possesses the mental reflexivity that is in Locke's view essentially constitutive of all 'thinking' (i.e. all experience) and is in addition fully and explicitly self-conscious in the way that human beings are and dogs and foxes aren't, so that it can consider itself specifically as itself in the past and future. It has, however, no capacity for happiness or misery and therefore no Concernment, nor any grasp of a law. Such a subject of experience is certainly not a Person on Locke's view.[24]

12.11 Consciousness isn't Memory

It's already clear that Consciousness isn't the same as memory. But this is not just because Consciousness is essentially accompanied by Concernment, in addition to its purely cognitive features. The principal point is much simpler: the primary case of Consciousness involves no memory at all, according to Locke, for it's the Consciousness that one has of one's own experience and action in the present. It's the Consciousness that is 'inseparable from thinking' (i.e. experience), 'essential to it', essentially constitutive of it. 'Thinking consists in being conscious that one thinks',

---

[23] Compare Leibniz 1686: §34, c.1704: 2.27.9.

[24] Some, perhaps, have supposed that Locke means something merely cognitive by the word 'thinking', and so has only the cognitive aspect of memory in mind when considering Consciousness of the past. As already noted, however, Locke uses 'thinking' in the wide Cartesian sense, as is shown by the immediate continuation of the famous passage: 'it being impossible for any one to perceive, without perceiving, that he does perceive. When we see, hear, smell, taste, feel, meditate, or will anything, we know that we do so. Thus it is always as to our present sensations and perceptions: and by this every one is to himself, that which he calls self . . . consciousness always accompanies thinking, and 'tis that, which makes every one to be, what he calls self' (§9). It's a pity that many encounter the famous passage only lifted out of context and quoted in a truncated form.

Locke writes, just as 'hunger consists in that very sensation' (2.1.19). One could be fully Conscious in this fundamental way throughout one's life and have no memory at all, or only a few seconds' worth.[25] The case of Consciousness of *past* actions and experiences, which does of course involve memory, is explicitly explained and characterized by reference to the primary and fundamental case of present Consciousness. Personal identity 'extends itself beyond present [conscious] existence' (where Consciousness is certainly in place, because it is essentially constitutive of the very existence of experience)

only by consciousness, whereby it becomes concerned and accountable; owns and imputes to itself past actions, *just upon the same ground, and for the same reason, that it does the present* [actions]. (§26)

As far as any intelligent being can repeat the idea of any past action with the same consciousness it had of it at first, and with *the same consciousness it has of any present action*; so far it is the same personal self. For it is by the consciousness it has of its present thoughts and actions, that it is self to itself now, and so will be the same self as far as the same consciousness can extend to actions past or to come. (§10)[26]

The fundamental reference point for all attributions of Consciousness is the subject considered in the present moment.

It may be said that Consciousness *of the past*, at least, is the same as memory, on Locke's view. Or rather, it may be said that Locke wouldn't have felt any need to distinguish memory and Consciousness if he had restricted attention to autobiographical from-the-inside memory. But he might have rejected even this identification if he had thought (as I do) that there can be from-the-inside memory without Concernment.[27] One can identify Consciousness of the past with from-the-inside memory only if one accepts that from-the-inside memory is truly inseparable from moral-affective Concernment.

Some years ago, Schechtman observed that almost all commentators on Locke think of Consciousness as merely

a faculty of *knowing*, and this makes the interpretation of consciousness of the past as memory almost irresistible. This is not, however, the aspect of consciousness that Locke most emphasizes in his discussion of personal identity. Instead he stresses the *affective* side of consciousness. (1996: 108)

She put a very good question: if Locke means memory when he talks of Consciousness, why doesn't he say so? Why doesn't he simply talk of memory? Why does he 'never *say* . . . . that memory connections constitute personal identity if this is what he means?' (1996: 107). There's an extended discussion of memory in 2.10 of the *Essay*, and Locke uses the word many times in his discussion of personal identity, and yet 'when he tells us what personal identity consists in, which he does many times

---

[25] Such cases are found in clinical neurology; see e.g. Damasio 1999, 2000.

[26] Note that 'with the same consciousness it had of it at first' makes this, at least on one reading, an implausibly strong requirement.

[27] See e.g. Strawson 1997: §8, 2004: §4.

throughout the chapter, he *always* talks about extension of consciousness and *never* about memory connections' (ibid.).

The principal reason for this has been given: Consciousness has nothing essentially to do with memory. But the point Schechtman stresses is also important—the fact that 'we extend [Lockean] consciousness back in time to some past action or experience by caring about it in the appropriate way' (ibid. p. 109). Certain 'past events can become part of present [Lockean] consciousness by affecting us in the present along the dimension of pleasure or pain' (ibid. p. 112). That said, it should be noted that caring or affective concern (Concernment) is not strictly part of Consciousness, on Locke's view, only an inevitable accompaniment of it. It's also arguable that one may be Conscious of a past experience in the present simply insofar as one experiences it as one's own, while having no particular feelings of pleasure or pain with regard to it; just as one can be Conscious of a part of one's body as one's own while having no particular present feelings of pleasure or pain with regard to it. One may also, perhaps, remember stealing plums and being flogged as a boy with some amusement, and hence with whatever pleasure and emotion is inseparable from amusement, while no longer being Conscious of it in the accountability-engaging sense.

Another case involves a complication Locke didn't consider, and which arguably raises a doubt about the adequacy of his account. Suppose one is given to guilt. It seems plain that one can continue to feel guilty about an action performed as a child although one is *not* in fact still related to it—emotionally implicated in it—in an accountability-engaging way. Guilt, however, is a form of Concernment, and entails Consciousness in Locke's sense, and Consciousness entails Personal identity or same-Personhood, and same-Personhood entails present accountability and punishability. So it seems that a current feeling of guilt entails accountability and punishability even when the feeling is inappropriate or absurd.

A quick answer to this in the spirit of Locke's theory is that one will be all right on the Day of Judgement, because one's conscience on that awesome occasion will get things in proportion and excuse one (§22) for one's childish misdeed. It will show that one is no longer really Concerned in it. One will see how things are and no longer feel guilty. Alternatively one may suppose that one's childish misdemeanour will indeed feature on the long list of things for which one is *accountable*, simply insofar as one is Conscious of it, but that it certainly won't follow that one will actually be *punished* for it. (God, for one, wouldn't dream of doing such a thing.)

12.12 Personal Identity: the Canonical Question

I'll take these issues a little further below. First consider the canonical personal identity question mentioned in §12.1: What are the necessary and sufficient conditions of the truth of the claim that a person considered at time t_1—whom we may call P_1—is the same person as a person considered at a different (later) time t_2—whom we may call P_2? What has to be true if it is to be true that P_1 is indeed the same person as P_2? The present claim is that Locke doesn't address this question—or not as it's ordinarily understood. He simply assumes—takes it for granted—that he's dealing with a continuously existing thing, a continuously existing subject of experience, a continuously existing 'consciousness' (in the special count-noun use of 'consciousness' in §23) that is of such a kind that it qualifies as a Person. Having taken the existence of continuously existing subjects of experience for granted, and having specified what they have to be capable of to qualify as Persons (= answering question [B]), and what they consist of ontologically, at any given time (= answering question [A]), he raises question [D]: the question of what the *Personal identity*—i.e. the forensic identity—of such entities consists in.[28]

He also raises and answers question [C]: the question of what sorts of substantial changes subjects of experience like S that qualify as Persons can undergo while continuing to exist. He argues that, as far as we know, they may possibly survive complete replacement of any parts that substantially realize them at any time— whatever those parts are. S may for example survive a complete change of body or body parts ([1] parts), and/or a complete change of immaterial soul (a [2] part). In telling us what sorts of changes and replacements he thinks Persons can survive, Locke makes it clear that he's conceiving of them as things whose continuing existence essentially involves the continuing existence, through all possible changes of substantial realization, of *something that remains in possession of psychological capacities [i]–[vii]—the psychological capacities specified in answer to question [B].*[29]

I'll repeat this. Locke is simply *assuming*, and operating with, a conception of *continuously existing psychological-capacity-preserving subject-of-experience-hood* that allows that a single persisting subject of experience may survive replacement of all its substantially realizing parts. He's not giving an account of what the continuity of this same-subject-of-experience-hood consists in (as most accounts of personal identity aim to do) in giving his special forensic account of Personal identity. He's assuming the existence of entities like S that have this sort of continuity, and taking it that we are ourselves things of this kind, in order to raise the issue that then concerns him: the issue of the Personal identity of such things, including most notably ourselves; that is, the question of the *moral standing*—the *forensic identity*— of such things; that is, the question of which parts of their past still count as theirs forensically speaking; and therefore still count as part of the Person they are. Equivalently: he's asking which parts of the past of the continuing *subjects of experience* that they are *no longer* count as part of the continuing *Persons* they are.

This is the point at which these things' capacity for Concernment-involving Consciousness of their past actions and experiences becomes crucial—because it provides the answer to question [D]. But there's no sense in which possession of this capacity constitutes one of these subjects of experience, say S, as a continuously existing thing. The subject of experience S is simply given as a continuously existing thing that possesses this capacity, and it would continue to exist as the same *subject of experience* even if it lost this capacity, and so ceased to be a full *Person*. Nor does the set of things of which S is Conscious at any given time, in virtue of its possession of

---

[28] He doesn't have much to say about what might preserve the identity of subjects of experience between death and resurrection. See further note 31.

[29] Here there is an interesting connection to Dainton's conception of the self: 'a subject', he says, 'is essentially a continuous potential for consciousness' (2008: 251); 'the essence of subjects is the *capacity to be conscious*' (2013: ch. 6).

this capacity (i.e. [1] ± [2] + [3]), constitute it as a continuously existing thing. Its material and immaterial parts ([1] and [2]) may completely change, compatibly with its continuing to exist. As for [3], the past actions and experiences of which it is Conscious, these do not in fact constitute a temporally continuous series. The subject of experience, once again, is simply given as a continuously existing thing. Some but certainly not all of the subject of experience's past actions and experiences are still part of the Person it is.

So Locke doesn't answer the canonical personal identity question. But he does give a full account of what one is considered specifically as a Person: [1] ± [2] + [3]. Why is [1] ± [2] literally part of what constitutes one, considered specifically as a Person, in spite of the fact that it's the persistence of one's psychological capacities that is essential to one's persistence as a Person? Two answers are possible and correct: [i] because [1] ± [2] is situated in the field of one's Consciousness, and hence in the field of one's Concernment; [ii] because one is (one's actions and experiences apart) what actually substantially constitutes one at any given time.

The first answer is primary for Locke: *one is constituted as a Person by whatever lies in one's field of Consciousness.*[30] That's it. And that's the answer to question [D], although it's only [3] (the set of actions and experiences one is Conscious of) that matters, not [1] and [2] (one's substantial realization), when it comes to [D], the question of responsibility. Locke's famous claim that 'Consciousness makes personal identity' (§10) is not in any sense a claim that something merely mental or psychological constitutes Personal identity in the sense of making up its whole being. It is rather and precisely the theoretically elegant claim I've just italicized. Given a subject of experience, a thinking intelligent agent, considered at a particular time *t*, it's the reach of that subject of experience's Consciousness at *t* that wholly determines and settles the question of which or what Person that subject of experience is at *t*; where this includes, of course, the question of what constitutes the Person substantially speaking (materially ± immaterially). Everything that one's Consciousness touches or 'can join itself ... with', everything that is 'comprehended under' one's Consciousness in this sense, is a part of the person one is.[31] This and only this settles the question of the subject of experience's Personal identity, or Personhood, which is also (given [3]) question [D], the question of its forensic identity, at *t*. Certainly one needn't know exactly what is comprehended under one's Consciousness. (One may not for example know something Locke knew himself not to know, i.e. whether an immaterial substance is comprehended under one's Consciousness, or whether instead materialism is true.)

I hope the picture is now clear. The material ± immaterial substance that actually makes you up now, substantially, is literally part of what constitutes you, the Person

---

[30] Nothing can lie in the field of Consciousness of more than one person.

[31] Note that this includes one's body, in Locke's account, even though Consciousness is standardly and primarily defined as a reflexive property of experience. See e.g. §11: 'cut off a hand, and thereby separate it from that consciousness, we had of its heat, cold, and other affections; and it is then no longer a part of that which is *himself*'. See also §17: 'thus every one finds that, whilst comprehended under that consciousness, the little finger is as much a part of himself as what is most so. Upon separation of this little finger, should this consciousness go along with the little finger, and leave the rest of the body, it is evident the little finger would be the person, the same person'.

you are now. What about the past? Which parts or aspects of the past of you-the-continuing-subject-of-experience are now part of the Person you are? None of the material particles that have previously constituted your body are, given that they no longer lie in your field of Consciousness (or Concernment). Only those that are now part of your body do so. The same goes if there has been any change in your immaterial substance. Only the immaterial soul or soul-substance that is currently part of you lies in your field of Consciousness (and Concernment) and is therefore part of the Person you now are.

So far as its substance is concerned, then, a subject of experience S who is a Person consists of S's present substantial realization—which may be wholly different from S's substantial realization at some previous time. One may certainly say, in spite of this, that S is a diachronically extended entity, but one must cancel any implication that diachronic extension implies any kind of same-substance-involving diachronic continuity. Most essentially, S is a diachronically continuous stream of memory-and-disposition-rich mental being ('a consciousness' in the count-noun use). S is always carried by something, substance-wise, but it doesn't matter what substantial realization S has at any given time. It doesn't matter what substantial realization S has although S must of course always have some substantial realization or other in order to exist at all. For on the one hand S may have switched bodies, according to Locke, as in the case of the cobbler and the prince; on the other hand S's whole mental being (memory, Consciousness, personality, and so on) may have transferred from one portion of soul-substance to another, as in the case Locke considers in §13.[32] S is indeed—as ever and without qualification—a whole single subject of experience, metaphysically speaking, and it is as such that S will report for inspection, fully embodied, on the Day of Judgement. But there's also a *sense* in which S may be said to be a gappy entity metaphysically speaking, when considered as a Person, because the temporally scattered actions and experiences that S is still Conscious of are literally part of what constitutes S as a Person so far as S's (forensic) Personal identity is concerned. In this forensic respect, one's Consciousness-constituted Personal identity resembles the contrail of an aeroplane most of whose parts have faded to nothing while some indelibly remain.

Suppose we draw an unbroken line (Figure 12.2) to represent my actual life as a subject of experience, from my first coming into existence as a human being. We may then consider the segment from t_1, a moment ten years ago, to t_2, a moment five years ago:

t_1 t_2

Figure 12.2 My life from t_1 to t_2

---

[32] This is part of Locke's campaign against those of his contemporaries who argue that belief in Resurrection requires belief in an immaterial soul, because personal identity between death and Resurrection requires the persistence of single continuing substance.

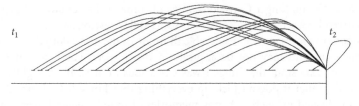

Figure 12.3 The view of t_1–t_2 from t_2; my (forensic) Consciousness at t_2 with respect to t_1–t_2

We can now add a line above my basic lifeline (Figure 12.3) to represent schematically the *Person* that I am at t_2 considered specifically with respect to [3] my actions and experiences between t_1 and t_2.[33] This will be a broken line and will look something like this.

The dashes of the fragmented upper line represent pieces of the lower line: action-and-experience-involving pieces of which I am now Conscious. The curving lines represent the fact that I am at t_2 Conscious of some of the periods of time between t_1 and t_2. The loop from t_2 back to t_2 represents my present Consciousness of my currently occurring experiences at t_2 ('thinking consists in being conscious that one thinks', 2.1.19).

Now consider the view of t_1–t_2 from t_3, the present moment (Figure 12.4), and see what the passing of time has done.

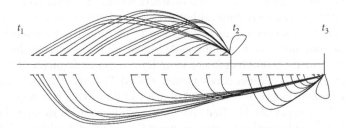

Figure 12.4 The view of t_1–t_2 from t_3; my (forensic) Consciousness at t_2 and t_3 with respect to t_1–t_2

The view from t_2 is represented as before by the gappy line above my continuous lifeline; the view from t_3 is represented by the gappy line below it. (The vertical line cutting the continuous horizontal lifeline marks the Person I was at t_2.) The key change in my (forensic or [3]-related) Consciousness from t_2 to t_3—the change so far as the period from t_1 to t_2 is concerned—is marked by the fact that the lower gappy line is sparser than the higher gappy line. This represents the fact that I am at t_3 Conscious of fewer of the experiences that occurred between t_1 and t_2 than I was at t_2. So the Person that I am at t_3, the moral unit that I am, has changed not only because I've performed new actions and undergone new experiences between t_2 and t_3 but

---

[33] And so not considered with respect to my substantial composition between t_1 and t_2, insofar as this involves more than the existence of the relevant actions and experiences.

also because I'm no longer Conscious, at t_3, of some of the actions and experiences that occurred between t_1 and t_2 of which I was still Conscious at t_2.

The diagram represents a considerable thinning of the lower dotted line relative to the higher one, and may not be accurate in this respect. For I may at t_3 still be Conscious of almost all the things I was Conscious of at t_2. If we slightly redefine 'Conscious' so that it doesn't pick up everything that I'm still Concerned or emotionally implicated in, such as happy memories of morally neutral experiences, but only picks up morally relevant items, then it may be that not much has changed at t_3, Consciousness-wise, when it comes to the period between t_1 and t_2. In particular, it may be that not much has changed in my 'heart'—all of whose secrets will be 'laid open' on the Day of Judgement. I think that Locke doesn't expect the field of my Consciousness to change much from t_2 to t_3 so far as the morally important events in my life prior to t_2 are concerned.

That said, it's important that his view allows change in the content of my field of Consciousness over time, relative to the actions and experiences of any period of past time. I may for example steal plums between t_1 and t_2 and no longer be Conscious of this action at t_3—and so no longer be properly punishable for it at t_3 (which may be the Day of Judgement). A Person's Consciousness may contain an involuntary natural mechanism that operates somewhat like a statute of limitations. One may forget many things precisely because they can appropriately be forgotten, because one is no longer Concerned in them (rather than ceasing to be Concerned in them simply because one has irretrievably forgotten them and is therefore no longer Conscious of them). And one may perhaps *remember* things although one is no longer *Conscious* of them in the relevant sense, no longer Concerned in them in the moral-responsibility-engaging sense. One may not have to ask for 17,033 other minor offences to be taken into consideration on the Day of Judgement, when receiving one's doom (i.e. all the offences of the human subject of experience = person$_1$ one is). For even if one then remembers them one may no longer be Concerned in many of them. One may hope that Reid's general will not be punished by God on the Day of Judgement for stealing plums when he was a boy,[34] for he neither remembers nor is Conscious of the theft, and the theft is therefore not part of the Person he is, on the Day of Judgement. In fact he won't be punished for it even if he does remember it—so long as he isn't still Conscious of it, i.e. so long as he isn't still morally or affectively concerned or implicated in it. For in this case it will again not be part of the Person he is: 'whatever past actions [he] cannot reconcile or appropriate to that present self by consciousness, [he] can be no more concerned in, than if they had never been done' (§26).

It seems to me that the general shouldn't be punished even if he not only remembers it but still feels bad about it, and is to that extent still Concerned in it in such a way that it is still part of the Person he is. For in childhood we have not yet attained the 'age of responsibility', and this is a fact to which divine law will surely not pay less attention than human. There are vicious eschatologies that demand punishment of young children and of all wrong acts performed in childhood, but what will presumably happen on the Great Day, as remarked earlier, is that the general's

---

[34] Even leaving aside the fact that he was at the time soundly flogged for doing so.

conscience, enlightened by the grandeur of the occasion, will excuse him, and so surely and in any case will God.

It may help to introduce the notion of one's *account*—the bill, the tab, the list of chargeable items that the subject of experience that one is will have on the Day of Judgement.[35] Only things (actions) that are on one's account will be punished or rewarded. What is on one's account will be a function of what one is Conscious of, where Consciousness (as always) brings with it moral-emotional Concernment.[36] To work out one's Personal account one starts out from the complete set of the past actions of the continuing subject of experience one is, i.e.—in our own case—the human person$_1$ that one is. Plainly not all of these actions are on one's account. In fact very few of them are. The question, question [D] (familiarly by now), is this: which of these actions does one still feel involved in, involved in in such a way as to feel that it is something that *one* did—where this '*one*' in italics denotes the Person one is now or if you like the person$_2$ one is now? This tiny subset of the actions of the person$_1$ that one is contains all the actions that are on one's account and that actually constitute the Person one now is so far as one's past actions are concerned (i.e. so far as [3] rather than [1] $\pm$ [2] is concerned): 'that with which the *consciousness* of this present thinking thing can join itself, makes the same person, and is one self with it, and with nothing else' (§17). And although being on one's account is a necessary condition of attracting punishment or reward, it is not a sufficient condition, for many things—like warm memories—will be morally neutral; and God has a reputation for mercy.

12.13 Psychological Connectedness

The point can be re-expressed in Parfitian terms, according to which a person P$_7$ at t_7, e.g. now, is (directly) *psychologically connected* to a person P$_1$ at some past time t_1 if— to take the case of memory—P$_7$ can now remember having some of the experiences that P$_1$ had at t_1; while P$_7$ is *psychologically continuous* with P$_1$ if there is an overlapping chain of such direct connections (e.g. P$_7$ is psychologically connected to P$_6$, P$_6$ to P$_5$, P$_5$ to P$_4$, and so on unbrokenly back to P$_1$). Clearly P$_7$ can be psychologically continuous with P$_1$ even if P$_7$ is not psychologically connected to P$_1$. Equally clearly, P$_7$ can be psychologically connected with P$_1$ even if not psychologically continuous with P$_1$.[37]

In these terms we may say that Locke isn't interested in the (transitive) relation of psychological continuity when it comes to the question of personal identity. He's only interested in the (non-transitive) relation of psychological connectedness. It is accordingly misleading to call those who seek to give an account of personal identity principally in terms of psychological continuity 'neo-Lockeans'. It's true that Locke

---

[35] At one point Locke imagines a thinking being losing all consciousness of its past, 'and so as it were beginning a new account from a new period' (§14).

[36] One might say, in other terms, it will be a matter of what one still identifies with in the past, where this identification is not necessarily a matter of having a positive attitude to something, nor a matter of choice or intentional action.

[37] Cf. Parfit 1984: 205–6.

gives an essentially psychological account of the conditions of Personal identity (an account in terms of Consciousness) but the resemblance between Locke and the neo-Lockeans ends there.

The psychological connectedness that matters to Locke is furthermore narrower—more fine-grained—than psychological connectedness as ordinarily understood; and this isn't simply because Consciousness isn't the same as memory (it's not the same as memory even when we restrict attention to Consciousness of the past). The point was made in §12.10 but it's worth repeating. Suppose P_1 performs two actions a_1 and a_2 at the same time at t_1.[38] Locke's position, which is clearly correct given the constantly reiterated point of his account of Personal identity, is that P_7 at t_7 can be Conscious of a_1, and so psychologically connected to P_1 at t_1 as the performer of a_1 in such a way as to be the same Person as P_1 at t_1, and so morally responsible for a_1, while not being Conscious of a_2—not psychologically connected to P_1 at t_1 as the performer of a_2 in such a way as to be the same Person as P_1 at t_1. Plainly, then, P's Consciousness connection at t_1 to P_1 at t_1 is not a connection to P_1 at t_1 überhaupt, for if it were this would yield a contradiction. The Consciousness connection is to the doing of a_1 at t_1 and not to the doing of a_2. On Locke's theory it doesn't matter that there is only one human being involved. P can be the same Person as P_1-doing-a_1 ('P_{1a1}') and not the same Person as P_1-doing-Y ('P_{1a2}').

Objection. 'This isn't possible. P_{1a1} is not only the same *human being* as P_{1a2} but also the same *Person*, because she is (we may suppose) fully Conscious of what she is doing at t_1. And this means that we can generate a contradiction. For even if we allow ourselves for purposes of argument to treat P_{1a1} and P_{1a2} as potentially different Persons, in spite of the fact that there's only one human being, so that P_7 at t_7 can be the same Person as P_{1a1} and not the same Person as P_{1a2}, still P_{1a1} and P_{1a2} must be the same Person *by Locke's own Consciousness criterion*, given that P_1 is fully Conscious of what she is doing at t_1; so P_1 can't be identical with P_{1a1} and not also with P_{1a2}.'

Reply. There is perhaps no better way to understand Locke's theory of personal identity than to realize that is not any sort of objection to it. 'Person...is a forensic term, appropriating actions and their merit.'[39]

---

[38] 'Do an action' seems incorrect in modern English, outside philosophy, but I follow Locke's usage.

[39] In Strawson 2014 I go into more detail. I also analyse the 'fatal error' passage in §13 of Locke's chapter. I'm grateful to Ruth Boeker and Mohan Matthen for comments on a draft of this paper, and to audiences at Reading University, the American University of Beirut, and the Royal Institute of Philosophy.

13

'When I enter most intimately into what I call *myself*'
Hume on the Mind 1

13.1 Introduction

In this paper I focus on Hume's initial discussion of personal identity in section 1.4.6 of his *Treatise of Human Nature*. I argue for three controversial theses: first, that Hume doesn't think that the mind is just a 'bundle' of perceptions; second, that the bundle account of the mind that he expounds in 1.4.6 doesn't involve any sort of denial of the existence of subjects of experience; third, that he never claims that the subject of experience isn't encountered in experience.

I don't here consider Hume's partial repudiation of his account of personal identity in the Appendix to the *Treatise*; but he doesn't in the Appendix find any fault in his phenomenological account in 1.4.6 of what he comes across when he engages in mental self-examination by 'entering intimately into what I call *myself*'. Nor, I believe, does he find any fault in his treatment of the other main topic of 1.4.6: his account of how we come to believe in the existence of a persisting self as a result of the mind's 'sliding easily' along certain series of perceptions.[1]

13.2 The Experience/Experiencer Thesis

I begin with a point stressed by many philosophers and taken for granted by many others, including Hume; reasonably so, because it's a necessary truth. Frege puts it straightforwardly: 'an experience is impossible without an experiencer' (1918: 27). Shoemaker remarks that it's 'an obvious conceptual truth that an experiencing is necessarily an experiencing by a subject of experience, and involves that subject as intimately as a branch-bending involves a branch' (1986: 10).

I'll call this the *Experience/Experiencer Thesis*.[2] Note that it doesn't commit one to any particular metaphysical view about the ultimate nature of the subject of

---

[1] I discuss the famously difficult issue of what happens in the Appendix to the *Treatise* in the next essay, and (in more detail) in Strawson 2011a: Part 3. When I cite a work by someone other than Hume I give the first publication date or (occasionally) estimated date of composition, while the page reference is to the published version listed in the Bibliography. When quoting I mark the author's emphases by **bold italics** and my own by *italics*.

[2] In other work I call it 'Frege's Thesis' (Strawson 1994: 129–34) and the 'Subject Thesis' (Strawson 2009: 271–6).

experience. One can be as uncommitted on this question as Descartes is in his *Second Meditation*.[3] One can, for example, fully accept the Experience/Experiencer Thesis without supposing that a subject of experience is something that lasts longer than a single experience or 'perception'.

One way to mark this point is to say that the Experience/Experiencer Thesis isn't something that Buddhists deny. Another is to say that the notion of the subject that features in the necessary truth doesn't allow that one can say something true and weaker by saying 'the existence of experience entails the existence of subjectivity, but not the existence of a subject of experience'. This is because the presence of subjectivity already entails the presence of a subject of experience, given the present metaphysically uncommitted notion of a subject of experience. (I'll consider a challenge to this proposal at the end of §13.3.)

The point can be re-expressed by saying that experience is necessarily experience-*for*—experience for or on the part of someone or something. Consider pain, a familiar case of experience. It is, essentially, a feeling, and a feeling is just that, a *feeling*, i.e. a feel-ing, a being-felt, and a feel-ing or being-felt can't possibly exist without there being a feel-er. Again I'm only interested in the sense in which this is a necessary truth. The noun 'feeler' doesn't import any metaphysical commitment additional to the noun 'feeling'. It simply draws one's attention to the full import of 'feeling'. The sense in which it's necessarily true that there's a fee*ling*, and hence a fee*ler*, of pain, if there is pain at all, is the sense in which it's necessarily true that there's a subject of experience if there is experience, and hence subjectivity, at all. These truths are available prior to any particular metaphysics of object or property or substance or accident or process or event or state.

Kant endorses the Experience/Experiencer Thesis when he writes to Herz that 'the thinking or the existence of the thought and the existence of my own self are one and the same' (1772: 75), or (substituting 'experience' for 'thinking' and 'thought'—a better translation, all in all) 'the experiencing, or existence of the experience, and the existence of my own self are one and the same'. Kant's claim here, which one might call the *Experience/Experiencer Identity Thesis*, is much stronger than the Experience/Experiencer Thesis, and entails it.

13.3 The 'Bundle Theory of Mind'

The Experience/Experiencer Identity Thesis is endorsed by many philosophers, including Descartes, as I read him,[4] and William James in his *Principles of Psychology*. It seems useful to put it on the table now, if only because it appears to be cognate with an outright ontological claim often attributed to Hume: the claim that the subject, or self, or mind, or 'person', conceived of as something that persists through time, is

---

[3] 'I know that I exist; the question is, what is this *I* that I know? I do not know.' I do not know that I'm not just a 'human body', or 'some thin vapour which permeates my limbs—a wind, fire, air, breath'. 'But whatever I suppose, and whatever the truth is, for all that I am still something' (1641: 18). Descartes does not at this stage commit himself on the question of ontological category.

[4] See e.g. Strawson 2017.

identical to a series of experiences, and is therefore—presumably—identical to a single (possibly complex) experience, at any particular time that it exists.

Hume, however, doesn't make this ontological claim. He is, after all, a sceptic. As such, he doesn't claim to know the ultimate nature of things (other than experiences or 'perceptions', conceived in the traditional 'internalist' way). He is clear on the point that 'the essence of the mind' is unknown to us; it is 'equally unknown to us with that of external bodies' (Int§8/xvii). The closest he comes to the outright ontological claim is when he makes the following far more modest semantico-epistemological claim: all the directly empirically warranted content we can give to the idea of a mind or self or person,[5] and hence all the content we can give to these ideas insofar as they have a legitimate employment in philosophy, which must restrict itself to clear and distinct ideas,[6] is the idea of a perception or experience, or series of perceptions or experiences. The mind '*as far as we can conceive it*, is nothing but a system or train of different perceptions' (Abs§28/657, my emphasis). We have no 'notion of...self..., *when conceiv'd distinct from* particular perceptions... we have *no notion* of...the mind..., distinct from the particular perceptions' (App§§18,19/635, my emphasis).[7]

These are explicitly epistemologically qualified statements of what has come to be known as the 'bundle theory of mind'. They're claims to the effect that this is all we can know or clearly conceive of the mind.

But we also find many (mostly earlier) epistemologically unqualified ontological formulations of the bundle theory of mind. Minds or selves or persons, Hume says, are 'nothing but a bundle or collection of different perceptions' (1.4.6.4/252). 'They are the successive perceptions only, that constitute the mind' (1.4.6.4/253). A 'succession of perceptions...constitutes [a] mind or thinking principle' (1.4.6.18/260). It is a 'chain of causes and effects, which constitute our self or person' (1.4.6.20/262).[8] A 'composition of...perceptions...forms the self' (App§15/634). A 'train...of...perceptions...compose a mind' (App§20/635). Hume couldn't be more plain: 'what we call a mind, is nothing but a heap or collection of different perceptions, united together by certain relations' (1.4.2.39/207). It is a 'connected mass of perceptions, which constitute a thinking being' (1.4.2.39/207), 'a connected heap of perceptions' (1.4.2.40/207). It is a 'succession of perceptions, which constitutes our self or person' (1.4.7.3/265). 'It must be our several particular perceptions, that compose the mind. I say, compose the mind, not belong to it' (Abs§28/658).[9]

---

[5] In his discussion of personal identity in Book 1 of the *Treatise*, Hume uses the words 'mind', 'self', and 'person' interchangeably. So he uses 'person' to denote himself considered simply in his mental being (see e.g. Penelhum 1955, Pike 1967, Biro 1993), and this is also what he refers to when he speaks of 'myself'. The term 'person' builds in the idea of something that has 'personality', i.e. (this is the eighteenth-century use of 'personality') diachronic continuity considered as a person.

[6] For Hume's use of this criterion see e.g. 1.1.7.6/19, 1.2.4.11/43; see also 12.20/157, 12.28/164, 4.18/35. The conventions for referring to Hume's work are given on p. xiii above.

[7] All mental occurrences are perceptions, in Hume's terminology—thoughts, sensations, emotions, ideas, and so on—and they're all (by definition) conscious. The word that now corresponds most closely to Hume's word 'perceptions', in this use, is 'experiences'.

[8] Here the 'causes and effects' are particular perceptions.

[9] Six of these eleven quotations are from passages where Hume is discussing something else, or summarizing the view and stating it in a particularly compressed form. See also 2.1.2.2/277.

How should we take these remarks? We should remember that Hume's central project in *Treatise* and the first *Enquiry* is a 'mental geography, or delineation of *the distinct parts and powers of the mind*'. 'It cannot be doubted', he says, 'that *the mind is endowed with several powers and faculties,* [and] that these powers are distinct from each other'. His hope is that 'philosophy...may...discover, at least in some degree, *the secret springs and principles, by which the human mind is actuated in its oper- ations*' (1.15/13–14, my emphases). 'At least in some degree': he thinks that there is only so much that philosophy can do: for, again, 'to me it seems evident, that the essence of the mind [is] equally unknown to us with that of external bodies' (Int§8/ xvii). The mind, then, can't be just a series of experiences, on Hume's view, if only because he holds that 'the [experiences] of the mind are perfectly known' (2.2.6.2/ 366), and nothing can be both unknown and perfectly known. Nor can a thing have any 'secret springs and principles' that are at best only partially discoverable if it's just a series of perfectly known experiences.[10]

Hume regularly makes the point that nothing is hidden, so far as experiences are concerned, noting, for example, that 'since all actions and sensations of the mind are known to us by consciousness, they must necessarily appear in every particular what they are, and be what they appear'; for 'consciousness never deceives' (1.4.2.7/ 190, 7.13/66). They can't, then, be all there is to the mind, as the ontological bundle theory asserts. Hume doesn't for a moment intend the above ontological claims without restriction, as stating the essential nature of the mind. They are, again, claims about the mind so far as we have any empirically—and hence philosophically— respectable knowledge of it. They're claims about the maximum legitimate content of any claims about the nature of the mind that can claim to express knowledge of the mind.[11]

I'm going to assume that we are now in the twenty-first century sufficiently reconciled with the eighteenth (after the confusions of the nineteenth, and madnesses

---

[10] Here Hume takes up a (Newtonian) methodological position parallel to that of the early behaviour- ists. Just as it didn't occur to the original behaviourists to deny the existence of inner mental states of consciousness—they simply chose to restrict their experimentation to the recording and measuring of publicly observable phenomena—so too Hume doesn't deny the existence of the mind considered as something more than a series of perceptions. It's just that the essence of the mind is unknown to us, and that it's 'impossible to form any notion of its powers and qualities otherwise than from careful and exact experiments, and the observation of those particular effects, which result from its different circumstances and situations' (Int§8/xvii).

[11] 'The outright ontological claims about the mind may be said to be literally true when made strictly within the philosophical framework of ideas constituted by empirically warranted clear and distinct ideas, since they just repeat the definition of the empirically warranted clear and distinct idea of the mind.' True; the point is then that this empirically warranted framework of ideas is in Hume's philosophy rightly and crucially embedded within a larger, sceptical framework of ideas. In the larger sceptical framework of ideas it's acknowledged that there may be and indeed is more to reality than what we can form empirically warranted clear and distinct ideas of. Words like 'mind' and 'bodies' are accordingly used in a larger sense in a way already illustrated: 'the essence of the *mind*' is 'equally unknown to us with that of *external bodies*' (Int§8/xvii); 'the perceptions of the *mind* are perfectly known', but 'the essence and composition of *external bodies* are so obscure, that we must necessarily, in our reasonings, or rather conjectures concerning them, involve ourselves in contradictions and absurdities' (2.2.6.2/366); ''Tis in vain to ask, Whether there be *body* or not? That is a point, which we must take for granted in all our reasonings' (1.4.2.1/187). Note that exactly the same is true of Hume's use of words like 'cause', 'power', 'force', and so on. See e.g. Strawson 2011a: 45 n.

of the twentieth) to have passed beyond the point at which we think that Hume was in his discussion of personal identity centrally concerned to make an outright ontological claim about the nature of the self. If there's one thing we know about him, it is that he is a sceptic who doesn't claim to know the ultimate nature of any reality, other than the reality of perceptions or experiences.

13.4 '...when I enter most intimately into what I call *myself*'

With the Experience/Experiencer Thesis in place, consider what is perhaps Hume's most famous remark:

when I enter most intimately into what I call *myself*, I always stumble on some particular perception or other.... I never can catch *myself* at any time without a perception, and never can observe any thing but the perception.   (1.4.6.3/252)

I'm going to vary Hume's wording in a number of ways, after stressing a point that no serious person will dispute: the point that the word 'perception' refers here to an actual occurrence, an actual episode of perceiving that occurs at a particular time.

The first variation accordingly substitutes 'episode of perceiving' or 'perceiving' for 'perception':

when I enter most intimately into what I call myself, I always stumble on some particular episode of perceiving or other.... I never can catch *myself* at any time without an episode of perceiving, and never can observe any thing but the perceiving.

The second variation substitutes 'come across' for 'catch' in the first variation, in the attempt to make things clearer:

when I enter most intimately into what I call myself, I always stumble on some particular episode of perceiving or other.... I never can come across *myself* at any time without [coming across] an episode of perceiving, and never can observe any thing but the perceiving.

The third variation substitutes 'episode of experience' or 'experience' or 'experiencing' for 'perception':

when I enter most intimately into what I call *myself* I always stumble on some particular episode of experience or other.... I never can come across *myself* at any time without [coming across] an experience, and never can observe anything but the experience (experiencing).

I'll regularly substitute 'experience' for 'perception' in what follows, because one natural use of 'experience' in present-day philosophical discourse corresponds very well to what Hume means by 'perception', a term he uses in an entirely general way to cover any sort of conscious mental occurrence. The substitution may help to suspend certain standard interpretative reflex reactions which seem to have sunk into the very words of the text in such a way that we no longer have clear access to the original. 'Experiencing' is also helpful, because it makes it clear that an actual occurrence of experience is in question.

I believe that Hume's meaning is wholly preserved in these variations of the original passage. What does the passage say? It's a strictly phenomenological claim. It says that when I consider myself in my mental being, when I engage in a certain kind of mental self-examination, two things are true.

[1] I never catch or come across myself without also catching or coming across an experience (the *No Bare View Thesis*).

[2] I never observe anything other than the experience—the experiencing, the episode of experience (the *Nothing But An Experience Thesis*).

These two claims are linked but different. According to [1], the weaker claim, I never get a *bare view* of the self or subject of experience. That is, I never get a view of the subject alone. I do of course always catch *myself*, the subject of experience, when I enter most intimately into what I call myself and observe an experience, for an experience encountered in this way is indeed an *experience*, an actual concrete episode of experienc*ing*, and therefore always and essentially involves an experienc*er*, for an experiencing is necessarily an *experiencing-by-an-experiencer*, as the Experience/Experiencer Thesis states (a perception is indeed a *perception*, an actual concrete perceiv*ing*, and therefore essentially involves a perceiv*er*, for a perceiving is essentially a *perceiving-by-a-perceiver*). True. And the claim that an experience or experiencing necessarily involves an experienc*er* isn't just the claim that it presupposes one, as a possibly unencountered, transcendental condition of its possibility. To think clearly about what an actual experiencing is is to see that it's not possible to encounter an experiencing, in mental self-examination, without also encountering an experiencer.[12] Nevertheless, I never catch or come across myself at any time pure, as it were, i.e. 'without a perception' or experience. Nor, therefore, and crucially, given Hume's purposes, do I ever catch anything that presents itself as capable of existing apart from the experience in such a way as to have a chance of qualifying for the title 'substance' as traditionally understood.[13]

According to [2], the stronger claim, when I catch myself in this way I never observe anything but the experience—the experience-event, the episode of experience. The experience-event is, to be sure, an experiencing. It's a necessarily-subject-of-experience-involving thing, a thing whose existence is, necessarily, partly *constituted* by the existence of a subject of experience. So I do indeed catch myself, the self or person or subject, in catching the experience. But no self or subject presents in such a way that it can be taken to be distinct from the overall experience-event *in any way at all*, as the philosophical tradition of Hume's time uniformly supposes the self or subject (or soul) to be. There's no impression of any such thing to be had, and there is therefore (for a Humean empiricist) no warrant for taking there to be such a thing in one's philosophy, when aiming to make claims about the nature of reality. Nothing presents as a subject that is distinct or distinguishable from the episode of experience in such a way that it can be taken to be ontologically separate from the episode of

---

[12] Phenomenologists should note that this claim is not at odds with Sartre's and Gurwitsch's insistence on the 'non-egological' character of experience (see e.g. Gurwitsch 1941). See also §10.4 above, p. 193.

[13] According to one central traditional metaphysical definition a substance is something that can exist by itself without dependence on any other created or contingently existing thing.

experience on the terms of Hume's fundamental Separability Principle.[14] It's not just that nothing presents as a *simple, unchanging, persisting (continuously existing)* subject distinct from the episode of experience, although this—the traditional conception of the soul—is Hume's principal point and target. It's that no subject of any sort, not even a fleeting one, presents as distinct from the episode of experience in the required way.

One might re-express the point by saying that for any given individual experience E encountered in reflection on one's mental being, when E is strictly examined, no subject presents as in any way *E-transcendent*.[15] To say this, though, is not—not at all—to say that a subject or self is not encountered in any way at all. To say that all that we encounter in mental self-examination, so far as the mind or self or subject of experience is concerned, is a series of experiences or experiencings, is certainly not to say that we don't encounter a subject of experience in any sense at all, for an experience is a necessarily-subject-involving occurrence. Even the outright ontological (and therefore non-Humean) claim that the mind or self is nothing but a series of experiences is not—not at all, not in any way—the claim that it doesn't involve any subject of experience, or any subjects of experience. For, once again, the existence of an experience, an actual experiencing, obviously and necessarily involves the existence of a subject of experience.

I think Hume is right about both [1] and [2]. He gives a very accurate report of what one finds when one engages in this sort of mental self-examination. The phenomenological facts are waiting for anyone to discover, and are well recognized in the tradition of philosophy deriving from Husserl. When Kant says that 'I do not know myself through being conscious of myself as experiencing, but only when I am conscious of the intuition of myself as determined with respect to the function of experiencing' (1781/7: B406), he has more in mind than Hume, but he is also expressing something like [1], and, in effect, [2]. William James affirms [2] when, using 'thought' in Descartes's entirely general sense to mean any kind of conscious experience, he says that 'the passing Thought itself is the only *verifiable* thinker'.[16]

---

[14] 'Whatever is distinct, is distinguishable; and whatever is distinguishable, is separable by the thought or imagination...and may be conceiv'd as separately existent, and may exist separately, without any contradiction or absurdity' (App§12/634). See Garrett 1997: ch. 3.

[15] One can say the same for any series of experiences E* so encountered: nothing presents as in any way E*-transcendent.

[16] 1890: 1.346 (for James's explicit adoption of the Cartesian use of 'thought' to mean 'every form of consciousness indiscriminately', see e.g. 1890: 1.224). Compare Reid in a manuscript note of 1 December 1758: '...it seems utterly inexplicable how we come by the very Idea of a Subject or to imagin that these thoughts have a necessary Relation to some thing else which we call their Subject. We are onely conscious of the thoughts, yet when we reflect upon them there arises necessarily and unavoidably a Notion of a thinking thing, & that this thought we are conscious of is its Operation or Act.... If any Man will affirm that thought may exist without a Subject & that the conceiving it as an Act or Operation of some Being is a vulgar or a Philosophical Prejudice, I do not see how he can be confuted but by appealing to his own Sense or the Common Sense of Mankind' (Reid 1764: 320-1; note the use of the word 'notion', following Berkeley's use in his *Principles*). On this view, a subject is a transcendental condition of an experience in Kant's sense, and can be known to be so, and accordingly can be known to exist when an experience is known to exist; but we don't have any experiential encounter with the subject in being conscious of our thoughts.

Hume, then, never denies the existence of the, or a, self or subject of experience, contrary to what some have suggested. If, however, one defines a self or subject of experience as something that persists for a considerable period of time—in a way that was then, and still is now, the natural understanding of the term—then Hume does of course deny that we can know there to be such a thing; and he also, of course, and connectedly, and centrally, denies that we can take the idea or term *self* (or *mind* or *person*) to mean such a thing when we purport to make knowledge claims in philosophy. For we must in such cases restrict ourselves to clear and distinct (fully 'intelligible') ideas. We can, when doing philosophy, sufficiently characterize what the 'metaphysicians' (1.4.6.4/252) take themselves to have in mind when they use the term *self* or *person*, even though these terms are not clear and distinct (or therefore 'intelligible') by Hume's empiricist standards. When knowledge claims are in question, however, the idea of the self, understood to pick out something that persists for a considerable period of time, can have no more legitimate meaning or content than the idea of a (possibly gappy) series of experiences.

13.5 A Troublesome Ambiguity

It's the above reading of [2] that analytic philosophers find most difficult, given the existing tradition of Hume commentary. I suspect that the difficulty derives in part from the fact that words like 'perception' or 'experience' have a natural dual use, which is harmless in many contexts, but potentially misleading in others. The primary use of the word 'perception' or 'experience' is to denote an actual, particular, 'token' episode of conscious experience occurring at a particular time, as when I say I'm now having a perception of red, an experience of red. But we can also use the expression 'perception of red' or 'experience of red' to denote a type of experience that both you and I and many others can have, or might have but have never had in fact, and so on. And Hume does sometimes use 'perception' (or rather, much more commonly, 'impression' and 'idea') in just this way: not as a word for an actual concrete occurrence, an actual perceiving, an actual experiencing, a given particular token instance of experiential content of a certain type, occurring at noon, say, or ten to three, but as a word for a type of experiential content, e.g. the experience of *red*, or *pain*, or *the taste of pineapple*, or the thought *twice two is four* or *what on earth is he saying?*[17] Of the fifty-nine occurrences of the word 'perception' in the passages of Hume's writing that primarily concern us now ('Of personal identity', paragraphs 10–21 of the Appendix, and paragraph 28 of the Abstract) only two are even prima facie candidates for being type uses,[18] but there are type uses elsewhere in the *Treatise*

---

[17] I take conscious thought to be a matter of experience, just as sensory experience is, although (unlike Hume) I don't think it need involve sensory phenomenology. See e.g. Strawson 1994: 5–13, 2011b.

[18] When Hume talks of the 'sub-oyster' that has only 'one perception' (App§16/634), he could mean that the sub-oyster has only one type of perception, not just one perception. Secondly, Hume holds that there can be complex perceptions (see e.g. 1.1.1.4/3, 1.4.5.12/237), and when he considers the case in which 'several perceptions...mingle' (1.4.6.4/253), it's plausible that his idea is that they may mingle in such a way as to form a single complex perception. Now it's clear that 'perceptions' still refers to actual occurrences, in the phrase 'several perceptions...mingle', but if we fix on the idea that there is one complex perception, then, relative to that idea, we may say that 'perception' has a type use in describing the

(especially of 'impression' and 'idea'), and it may be that the availability of such uses to mean *red* as a type of experiential content rather than an actual, lived, clockable experiencing of red removes a crucial barrier on the route to the false view that Hume's famous claim is that all he comes across, when he comes across a perception or experience in mental self-examination, is, as it were, a mere patch of content, a patch of content considered abstractly, as it were, rather than as a concrete occurrence of necessarily-experiencer-involving experiencing-content (necessarily perceiver-involving perceiving-content).

It's hard to know quite what to make of this view, but it seems to involve attributing to Hume the idea that one could come across occurrent experiential/ perceptual content, an actual occurrence of redness-experience, say, existing at a given particular time, without in any sense coming across a subject of experience. And this, of course, has been extended into the claim that Hume denies the existence of a subject. It seems, however, enough to read and understand the words 'when I enter most intimately into what I call *myself*...' to be clear on the point that Hume believes in the existence of a subject of experience of some sort—as H. H. Price remarks.[19] What Hume denies is that there is any empirically respectable evidence for the view that there is a subject of experience that lasts longer than any given fleeting necessarily-subject-involving perception; let alone a subject of experience that is metaphysically simple and absolutely unchanging through time (1.4.6.1–2/251).

He's quite right about this, on his own empiricist terms. But if one thing is certain, it is that the 'bundle' account of the mind or self or subject—which records all the empirically legitimate content that can be given to the idea of the mind or self or subject, and hence all the content that it can be allowed to have in any purported knowledge claim in a strict empiricist philosophy—doesn't conceive the mind, incoherently, as a bundle of subject-of-experienceless but none the less occurrent experiential-content patches. It conceives it as a bundle of necessarily-subject-involving experiential-content patches. The claim, again, is that insofar as we take it that *the self or subject is something that persists through a long stretch of time*, the only empirically warranted and therefore clear and distinct content of our conception of that entity is: a bundle or succession of numerically distinct *selves* or *subjects*: lots of subjects, not just one. One can put this equally well by saying that the empirically warranted content of our conception of a persisting self or subject is: a (temporally gappy) bundle of numerically distinct experiences; as Hume does. But if one puts it this way one must be clear on the point that these experiences are necessarily subject-of-experience-involving experiences. Lots of numerically distinct experiences mean lots of numerically distinct subjects.

Has anyone ever really taken the 'no-ownership' view to be the denial that experiences necessarily have subjects at least in the sense that they are necessarily

---

different types of content in that single perception (sound, smell and taste, say, or the ideas *grass* and *green* in the thought that grass is green).

[19] 1940: 96–7; see also Chisholm 1969: 97.

experiences-*for*? I don't know (I fear so). The view is for all that incoherent, and as foreign to Hume as it is to Buddhists.

—The idea that there could be an actual occurrence of redness-experience without any *subjectivity* is indeed and of course incoherent. The idea of an actual occurrence of redness-experience without a *subject* isn't. And this is precisely Hume's point in the passage in question. You've simply laid it down that you're going to use 'subject' in a metaphysically non-committal way which has the consequence that the existence of subjectivity entails the existence of a subject. To do this, though, is to deprive yourself of the terms you need to make Hume's point. More seriously, it's to make the correct objection to your claim invisible.

I don't think many participants in the 270-year discussion of Hume's account of personal identity have had this point in mind, but it's worth registering none the less. There's a sense in which it's correct, given that Hume has the then universally accepted idea of a *persisting* mind or self or person or subject or 'thinking being' firmly in mind, in his discussion of 'personal identity'. For, relative to that idea of the subject, the suggestion that a fleeting perception involves only subjectivity, and not *a* subject, can be given a reasonable sense. It isn't, however, correct as an interpretation of Hume. That is, he wouldn't have allowed that there could be subjectivity without there being (*ipso facto*) a subject of experience, once the assumption that subjects are long lived had been cancelled. When he says that a single experience (perception) may qualify as a substance, so far as we have any empirically warranted conception of a substance, he doesn't mean that a single experience—a patch of subjectivity—could exist without a subject of experience for whom it was an experience.

It's helpful to consult Hume's sub-oyster on this issue—the minimal 'thinking being' of his Appendix. I'll return to it in the next section.

13.6 What is Given in Experience

Let me now re-present the point using a primitive symbolism in which 'S' stands for a *subject of experience,* 'E' for an *experience* (or perception), and 'C' for a *content*, i.e. an occurrent experiential content (an occurrent perception content). The curly brackets constitute a *phenomenological* context. That is, anything inside the curly brackets is a representation of *what is phenomenologically given, given in experience.*[20]

The No Bare View Thesis, [1], can be expressed as follows. When I engage in mental self-examination I do not encounter any experience or impression that can be represented simply as

{S}.

I have, in other words, no sort of experience or impression of a subject alone, let alone an experience or impression of some continuing unchanging subject alone. I do of course (necessarily, trivially) encounter a subject of experience, in encountering an

---

[20] I introduced this scheme in Strawson 2001.

experience, but all experiences or impressions of the subject are experiences or impressions of the subject *with*, or *involved in*, an (episode of) experience. That is, they are at the very least of the form

{S+E}

where 'E' stands for whatever particular experiential content you encounter when you try to catch yourself in the moment of experiencing something, which cannot be supposed to be simply S, given that {S} has been ruled out.

But experiences of the subject aren't really of this additive {S+E} form either. For according to the Nothing But An Experience Thesis, [2], the experience of the subject that is necessarily involved in any coming upon an actual experience in Humean mental self-examination doesn't present the subject as something distinct from the experience in such a way as to legitimize any sense in which I can be said to encounter the subject *on the one hand*, and the experience *on the other hand*. Hume expresses this last point strikingly and accurately by saying that there's a fundamental sense in which what I observe or catch is *just the experiencing*, i.e.

{E}.

And there is a fundamental sense, acknowledged by Kant, in which this claim is phenomenologically correct. It has however caused confusion, because something that Hume takes for granted—reasonably enough, because it's a necessary truth—has been suppressed by commentators and accordingly discounted by many readers.

This (of course, and again) is the Experience/Experiencer thesis, the point that an experience that is come upon in this way is indeed an *experience*, i.e. an experien*cing*. Such an experience isn't just an experiential content type—it's not just an experiential content in any sense that allows that an experiential content can somehow concretely occur or be detected without an experiencer also existing and being detected. An experience, once again, is an experiencing, and to come across an experiencing is necessarily to come across an experiencer. In Hume's terms: a perception, an actual temporally situated occurrence, a concrete mental event, isn't just a perceptual content. A perception is a *perception*, an actual perceiv*ing* of something which necessarily involves a perceiv*er*, a subject of experience.

A necessary truth needn't of course be phenomenologically apparent, even in one who takes it for granted—a point to which I will return. The present claim is not that Hume takes a certain theoretical point (a necessary truth) for granted, and automatically applies it in his report of the deliverances of mental self-examination. Nor is it that Hume's experience, when he engages in mental self-examination, is influenced by his theoretical appreciation of the necessary truth in question. The present claim is a very simple claim about what he means by the word 'perception' ('experience') in this context. One might express it by saying that {E} can and should be represented as follows:

{S:C}

where ':' has some kind of intense-intimacy-intimating function which we need not at present specify further. It's {S:C}—a subject-experiencing-a-content—that I catch or observe, in some way that does not involve any full or explicit differentiation of

S and C (but see further below), when I catch or observe an experience or experiencing {E} and can observe nothing but {E}. For {E} is {S:C}.[21]

In these terms, one can say that the error in the traditional interpretation (especially its 'no ownership' division) is to think that when Hume says he 'never can observe anything but the experience' he means that all he encounters when he encounters the experience is

{C},

a 'mere content', as it were, a visual presentation as of a tiger, say, a mere content that is somehow given wholly independently of its being an actual episode of experiencing, an experience on the part of some subject of experience—even though it is given as a concretely occurring phenomenon. But: to log a content in this sense is not to log an experience in the sense (in the way) that concerns Hume in this passage. It's not to take notice of an actual episode of experiencing (perception) at all. It's not to register an actual perceiving, an actual experiential episode considered specifically as such, as one is bound to if one is seriously engaged in the focused exercise of mental self-apprehension that Hume is engaged in. A simple way to see this is to consider the difference between

[a]   what it is to experience or think about a patch of red

in a completely unreflective way, and

[b]   what it is to consider an experience of or thought about a patch of red and consider it specifically as such, i.e. as a thought or experience.[22]

In entering intimately into himself in mental self-examination, a thing which can be difficult to do, as Reid points out,[23] Hume is wholly focused on [b]. And when you do something of the sort specified in [b], to come upon the experience is necessarily to come upon the subject of experience.

Some may agree that an experience is a necessarily-subject-involving entity, a subject-entertaining-a-content or S:C entity, while continuing to insist that it's just the C-ness of the necessarily-S-involving experience that Hume claims to come upon in claiming to come upon nothing but {E}. The idea is that Hume abstracts away from the necessarily-subject-involving reality of the experience considered as a concrete whole, even when engaged in this specially focused act of investigative entry into his mental being, and somehow considers only the abstract content(-type) C. Hume, however, explicitly rejects this view: 'in thinking of our past thoughts, we not only delineate out the objects, of which we were thinking, but also conceive the action of the mind in the meditation, that certain

---

[21] Recall that experiential content is wholly 'internalistically' conceived, here, as concrete occurrent mental content (for those who know about philosophical 'Twins', it's that in respect of which you and your 'Twin' on 'Twin Earth' are qualitatively identical).

[22] Harry Frankfurt provided this case during a discussion in Princeton in 2001.

[23] The 'sensation of hardness may easily be had, by pressing one's hand against the table, and attending to the feeling that ensues, setting aside, as much as possible, all thought of the table and its qualities, or of any external thing. But it is one thing to have the sensation, and another, to attend to it, and make it a distinct object of reflection. The first is very easy; the last, in most cases, extremely difficult' (1764: 55–6).

je-ne-scai-quoi, of which 'tis impossible to give any definition or description, but which every one sufficiently understands' (1.3.8.16/106). The view that Hume claims to find nothing but {C} seems to be nothing but an old prejudice, facilitated by the fact, already noted, that the word 'perception' and other similar words can be understood to have not only a concrete-occurrence use but also a content-type use.

The weight of the traditional interpretation is so great that many may not be convinced. Here it may help to consult the imagined sub-oyster of Hume's Appendix, a creature that is, Hume supposes, even less sophisticated than an oyster, but is none the less a 'thinking being' in the wide Cartesian sense of 'thinking', i.e. an experiencing or conscious being, a subject of experience, although it has 'only one [experience], as of thirst or hunger'.[24] 'Consider it in that situation', he says. 'Do you conceive any thing but merely that [experience]?' No, he answers. But you do indeed conceive an experience, i.e. something that is a conscious episode by definition, an actual episode of experiencing; you do (trivially) conceive or come upon a thinking-being-involving phenomenon and hence upon a 'thinking being', a subject of experience.[25] And Hume's claim is then the same as before: nothing more is given to observation or conception, in the thinking being's being given, than the experience. There is nothing that gives reason to believe in any 'self or substance' that endures and could possibly exist apart from the experience. But to say this is in no way to say that you don't come upon a thinking being, a thinking being considered in its mental being, when you come upon the experience—the experiencing.[26]

So if I follow Hume and enter intimately into what I call myself, I get no view of a bare self—{S}—, a self or subject that is not having any experience. True. Nor do I get a view of a subject having an experience in which the subject is given apart from the overall experience-event as something clearly distinguishable from it—{S+E}. True. And I certainly don't get a view of some enduring unchanging perfectly simple subject that is fully ontologically distinct from the experience—of {$}, as it were, the subject that is the explicit principal target of Hume's scepticism, the soul beloved of the philosophers he's criticizing. True. What I come upon is {E}, nothing but {E}, where {E} is {S:C}, an experiencing-of-a-content-by-an-experiencer.

This is certainly not to say that the subject is encountered as some sort of personalitied entity, when {E} is come upon. It isn't. Nor is it to say that it's encountered as an express object of attention, if this is taken to mean that it has some special, separate salience as object of attention over and above the experience-event considered as a whole. Hume's crucial and wholly correct phenomenological point is, once again, precisely that it isn't. How then is it encountered? This is a question which has been well treated in the Phenomenological tradition, and I will shortly say more about it.

---

[24] App§16/634. This may concern a type or a token of experience. Oysters were a popular example, used also by Descartes and Locke.

[25] A subject that you are, in Hume's thought-experiment, considering specifically and only in its mental being. See n. 5.

[26] As noted (n. 18), the first occurrence of the word 'perception' in App§16 may seem to invite a type reading—the sub-oyster has only one type of perception—while the second occurrence seems to be part of an invitation to consider one single particular 'token' perception. But this isn't any kind of error on Hume's part.

Some may think that this account of what Hume is saying is sophistical, or attributes something too complicated to him. I think it will look sophistical only to those who have been conditioned by the traditional interpretation of Hume. All that the account attributes to Hume is phenomenological perspicacity and honesty and accuracy of expression. True, he was dead against immortal souls, but there's no reason to think that his description of his experience of mental self-examination is influenced by any theoretical prejudice. The point that we have no impression or impression-based idea of the self or subject had already been very clearly made by Berkeley, for one.

13.7 Subject or Subjectivity?

Some may again question whether a *subject* is come upon, experientially, when {E} is come upon. What is come upon, they may say, what is knowably come upon, is, at bottom, just *subjectivity*. '{E} is {S:C}' can be allowed to stand as correct, then, only on condition that one read 'S' simply as 'subjectivity'. What we have is C-flavoured subjectivity. Meditators may agree, claiming that an event of experience encountered in attentive meditative mental self-examination presents merely as something that is intrinsically both subjectivity-involving and content-involving, not as something intrinsically subject-involving.[27]

As before, I think this challenge is worthwhile. But there's no reason to think that Hume thought along these lines, or ever thought there could be a perception or experience—a subjectivity-event—without a 'thinking being'. He finds a thinking being, i.e. a conscious being, even in the case of the sub-oyster, as remarked. The sub-oyster says: a perception (i.e. a perceiving) entails a thinking (conscious) being. No thinking (conscious) being, no perception. This, converted into my terms, says: a subjectivity-involving event entails a subject. No subject, no subjectivity-involving event.

It may be objected that 'subject' is a count noun, whereas 'subjectivity' is a mass term which is as such intrinsically less metaphysically committed. But my non-committal use of 'subject' makes no assumptions about the ontological category of subjects (like Descartes in his *Second Meditation*—see note 3 above). As I understand the term 'subject', to say that subjectivity is knowably present, or experientially given, is already to allow that a subject is knowably present, experientially given.[28] Hume holds that we have to do with a thinking (or conscious) being when we contemplate the sub-oyster's experience, even as he rejects the whole traditional metaphysical framework of substance and accident and, to that extent, anticipates Kant on the point that insofar as we accept to use the categories of traditional metaphysics at all, we can't even know that the thinking being (which certainly exists) is substantial in

---

[27] See e.g. Shear 1998, Rosch 1997. See also Stone 1988, 2005. Hume is not of course concerned with some specially trained practice of mental self-examination.

[28] This re-expresses the point that experience is necessarily experience-*for*; but note further that if one allows that there is subjectivity where I am, and non-overlapping subjectivity where you are, and again where your friend is, one is in effect committed to a count noun—something like 'patch of subjectivity', or 'episode' or 'stream' of subjectivity—i.e. *a* subject.

nature, and not in some way 'just' an accident or property.[29] He doesn't, then, think that any particular traditional substantial metaphysical commitment is built into the admittedly grammatically substantival noun phrase 'thinking being', and holds that individual experiential episodes themselves pass the traditional test for being a substance, so far as our knowledge goes.[30] His position is plain: if there is indeed a experience, then there is indeed a thinking being. There is, in other words, a subject of experience. The presence of experience or subjectivity is sufficient for the presence of a subject of experience.[31]

If the view that you can't have experience (subjectivity) without a subject were doubtful, it might seem improper to hang it on the sub-oyster. There is, though, a comfortable, central, metaphysically uncommitted sense in which it's necessarily— trivially—true (experience is necessarily experience-*for*), and the attribution of it to Hume certainly doesn't hang only on the sub-oyster.

13.8 Metaphysics and Phenomenology

Whatever the phenomenological facts, it is in my terms a straightforward metaphysical truth that an experience necessarily involves a subject of experience as well as a content. Using square brackets for straightforwardly metaphysical propositions, and an arrow to indicate metaphysical entailment, one can represent it as follows:

$$[E \rightarrow [S \& C]].$$

Having done so, it's natural to ask how this metaphysical claim—I'll call it the *ESC Thesis*—relates to the structurally cognate phenomenological claim, made in the last section, that an event of experience genuinely grasped in mental self-examination presents as both subject-involving and content-involving, which I represented as

$$\{E\} = \{S:C\}.$$

I will now consider this question, both for its own sake and for the further light that considering it may throw on Hume's position.

Let me first strengthen the representation of the metaphysical ESC thesis to bring it formally into line with the phenomenological thesis:

$$[E = S:C].$$

This states that an experience (a Humean perception) consists, metaphysically, of a subject entertaining (experiencing, standing in the relation of haver-of to, etc.) a content.[32] I think this is in fact the best thing to say, with Kant in 1772, when the notion of the subject is taken in Hume's way, i.e. narrowly and mentalistically, as it is

---

[29] It is, Kant says, 'quite impossible' for me, given my experience of myself as a mental phenomenon, 'to determine the manner in which I exist, whether it be as substance or object or as accident or property' (1787: B420). Compare Descartes in note 2 above.

[30] 1.4.5.5/233, App§19/634. Hume likes this point.

[31] For a doubt about this approach to the sub-oyster, see Garrett 1997: 180.

[32] The 'intimacy-intimating colon' is designed to sweep up all these phrases; different theories may give different accounts of its force, which is now metaphysical, not phenomenological.

here. But one needn't accept this very difficult idea in order to consider the question of how the two claims, curly and straight bracketed, phenomenological and meta-physical, relate.[33]

It may first be said that the phenomenological claim can be false even if the metaphysical claim is true. It may be said that even if [E = S:C] is true it's possible to have an experience, of a tiger, say, and to be aware of it specifically as an experience, an occurring experiential content (so that one is not merely aware of the outside world, but also of one's experience of it), without being in any way aware of a subject of experience, or even subjectivity; let alone necessarily aware of it. The idea, then, is that

[i] one turns one's attention on an experience, so that it's true to say that what is presented to one is an experience, {E},

and

[ii] the object of one's attention, E, has in fact the metaphysical structure [S:C],

but

[iii] the actual phenomenological content of one's experience of the experience, i.e. {E}, is fully conveyed just by {C}.

I think this claim may still sound plausible to some in the analytic tradition; and some non-philosophers may agree. But even if it were true (I'll consider it further below), its truth wouldn't be relevant to the present discussion of Hume. This is because the question that concerns us at present isn't just about having an—any—experience. It's much more specific. It's about what happens when, like Hume, one sets out in pursuit of a certain very special kind of experience—when one sets out specifically to observe oneself having an experience and in this way 'enters intimately' and attentively into oneself (this is the point made with [a] and [b] in §13.6 above, p. 264). It's about what one finds, in the way of mental phenomena, when one does this rather unusual thing. And here I think it is quite clear that to log the experiencing properly—genuinely to grasp something as an experience, as an experiencing—is, necessarily, to log the experiencer. The experience consists of an experiencer experiencing a content, and focused attention to the experience—to the experience considered specifically as an episode of experience—is (I propose) bound to involve cognizance of this fact. This is so even if—even though—the focused attention needn't involve any thought or grasp that the experiencer is oneself, i.e. any fully or expressly self-conscious thought.[34]

[33] I argue for this view in Strawson 2008a: Essay 6, and Strawson 2009: Part 7. With the William James of *The Principles of Psychology*, I think the best thing to say, when we operate with the 'thin', mentalistic notion of the subject, is that every numerically distinct experience has a different subject. As it stands, however, the symbolism does not exclude saying that numerically distinct experiences occurring in a human being have the same subject. Thus we might have $[E_1 = S_1:C_1]$, $[E_2 = S_1:C_2]$, $[E_3 = S_1:C_3]$ and so on.

[34] Full or express self-consciousness is consciousness of oneself that involves grasping oneself expressly *as oneself* and, not, say, just as the child of X and Y, or the person obliquely reflected in the glass. It's a familiar point that it is possible for one to be wrong—or unaware—that the person one is thinking about is in fact oneself in every case except the case in which one is thinking about oneself specifically as oneself. See, classically, Castañeda 1966, Shoemaker 1968, Perry 1979.

13.9 Thetic and Non-thetic

This may still be doubted. So let me restate the point—first of all in an intentionally imperfect way. The claim is not that the subject (the subject-as-such, as it were) must present (verb) as an express object of attention.[35] It's not that the subject must be apprehended in a 'thetic' way, in the language of the Phenomenologists, i.e. expressly apprehended as an object of attention in the 'focus' of consciousness.[36] On the contrary: it seems clear that the best thing to say, in many contexts of enquiry, *given the way in which the conception of what it would be to apprehend the (mental) subject is set up in those contexts*, is that the subject is not apprehended—not even in a specially attentive act of Humean mental self-examination. For any awareness of the subject is in this case 'non-thetic': in no way in the focus of attention, in no way 'express', as I am currently using this word. Many sincere self-observers will accordingly truthfully deny that they encounter any such thing as the subject in the Humean thought-experiment; and they will be right. For this is the sense in which Hume's phenomenological report, according to which all he finds is {E}, is correct: there is indeed no thetic presentation of the subject as such. The natural idea is that any such presentation would *ipso facto* be presentation of the subject as something in some way distinct from the experience as a whole; that this is what a thetic focusing of attention on the subject would inevitably amount to, a singling out of the subject; and this, as Hume rightly says, is precisely what does not happen. And yet there is, nevertheless, awareness of the subject. Successful focusing on the whole phenomenon of an experience, an actual episode of experiencing, can't deliver just the content of the experience without delivering any sort of awareness of the subject, any more than successful focusing on the whole phenomenon of a page with words written on it can deliver just the content of the words.

Actually, the last paragraph is too concessive. The concession lies in the (in my view mistaken) supposition that the notion of being apprehended as an *express* or *thetic* object of attention is equivalent to the notion of being apprehended as an express *and distinct* object of attention. One can specifically exclude the distinctness claim from the definition of 'thetic', to get 'apprehended as an express but not necessarily distinct object of attention', but even then the claim that the subject is not thetically apprehended may be too concessive. This is because there is after all (I propose) a fundamental sense in which the subject is indeed an express object of my attention, and necessarily so, when I apprehend the experience. The experience I apprehend is indeed an experience, an experiencing, a necessarily-subject-involving thing (not just a content), and I can't possibly genuinely and expressly apprehend it as such, as an experiencing, without also in some way expressly apprehending the subject necessarily involved in the experiencing. I can no more do this than I can fully and carefully and expressly apprehend an actual walking without expressly apprehending a walker ('necessarily involved in' is putting it mildly).

---

[35] I use 'express' where many would use 'explicit' because I prefer to give 'explicit' a weaker than normal use in discussions of this topic.

[36] It doesn't matter whether this apprehension is supposed to be active or passive.

It may be objected that even if this is so—even if I do necessarily apprehend a subject, in apprehending an experience in focused mental self-examination, and even if there is a sense in which I apprehend the subject *expressly* in so doing, although I do not apprehend it as a *distinct* object of attention—still I do not expressly apprehend the subject *as such* as part of the object of my attention, in expressly apprehending the experience. And it may then be said that this as-such-ness is central to one conception of what expressness or theticity is. In fact, though, this claim too is highly debatable. It brings up the distinctness issue again, because there are two readings of 'apprehend as'. Thus it may be reasonably said that although I do not apprehend the subject expressly as the object of my attention by any process of consciously deploying a concept of the subject, I do none the less apprehend the subject expressly as such in apprehending what is in fact the object of my attention—the experience, the experiencing—expressly *as an experience*, an experiencing; and even though I don't apprehend the subject as in any way distinct from the whole experiencing. And I think this is right.

—I understand your phenomenological claim and I still don't agree with it. The claim that you can't observe an experience without also observing an experiencer is doubtless true when taken merely referentially or 'relationally': if an experience consists metaphysically of a subject experiencing a content, then awareness of an experience is necessarily awareness of a subject. But why should I accept the claim when it's taken 'notionally', i.e. as a phenomeno-logical claim, a claim about the experiential character that my experience has for me when I set out on the Humean project of mental self-examination and deliberately take one of my experiences as the object of my attention?[37]

I do indeed mean it to be taken 'notionally' or phenomenologically, and not just referentially or relationally. Perhaps it will help to distinguish two versions of the phenomenological claim, i.e. the claim that any conscious episode of mental self-examination whose principal phenomenological content is such that it is

[1]   awareness of an experience

(awareness 'from the inside', as we say) will also and necessarily be such that its *phenomenological* content involves

[2]   awareness of a subject of experience

even though [2] need not (Hume's point) involve any presentation of the subject as a distinct object of awareness, and may amount simply to a genuine grasp of the fact that the experiential content is live, is actually being lived, had, experienced.

The first and weaker version of this two-point claim restricts attention to those cases in which, with Hume, one undertakes to engage in the special attentive activity of entering intimately into what one calls oneself. The second and stronger version has it that any mental episode at all whose primary content is [1] necessarily also involves [2]; however non-thetic the awareness of the subject may be. The stronger

---

[37] For the relational-notional distinction see Quine 1955; remember that phenomenological content properly understood is no less cognitive than sensory.

version greatly increases the number of relevant cases, for mental episodes that include [1], awareness of an experience, often occur when one isn't involved in specially focused and intentionally directed intimate self-examination. There are, for example, cases in which one is aware of the fact that one is experiencing pinkness when looking at a white table under red light and judging the table to be white, or in which one looks at oneself in a mirror under fluorescent light and thinks that one isn't really that colour. This awareness of experience-as-such may be marginal, *en marge*, ἐν παρέργῳ, in Aristotle's phrase,[38] but it is none the less real, a real concrete occurrence, part of the actual course of one's experience.

I think we should all grant the weaker version of the two-point claim, and I think that it is the beginning of wisdom in these matters to see that the second, stronger version is also true.[39] The simplest way to realize this, perhaps, is to consider again the difference between what it is to think of or otherwise apprehend a patch of red and what it is to think of or otherwise apprehend a thought or experience (on one's own part) of a patch of red.

Some philosophers, including most Phenomenologists, favour an even stronger phenomenological claim, which I mentioned earlier and put aside. This is the claim that all experiences whatever—not just experiences that involve some kind of concerted or explicit reflection on experience—necessarily involve [2] some sort of non-thetic awareness of the subject simply insofar as they necessarily involve [1] some sort of awareness of themselves.

I think this is true. The question is of great interest when one considers the many issues raised by Hume's discussion of personal identity and mental self-examination. But it is a topic for another time.[40]

13.10 Russell and Foster

I've been arguing that Hume doesn't claim that the subject of experience isn't encountered in experience. Since taking up this cause,[41] I've found that I'm not alone. If I haven't convinced you, perhaps Russell will. He considers the Humean project of mental self-examination and makes the point helpfully in his own terms in *The Problems of Philosophy*:

When we try to look into ourselves we always seem to come upon some particular thought or feeling, and not upon the 'I' which has the thought or feeling. Nevertheless there are some reasons for thinking that we are acquainted with the 'I', though the acquaintance is hard to disentangle from other things. To make clear what sort of reason there is, let us consider for a moment what our acquaintance with particular thoughts really involves. When I am acquainted with 'my seeing the sun', it seems plain that I am acquainted with two different things in relation to each other. On the one hand there is the sense-datum which represents the sun to me, on the

---

[38] '...knowledge and perception and opinion and understanding have always something else as their object, and themselves only by the way' (*Metaphysics* 12.9.1074b35–6).

[39] Note that it applies at least as well in the case of experiences that are not one's own as in the case of experiences that are one's own, although the former case is not at present of concern.

[40] See Ch. 8 above.

[41] In a talk given to the Hume Society in Cork in 1999.

other hand there is that which sees [has] this sense-datum. All acquaintance . . . seems obviously a relation between the person acquainted and the object with which the person is acquainted. When a case of acquaintance is [itself something] with which I can be acquainted (as I am acquainted with my acquaintance with the sense-datum representing the sun) it is plain that the person acquainted is myself. Thus, when I am acquainted with my seeing the sun, the whole fact with which I am acquainted is 'self-acquainted-with-sense-datum'. . . . It does not seem necessary to suppose that we are acquainted with a more or less permanent person, the same today as yesterday, but it does seem as though we must be acquainted with that thing, whatever its nature, which sees the sun and has acquaintance with sense-data. Thus, in some sense it would seem we must be acquainted with our Selves as opposed to our particular experiences.[42]

And when John Foster writes that

a natural response to Hume would be to say that, even if we cannot detect ourselves *apart from* our perceptions (our conscious experiences), we can at least detect ourselves *in* them—that when I introspectively detect an experience, what is revealed is the complex of myself-experiencing-something or myself experiencing-in-a-certain-manner. Indeed, it is not clear in what sense an experience *could* be introspectively detected without the detection of its subject[43]

his only error, in my view, is to think that Hume ever thought otherwise. Hume's target was the simple unchanging persisting subject of the philosophers and the church, nothing less and nothing more.[44]

13.11 Is Hume Right about Intimate Entrance?

How does Hume come out of all this? Wonderfully well, I think. In his admittedly imperfect terms, he is making an extremely perceptive claim—a completely accurate claim, as far as I can see—about what it's actually like to encounter oneself as a (mental) subject of experience when one has decided to go looking for oneself considered specifically as a (mental) subject of experience.

How does one proceed in such a case? The most natural thing to do at first, I think, is to try to catch oneself on the fly in one's experience in the present moment (it's a familiar claim that the act of trying to take one's present experience as the explicit or

---

[42] 1912: 27–8; Sydney Shoemaker tells me that this passage was the subject of his first paper, and it is worth bearing in mind Shoemaker's demolition of the 'view, which motivates "bundle", "logical construction", and "no subject" theories of the self, that from an empiricist standpoint the status of the self (the subject of experience) is suspect compared with that of such things as sensations, feelings, images, and the like' (1986: 24). At the same time, Shoemaker thinks that the standard perceptual model of introspection favoured by such empiricists is incorrect, and his claim is accordingly conditional: *if* one accepts such a model at all then 'the view that we have introspective perception of individual mental happenings but not of a self is indefensible' (ibid.).

[43] 1991: 215; see also 215–19.

[44] Objection: 'I still favour the only-{C} reading because I think that that Hume might have been happy to agree with what Kant is trying to express when he says such things as that "the representation of [empirical] apperception is nothing more than feeling of an existence" (1783: §46n), or that "the consciousness of myself in the representation *I* is no intuition at all, but a merely *intellectual* representation of the self-activity [*Selbsttätigkeit*] of a thinking subject" (Kant 1781/7: B228).' Reply: to the extent that this is right, it seems to me to strengthen the rejection of the only-{C} reading.

thetic object of one's attention inevitably induces a delay which means that what one actually catches is the immediate past experience).[45] And this is probably what Hume did. One may also conduct one's investigation by having, or staging, in expressly introspective mode, an individual, explicitly self-conscious mental episode; by thinking, now, 'I'm reading a book' or 'I'm bored', 'I'm now thinking about my thinking'; and he may also have tried this. The result is the same. There is, as Hume says, [1] no *bare* or naked view or apprehension of the subject. There is, as he says, [2] no view or apprehension of the subject as something saliently experientially distinct from the episode of experiencing considered as a whole. There is, as he says, [3] nothing that presents both as the subject of the apprehended experience and as an intrinsically persisting (or experience-transcendent) thing. There is, nevertheless (and of course, so that it is not explicitly mentioned) [4] apprehension of the subject, not only 'relationally' speaking but also 'notionally' speaking (§13.9 above, p. 270), in the apprehension of the experience in present-moment mental self-examination. When Hume carries out this exercise, what he apprehends is as he says himself, '*myself*', by which he means specifically himself considered as mental subject, the mental subject that necessarily exists when experiences exist.

To say that the self or mental subject doesn't present as an intrinsically persisting thing is not of course to say that people don't *believe* that it's an intrinsically persisting thing. They do, as Hume knows; and they may well also believe that they have direct experience of there being such a thing, or at least experience that strongly backs up the belief that there is such a thing, as Hume remarks. If, however, we consider how the mental subject is given in unprejudiced mental reflection of the sort Hume is engaged in, we find nothing of the sort—as he says. This, after all, is why he devotes most of 'Of personal identity' to explaining the various mechanisms by which we come to believe in a persisting subject of experience in spite of the fact that no such thing presents itself as such when we engage in reflection of this kind.

---

[45] I question this claim in Ch. 10 above.

14

'All my hopes vanish'
Hume on the Mind 2

14.1 'The essence of the mind [is] unknown'

Hume holds that 'the essence... of external bodies' is unknown, and that 'the essence of the mind [is] equally unknown to us with that of external bodies'.[1] His aim in section 1.4.6 of his *Treatise*, which addresses the question of the nature of the mind (after having dismissed the traditional debate between the materialists and immaterialists in the preceding section), is accordingly modest. It is, first, to provide an account of the content of

[1] the *empirically warranted* idea of the mind (or self or person),

given that we cannot know the *essence* of the mind, and, second, to provide a causal psychological account of the origin of

[2] our belief in a single diachronically persisting mind (or self or person),

given that the account of [1] turns out to show that no idea of the mind as a single diachronically persisting entity is empirically warranted.[2] More particularly, it is to provide a psychological account of how each of us individually comes to believe that that he or she is a single persisting person or self or has a single persisting mind.

When Hume returns to this topic in §§10–21 of the Appendix to the *Treatise*, he can find no fault in his accounts of [1] and [2]. The consequence, in his own words, is that his 'hopes vanish'.

Why is this? He remains entirely happy with his account of [2], and reaffirms it in the Appendix (App§20/635).[3] The trouble lies in his account of [1]. But the trouble is not that the account of [1] is wrong. On the contrary: Hume can't see how it can be

---

[1] Int§8/xvii (in the case of the *Abstract*, the Appendix and the Introduction to the *Treatise*, I refer to their seventh paragraphs (e.g.) as 'Abs§7', 'App§7' and 'Int§7' respectively). When I cite a work by someone other than Hume I give the first publication date or estimated date of composition, while the page reference is to the published version listed in the Bibliography. When quoting I mark my emphases by italics, and the author's by **bold italics**.

[2] In Book 1 of the *Treatise* Hume takes 'person' to have a merely mental reference, and uses it interchangeably with 'mind' and 'self' (and sometimes 'soul'). See e.g. Pike: 'when Hume uses the term... "person", he generally means to be referring only to the mind' (1967: 161), at least in Book 1 of the *Treatise*. See also §2/251, §5/253, §20/262, 'self or person'; §17/260, 'mind or thinking person'.

[3] Most commentators have thought his problem lies in his account of [2]. See Ellis 2006 for an interesting recent defence of this view. For the opposing view (other than this paper), see e.g. Stroud 1977, and, more recently, Garrett 2011, Strawson 2011a: §§3.4, 3.10.

wrong, on his empiricist terms, and he reaffirms it, too, in the Appendix (App§§15–19/634–5). The trouble is that his philosophy as a whole makes essential use of a conception of mind that isn't empirically warranted, according to [1]. Since he is committed to an empiricist approach, he needs to get more into his account of the empirically warranted idea of the mind. But he can't. So his hopes vanish.

14.2 The Empirically Warranted Idea of the Mind

What is the empirically warranted idea of the mind, the account of the mind that any philosophy that aims at clarity and distinctness must aim at, given that the essence of the mind is unknown?[4] Hume's answer is plain: the mind '*as far as we can conceive it*, is nothing but a system or train of different perceptions' (Abs§28/657). We have no 'notion of... self..., *when conceiv'd distinct from* particular perceptions... we have *no notion* of... the mind..., distinct from the particular perceptions' (App§§18,19/635).[5]

These are explicitly epistemologically qualified statements of what has come to be known as 'the bundle theory of mind'. They're claims to the effect that this is all we can know of the mind. But we also find many (mostly earlier) epistemologically unqualified ontological formulations of the bundle theory of mind. Minds or selves or persons or thinking beings, Hume says, are 'nothing but a bundle or collection of different perceptions' (1.4.6.4/252). 'They are the successive perceptions only, that constitute the mind' (1.4.6.4/253) A 'succession of perceptions... constitutes [a] mind or thinking principle' (1.4.6.18/260). It is a 'chain of causes and effects, which constitute our self or person'.[6] A 'composition of... perceptions... forms the self' (App§15/634). A 'train... of... perceptions... compose a mind' (App§20/635). Hume couldn't be more plain: 'what we call a mind, is nothing but a heap or collection of different perceptions, united together by certain relations' (1.4.2.39/207). It is a 'connected mass of perceptions, which constitute a thinking being' (1.4.2.39/

Hume later comes to think that Kames gives a better account of the origin of [2] than he does. Reading a draft of Kames's *Essays* in 1746, Hume writes to Kames that 'I likt exceedingly your Method of explaining personal Identity as more satisfactory than any thing that had ever occurr'd to me' (1746: 20). I suspect that Hume here means Kames's account of the origin of our idea of or belief in a persisting self—'man... has an original feeling, or consciousness of himself, and of his existence, which for the most part accompanies every one of his impressions and ideas, and every action of his mind and body' (Kames 1751: 231–2). For Kames's further remarks (e.g. 'this consciousness or perception of self is, at the same time, of the liveliest kind. Self-preservation is everyone's peculiar duty; and the vivacity of this perception, is necessary to make us attentive to our own interest' (1751: 232)) are very close to Hume's own published views in Book 2 and 3 of the *Treatise* (see e.g. 2.1.11.4/317, 2.1.11.8/320, 2.2.2.15–16/339–40, 2.2.4.7/354, 2.3.7.1/427).

[4] Hume holds, of course, that only an empiricist philosophy deals only in clear and distinct ideas. He uses 'clear and distinct' a couple of times in the *Treatise* when discussing geometrical concepts (1.1.7.6/19, 1.2.4.11/43). He uses 'clear and distinct... idea' and 'clear, distinct idea' in the *Enquiry* (see 12.20/157, 12.28/164), also 'clearly and distinctly' (4.18/35); otherwise he uses 'clear' and 'distinct' separately. He also uses 'clear and precise' (648/Abs§7, 52/1.3.1.7).

[5] All mental occurrences are perceptions, in Hume's terminology—thoughts, sensations, emotions, ideas, and so on—and they're all (by definition) conscious. The word that now corresponds most closely to Hume's word 'perceptions', in this use, is 'experiences'.

[6] 262/1.4.6.20. Here the 'causes and effects' are particular perceptions.

207), 'a connected heap of perceptions' (1.4.2.40/207). It is a 'succession of perceptions, which constitutes our self or person' (1.4.7.3/265). 'It must be our several
particular perceptions, that compose the mind. I say, compose the mind, not belong
to it' (Abs§28/658).[7]

How should we take these remarks? Well, Hume holds that 'the perceptions of
the mind are perfectly known' (2.2.6.2/366), and he also holds that the essence of the
mind is unknown. So he certainly doesn't intend these outright ontological claims
without restriction, as stating the essence of the mind. They're claims about the mind
so far as we have any empirically—and hence philosophically—respectable knowledge of it.[8] They're claims about the empirically legitimate content of any claims
about the nature of the mind that can claim to express knowledge of the nature of the
mind. Hume is a sceptic, and a sceptic, even a moderate sceptic like Hume, doesn't go
around claiming to have certain a posteriori knowledge of the ultimate metaphysical
nature of the concrete constituents of the universe (other than perceptions). He
doesn't claim to have certain a posteriori knowledge either of the essence of the mind,
or of the essence of objects.

—The outright ontological claims about the mind are literally true when they are made strictly
within the philosophical framework of ideas constituted by empirically warranted (and hence
clear and distinct) ideas, since they just repeat the definition of the empirically warranted clear
and distinct idea of the mind.

True. The point is then that this framework of empirically warranted (and hence
clear and distinct) ideas is in Hume's philosophy rightly and crucially embedded
within a larger sceptical framework of ideas. In the larger sceptical framework of
ideas it's acknowledged that there may be and indeed is more to reality than what we
can comprehend in empirically warranted ideas, and words like 'mind' and 'bodies'
are accordingly used in a larger sense: 'the essence of the *mind*' is 'equally unknown
to us with that of *external bodies*' (Int§8/xvii), and 'the essence and composition of
external bodies are so obscure, that we must necessarily, in our reasonings, or rather
conjectures concerning them, involve ourselves in contradictions and absurdities'.[9]

14.3 Why isn't the Empirically Warranted Idea
of the Mind Enough for Hume?

Why isn't the empirically warranted idea of the mind enough for Hume? Before
trying to answer this question, we should consider Hume's statement of what he
would need in order to be able to put things right, now that his hopes have vanished.

---

[7] 1.4.6.4/252, 1.4.6.4/253, 1.4.6.18/260, 1.4.6.20/262, App§15/634, App§20/635, 1.4.2.39/207, 1.4.2.39/
207, 1.4.2.40/207, 1.4.7.3/265, Abs§28/658. Six of these eleven quotations are from passages where Hume is
discussing something else, or summarizing the view and stating it in a particularly compressed form. See
also 2.1.2.2/277.

[8] On this see in particular Craig 1987: 111–20.

[9] 2.2.6.2/366. ''Tis in vain to ask, Whether there be body or not? That is a point, which we must take for
granted in all our reasonings' (1.4.2.1/187). Note that exactly the same is true of Hume's use of words like
'cause', 'power', 'force', and so on. See e.g. Strawson (2011a: 45n).

He is very straightforward about this:

Did our perceptions either inhere in something simple and individual, or did the mind perceive some real connexion among them, there wou'd be no difficulty in the case. (App§21/636)

If we could appeal to the idea that our perceptions inhered in something simple and individual, all would be well. But in that case we would of course have to have empirical warrant for the view that our perceptions inhere in something simple and individual, and that, Hume thinks (rightly, on his terms), is something we'll never have.

We'd also be able to put things right if we could perceive 'some real connexion' among our perceptions. For in that case the idea of real connection among perceptions would be empirically warranted (because perceived), and could accordingly feature as part of the empirically warranted idea of the mind. But that, Hume says (again rightly, on his terms), is something that will never happen.

14.4 What Does Hume Need to Do That he Can't Do?

If either of the two options specified in the previous quotation were available, Hume would be all right, given what he needs to do. What does he need to do? He's very straightforward about this too. He needs to explain something. What does he need to explain? He states what he needs to explain in two different ways in a single paragraph (App§20/635–6). It's slightly confusing, because he speaks of principles first in the singular and then in the plural, although he has the same thing in mind in both cases. He needs

to explain the *principle* of connexion, which binds [our perceptions] together, and makes us attribute to them a real simplicity and identity. (App§20/635)

He needs in other words

to explain the *principles*, that unite our successive perceptions in our thought or consciousness. (App§20/636)

One finds exactly the same shift between the singular and the plural in the passage about the mind (in particular the 'imagination') in which his problem originates, and to which one must turn first when trying to say what his problem was:[10]

nothing wou'd be more unaccountable than the operations of [the imagination], were it not guided by some *universal principles*, which render it, in some measure, uniform with itself in all times and places. Were ideas entirely loose and unconnected, chance alone wou'd join them; and 'tis impossible the same simple ideas should fall regularly into complex ones (as they

---

[10] As Garrett remarks, the question of what Hume's problem was—the question of what Hume thought his problem was—'has received what is surely a far greater number of distinct answers—well over two dozen, even by a conservative count—than has any other interpretive question about Hume's philosophical writings' (2011: 16). I don't think this would have happened if the discussion had started out from 1.1.4.

commonly do) without some bond of union among them, some associating quality, by which one idea naturally introduces another. This *uniting principle* among ideas . . .   (1.1.4.1/10–11)

Why does he need to explain this principle, or these principles, and what exactly does he mean by 'explain'? At the very least, he means that he needs to make the existence of these principles readily intelligible. Why so? Well, for one thing, they're his fundamental explanatory posits. The fact that the mind is governed by these principles—the fact that the mind is a Principle-Governed Mind—is the fundamental explanatory posit of Hume's whole philosophy. He needs to explain the Principle-Governed Mind—to make its existence readily intelligible.

As a sceptic, Hume is clear on the point that he doesn't have to explain everything. He's clear that many things about the nature of the universe lie beyond the reach of human understanding. In fact he's clear on the point that he doesn't have to explain everything about the very principles that are in question when his hopes vanish. When we consider these principles, he says, 'the principles of union or cohesion among our simple ideas' (1.1.4.6/12), we encounter

'a kind of ATTRACTION, which in the mental world will be found to have as extraordinary effects as in the natural. . . . [11] Its effects are every where conspicuous; but as to its causes, they are mostly unknown, and must be resolv'd into *original* qualities of human nature, which I pretend not to explain.

'Nothing is more requisite for a true philosopher', he continues:

than to restrain the intemperate desire of searching into causes, and having establish'd any doctrine upon a sufficient number of experiments, rest contented with that, when he sees a farther examination would lead him into obscure and uncertain speculations. In that case his enquiry wou'd be much better employ'd in examining the effects than the causes of his principle.'[12]

Quite so. This is clear. But Hume is no less clear on the fact that there's something about these principles, about the Principle-Governed Mind, that he needs to explain and can't explain; something that he needs to make readily intelligible, and can't.

14.5 What Has Caused His Difficulty to Arise in the First Place?

What has caused his difficulty? Hume is clear on this point too. It's the fact that he has 'loosen'd all our particular perceptions':

But having thus loosen'd all our particular perceptions, when[13] I proceed to explain the principle of connexion, which binds them together, . . . I am sensible, that my account is very defective . . .   (App§20/635)

---

[11]   Here he is referring to gravity.

[12]   1.1.4.6/12–13. The reference to 'simple' in 'the principles of union or cohesion among our simple ideas' could be dropped.

[13]   There is a footnote reference letter ('a') attached to the word 'when' in Hume's text. The note refers the reader to 'Vol. I. Page 452.' This falls wholly on p. 260 in the Selby-Bigge edition, beginning with '. . . if disjoin'd by the greatest difference' (1.4.6.16) and ending with '. . . amidst all its variations' (1.4.6.18).

Why is this loosening a problem? Because, he says, in a passage already quoted:

were ideas entirely loose and unconnected, chance alone wou'd join them; and 'tis impossible the same simple ideas should fall regularly into complex ones (as they commonly do) without some bond of union among them, some associating quality, by which one idea naturally introduces another. (1.1.4.1/10)[14]

It seems, then, that he shouldn't have loosened all our perceptions. If he hadn't he wouldn't have this problem. But when he asks what an empirically warranted idea of the mind looks like, he finds he has to loosen them. For all that is observable of the mind is a 'train of perceptions' with no observable connection between them. This is his problem.

In another well-known passage, Hume writes that

the true idea of the human mind, is to consider it as a system of different perceptions or different existences, which are link'd together by the relation of cause and effect and mutually produce, destroy, influence, and modify each other. (1.4.6.19/261)

Doesn't he here claim that he has the 'real connexion' he needs? No. This reference to the relation of cause and effect brings in nothing more than the empirically warranted idea of cause and effect, and this, of course, is not an idea of real connection.[15] Hume is clear on the point. The 'true', i.e. empirically warranted, idea of the human mind, which is characterized in terms of causal links, as above, is an account of the mind in which 'all our particular perceptions' are 'loosen'd' (App§20/635). He can't explain the existence of the principle/principles whose existence needs to be explained if all he has are loose perceptions—which are all his empirically warranted account of the mind gives him. He needs observable 'real connexion' between the perceptions, or their inherence in 'something simple and individual', which is in effect just a particularly strong form of real connexion (App§21/636). That's what he says. He could hardly be more clear on the point.

14.6 The Heart of the Problem

We can put Hume's problem in a suitably painful way as follows. He uses a certain theoretical conception of the mind—the Principle-Governed Mind described in 1.1.4—with tremendous success in 1.3.14 ('Of the idea of necessary connexion'), in his psychological account of how it is that we come to believe we experience

---

[14] Note that the problem is not just that he can't give an account of the fact that 'the same simple ideas should fall regularly into complex ones'. That's simply the first point he considers in 1.1.4, 'Of the connexion or association of ideas'. He also needs to give an account of the operation of the other associations of ideas that the 'uniting principle' accounts for, the associations of ideas based on resemblance, contiguity, and causation, which he sets out in the rest of the section. (I think Hume may have turned up this section when sketching his difficulty in the Appendix.)

[15] As Garrett says, 'by "real connexion" used as a technical term, Hume means (at least) a connection between two objects that is more than simply an associative relation in the imagination' (1997: 181). Hume's principal example of a 'real connexion' is causal necessity realistically and naively figured as something that exists quite independently of any activity of the fiction-generating 'imagination'.

causal necessity or power in the world, and of how it is that we do this in spite of the fact that the actual legitimate empirical content of our experience of causation in the world contains no experience of causal necessity or power in the world. He uses this conception of the Principle-Governed Mind again in 1.4.2 ('Of scepticism with regard to the senses'), and with equal success, in his psychological account of how it is that we come to believe in external objects that continue to exist independent and unperceived, and of how it is that we come to do this in spite of the fact that this property of continuous independent unperceived existence can't be part of our experience, or, therefore, part of the actual legitimate empirical content of our idea of an external object. His conception of the Imagination—the capital letter marks Hume's use of 'imagination' as a theoretical term—effectively contains the whole conception of the Principle-Governed Mind. It drives his account of how, given only

[3]   the actual or empirically warranted content of the idea of causation

we none the less acquire

[4]   our belief that we experience causal power in external objects,

as just remarked, and equally of how, given only

[5]   the actual empirically warranted content of the idea of an external object,

we none the less acquire

[6]   our belief in external objects.

Appeal to the Imagination works beautifully, on its own terms, in explaining [4] and [6]. The crash comes only when Hume turns (in 1.4.6) to give his account of how we acquire

[2]   our belief in a single diachronically persisting mind,

given only

[1]   the actual empirically warranted idea of the mind.

For then he finds that [1], the actual empirically warranted idea of the mind, doesn't furnish the materials—the machinery, one might say—he needs to drive his account of how we acquire [2]. Nor does it contain the machinery he has already used to drive his accounts of how we acquire [4] and [6]. His account of [1], the actual empirically warranted idea of the mind, the only one he can use in his philosophy, on his own terms, forbids him to appeal to the Principle-Governed Mindaka the Imagination, the very thing that drives all the most original parts of his philosophy: the accounts of how we acquire [4], [6], and [2]. The problem is stark: the Imagination can't have any real existence if all there is to the mind is a bundle of perceptions. There is nowhere for it to be. More moderately, and more precisely to the point: we can't make use of the notion of the Imagination or the Principle-Governed Mind *in our philosophy*, if our philosophy rules that the only idea of the mind that is suitably clear and distinct, and can therefore be legitimately used in philosophy to make knowledge claims, is the bundle theory of mind. No doubt what we need *exists*. It exists in reality—it's the 'essence of the mind'. But 'the essence of the mind [is] unknown', and we can't make use of it in our empiricist philosophy.

In sum: when Hume comes to give his empiricist account of the mind, his philosophy shoots itself in the foot. That's why his hopes vanish. His particular brand of empiricism is unsustainable.[16]

In the first *Enquiry* he endorses the claim that prompts his confession of failure in the Appendix to the *Treatise*, when, in his only direct reference to the abandoned problem, he observes, briefly but decisively, that

it is evident that there is a principle of connexion between the different thoughts or ideas of the mind. (3.1/23)

Here he refers to a real connection of precisely the sort that the empiricistically 'true' idea of the human mind can't countenance.[17] This is the very same 'principle of connexion' that he refers to in the Appendix, the principle of connexion that, he says, makes 'my hopes vanish... when I proceed to explain' it (App§20/635). He can't explain it on the terms of his empiricist theory of ideas. In turning his attention to our idea of the mind in 1.4.6—after having devoted detailed attention to our idea of causation in 1.3.14, and our idea of external bodies in 1.4.2—Hume finds himself obliged to deprive himself of 'the uniting principle' (1.1.4.1/10) that he had relied on in 1.3.14 and 1.4.2: 'the principle of connexion, which binds... all our particular perceptions together' (App§20/636). It can't be part of the empirically warranted idea of the mind. It can't be part of the empirically warranted idea of the mind whether it's thought of as a 'real connexion' of some sort or as something 'simple and individual', because neither of these things is given in experience.[18]

---

[16] For independent proof that Hume takes there to be more to the mind than perceptions, see e.g. Strawson 1989: 130, Strawson 2011 §2.6. (Briefly: call a simple impression of A an *A-impression*, and a simple idea of A an *A-idea*. According to Hume, an A-idea can arise in my mind only if I've already had an A-impression. What happens is that 'there is a copy taken by the mind, which remains after the impression ceases; and this we call an idea' (1.1.2.1/8). But if the mind is just a bundle of distinct experiences with no hidden content (their contents are 'perfectly known'), then there is no possible way in which this can happen. For where does the A-idea 'remain... after the impression ceases'—given that I then go on to experience or think about, B, C, and many other things, and have no conscious thought of A?

[17] See also 5.14/50: 'nature has established *connexions* among particular ideas.... These principles of connexion or association we have reduced to three, namely, **Resemblance, Contiguity** and **Causation**; which are the only *bonds* that unite our thoughts together...'

[18] This proposed solution comfortably satisfies four of the five criteria for a successful solution that Garrett lists in Garrett 2011: the 'Crisis Criterion', the 'Origin Criterion', the 'Solution Criterion', and the 'Scope Criterion'. It questions whether the fifth criterion—the 'Difficulty Criterion'—is correct, by proposing that Hume did not have any difficulty in stating his problem—although he could certainly have been clearer. The explanation of why Hume has been found obscure lies in the preconceived ideas about Hume that readers have brought to the Appendix. (The clause that has been most damagingly misread is 'when I proceed to explain the principle of connexion, which binds them together, and makes us attribute to them a real simplicity and identity'. On this see Strawson 2011a Part 3.)

14.7 The Unanswerable Objection?

Some may object that Hume doesn't really have the problem he thinks he has. I think Hume is not so foolish as to mistake his own situation, but the objection is worth addressing, and I'll do so in due course. First, I'll restate the issue.

We can start with the two fundamental theoretical principles that Hume says he can't renounce (App§21/636). I'll number them '[P1]' and '[P2]':

[P1] 'all our distinct perceptions are distinct existences' [so far as we know]

and

[P2] 'the mind never perceives any real connexion among distinct existences'.

These principles are very clear and familiar to any reader of Hume.

In the next sentence Hume states two options, already noted, either of which would in his opinion entirely solve his problem. The first is that [P1] is false—that

[O1] 'our perceptions ... inhere in something simple and individual'

The second, to spell it out a little, is that [P2] is false—that

[O2] although our perceptions are distinct existences, 'the mind perceive[s] some real connexion among them'.

Why would either of these two options solve his problem? Because both can sufficiently ground a fundamental theoretical commitment of his philosophy—his commitment to the real existence and operation of something he's just mentioned, i.e.

[P3] the principle of connexion, which binds ... our particular perceptions ... together (App§20/635)

or (in its plural version)

[P4] the principles, that unite our successive perceptions in our thought or consciousness (App§20/636),

i.e., most centrally, the principles of the association of ideas, the Resemblance principle, the Contiguity principle, and the Cause and Effect principle. The trouble is that [O1] and [O2] are ruled out for him. They have no empirical warrant. They're philosophically inadmissible from his empiricist point of view. The ideas of real or objective unity or connection that [O1] and [O2] appeal to are conceptually clear. They're 'perfectly distinct' as far as they go.[19] But they're 'unintelligible' in their application to concrete reality, i.e. experience furnishes no empirically legitimate content for them. So Hume can't appeal to them in his account of the nature of the mind. His hopes vanish.

This may not be the best way to put the point. It may be better to say that what happens in the Appendix is that Hume realizes that he has no answer, given his

---

[19] 'We have a distinct idea of an object, that remains invariable and uninterrupted thro' a suppos'd variation of time; and this idea we call that of *identity* or *sameness*. We have also a distinct idea of several different objects existing in succession, and connected together by a close relation; ... these two ideas of identity, and a succession of related objects [are] in themselves perfectly distinct' (1.4.6.6/253).

overall theory, to an objection that begins by citing [O1] and [O2] and then challenges him to deny that at least one of them (or perhaps their disjunction) is in effect built into what he means by 'mind', and is therefore built into what he is really taking to be the 'true idea' of the mind, although they're excluded from his official account of the 'true idea' of the mind.

On this account, Hume realizes that he faces what one might call the *Unanswerable Objection*:

Your philosophy taken as a whole commits you, Hume, to a view forbidden by your philosophy. More precisely, it commits you to a choice between one of two views. The first is that the self or mind is something like an ontologically (substantially) simple and individual persisting something, in which successive perceptions (i.e. experiences) inhere in such a way that it's not problematic that they are connected or united in the way you take them to be. If you reject this—as you must on your empiricist principles, given which we have (among other things) no warrant for believing in or appealing to the existence of anything that lasts longer than the duration of a single fleeting perception—and hold instead that the mind is something ontologically (substantially) multiple, you're no better off. For then you must hold that the mind is something whose existence involves 'real connexion' (and this is something that you have in effect already done), and also, crucially, given your own fundamental empiricist principles, that this real connection is *empirically knowable*, experienceable or perceivable by us. You must hold this because the idea of real connection is built into the conception of the Imagination-governed mind you make use of in your philosophy, so it must be empirically justified in order to be licensed for use. But you must also reject the view that it's empirically knowable, given those same fundamental empiricist principles, and you have indeed done so.

It seems that Hume agrees. He puts forward exactly the same two metaphysical options, [O1] and [O2], one straightforwardly ontological, the other ontological/epistemological, and then says that either would solve his problem, but that he can't have either.

It may be protested that Hume can't really be saying this, because he takes the idea of a persisting, simple and individual something and the idea of real connection to be 'unintelligible' *tout court*. But he is saying this. Even those who want to reject the quotation in note 17 from 1.4.6.6/253, in support of the claim that Hume thinks that both these two ideas are 'perfectly distinct', must concede that he's taking these two ideas to be *sufficiently intelligible to be available for use in an informative description of a situation in which he wouldn't face the philosophical difficulty he feels he does face.*[20] For Hume, 'unintelligible' means 'not understandable', 'incomprehensible'. It doesn't mean 'incoherent', and so necessarily non-existent, as it standardly does today in philosophy. It means 'not such that it has any empirically warrantable applicability to concrete reality', hence 'not clear in such a way that it can be appealed to in empiricist philosophy'.[21]

---

[20] Compare the move he makes in 1.4.5, discussed in Strawson 2011a: 50–1.

[21] Craig has an incomparable discussion of this issue; see in particular Craig 1987: 123–30, a decisive antidote to Millican's unfortunate recent attempts to re-equate Hume's use of 'unintelligible' with 'incoherent' (see e.g. 2009: 647–8). See also Strawson 1989: 49–58.

Some students of Hume have difficulty with the idea that he makes any use at all of the idea of objective or real connection. This is understandable, at least at first, but Hume's position is clear: if (once again) our ideas were

entirely loose and unconnected, chance alone wou'd join them; and *'tis impossible* the same simple ideas should fall regularly into complex ones (as they commonly do) without some *bond of union* among them, some associating quality, by which one idea naturally introduces another.[22]

In fact, 'the same simple ideas [do] fall regularly into complex ones', and one idea 'naturally introduce[s]' another (1.1.4.2/11). This is what actually happens, and it can't possibly happen, Hume says, unless there exists, as a matter of objective fact, a 'bond of union'—a 'uniting principle', 'principles of union or cohesion'—among our ideas (1.1.4.1/10, 1.1.4.6/13). The 'causes' of this phenomenon are he says 'mostly unknown, and must be resolv'd into *original qualities of human nature, which I pretend not to explain*'.[23] But this is not to say that these principles of cohesion aren't real. On the contrary, they are indeed real. All we can know of them are the observable regularities to which they give rise. Garrett states the general point robustly:

Hume is not forbidden by his empiricist principles from postulating the existence of unperceived *deterministic mechanisms* that would *underlie* the propensities of perceptions to appear in particular ways. He is forbidden by his principles only from trying to specify the nature of those mechanisms [in a way that goes] beyond what experience can warrant.

(1997: 171, my emphasis)

So it is that when he is discussing causal necessity, Hume says that he is

indeed, ready to allow, that there may be several qualities both in material and immaterial objects, with which we are utterly unacquainted; and if we please to call these *power* or *efficacy*, 'twill be of little consequence to the world. But when, instead of *meaning these unknown qualities*, we make the terms of power and efficacy signify something, of which we have a *clear idea*, and which is incompatible with those objects, to which we apply it [it's incompatible because it's just a feeling or impression], obscurity and error begin then to take place, and we are led astray by a false philosophy.[24]

14.8 Garrett's Objection

Many Hume commentators would reject Garrett's claim about Hume in this passage. I accept it, for reasons given at the end of §14.2 above, in spite of the fact that it suggests the following objection to the present account of Hume's problem.

---

[22] 1.1.4.1/10; my emphasis. See Strawson 2011a: 140–1 for a discussion of the point that these mental connections involve only a 'gentle force', and are not exceptionless.

[23] 1.1.4.6/13. He follows Newton, who states the law of gravitational attraction while adding that 'the cause of Gravity...I do not pretend to know' (1687: 3.240).

[24] 1.3.14.27/168. Notice the relative mildness of 'obscurity and error then begin'. Compare 2.3.2.4/ 409–10.

Look, as you say, Hume holds that 'the essence of the mind [is] unknown' (xvii/Int§8). He takes it for granted, in his philosophy considered as a whole, that there is in fact something more to the mind than just a series or bundle of perceptions. He never endorses the bundle theory of mind as the truth about the ultimate nature of the mind. All true. But this 'something more' isn't a problem for him, contrary to what you suggest. It's not a problem for him because he can treat it in the same way in which he treats many other things—as something not further explicable by us, something 'mostly unknown' that 'must be resolv'd into original qualities of human nature, which I pretend not to explain' (1.1.4.6/13), something that is part of the unknown essence of the mind, something 'wonderful and unintelligible' (i.e. not understandable) by us, as he says of reason (1.3.16.9/179), something 'magical', as he says of the Imagination. (1.1.7.15/24)

This is a very good objection, and it's raised explicitly, in one form, by Garrett, so I'll call it 'Garrett's objection'.[25] The principal difficulty for it can be put by saying that it seems to be an objection that must be put to Hume himself, because it's Hume himself who so plainly says that he has the problem that he doesn't have if Garrett's objection is correct.

When exactly do Hume's hopes vanish? They vanish when he comes 'to explain [P3] the principle of connexion, which binds...our particular perceptions... together', 'to explain [P4] the principles, that unite our successive perceptions in our thought or consciousness' (App§20–1/635–6). What does he mean by 'explain the principle of connexion which binds' or 'explain the principles that unite'? What failure of explanation does he have in mind? He tells us. It's his failure to explain the principles of connection that make us 'attribute...a real simplicity and identity' to our perceptions. It's his failure, in other words, to explain the existence and operation of the principles of the Imagination—I'll call the whole set of them *the I-Principles*, for short—that lead us to come to believe in a single continuing mind or self or subject. The problem, as he sees it, is that he can't make use of the fact of the existence of the I-Principles in his philosophy without thereby appealing to—or rather, without being open to the charge that he thereby appeals to—something he can't appeal to ([O1], the idea of the mind as 'something simple and individual', or [O2], some perceivable or experienceable 'real connexion' between perceptions).[26]

The lamented failure, then, is not a failure to explain how the I-Principles—in particular the Resemblance principle and the Cause and Effect principle—lead us to come to believe in a persisting mind or self.

---

[25] See Garrett 1997: 171. It's raised as an objection to Stroud (1977) and Beauchamp (1979). Garrett has changed his view about Hume's problem in the Appendix since he published *Cognition and Commitment* in 1997 (see Garrett 2011), and he and I are in agreement in one central respect.

[26] A full account of the I-Principles—the principles according to which the Imagination operates—must go beyond the three principles of the association of ideas (Resemblance, Contiguity, and Cause and Effect) and add the fundamental principle according to which the Imagination is unfailingly led to posit or 'feign' objective continuities (persisting objects, a persisting individual mind, and true causal continuities) on the basis of exposure to certain sorts of sets or series of ideas. See Strawson 2011a §3.4.

14.9 Could Hume's Problem
be the 'Problem of Detail'?

Many have supposed that this is the lamented failure. Subtle philosophers have done so. So let us grant for the moment that the 'when I come to explain...' passage can be read in this way, at least when it's taken in isolation from the rest of the text. Hume, then, is despairing of his account of how the idea of a persisting self arises in us, on the grounds that the I-Principles (in particular the Resemblance and Cause and Effect principles of association) can't really do the job.

I'll say that on this view Hume's problem is the *Problem of Detail*. Is this a defensible interpretation (loss of all hope seems a strangely extravagant reaction to such a problem)? The way to find out is to look at what he thinks might solve his problem.

But now we're back on the track already laid out in §14.3. One thing that will do the trick, he says, is (the right to appeal to) the existence of [O1], 'something simple and individual' in which our perceptions inhere; another is [O2], some perceivable or observable 'real connexion' between perceptions,[27] perceivable in such a way that *the deployment of the idea of it in one's philosophy when treating of concrete reality* is empirically warranted. Both [O1] and [O2] will provide Hume with the resources to explain the thing he has just said he can't explain. This, however, rules out the view that his problem is the Problem of Detail. For if anything is plain it is that neither [O1] nor [O2] can help the Resemblance and Cause and Effect principles of the association of ideas do their job in explaining our belief in a persisting mind or self.

Again this is a somewhat backwards way to put the point. A better way to put it, perhaps, is to say that what destroys Hume's hopes is his realization that he can't meet the objection that he has in effect appealed to one of [O1] and [O2] in placing the I-Principles at the very centre of his theory of human nature, in making them the great engine of his philosophy. He has in effect appealed to one of [O1] and [O2] although he can't appeal to either on his own terms.

One could put the point by saying that the passage parses like this:

when I proceed to explain [the principle of connexion, which binds them together, and makes us attribute to them a real simplicity and identity]; I am sensible, that my account is very defective...

The noun-clause inside the square brackets denotes his problem, the phenomenon that is to be explained. His problem is to explain the phenomenon that consists in the mind's operating according to the I-principles, not to explain how the I-principles (in particular Resemblance and Causation), once in place, can generate the belief in 'real simplicity and identity'. For, once again, the two ontological solutions to his problem that he offers in the next paragraph can't be construed as a solution to that problem (the Problem of Detail).

---

[27] Some connection which is not just an I-principles-generated connection in the Imagination, and is, therefore, essentially more than the relation of cause and effect so far as we have any empirically contentful notion of it. (As remarked in n. 14 above, Hume's prime example of 'real connexion' is causal necessity thought of as something that obtains quite independently of any action of the imagination.)

One could say that the word 'explain' is misread. It doesn't mean 'expound' or 'spell out'—expound or spell out the details of how the principle of connection that makes us attribute simplicity and identity to our perceptions does its job. It means 'account for the existence of': account for the existence and operation of the Imagination, aka the I-principles, given the resources of a strictly empiricist account of the mind. Hume's problem is to account for their existence given his commitment to the view that the bundle view is for philosophical purposes 'the true idea of the human mind'. Can't be done.[28]

14.10 'Explain'?

—No. Hume can and does treat the phenomenon of the existence and operation of the I-Principles in the same way that he treats other things, as something not further explicable by us, something 'mostly unknown' that 'must be resolv'd into *original* qualities of human nature, which I pretend not to explain' (1.1.4.6/13). The very fact that Hume uses the word 'explain' in the two crucial passages

'when I proceed to *explain* the principle of connexion, which binds them together'

and

'when I come to *explain* the principles, that unite our successive perceptions in our thought or consciousness'

proves that your interpretation can't be right. For your interpretation requires us to suppose that Hume is lamenting his inability to explain something that he has repeatedly said he can't and doesn't need to explain.

This is Garrett's objection, somewhat extended. I think it nearly succeeds, although it fails! Perhaps the best thing to do by way of reply is to start by considering points of agreement.

In operating in a way that is correctly described by the I-principles, the mind delivers all sorts of unity-and-connection experiences, which we may call *UC experiences* for short. It delivers *persisting-physical-object* unity-and-connection experiences, it delivers *necessary-causal-relation* unity-and-connection experiences, and it delivers *persisting-individual-self* unity-and-connection experiences. Is the existence of such experiences problematic for Hume? Not at all. He can fully explain the fact that we naturally believe in these sorts of unity and connection, even if our basic experience consists of nothing more than a series of distinct and fleeting perceptions, by appeal to the idea that the mind operates according to certain principles—the I-principles—that generate such ('fiction'-involving) UC experiences. We can't, however, explain the undoubtedly real phenomena that we refer to when we speak

---

[28] The clause 'which binds them together' can be read in two ways. On one reading it's about what the I-principles *do*: they lead us to put or bind experiences together in such a way as to take them to be parts or rather features of a single continuing object. On the other reading it is about the phenomenon of our experiences being actually bound together—united, connected—in being *governed* by the I-principles. On this second reading it's only the clause 'which makes us attribute to them' that is about what the I-principles do. Either way, the point remains: that the thing that Hume has to explain is the existence of 'the principle of connexion', not how it does what it does.

of the operation of the mind in accordance with the I-principles by reference to the operation of the mind in accordance with the I-principles, any more than we can use logic to prove the validity of logic. So the fact that the mind operates in accordance with the I-principles must be taken as a given (exactly as the conformity of physical phenomena to Newton's law of gravity is taken as a given).

Right. This is what Hume does. The causes of the mind's operation in accordance with the I-principles are, he says, 'mostly unknown, and must be resolv'd into *original* qualities of human nature, which I pretend not to explain'.[29] He could hardly be more clear: 'to explain the *ultimate* causes of our mental actions is impossible' (1.1.7.11/22).

Much is unknown, then, and must remain so. So far Hume, Garrett and I fully agree. And Garrett and I also agree—contrary to a cloud of commentators—that Hume does in fact appeal to real connections throughout book 1 of the *Treatise* in appealing as he does to the I-Principles—to the 'uniting principle' or 'bond of union' that exists—the 'uniting principles' that exist—between our different perceptions.[30] It's also plain that, pre-Appendix, Hume thinks that he can do this with impunity within his empiricist philosophy, because he can comfortably consign that in virtue of which the I-Principles exist to the 'unknown essence of the mind' in a thoroughly and indeed quintessentially Newtonian spirit.

14.11 Reply to Garrett's Objection

It's at this point that the agreement ends. For I think, as Garrett does not, that Hume's hopes vanish when he sees that there's an objection from which this large confession of ignorance—this affirmation of ignorance—can't protect him.[31] The affirmation of ignorance sweeps up almost everything, but it leaves a hole. Hume's position is vulnerable to the charge that if one relies on [P3/P4]—if one relies on the idea of the mind's operation in accordance with the I-principles—then one is obliged to accept that one of the two maximally general *positive metaphysical characterizations* of the mind's nature ([O1] or [O2]) must apply. But to accept this is to accept that one must allow the applicability of terms that are 'unintelligible' by Hume's empiricist principles [P1] and [P2]. This is how [P3/P4], [P1] and [P2], and [O1] and [O2] relate.[32] Acknowledgement that one of maximally general [O1] or [O2] must be

---

[29] 1.1.4.6/13. Hume would have loved modern neuroscience—although not as much as Descartes.

[30] 1.1.4.1/11, 1.4.6.16/260. Hume also mentions the 'uniting principle among our internal perceptions' at the heart of his principal discussion of causation (1.3.14.29/169). It is a matter of unintelligible real connection in just the same way as the uniting principle 'among external objects'.

[31] For Garrett's own account of Hume's problem in the Appendix, in terms of 'placeless perceptions', see Garrett 2011.

[32] All six occur in the space of eighty-seven words (of which they make up forty-eight): '... all my hopes vanish, when I come to explain [P3/P4] *the principles, that unite our successive perceptions in our thought or consciousness.* I cannot discover any theory, which gives me satisfaction on this head. In short there are two principles, which I cannot render consistent; nor is it in my power to renounce either of them, viz. [P1] *that all our distinct perceptions are distinct existences,* and [P2] *that the mind never perceives any real connexion among distinct existences.* Did [O1] *our perceptions either inhere in something simple and individual,* or [O2] *did the mind perceive some real connexion among them,* there wou'd be no difficulty in the case.'

the case is compatible with vast ignorance of the nature of things, but Hume needs one of them, for he won't otherwise be able to 'explain' the I-Principles ([P3/P4]) in the following highly general sense: he won't be able to account for how they exist at all. So he won't be able to make use of the idea that they exist. But they are central to his philosophy.

Note that to give an explanation of something X in this sense, to give an account of things that makes room for the bare fact of X's possibility, is not to attempt any further detailed explanation of X of the sort Hume thinks is impossible and is happy to leave as unknown.

There was a moment when it dawned sharply on Hume that he had a problem. He realized that the maximally general objection that one of [O1] and [O2], at least, is needed, and must in effect be allowed, given his account of the mind, can be most powerfully pressed against him. I suspect that it was the idea of others coming up with this objection that was most vivid for him as he wrote the Appendix. One thing he then wanted to do, most understandably, was to be the first to make the criticism (compare Wittgenstein's assault on his earlier position). His best defence was to show complete candour and to be the first to describe the fork—the either-a-single-thing-or-perceivable-real-connection fork—that others would seek to spike him on. Imagine how you yourself would feel, and what you might wish to do, if you discovered a serious difficulty in your just published and cherished theory. You would sit down and do something comparable to what Hume did when (probably hastily) he added the passage on personal identity to the Appendix.

One could put the point by saying that the existence and operation of the I-principles mean that some metaphysical description of the mind that Hume can't avail himself of is knowably applicable to the mind. He can't invoke the mind's 'unknown essence', treating this as a kind of explanation-sink that can absorb the whole difficulty, for—this is the direct reply to Garrett's objection—his opponents can happily grant that of course much must remain unknown, while continuing to insist that Hume has, in appealing to the I-Principles, invoked something—some sort of genuine metaphysical connection and continuity among the perceptions of the mind—whose existence he can make sense of only on one of two specific conditions neither of which is available to him.

It's hardly impressive (it's hopeless) for him, faced with such an objection, to answer again that much is 'unknown', 'magical', 'unintelligible', 'wonderful' and 'inexplicable'. 'Yes yes', his objectors reply in turn, 'we agree. The point we wish to make is much more general (it is, in twentieth-century parlance, a "logical" point). In relying on the I-Principles as you do you take a metaphysical step you can't take, given that you want to give an empiricist account of the *mind* as well as everything else. You incur a certain general metaphysical debt you can't repay on your own empiricist principles. You can't rely on the I-Principles as you do and simply refer everything else to the unknown essence of the mind, for you can't stop someone replying that your reliance on the I-Principles entails that there is at least one thing that can be known about the essence of the mind and that you can't allow to be known. The thing in question is in fact an either–or thing ([O1] or [O2]), but that doesn't help. You can't allow this either–or thing to be known, because it isn't possible to specify what it is without employing terms whose employment you can't allow, given your brand of empiricism, when it comes to making knowledge claims about the nature of concrete reality.'

'Specifically, and once again, your reliance on the I-Principles entails that the following high-level, either-or description of the essence of the mind—"persisting individual single thing or really connected plurality of things"—can be known to apply. You can't make room for this because you can't allow any empirical intelligibility or (therefore) concrete applicability to any idea of anything whose description entails that it lasts longer than a single fleeting perception. A fortiori you can't admit that any such idea has an indispensable employment in your philosophy, or that your philosophy presupposes that such an idea has valid application. But it does. Your philosophy entails—we're hammering the point—that we can know at least one thing more about the essence of the mind than you say we do or can: we can know something that we can't and mustn't claim to know on your empiricist principles. How else can it possibly be the case that perceptions come clumped in interacting groups as they do?'

To this Hume thinks, quite rightly, I believe, that he has no effective reply. He can't say what he actually believes, given the dialectical context of his discussion of personal identity. He can't say that the brain supplies all the needed real continuity. And even if he did, this wouldn't diminish his need to acknowledge real connection, for the brain is certainly not a simple substance (which is, after all, a property reserved to individual atoms and immaterial souls).

14.12 A Final Response

—You're seriously underestimating Hume's resources. He's 'not forbidden by his empiricist principles from postulating the existence of unperceived deterministic mechanisms that would underlie the propensities of perceptions to appear in particular ways. He is forbidden by his principles only from trying to specify the nature of those mechanisms [in a way that goes] beyond what experience can warrant.' But he doesn't try to do this, in the case of the mind, nor does he think he needs to. He is, again, happy to say that what you call the 'I-principles' are unintelligible, inexplicable, and wonderful. He has, therefore, no problem of the sort you describe.

This is another version of Garrett's objection, mostly in his own words.[33] I think I've answered it. Hume doesn't think he can plausibly reject the objection that he's committed to something like [O1] or [O2], caught in a fork according to which one at least of [O1] or [O2] is correct (he's caught because it's a maximally general and exhaustive fork). [O1] and [O2] are very general, but when we consider the mechanisms to which Hume can legitimately appeal, while holding them to be unknown, we see that [O1] and [O2] already 'specify the nature [or ground] or those mechanisms' in a metaphysical way that goes 'beyond what experience can warrant'.

---

[33] Garrett 1997: 171. Of course Garrett's text long predates, and is not a response to, the present one.

In conclusion, let me repeat the earlier suggestion that Garrett's objection has to be put to Hume himself, because it's Hume himself who thinks he has a problem that could be entirely solved if he were allowed to make use of the idea of a simple individual substance, or the idea of (empirically observable) real connections. This is the fundamental fixed point, when it comes to the interpretation of the Appendix. It's Hume himself who judges (sees) that he is in effect committed, in his philosophy, to the allowability of at least one of two very high-level metaphysical descriptions of the nature of the mind that can have no empirical warrant and are therefore officially excluded from any role in his philosophy. It's Hume himself who thinks that his empiricism allows him to ignore (delegate to the unknown, be agnostic about) all questions about the ultimate causes or sources of the patterns in our experiences that lead us to come to believe in physical objects and causal necessity, but doesn't allow him to do this when it comes to the mind itself. It's Hume himself who thinks he has a problem he can't solve even after he has stressed the unintelligibility and inexplicability (and 'wonderfulness' and 'magicality', 1.3.16.9/179, 1.1.7.15/24) of the workings of the mind—the mind whose principles of working are the great and indispensable engine of his whole empiricist programme—and who (again) thinks that he could solve the problem immediately if the principles of his philosophy allowed him to deploy the notion of a simple and individual substance, or to make empirically warranted use of the notion of real (non-'fictional', non-Imagination-generated) connections. The burden on those who favour what I'm calling Garrett's objection is to explain why Hume feels he has a problem he could solve if he could appeal to a persisting individual substance or make use of an empirically warranted notion of real connection. It's Hume himself who believes himself to be in a *Zugzwang*—a position where he would like to be able to make no move but feels he's obliged to make one (or admit that he has in effect already made one).

Old interpretative impulses may resurge: 'For Hume, the phenomenon of conformity to the I-principles is brute regularity; there is therefore no need or possibility of any further explanation of any sort, however general, in his scheme.' But it's far too late in the day for such a view of Hume, and there are two more particular replies. First, his problem stems from the fact that he has 'loosen'd all our particular perceptions' (App§20/635); but this loosening wouldn't cause a problem if he took it that the phenomenon of conformity to the I-principles were just a matter of brute regularity. Secondly, a reply already made: you have to contrapose: it's Hume himself who insists that the phenomenon of conformity to the I-principles does need some further explanation or grounding, however general, and who tells us that two things that are completely unavailable to him would do the trick: inherence in a single substance or real—non-regularity-theory—connections. It is not as if he wants to say any such thing, appealing to notions whose use in philosophy he has ruled out as 'unintelligible'.[34] It's just that he believes (sees) that the objection that he must admit some such thing is correct and unanswerable. When he moved on from [3] his empiricist account of the content of the idea of causation in 1.3.14 of the *Treatise*, and

---

[34] Recall again that he uses them constantly in a way that presupposes that they do have content and are to that extent intelligible, although they lack empirical warrant. He does not mean what present-day philosophers mean by 'unintelligible'.

[5] his empiricist account of the content of the idea of physical objects in 1.4.2, and took [1] the empirically warranted idea of the mind itself as his subject in 1.4.6, his general 'reductive' empiricist account of the origin of our belief in the objective continuities, persistences and connections that we take ourselves to encounter in experience was running beautifully. It was watertight on its own terms, and it must have seemed that it couldn't fail to deal also with the apparent or experienced continuity of the mind. And in a sense it did, and smoothly too: it gave at least as good an account of the origin of [2] our idea of ourselves as enduring selves or subjects as it did of the origin of [4] our ideas of causal power and [6] our ideas of physical objects (which is not to say that it was in fact empirically psychologically correct). But it relied on something more than [1] could supply. The whole system broke down when it came to [1], the empirically warranted idea of the mind. It's Hume himself—one more time—who believes that his account of the mind is 'very defective', indeed hopeless, and it's Hume himself who believes that his problem would be immediately solved by one of two metaphysical provisions that his empiricist philosophy rules out.[35]

[35] This paper descends from 'Hume on himself', a paper given at the Hume Society conference in Cork in 1999 and published 'too precipitately' (in Hume's words) in 2001. I'm grateful to Don Garrett for comments on a later (2003) version, and to Stephen Buckle for his comments on this one.

Bibliography

Adams, D. (1980/2009) *The Restaurant at the End of the Universe* (London: Pan Macmillan).

Albahari, M. (2009) 'Witness-Consciousness: Its Definition, Appearance and Reality', *Journal of Consciousness Studies* 16: 62–84.

Alexander, S. (1924) 'Preface to New Impression', in *Space, Time and Deity*, vol. 1 (London: MacMillan).

Alter, T., and Nagasawa, Y., eds. (2015) *Consciousness in the Physical World: Perspectives on Russellian Monism* (New York: Oxford University Press).

Amis, M. (2015) 'The Turbulent Love Life of Saul Bellow', *Vanity Fair*, May.

Anscombe, G. (1975/1994) 'The First Person', in *Self-Knowledge*, ed. Q. Cassam (Oxford: Oxford University Press).

Aristotle (*c*.350 BCE/1924) *Metaphysics*, trans. with commentary by W. D. Ross (Oxford: Oxford University Press).

Aristotle (*c*.340 BCE/1936) *De Anima*, trans. W. S. Hett (Cambridge, MA: Harvard University Press).

Aristotle (*c*.330 BCE/1953) *Nicomachean Ethics*, trans. J. Thomson (London: Penguin).

Aristotle (*c*.340 BCE/1957) *On the Soul; Parva Naturalia; On Breath*, trans. W. S. Hett (Cambridge, MA: Harvard University Press).

Armstrong, D. M. (1980/1997) 'Against "Ostrich Nominalism"', in *Properties*, ed. D. H. Mellor and A. Oliver (Oxford: Oxford University Press).

Arnauld, A. (1683/1990) *On True and False Ideas*, trans. with introduction by S. Gaukroger (Manchester: Manchester University Press).

Ayers, M. R. (1991) *Locke*, vol. 1 (London: Routledge).

Baars, B. (1996) *In the Theater of Consciousness: The Workspace of the Mind* (New York: Oxford University Press).

Balleine, B., and Dickinson, A. (1998) 'Consciousness: the interface between affect and cognition', in *Consciousness and Human Identity*, ed. John Cornwell (Oxford: Oxford University Press).

Barkow, J. H., Cosmides, L., and Tooby, J. (1992) *The Adapted Mind: Evolutionary Psychology and the Generation of Culture* (New York: Oxford University Press).

Barth, C. (2011) 'Bewusstsein bei Descartes', *Archiv für Geschichte der Philosophie* 93: 162–94.

Bayley, J. (1998) *Iris: A Memoir* (London: Duckworth).

Beauchamp, T. (1979) 'Self Inconsistency or Mere Self Perplexity?' *Hume Studies* 5: 37–44.

Beike, D. R., Lampinen, J. M., and Behrend, D. A. (2004) *The Self and Memory* (New York: Psychology Press).

Beiser, F. (2002) *German Idealism: The Struggle Against Subjectivism 1781–1801* (Cambridge, MA: Harvard University Press).

Bellow, S. (1959) *Henderson the Rain King* (New York: Viking Press).

Berkeley, G. (1707–8/1975) *Philosophical Commentaries*, in *Philosophical Works*, ed. M. R. Ayers (London: Dent).

Berkeley, G. (1707–10/1975) *Philosophical Works*, ed. M. R. Ayers (London: Dent).

Berkeley, G. (1713/1998) *Three Dialogues between Hylas and Philonous*, ed. J. Dancy (Oxford: Oxford University Press).

Berkeley, G. (1732/2008) *Alciphron: or the Minute Philosopher*, in *Philosophical Writings*, ed. D. Clarke (Cambridge: Cambridge University Press).

Bermúdez, J. L., Marcel, A., and Eilan, N., eds. (1995) *The Body and the Self* (Cambridge, MA: MIT Press).

Biro, J. (1993) 'Hume's new science of the mind', in *The Cambridge Companion to David Hume*, ed. D. F. Norton (Cambridge: Cambridge University Press).

Blachowicz, J. (1997) 'The Dialogue of the Soul with Itself', in *Models of the Self*, ed. S. Gallagher and J. Shear (Thorverton: Imprint Academic), 177–200.

Black, D. (1993) 'Consciousness and Self-Knowledge in Aquinas's Critique of Averroes's Psychology', *Journal of the History of Philosophy* 31: 349–85.

Blake, W. (*c.*1793/1905/2005) *William Blake: Collected Poems* (London: Routledge).

Blattner, W. (2000) 'Life is Not Literature', in *The Many Faces of Time*, ed. L. Embree and J. Brough (Dordrecht, Holland: Kluwer Publishers) 187–201.

Boethius (*c.*510 CE) *De Trinitate*, in *The Theological Tractates and The Consolations of Philosophy*, trans. H. F. Stewart and E. K. Rand (Cambridge, MA: Harvard University Press).

Bradley, F. (1893/1897) *Appearance and Reality*, 2nd edn (Oxford: Oxford University Press).

Brainard, J. (1970–3/2001) *I Remember* (New York: Granary Books).

Brentano, F. (1874/1995) *Psychology from an Empirical Standpoint*, 2nd edn, Introd. Peter Simons, trans. A. C. Rancurello, D. B. Terrell, and L. McAlister (London: Routledge).

Brison, S. (2002) *Aftermath: Violence and the Remaking of a Self* (Princeton, NJ: Princeton University Press).

Brook, A. (1998) 'Unified Consciousness and the Self', *Journal of Consciousness Studies* 5: 583–91.

Bruner, J. (1987) 'Life as Narrative', *Social Research* 54: 11–32.

Bruner, J. (1990) *Acts of Meaning* (Cambridge, MA: Harvard University Press).

Bruner, J. (1994) 'The "remembered" self', in *The Remembering Self: Construction and Accuracy in the Self-narrative*, ed. U. Neisser and R. Fivush (Cambridge University Press) pp. 55–77.

Bruner, J. (2002) *Making Stories: Law, Literature, Life* (New York: Farrar, Straus and Giroux).

Brüntrup, G., and Jaskolla, L., eds. (2016) *Panpsychism: Philosophical Essays* (New York: Oxford University Press).

Butler, J. (1736) First Appendix (*First Dissertation*) in *The Analogy of Religion*, 2nd edn (London: Knapton).

Butterworth, G. (1995) 'An ecological perspective on the origins of self', in *The Body and the Self*, ed. J. L. Bermúdez, A. Marcel, and N. Eilan (Cambridge, MA: MIT Press).

Butterworth, G. (1998) 'A Developmental-Ecological Perspective on Strawson's '"The Self"', *Journal of Consciousness Studies* 5: 132–40.

Campbell, A. (1994) 'Cartesian Dualism and the Concept of Medical Placebos', *Journal of Consciousness Studies* 1: 230–3.

Campbell, J. (1994) *Past, Space, and Self* (Cambridge, MA: MIT Press).

Campbell, J. (1995) 'The Body Image and Self-Consciousness', in *The Body and the Self*, ed. J. L. Bermúdez, A. Marcel, and N. Eilan (Cambridge, MA: MIT Press).

Camus, A. (1942/1946) *The Outsider*, trans. Joseph Laredo (London: Hamish Hamilton).

Camus, A. (1960/1995) *The First Man*, trans. David Hapgood (London: Hamish Hamilton).

Carey, S. (2009) *The Origin of Concepts* (Oxford: Oxford University Press, 2009).

Carrington, P. (1998) *Learn to Meditate: The Complete Course in Modern Meditation* (Rockport, MA: Element).

Cassam, A.-Q. A., ed. (1994) *Self-knowledge* (Oxford: Oxford University Press).

Cassam, A.-Q. A. (1997) *Self and World* (Oxford: Clarendon Press).

Cassam, A.-Q. A. (2014) *Self-knowledge for Humans* (Oxford: Oxford University Press).

Castañeda, H.-N. (1966/1994) 'On the Phenomeno-Logic of the I', in A.-Q. A. Cassam, ed., *Self-Knowledge* (Oxford University Press).

Caston, V. (2002) 'Aristotle on Consciousness', *Mind* **111**: 751–815.

Chalmers, D. and Clark, A. (1998) 'The extended mind', *Analysis* **58/1**: 7–19.

Chisholm, R. (1969/1994) 'On the Observability of the Self', in *Self-Knowledge*, ed. Q. Cassam (Oxford: Oxford University Press).

Chomsky, N. (1995) 'Language and Nature', *Mind* **104**: 1–61.

Chomsky, N. (2015) *What Kind of Creatures Are we?* (New York: Columbia University Press).

Chun, M., and Marois, R. (2002) 'The Dark Side of Visual Attention', *Current Opinion in Neurobiology* **12**: 184–9.

Clough, A. H. (1862/1974) 'The Mystery of the Fall', in *Poems* (Oxford: Oxford University Press).

Cockburn, C. (1702) *A Defence of the Essay of Human Understanding Written by Mr. Locke* (London: Turner).

Cohler, B. J., and Cole, T. R. (1996) 'Studying older lives: Reciprocal acts of telling and listening', in *Aging and Biography: Explorations in Adult Development*, ed. J. E. Birren et al. (New York: Springer).

Cole, J. (1997) 'On "being faceless": selfhood and facial embodiment', *Journal of Consciousness Studies* **4**: 467–84.

Coleman, S. (2006) 'Being Realistic, Why Physicalism May Entail Panexperientialism', in *Journal of Consciousness Studies* **13**: 40–52.

Collins, S. (1982) *Selfless Persons* (Cambridge: Cambridge University Press).

Cosmides, L., and Tooby, J. (1992) 'The Psychological Foundations of Culture', in *The Adaptive Mind*, ed. J. Barkow, L. Cosmides, and J. Tooby (New York: Oxford University Press).

Coventry, A., and Kriegel, U. (2008) 'Locke on Consciousness', *History of Philosophy Quarterly* **25**: 221–42.

Crabbe, J. ed. (1999) *From Soul to Self* (London: Routledge).

Craig, E. J. (1987) *The Mind of God and the Works of Man* (Cambridge: Cambridge University Press).

Currie, G. (2010) *Narratives and Narrators: A Philosophy of Stories* (Oxford: Oxford University Press).

Dabrowski, K. (1972) *Psychoneurosis is Not An Illness* (London: Gryf Publications) pp. 289–306.

Dainton, B. (2000) *Stream of Consciousness: Unity and Continuity in Conscious Experience* (London: Routledge).

Dainton, B. (2008) *The Phenomenal Self* (Oxford: Oxford University Press).

Dainton, B. (2013) *Self* (London: Penguin).

Damasio, A. (1994) *Descartes's Error: Emotion, Reason, and the Human Brain* (New York: Avon).

Damasio, A. (1999) *The Feeling of What Happens: Body and Emotion in the Making of Consciousness* (New York: Harcourt Brace).

Damasio, A. (2000) 'Interview', *New Scientist* **165**: 46–9.

Deikman, A. (1996) '"I" = Awareness' *Journal of Consciousness Studies* **3**: 350–6.

Dennett, D. (1988) 'Why everyone is a novelist', *Times Literary Supplement*, 16–22 Sept. pp. 1016, 1028–9.

Dennett, D. (1991) *Consciousness Explained* (Boston: Little, Brown).

Descartes, R. (1641/1985) *Meditations*, in *The Philosophical Writings of Descartes* vol. 2, trans. J. Cottingham et al. (Cambridge: Cambridge University Press).

Descartes, R. (1641–2/1985) *Objections and Replies* in *The Philosophical Writings of Descartes* vol. 2, trans. J. Cottingham et al. (Cambridge: Cambridge University Press).

Descartes, R. (1644/1985) *Principles of Philosophy*, in *The Philosophical Writings of Descartes*, vol. 1, trans. J. Cottingham et al. (Cambridge: Cambridge University Press).

Descartes, R. (1648) *The Passions of the Soul* in *The Philosophical Writings of Descartes*, vol. 1, trans. J. Cottingham et al. (Cambridge: Cambridge University Press).

Descartes, R. (1648/1976) *Conversations with Burman*, trans. with philosophical Introduction and commentary by J. Cottingham (Oxford: Clarendon Press).

Deschamps, L.-M. (1761, 1770–1772/1993) *La vérité, ou le vrai système* in *Œuvres philosophiques*, ed. and introduced by B. Delhaume (Paris: Vrin).

Dreyfus, G. (2010) 'Self and Subjectivity: A Middle Way Approach', in *Self, No Self?: Perspectives from Analytical, Phenomenological, and Indian Traditions*, ed. M. Siderits, E. Thompson, and D. Zahavi (Oxford University Press).

Dreyfus, G. and Thompson, E. (2007) 'Asian perspectives: Indian Theories of Mind', in *The Cambridge Handbook of Consciousness*, ed. M. Moscovitch, E. Thompson, and D. Zelazo (Cambridge: Cambridge University Press).

Dylan, B. (1997) 'Dylan Revisited', interview with David Gates, *Newsweek*, 5 October.

Eddington, A. (1928) *The Nature of the Physical World* (New York: Macmillan).

Edey, M. (1997) 'Subject and Object', in *Models of the Self*, ed. S. Gallagher and J. Shear (Thorverton: Imprint Academic), 441–6.

Einstein, A. (1931) 'About Free Will', in *The Golden Book of Tagore: A Homage to Rabindranath Tagore from India and the World in Celebration of His Seventieth Birthday*, ed. Ramananda Chatterjee (Calcutta: Golden Book Committee), pp. 77–84.

Eliot, T. S. (1936) 'Burnt Norton' (London: Faber).

Ellis, J., 'The Contents of Hume's Appendix and the Source of His Despair', *Hume Studies* 32 (2006), 195–231.

Emerson, R. W. (1835–38) *Journals and Miscellaneous Notebooks of Ralph Waldo Emerson*, vol. 5 (Cambridge, MA: Harvard University Press).

Emerson, R. W. (1832–60/1983) *Essays and Lectures* (New York: Library of America).

Emerson, R. W. (1841/1983) 'Self-Reliance', in *Essays and Lectures* (New York: Library of America).

Emerson, R. W. (1844/1983) 'Experience', in *Essays and Lectures* (New York: Library of America).

Erikson, E. (1968) *Identity: Youth and Crisis* (New York: Norton).

Evans, C. O. (1970) *The Subject of Consciousness* (London: Allen & Unwin).

Evans, G. (1982) *The Varieties of Reference* (Oxford University Press).

Farrell, B. (1996) Review of *The Body and the Self*, ed. J. L. Bermudéz, A. Marcel, and N. Eilan, *Journal of Consciousness Studies* 4: 517–19.

Fasching, W. (2008) 'Consciousness, self-consciousness, and meditation', in *Phenomenology and the Cognitive Sciences* 7: 463–83.

Feigl, H. (1963/1981) 'Physicalism, Unity of Science and the Foundations of Psychology', in *Inquiries and Provocations: Selected Writings 1929–1974* (Dordrecht: Reidel), 340.

Ferris, T. (1997) *The Whole Shebang* (London: Weidenfeld & Nicolson).

Feuerbach, L. (1843/1986) *Principles of the Philosophy of the Future*, trans. M. H. Vogel, Introd. T. E. Wartenberg (Indianapolis: Hackett).

Fichte, J. (1794–1802/1982) *The Science of Knowledge*, ed. and trans. P. Heath and J. Lachs (Cambridge: Cambridge University Press).

Fitzgerald, F. Scott (1945/1978) *The Notebooks of F. Scott Fitzgerald* (New York: Harcourt Brace Jovanovich).

Flanagan, O. (1991) *Varieties of Moral Personality* (Cambridge, MA: Harvard University Press).

Flanagan, O. (2003) *The Problem of the Soul* (New York: Basic Books).

Forman, R. (1998) 'What Does Mysticism Have to Teach Us About Consciousness?', *Journal of Consciousness Studies* 5: 185–201.

Foster, J. (1982) *The Case for Idealism* (London: Routledge).

Frank, M. (1991) *Selbstbewußtsein und Selbsterkenntnis* (Stuttgart: Reclam).

Frank, R. (1988) *Passions within Reason* (New York: Norton).

Frankfurt, H. (1987/1988) 'Identification and Wholeheartedness', in *The Importance of What We Care About* (Cambridge: Cambridge University Press).

Frege, G. (1918/1967) 'The Thought: A Logical Inquiry', in *Philosophical Logic*, ed. P. F. Strawson (Oxford: Oxford University Press).

French, S. (1998) 'Withering Away Physical Objects', in *Interpreting Bodies: Classical and Quantum Objects in Modern Physics*, ed. E. Castellani (Princeton: Princeton University Press).

Frisch, O. (1979) *What Little I Remember* (Cambridge: Cambridge University Press).

Gallagher S., and Marcel A. (1999) 'The self in contextualized action', *Journal of Consciousness Studies* 6: 4–30.

Gallagher, S. and Shear, J., eds. (1999) *Models of the Self* (Thorverton: Imprint Academic).

Gallagher, S., and Zahavi, D. (2007) *The Phenomenological Mind: an Introduction to the Philosophy of Mind and Cognitive Science* (London: Routledge).

Garrett, D. (1997) *Cognition and Commitment in Hume's Philosophy* (Oxford: Oxford University Press).

Garrett, D. (2003) 'Locke on Personal Identity, Consciousness, and "Fatal Errors"', *Philosophical Topics* 31: 95–125.

Garrett, D. (2009) 'Difficult Times for Humean Identity?', *Philosophical Studies* 146: 435–43.

Garrett, D. (2011) 'Rethinking Hume's Second Thoughts About Personal Identity', in *The Possibility of Philosophical Understanding: Essays for Barry Stroud*, ed. J. Bridges, N. Kolodny, and W. Wong (New York: Oxford University Press).

Gazzaniga, M. (1998) *The Mind's Past* (Berkeley: University of California Press).

Geertz, C. (1983) 'From the native's point of view: on the nature of anthropological understanding', in *Local Knowledge* (New York: Basic Books).

Gendler, T. (1998) 'Exceptional Persons: On the Limits of Imaginary Cases', *Journal of Consciousness Studies* 5: 592–610.

Gibson, E. (1993) 'Ontogenesis of the perceived self', in *The Perceived Self*, ed. U. Neisser (Cambridge: Cambridge University Press).

Gilbert, P. (1998) 'What is shame: some core issues and controversies', in *Shame: Interpersonal Behavior: Psychopathology, and Culture*, ed. P. Gilbert and B. Andrews (Oxford University Press).

Ginsberg, A. (1963) 'Statement to the *Burning Bush*', *Burning Bush II*.

Glover, J. (1988) *I: The Philosophy and Psychology of Personal Identity* (Harmondsworth: Penguin).

Goethe, J. G. (1809–32/1906) *The Maxims and Reflections of Goethe*, trans. B. Saunders (New York: Macmillan).

Goldman, A. (1970) *A Theory of Human Action* (Princeton, NJ: Princeton University Press).

Gray, S. (2008) *Coda* (London: Faber and Faber).

Greene, B. (2004) *The Fabric of the Cosmos* (New York: Knopf).

Greer, G. (1986) article in *The Times*, 1 February 1986.

Grice, P. (1941) 'Personal identity', *Mind* 50: 330–50.

Griffin, D. R. (1998) *Unsnarling the World-Knot: Consciousness, Freedom, and the Mind-Body Problem* (Berkeley, CA: University of California Press), http://ark.cdlib.org/ark:/13030/ft8c6009k3

Grimes, J. (1996) 'On the Failure to Detect Changes in Scenes across Saccades', in *Perception*, ed. K. Akins (Oxford: Oxford University Press) pp. 89–110.

Grove, H. (1718/1748) *An Essay towards a Demonstration of the Soul's Immateriality* in *Works* vol. 3 (London: Waugh).

Gupta, B. (2003) *Cit Consciousness* (New Delhi: Oxford University Press).

Gurwitsch, A. (1941/1966) 'A non-egological conception of consciousness', in *Studies in Phenomenology and Psychology* (Evanston: Northwestern University Press).

Happé, F. G. E. (1991) 'The autobiographical writings of three Asperger syndrome adults: problems of interpretation and implications for theory', in *Autism and Asperger syndrome*, ed. U. Frith (Cambridge: Cambridge University Press).

Hardy, T. (1912–13/2010) *Unexpected Elegies: Poems of 1912–13 and Other Poems About Emma*, ed. C. Tomalin (New York: Norton).

Hayward, J. (1998) 'A rDzogs-chen Buddhist Interpretation of the Sense of Self', *Journal of Consciousness Studies* 5: 611–26.

Heller-Roazen, D. (2007) *The Inner Touch* (Brooklyn, NY: Zone Books).

Herbart, J. F. (1816/1891) *Textbook of Psychology*, trans. M. K. Smith (New York: D. Appleton).

Hermer, L., and Spelke, E. (1996) 'Modularity and development: The case of spatial reorientation' *Cognition* 61(3): 195–232.

Hirst, W. (1994) 'The remembered self in amnesics', in *The Remembering Self: Construction and Accuracy in the Self-narrative*, ed. U. Neisser and R. Fivush (Cambridge: Cambridge University Press).

Hirstein, W. (2005) *Brain Fiction: Self-Deception and the Riddle of Confabulation* (Cambridge: Cambridge University Press).

Hobbes, T. (1651/1996) *Leviathan*, ed. Richard Tuck (Cambridge: Cambridge University Press).

Holub, M. (1990) *The Dimension of the Present Moment* (London: Faber).

Hopkins, G. M. (1880/1959) 'Commentary on the Spiritual Exercises of St Ignatius Loyola', in *Sermons and Devotional Writings*, ed. C. J. Devlin (London: Oxford University Press).

Horgan, T., and Potrč, M. (2008) *Austere Realism: Contextual Semantics Meets Minimal Ontology* (Cambridge, MA: MIT Press).

Hornsby, J. (1981/1997) 'Which Mental Events Are Physical Events?', in J. Hornsby, *Simplemindedness* (Cambridge, MA: Harvard University Press).

Hughes, R. (1929) *A High Wind in Jamaica* (London: Chatto and Windus).

Hume, D. (1737–76/1978) *New Letters of David Hume*, ed. R. Klibansky and J. V. Price (Oxford: Clarendon Press).

Hume, D. (1739–40/1978) *A Treatise of Human Nature*, ed. L. A. Selby-Bigge and P. H. Nidditch (Oxford: Oxford University Press).

Hume, D. (1739–40/2000) *A Treatise of Human Nature*, ed. D. F. Norton and M. Norton (Oxford: Clarendon Press).

Hume, D. (1746) Letter to Lord Kames (24 July) in *New Letters of David Hume*.

Hume, D. (1748–51/1975) *Enquiries Concerning Human Understanding*, ed. L. A. Selby-Bigge and P. H. Nidditch (Oxford: Oxford University Press).

Hume, D. (1748–51/1999) *An Enquiry Concerning Human Understanding*, ed. T. L. Beauchamp (Oxford: Oxford University Press).

Hume, D. (1749–76/1947) *Dialogues Concerning Natural Religion*, ed. N. Kemp Smith (Edinburgh: Nelson).

Hurlburt, R. (2011) *Investigating Pristine Inner Experience: Moments of Truth* (Cambridge: Cambridge University Press).

Hurlburt, R. (2011) *Investigating Pristine Inner Experience: Moments of Truth* (Cambridge: Cambridge University Press).

Hurlburt, R., Happé, F., and Frith, U. (1994) 'Sampling the form of inner experience in three adults with Asperger syndrome', *Psychological Medicine*, 24: 385–95.

Hurlburt, R., and Schwitzgebel, E. (2007) *Describing Inner Experience?* (Cambridge, MA: Bradford Books).

Husserl, E. (1907–9/1991) *On the Phenomenology of the Consciousness of Internal Time (1893–1917) Husserliana 10*, trans. J. Brough (Dordrecht: Kluwer).

Husserl, E. (1921–8/1973) *Zur Phänomenologie der Intersubjectivität. Texte aus dem Nachlass. Zweiter Teil: 1921–8* (The Hague: Martinus Nijhoff).

Husserl, E. (1923–4/1959) *Erste Philosophie II (1923–24) Husserliana 8* (Den Haag: Nijhoff).

Husserl, E. (1931/1973) *Cartesian Meditations*, trans. D. Cairns (The Hague: Nijhoff).

Isen, A., and Levin, P. (1972) 'Effect of Feeling Good on Helping: Cookies and Kindness', *The Journal of Personality and Social Psychology* 21: 384–8.

Jackson, F. (1994) 'Metaphysics by Possible Cases', in *Monist* 77: 93–110.

James, H. (1864–1915/1999) *Henry James: A Life in Letters*, ed. Philip Horne (London: Penguin).

James, H. (1899) *The Awkward Age* (New York: Harpers).

James, W. (1890/1950) *The Principles of Psychology*, 2 vols (New York: Dover).

James, W. (1892/1984) *Psychology: Briefer Course* (Cambridge, MA: Harvard University Press).

James, W. (1904/1996) 'Does Consciousness Exist?', in *Essays in Radical Empiricism* (Lincoln, NE: University of Nebraska Press).

Johnston, M. (2010) *Surviving Death* (Princeton, NJ: Princeton University Press).

Joyce, J. (1986) *Ulysses* (Harmondsworth: Penguin).

Kahane, G. (2014) 'Our Cosmic Insignificance', *Nous* 48: 745–72.

Kahneman, D. (2011) *Thinking, Fast and Slow* (New York: Farrar, Strauss, and Giroux).

Kames, Lord (Henry Home) (1751) 'Of the idea of self and of personal identity', in *Essays on the Principles of Morality and Natural Religion* (Edinburgh: Fleming).

Kant, I. (1766/1992) *Dreams of a Spirit Seer Elucidated by Dreams of Metaphysics*, trans. D. Walford (Cambridge: Cambridge University Press).

Kant, I. (1772/1967) Letter to Marcus Herz (21 February) in *Kant: Philosophical Correspondence 1759–99*, ed. and trans. A. Zweig (Chicago: University of Chicago Press).

Kant, I. (1781–7/1933) *Critique of Pure Reason*, trans. N. Kemp Smith (London: Macmillan).

Kant, I. (1781–7/1996) *Critique of Pure Reason*, trans. W. S. Pluhar (Indianopolis: Hackett).

Karma Chagme (c.1660/1998) *A Spacious Path to Freedom*, trans. A. Wallace (Ithaca, NY: Snow Lion).

Keats, J. (1817/1958) Letter to George and Tom Keats (21 December) in *The Letters of John Keats* (Cambridge, MA: Harvard University Press).

Keats, J. (1819/1958) Letter of 14 February–3 May 1819 to George and Georgiana Keats, in *The Letters of John Keats, 1814–1821*, 2 vols, ed. H. Rollins (Cambridge, MA: Harvard University Press).

Kenny, A. (1988) *The Self* (Marquette: Marquette University Press).

Kenny, A. (1989) *The Metaphysics of Mind* (Oxford: Clarendon Press).

Kenny, A. (1999) 'Body, Soul, and Intellect in Aquinas', in *From Soul to Self*, ed. J. Crabbe (London: Routledge).

Kierkegaard, S. (1843/1967) *Journals and Papers Vol. 1*, trans. H. V. Hong and E. H. Hong (Bloomington: Indiana University Press).

Kierkegaard, S. (1847/1995) *Works of Love*, trans. H. V. Hong and E. H. Hong (Princeton, NJ: Princeton University Press).

Kierkegaard, S. (c.1847/1995) *The Book on Adler*, trans. H. V. Hong and E. H. Hong (Princeton, NJ: Princeton University Press).

Kipling, R. (1895/1910) 'If', in *Rewards and Fairies* (London: Macmillan and Co.).

Klee, P. (1965) *The Diaries of Paul Klee, 1898–1918* (London: Peter Owen).

Knight, R. T., and Grabowecky, M. (1995) 'Escape from Linear Time: Prefrontal Cortex and Conscious Experience', in *The Cognitive Neurosciences*, ed. M. Gazzaniga (Cambridge, MA: MIT Press).

Krauss, L. (2012) *A Universe from Nothing: Why there is Something Rather than Nothing* (New York: Free Press).

Kriegel, U. (2009) *Subjective Consciousness: A Self-Representational Theory* (New York: Oxford University Press).

Kriegel, U., and Williford, K. (2006) 'Introduction', in *Self-Representational Approaches to Consciousness*, ed. U. Kriegel and K. Williford (Cambridge, MA: MIT Press).

La Forge, L. de (1666/1670) *Traité de l'esprit de l'homme* (Amsterdam: Abraham Wolfgang).

Ladyman, J., and Ross, D. (2007) *Every Thing Must Go: Metaphysics Naturalized*, with D. Spurrett and J. Collier (Oxford: Clarendon Press).

Lampinen, J., Odegard, T., and Leding, J. (2004) 'Diachronic disunity', in *The Self and Memory*, ed. D. Beike, J. Lampinen, and J. Behrend (New York: Psychology Press).

Langton, R. (1998) *Kant's Humility* (Oxford: Oxford University Press).

Larkin, P. (2003) 'Continuing to live', *Collected Poems* (London: Faber and Faber).

Law, E. (1769/1823) *A Defence of Mr. Locke's Opinion Concerning Personal Identity, in Answer to the First Part of a late Essay on that Subject*, in *The Works of John Locke*, vol. 3 (London: T. Tegg).

Laycock, S. (1998) 'Consciousness It/Self', *Journal of Consciousness Studies* 5: 141–52.

Legerstee (1998) 'Mental and Bodily Awareness in Infancy: Consciousness of Self-existence', *Journal of Consciousness Studies* 5: 627–44.

Leibniz, G. (1686/1988) *Discourse on Metaphysics,* trans. R. Martin, D. Niall, and S. Brown (Manchester: Manchester University Press).

Leibniz, G. (c.1704/1996) *New Essays on Human Understanding*, ed. and trans. J. Bennett and P. Remnant (Cambridge: Cambridge University Press).

Levine, J. (1983) 'Materialism and Qualia: The Explanatory Gap', *Pacific Philosophical Quarterly* 64: 354–61.

Levine, R. (1998) *A Geography of Time: The Temporal Misadventures of a Social Psychologist* (New York: Basic Books).

Lewis, D. (1979) 'Attitudes De Dicto and *De Se*', *Philosophical Review* 88: 513–43.

Lewis, D. (2002/2003) 'Things qua Truthmakers', in *Real Metaphysics: Essays in Honour of D.H. Mellor*, ed. H. Lillehammer and G. Rodriguez-Pereyra (London: Routledge).

Locke, J. (1689–1700/1975) *An Essay Concerning Human Understanding*, ed. P. Nidditch (Oxford: Clarendon Press).

Locke, J. (1694) *An Essay Concerning Human Understanding*, 2nd edn (London: Dring and Manship).

Lockwood, M. (1989) *Mind, Brain, and the Quantum* (Oxford: Blackwell).

Lockwood, M. (2005) *The Labyrinth of Time* (Oxford: Oxford University Press).

Lonergan, B. (1967) *Collection*, ed. F. Crowe (New York: Herder and Herder).

Lowe, E. J. (1996) *The Subject of Experience* (Cambridge: Cambridge University Press).

Lucretius (c.50 BCE/2007) *The Nature of Things*, trans. A. Stallings (London: Penguin).

MacIntyre, A. (1981) *After Virtue* (London: Duckworth).

MacKenzie, M. (2007) 'The Illumination of Consciousness: Approaches to Self-Awareness in the Indian and Western Traditions', *Philosophy East and West* 57: 40–62.

Mackie, J. L. (1976) *Problems from Locke* (Oxford: Clarendon Press).

MacNeice, L. (1941/2007) 'Plant and Phantom', in *Collected Poems* (London: Faber).

Malebranche, N. (c.1680–90) *Oeuvres complètes, tomes 6 et 7. Recueil de toutes les réponses à M. Arnaud* (Paris: Vrin).

Marcus Aurelius (c.170/1964) *Meditations (Notes to himself)*, trans. M. Staniforth (Harmondsworth: Penguin).

Margolis, J. (1988) 'Minds, Selves, and Persons', *Topoi* 7: 31–45.

McAdams, D. (2004) 'The Redemptive Self: Narrative Identity in America Today', in *The Self and Memory*, ed. D. R. Beike, J. M. Lampinen, and D. A. Behrend (New York: Psychology Press), pp. 95–115.

McAdams, D. (2005) *The Redemptive Self: Stories Americans Live By* (New York: Oxford University Press).

McAdams, D., Josselson, R., and Lieblich, A. (2006) 'Introduction', in *Identity and Story: Creating Self in Narrative* (American Psychological Association).

McCarthy, M. (1962/1964) 'The Art of Fiction, No. 27', in *Writers at Work: the Paris Review Interviews, Second Series*, ed. G. Plimpton (New York: Viking Press).

McGinn, C. (1995/2004) 'Consciousness and Space', in *Consciousness and its Objects* (Oxford: Oxford University Press), 93–115.

McGinn, C. (1999) *The Mysterious Flame* (New York: Basic Books).

Meek, J. (2013) 'Memories We Get to Keep', *London Review of Books*, 20 June.

Merian, J. (1793/1997) 'On the Phenomenalism of David Hume', *Hume Studies* 23: 178–91.

Midgley, M. (1984) *Wickedness: A Philosophical Essay* (London: Ark).

Millican, P. (2009) 'Hume, Causal Realism, and Causal Science', *Mind* 118: 647–712.

Milne, A. A. (1928) *The House at Pooh Corner* (London: Methuen).

Montague, M. (2007) 'Against Propositionalism', *Nous* 41: 503–18.

Montague, M. (2009) 'Perceptual experience', in *Oxford Handbook in the Philosophy of Mind*, ed. A. Beckermann and B. McLaughlin (Oxford: Oxford University Press), pp. 494–511.

Montague, M. (2014) 'The Life of the Mind', in *The Nature of Phenomenal Qualities*, ed. P. Coates and S. Coleman (Oxford University Press).

Montaigne, M. de (1562–92/2003) *The Complete Works*, trans. D. Frame (New York: Everyman's Library).

Montaigne, M. de (1563–92/1991) *The Complete Essays*, trans. M. A. Screech (London: Penguin).

Moore, G. E. (1903) 'The Refutation of Idealism', *Mind* 12: 433–53.

Moore, G. E. (1959) 'Wittgenstein's Lectures in 1930–33', *Philosophical Papers* (London: Allen and Unwin).

Munro, A. (2001) 'Go Ask Alice', interview, *New Yorker*, 19 February.

Murdoch, I. (1954/2002) *Under the Net* (London: Vintage).

Murdoch, I. (1969/1970) 'On "God" and "Good"', in *The Sovereignty of Good* (London: Routledge and Kegan Paul).

Nāgārjuna (c.150/1995) *The Fundamental Wisdom of the Middle Way*, trans. with commentary by Jay Garfield (Albany, NY: SUNY Press).

Nagel, T. (1979) 'Panpsychism', in *Mortal Questions* (Cambridge: Cambridge University Press).

Nagel, T. (1986) *The View From Nowhere* (New York: Oxford University Press).

Nehamas, A. (1985) *Life as Literature* (Cambridge, MA: Harvard University Press).

Neisser, U. (1994) 'Self-narratives: True and false', in *The Remembering Self: Construction and Accuracy in the Self-narrative*, ed. U. Neisser and R. Fivush (Cambridge: Cambridge University Press).

Newton, I. (1687/1934) *Principia*, trans. A. Motte and F. Cajori (Berkeley: University of California Press).

Nietzsche, F. (1874/1988) 'Schopenhauer als Erzieher', in *Unzeitgemässe Betrachtungen*, *Sämtliche Werke Kritische Studienausgabe*, vol. 1, revised edn. (Berlin: De Gruyter).

Nietzsche, F. (1874a/1988) 'Schopenhauer als Erzieher', in *Unzeitgemässe Betrachtungen*, *Sämtliche Werke Kritische Studienausgabe*, vol. 1, revised edn (Berlin: De Gruyter).

Nietzsche, F. (1874b/1997) 'Schopenhauer as Educator', in *Unfashionable Observations*, trans. R. Gray (Stanford, CA: Stanford University Press).

Nietzsche, F. (1882/2001) *The Gay Science*, ed. B. Williams, trans. J. Naukhoff and A. del Caro (Cambridge University Press).

Nietzsche, F. (1883–5/1961) *Thus Spoke Zarathustra: A Book for All and None*, trans. R. J. Hollingdale (London: Penguin).

Nietzsche, F. (1885–8/2003) *Writings from the Late Notebooks*, trans. Kate Sturge, ed. Rüdiger Bittner (Cambridge: Cambridge University Press).

Nietzsche, F. (1888/2005) *Twilight of the Idols*, ed. A. Ridley and J. Norman, trans. J. Norman (Cambridge University Press).

Niven, L. (1970) *Ringworld* (New York: Ballantine Books).

Nozick, R. (1981) *Philosophical Explanations* (Oxford: Clarendon Press).

Nozick, R. (1989/1990) *The Examined Life: Philosophical Meditations* (New York: Touchstone).

Olson, E. (1997) *The Human Animal* (Oxford: Oxford University Press).

Olson, E. (1998/1999) 'There is No Problem of the Self', in *Models of the Self*, ed. S. Gallagher and J. Shear (Thorverton: Imprint Academic).

Panskepp, J. (1998) 'The Periconscious Substrates of Consciousness: Affective States and the Evolutionary Origins of the Self', *Journal of Consciousness Studies* 5: 566–82.

Parfit, D. (1984) *Reasons and Persons* (Oxford: Clarendon Press).

Parfit, D. (1995) 'The Unimportance of Identity', in *Identity*, ed. H. Harris (Oxford: Clarendon Press).

Parfit, D. (1998a/2011a) 'Why Anything? Why This?', In *On What Matters*, vol. 2, Appendix D (Oxford: Oxford University Press).

Parfit, D. (1998b) 'Experiences, Subjects, and Conceptual Schemes', in *Philosophical Topics* 26: 217–20.

Parfit, D. (2012) 'We Are Not Human Beings', *Philosophy* 87: 5–28.

Penelhum, T. (1955) 'Hume on Personal Identity', *Philosophical Review* 64: 575–86.

Perec, G. (1978) *Je me souviens* (Paris: Hachette).

Perlis, D. (1997) 'Consciousness as Self Function', in *Models of the Self*, ed. S. Gallagher and J. Shear (Thorverton: Imprint Academic), pp. 131–47.

Perry, J. (1979/1994) 'The Problem of the Essential Indexical', in A.-Q. A. Cassam, ed., *Self-Knowledge* (Oxford: Oxford University Press).

Pessoa, F. (1914/1998) 'The Keeper of Sheep', in *Fernando Pessoa & Co., Selected Poems*, ed. and trans. R. Zenith (New York: Grove Press).

Pessoa, L. and De Weerd, P. (2003) *Filling-In: From Perceptual Completion to Cortical Reorganization* (Oxford: Oxford University Press).

Pickering, J. (1999) 'The Self is a Semiotic Process', in *Models of the Self*, ed. S. Gallagher and J. Shear (Thorverton: Imprint Academic), pp. 63–79.

Pike, N. (1967) 'Hume's Bundle Theory of the Self: A Limited Defense', in *American Philosophical Quarterly* 4: 159–65.

Pinker, S. (1997) *How the Mind Works* (London: Allen Lane).

Pitt, D. (2004) 'The Phenomenology of Cognition, or What is it Like to Think That p?', *Philosophy and Phenomenological Research* 69/1: 1–36.

Platner, E. (1772) *Anthropologie für Ärzte und Weltweise* (Leipzig: Dyck).

Plato (399 BCE/2002) *Apology*, in *Five Dialogues: Euthyphro, Apology, Crito, Meno, Phaedo*, 2nd revised edn, trans. G. Grube (Indianopolis: Hackett).

Plutarch (1939) 'On Tranquillity of Mind', in Plutarch, *Moralia*, vol. 6, trans. W. C. Helmbold (Cambridge, MA: Harvard University Press).

Poincaré, H. (1903/1905) *Science and Hypothesis* (London and Newcastle-upon-Tyne: The Walter Scott Publishing Company).

Pöppel, E. (1978) 'Time Perception', in R. Held, H. W. Leibovitz, and H. L. Teuber, eds., *Handbook of Sensory Physiology*, Vol. VIII (New York: Springer).

Post, H. (1963) 'Individuality and Physics', *Listener* 70: 534–7.

Potter, B. (1909) *The Tale of The Flopsy Bunnies* (London: Frederick Warne and Co).

Price, H. H. (1940) *Hume's Theory of the External World* (Oxford: Oxford University Press).

Priestley, J. (1777/1965) *Priestley's Writings on Philosophy, Science and Politics*, ed. J. A Passmore (New York: Collier).

Pritchett, V. S. (1979) *The Myth Makers* (London: Chatto and Windus).

Proust, M. (1919–27/1987) À la recherche du temps perdu (Paris: Pléiade).

Proust, M. (1920–1/2003) The Guermantes Way, trans. with Introd. Mark Treharne, vol. 2 of In Search of Lost Time (London: Penguin).

Proust, M. (1920–1/1987) Le Côté de Guermantes 1, in À la recherche du temps perdu, vol. 2 (Paris: Pléiade).

Proust, M. (1923–5/2003) The Prisoner and the Fugitive, trans. and Introd. Carol Clark, vol. 5 of In Search of Lost Time (London: Penguin).

Proust, M. (1925/1987) Albertine disparue, in À la recherche du temps perdu, vol. 4 (Paris: Pléiade).

Proust, M. (1927/1987) Le temps retrouvé, in À la recherche du temps perdu, vol. 4 (Paris: Pléiade).

Proust, M. (1927/2003) Finding Time Again, trans. and Introd. Ian Patterson, vol. 6 of In Search of Lost Time (London: Penguin).

Prufer, T. (1975) 'An outline of some Husserlian distinctions and strategies, especially in the Crisis', Phänomenologische Forschungen 1: 189–204.

Quine, W. V. (1955/1966) 'Quantifiers and Propositional Attitudes', in The Ways of Paradox (New York: Random House).

Radden, J. (1998) 'Pathologically Divided Minds, Synchronic Unity and Models of the Self', Journal of Consciousness Studies 5: 658–72.

Ram-Prasad, C. (2010) 'Situating the Elusive Self of Advaita Vedānta', in Self, No Self?: Perspectives from Analytical, Phenomenological, and Indian Traditions, ed. M. Siderits, E. Thompson, and D. Zahavi (Oxford: Oxford University Press), pp. 217–38.

Ramachandran, V., And Hirstein, W. (1997) 'Three Laws of qualia: what neurology tells us about the biological functions of consciousness', Journal of Consciousness Studies, 4: 429–57.

Ramsey, F. (1925/1997) 'Universals', in Properties, ed. D. H. Mellor and Alex Oliver (Oxford: Oxford University Press).

Reed, G. (1987) 'Time-Gap Experience', in The Oxford Companion to the Mind (Oxford: Oxford University Press).

Reid, T. (1748/2000) 'On the self', in An Inquiry into the Human Mind on the Principles of Common Sense, ed. D. Brookes (Edinburgh: Edinburgh University Press).

Reid, T. (1764/2000) An Inquiry into the Human Mind, ed. D. Brookes (Edinburgh: Edinburgh University Press).

Reid, T. (1785/2002) Essays on the Intellectual Powers of Man, ed. D. Brookes (Edinburgh: Edinburgh University Press).

Richardson, D. (1979) Pointed Roofs, Pilgrimage, vol. 1 (London: Virago Press).

Ricoeur, P. (1985/1988) Time and Narrative, vol. 3 (Chicago University Press).

Ricoeur, P. (1990/1992) Oneself as Another, trans. Kathleen Blamey (Chicago: Chicago University Press).

Rimbaud, A. (1871/1972) Oeuvres complètes (Paris: Gallimard).

Robinson, H. (2002) Matter and Sense: a Critique of Contemporary Materialism (Cambridge: Cambridge University Press).

Rosch, E. (1997) 'Mindfulness meditation and the private (?) self', in The Conceptual Self in Context: Culture, Eexperience, Self-understanding, ed. U. Neisser and R. Fivush (Cambridge: Cambridge University Press).

Rosenthal, D. (1986) 'Two Concepts of Consciousness', Philosophical Studies 49: 329–59.

Rosenthal, D. (2005) Consciousness and Mind (Oxford: Oxford University Press).

Rozemond, M. (1998) Descartes's Dualism (Oxford: Oxford University Press).

Roth, P. (1986/2005) The Counterlife (London: Vintage).

Rotter, J. B. (1966) 'Generalized expectancies for internal versus external control of reinforcement', Psychological Monographs 80 (1, Whole Number 609).

Rowlands, M. (2011) 'Jean-Paul Sartre's Being and Nothingness', Topoi 30: 175–80.

Ruhnau, E. (1995) 'Time Gestalt and the Observer', in T. Metzinger, ed., *Conscious Experience* (Thorverton: Imprint Academic).

Russell, B. (1927a/1995a) *The Analysis of Matter* (London: Allen and Unwin).

Russell, B. (1927b/1995b) *An Outline of Philosophy* (London: Allen and Unwin).

Russell, B. (1940) *An Inquiry Into Meaning and Truth* (London: George Allen and Unwin).

Ryle, G. (1949) *The Concept of Mind* (New York: Barnes and Noble).

Sacks, O. (1984) *A Leg to Stand On* (London: Picador).

Sacks, O. (1985) *The Man Who Mistook His Wife For A Hat* (London: Duckworth).

Salter, J. (1975) *Light Years* (New York: Vintage International).

Sartre, J.-P. (1936–7/2004) *Transcendence of the Ego*, trans. Andrew Brown, Introd. Sarah Richmond (London: Routledge).

Sartre, J.-P. (1938/1996) *La nausée* (Paris: Gallimard).

Sartre, J.-P. (1943/1969) *L'être et le néant* (*Being and Nothingness*), trans. H. Barnes (London: Methuen).

Sartre, J.-P. (1948) 'Conscience de soi et connaissance de soi,' *Bulletin de la Société Française de Philosophie* **42**: 49–91.

Sartre, J.-P. (1948/1967) 'Consciousness of Self and Knowledge of Self', in N. Lawrence and D. O'Connor, eds., *Readings in Existential Phenomenology* (Englewood Cliffs, NJ: Prentice-Hall), pp. 113–42.

Sass, L. (1998) 'Schizophrenia, Self-consciousness and the Modern Mind', *Journal of Consciousness Studies* **5**: 543–65.

Schaffer, J. (2009) 'Spacetime: the one substance', *Philosophical Studies* **145**: 131–48.

Schaffer, J. (2010) 'Monism: the Priority of the Whole', *The Philosophical Review* **119**: 31–76.

Schechtman, M. (1996) *The Constitution of Selves* (Ithaca: Cornell University Press).

Schechtman, M. (2001) 'Empathic Access: The Missing Ingredient in Personal Identity', *Philosophical Explorations* **4**: 95–111.

Schechtman, M. (2005) 'Self-expression and Self-control', in *The Self?*, ed. G. Strawson (Oxford: Blackwell).

Schechtman, M. (2007) 'Stories, Lives, and Basic Survival', in *Narrative and Understanding Persons*, ed. Daniel D. Hutto (Cambridge: Cambridge University Press).

Schechtman, M. (2014) *Staying Alive* (Oxford: Oxford University Press).

Schopenhauer, A. (1819–1859/2010) *The World as Will and Representation*, trans. J. Norman et al. (Cambridge: Cambridge University Press).

Schopenhauer, A. (1847) *Über die vierfache Wurzel des Satzes vom zureichenden Grunde* (*On the Fourfold Root of the Principle of Sufficient Reason*), revised 2nd edn (Frankfurt am Main).

Schulkind, J. (1978) 'Introduction', in *Virginia Woolf: Moments of Being*, ed. Jeanne Schulkind (London: Hogarth Press).

Scoville, W. B., and Milner, B. (1957) 'Loss of recent memory after bilateral hippocampal lesions', *Journal of Neurology, Neurosurgery, and Psychiatry* **20**: 11–21.

Searle, J. (1983) *Intentionality* (Cambridge: Cambridge University Press).

Searle, J. (1992) *The Rediscovery of the Mind* (Cambridge, MA: MIT Press).

Shakespeare, W. (1599–1600/2004) *As You Like It*, ed. J. Dusinberre (Arden Shakespeare, London: Bloomsbury).

Shear, J. (1998) 'Experiential Clarification of the Problem of Self', *Journal of Consciousness Studies* **5**: 673–86.

Sheets-Johnstone, M. (1999) 'Phenomenology and agency', *Journal of Consciousness Studies*, **6**: 48–69.

Shelley, P. (1818a/2003) 'Lines Written Among The Euganean Hills', in *Percy Bysshe Shelley: The Major Works*, ed. Z. Leader and M. O'Neill (Oxford: Oxford University Press).

Shelley, P. (1818b/2003) *Revolt of Islam,* 'Dedication: To Mary—', in *Percy Bysshe Shelley: The Major Works,* ed. Z. Leader and M. O'Neill (Oxford: Oxford University Press).

Sherlock, W. (1690) *A Vindication of the Doctrine of the holy and Ever Blessed Trinity* (London).

Shoemaker, S. (1968/1994) 'Self-Reference and Self-Awareness', in *Identity, Cause, and Mind* (Cambridge University Press) and in *Self-Knowledge,* ed. Q. Cassam (Oxford University Press).

Shoemaker, S. (1970) 'Persons and their Pasts', *American Philosophical Quarterly* 7: 269–85.

Shoemaker, S. (1986/1996) 'Introspection and the Self', in *The First-Person Perspective and Other Essays* (Cambridge: Cambridge University Press).

Shoemaker, S. (1999a) 'Self, Body, and Coincidence', *Proceedings of the Aristotelian Society, Supplementary Vol. 73.*

Shoemaker, S. (1999b) Review of *The Human Animal,* by Eric Olson in *Nous* 33: 496–504.

Siderits, M. (2010) 'Buddhas as Zombies: A Buddhist Reduction of Subjectivity', in *Self, No Self?: Perspectives from Analytical, Phenomenological, and Indian Traditions,* ed. M. Siderits, E. Thompson, and D. Zahavi (Oxford University Press), pp. 308–31.

Simic, C. (2011) 'Grass: The Gold and the Garbage', *New York Review of Books,* 24 March, p. 23.

Simons, D., and Levin, D. (1997) 'Change blindness', in *Trends in Cognitive Sciences* 1: 261–7.

Smith, B. (2012) 'Complexities of taste', *Nature* **486**: 21 June.

Smith, D. W. (1989) *The Circle of Acquaintance: Perception, Consciousness, and Empathy* (Dordrecht: Kluwer).

Somerset Maugham, W. (1949) *A Writer's Notebook* (London: Heinemann).

Sorabji, R. (2006) *Self: Ancient and Modern Insights about Individuality, Life and Death* (Oxford: Clarendon Press).

South, R. (1693) *Animadversions upon Dr. Sherlock's Book Entituled A Vindication of the Holy and Ever Blessed Trinity* (London).

Spenser, E. (*c.*1594/1989) *Amoretti,* in *Shorter Poems* (New Haven: Yale University Press).

Spinoza, B. de (1677/1985) *Ethics,* in *The Collected Works of Spinoza,* ed.and trans. E. Curley (Princeton: Princeton University Press).

Sprigge, T. L. S. (1983) *The Vindication of Absolute Idealism* (Edinburgh: Edinburgh University Press).

Sprigge, T. L. S. (2006) *The God of Metaphysics* (Oxford: Oxford University Press).

Squire, L., and E. Kandel (1999) *Memory: From Mind to Molecules* (New York: Scientific American Library).

Stedman's (2005) *Stedman's Medical Dictionary for the Health Professions and Nursing,* 5th edn (Baltimore, MD: Lippincott Williams and Wilkins).

Stern, D. (1985) *The Interpersonal World of the Infant* (New York: Basic Books).

Stokes, P. (2008) 'Locke, Kierkegaard and the Phenomenology of Personal Identity', *International Journal of Philosophical Studies* 16: 645–72.

Stokes, P. (2010) 'What's Missing in Episodic Self-Experience? A Kierkegaardian Response to Galen Strawson', *Journal of Consciousness Studies* 17: 1–25.

Stone, J. (1988) 'Parfit and the Buddha: Why There Are No People', *Philosophy and Phenomenological Research* 48: 519–32.

Stone, J. (2005) 'Why There Still Are No People', *Philosophy and Phenomenological Research* 70: 174–92.

Strawson, G. (1986/2010) *Freedom and Belief,* 2nd edn (Oxford University Press).

Strawson, G. (1989/2014) *The Secret Connexion,* 2nd edn (Oxford: Clarendon Press).

Strawson, G. (1994) *Mental Reality* (Cambridge, MA: MIT Press).

Strawson, G. (1997) 'The Self', *Journal of Consciousness Studies* 4: 405–28.

Strawson, G. (1999a) 'Realistic Materialist Monism', in *Towards a Science of Consciousness III,* ed. S. Hameroff et al. (Cambridge, MA: MIT Press), pp. 23–32.

Strawson, G. (1999b) 'The self and the sesmet', *Journal of Consciousness Studies* 6: 99–135.

Strawson, G. (1999c) 'Self, body and experience', *Proceedings of the Aristotelian Society* **73**: 308–31.

Strawson, G. (1999d) 'The Sense of the Self', in *From Soul to Self*, ed. J. Crabbe (London: Routledge).

Strawson, G. (2001) 'Hume on himself', in *Essays in Practical Philosophy: From Action to Values*, ed. D. Egonsson et al. (Aldershot: Ashgate Press).

Strawson, G. (2002/2008) 'Can we Know the Nature of Reality as It is in Itself?', in *Real Materialism and Other Essays* (Oxford: Oxford University Press).

Strawson, G. (2003a) 'Real materialism', in L. Antony and N. Hornstein, eds., *Chomsky and his Critics* (Oxford: Blackwell).

Strawson, G. (2003b) 'What is the relation between an experience, the subject of the experience, and the content of the experience?', *Philosophical Issues* **13**: 279–315, revised version see (2008b).

Strawson, G. (2004/2008) 'Against Narrativity', in G. Strawson, *Real Materialism and Other Essays* (Oxford: Oxford University Press).

Strawson, G. (2005/2008) 'Intentionality and Experience: Terminological Preliminaries', in G. Strawson, *Real Materialism and Other Essays* (Oxford: Clarendon Press), pp. 255–79.

Strawson, G. (2006a) 'Realistic monism: why physicalism entails panpsychism', in *Consciousness and its Place in Nature*, ed. A. Freeman (Thorverton: Imprint Academic), pp. 3–31.

Strawson, G. (2006b) 'Reply to commentators, with a celebration of Descartes', in *Consciousness and its Place in Nature*, ed. A. Freeman (Thorverton: Imprint Academic), pp. 184–280.

Strawson, G. (2007) 'Episodic Ethics', in *Narrative and Understanding Persons*, ed. D. Hutto (Cambridge: Cambridge University Press), pp. 85–115.

Strawson, G. (2008a) *Real Materialism and Other Essays* (Oxford: Clarendon Press).

Strawson, G. (2008b) 'Real Intentionality 3', in *Theorema* 27 and in G. Strawson, *Real Materialism and Other Essays* (Oxford: Clarendon Press).

Strawson, G. (2008c) 'The identity of the categorical and the dispositional', *Analysis* **68(4)**: 271–82.

Strawson, G. (2009/2011) *Selves: An Essay in Revisionary Metaphysics*, 2nd edn (Oxford: Oxford University Press).

Strawson, G. (2010) 'Radical Self-Awareness', in *Self, No Self?: Perspectives from Analytical, Phenomenological, and Indian Traditions*, ed. M. Siderits, E. Thompson, and D. Zahavi (Oxford: Oxford University Press).

Strawson, G. (2011a/2013) *The Evident Connexion: Hume on Personal Identity*, 2nd edn (Oxford: Oxford University Press).

Strawson, G. (2011b) 'Cognitive phenomenology: real life', in *Cognitive Phenomenology*, ed. T. Bayne and M. Montague (Oxford: Oxford University Press).

Strawson, G. (2011c/2014) *Locke on Personal Identity: Consciousness and Concernment*, 2nd edn (Princeton, NJ: Princeton University Press).

Strawson, G. (2011d) 'The minimal self', in *Oxford Handbook of the Self*, ed. S. Gallagher (Oxford University Press).

Strawson, G. (2012a) 'All My Hopes Vanish: Hume's Appendix', in *The Continuum Companion to Hume*, ed. A Bailey and D. O'Brien (London: Continuum).

Strawson, G. (2012b) 'Real naturalism', Romanell Lecture in *Proceedings of the American Philosophical Association* **86**: 125–54.

Strawson, G. (2014) *Locke on Personal Identity: Consciousness and Concernment*, 2nd edn (Princeton, NJ: Princeton University Press).

Strawson, G. (2015) 'Real direct realism', in *The Nature of Phenomenal Qualities*, ed. P. Coates and S. Coleman (Oxford University Press).

Strawson, G. (2016) 'Mind and Being: The Primacy of Panpsychism', in *Panpsychism: Philosophical Essays*, ed. G. Bruntrup and L. Jaskolla (Oxford University Press).

Strawson, G. (2017) 'Descartes's mind', in *Descartes and Cartesianism: Essays in Honour of Desmond Clarke*, ed. S. Gaukroger and C. Wilson (Oxford: Oxford University Press).

Strawson, G. (2018) *Things That Bother Me* (New York: New York Review Books).

Strawson, P. F. (1959) *Individuals* (London: Methuen).

Strawson, P. (1966) *The Bounds of Sense* (London: Methuen).

Strawson, P. F. (1969/1971) 'Meaning and Truth', in P. F. Strawson, *Logico-linguistic Papers* (London: Methuen).

Stroud, B. (1977) *Hume* (London: Routledge).

Tani, J. (1998) 'An Interpretation of the "Self" from the Dynamical Systems Perspective: A Constructivist Approach', *Journal of Consciousness Studies* 5: 516–42.

Taylor, C. (1989) *Sources of the Self* (Cambridge: Cambridge University Press).

Taylor, H. (1836) *The Statesman* (London: Longman, Rees, Orme, Brown, Green, & Longman).

Thiel, U. (1998) 'Personal Identity', in *The Cambridge History of Seventeenth-Century Philosophy*, vol. 1, ed. M. R. Ayers and D. Garber (Cambridge: Cambridge University Press).

Thiel, U. (2011) *The Early Modern Subject: Self-consciousness and Personal Identity from Descartes to Hume* (Oxford: Oxford University Press).

Thomas, L. (1983) 'The Attic of the Brain', in *Late Night Thoughts on Listening to Mahler's Ninth Symphony* (New York: Bantam Books).

Thompson, E. (2010) 'Memory and Reflexive Awareness', in *Self, No Self?: Perspectives from Analytical, Phenomenological, and Indian Traditions*, ed. M. Siderits, E. Thompson, and D. Zahavi (Oxford University Press) pp. 157–75.

Tolstoy, L. (1886/2008) 'The Death of Ivan Illich', in *The Death of Ivan Ilyich and Other Stories*, trans. D. McDuff (London: Penguin).

Traherne, T. (1637–74/1903) *Poetical Works* (London).

Trivers, R. (1985) *Social Evolution* (Menlo Park, CA: Benjamin/Cummings).

Tulving, E. (1985) 'Memory and Consciousness', *Canadian Psychology/Psychologie Canadienne* 26: 1–12.

Twain, M. (1902/1992) 'Does the Race of Man Love a Lord?', *North American Review* 174(4) in *Collected Tales, Sketches, Speeches and Essays: 1891–1910* (New York: Library of America).

Tyndall, J. (1874) *Address Delivered Before the British Association Assembled at Belfast, With Additions* (London: Longmans, Green, and Co.

Updike, J. (1989) *Self-Consciousness* (London: Deutsch).

Updike, J. (1999) 'One Cheer for Literary Biography', *The New York Review of Books*, 4 February.

Updike, J. (2000) *Gertrude and Claudius* (New York: Knopf).

van Cleve, J. (2005) 'Troubles for Radical Transparency', http://www-rcf.usc.edu/~vancleve

van Inwagen, P. (1990) *Material Beings* (Ithaca, NY: Cornell University Press).

Velleman, D. (2005/2006) 'The Self as Narrator', in D. Velleman, *Self to Self* (Cambridge: Cambridge University Press).

Waggenaar, W. (1994) 'Is memory self-serving?', in *The Remembering Self: Construction and Accuracy in the Self-narrative*, ed. U. Neisser and R. Fivush (Cambridge: Cambridge University Press).

Watson, D. R. (1998) 'Ethnomethodology, Consciousness and Self', *Journal of Consciousness Studies* 5: 202–23.

Wegner, D. M. (2002) *The Illusion of Conscious Will* (Cambridge, MA: MIT Press).

Weinberg, S. (1997) 'Before the Big Bang', *The New York Review of Books* 44(10).

Weinberg, S. (2008) 'The Coherence of Consciousness in Locke's *Essay*, *History of Philosophy Quarterly* 25: 21–39.

Whitehead, A. (1938/1969) *Modes of Thought* (New York: The Free Press).

Wilkes, K. (1998) 'GNOTHI SEAUTON (Know Thyself)', *Journal of Consciousness Studies* 5: 153–65.

Williamson, T. (2002) *Knowledge and its Limits* (Oxford: Oxford University Press).

Williford, K. (2006) 'The Self-Representational Structure of Consciousness', in *Self-Representational Approaches to Consciousness*, ed. U. Kriegel and K. Williford (Cambridge, MA: MIT Press).

Wilson, R. (2004) *Boundaries of the Mind: The Individual in the Fragile Sciences* (Cambridge: Cambridge University Press).

Wilson, T. (2002) *Strangers to Ourselves: Discovering the Adaptive Unconscious* (Cambridge, MA: Harvard University Press).

Wittgenstein, L. (1916/1961) entry of 5 August 1916, *Notebooks 1914–1916* (Oxford: Blackwell).

Wittgenstein, L. (1933–5/1958) *The Blue and Brown Books* (Oxford: Blackwell).

Wittgenstein, L. (1948/1980) *Culture and Value* (Oxford: Blackwell).

Wollheim, R. (1984) *The Thread of Life* (Cambridge, MA: Harvard University Press).

Woolf, V. (1925) *Mrs Dalloway* (London: Hogarth Press).

Woolf, V. (1925/2008) 'Modern Fiction', in *The Essays of Virginia Woolf. Volume 4: 1925 to 1928*, ed. A. McNeillie (London: Hogarth Press).

Woolf, V. (1926) undated, see entry of 25 July, *The Diary of Virginia Woolf 1925–30*, vol. 3 (London: Penguin).

Woolf, V. (1927) *To the Lighthouse* (London: Hogarth Press).

Woolf, V. (1931) *The Waves* (London: Hogarth Press).

Woolf, V. (1939/1978) *A Sketch of the Past*, in *Virginia Woolf: Moments of Being*, ed. and Introd. Jeanne Schulkind (London: Hogarth Press).

Woolf, V. (1941) *Between the Acts* (London: Hogarth Press).

Wu Cheng-en, attrib. (1592/1993) *Xiyouji (Journey to the West)*, vol.1, trans. W. J. F. Jenner (Beijing: Foreign Languages Press).

Wundt, W. (1874/1911) *Principles of Physiological Psychology*, trans. E. B. Titchener (New York: Macmillan).

Yaffe, G. (2009) 'Thomas Reid on Consciousness and Attention', *Canadian Journal of Philosophy* 39(2): 165–94.

Yeats, W. B. (1933/1967) 'Vacillation', in *The Collected Poems of W. B. Yeats* (London: Macmillan).

Zahavi, D. (1999) *Self-Awareness and Alterity: A Phenomenological Investigation* (Evanston, IL: Northwestern University Press).

Zahavi, D. (2005) *Subjectivity and Selfhood: Investigating the First-person Perspective* (Cambridge, MA: MIT Press).

Zahavi, D. (2006a) 'Thinking about self-consciousness: phenomenological perspectives', in U. Kriegel and K. Williford, eds., *Consciousness and Self Reference* (Cambridge, MA: MIT Press).

Zahavi, D. (2006b) 'Two Takes on a One-Level Account of Consciousness', *Psyche* 12(2): 1–9.

Zahavi, D. (2007) 'The Heidelberg School and the Limits of Reflection', in S. Heinämaa, V. Lähteenmäki, and P. Remes, eds., *Consciousness: from Perception to Reflection in the History of Philosophy* (Dordrecht: Springer), pp. 267–85.

Zahavi, D. (2007) 'Self and Other: The limits of narrative understanding', in *Narrative and Understanding Persons*, ed. D. Hutto (Cambridge: Cambridge University Press).

Zahavi, D. and Parnas, J. (1998) 'Phenomenal Consciousness and Self Awareness: A Phenomenological Critique of Representational Theory', *Journal of Consciousness Studies* 5: 687–705.

Zenith, R. (2002) 'Introduction', in F. Pessoa, *The Book of Disquiet* (London: Penguin).

Zimbardo, P. and Boyd, J. (2008) *The Time Paradox* (New York: Random House).

Name Index

Subject Index

This index does not cite every occurrence of every listed term or topic. Page numbers in bold indicate the place at which an entry is introduced or defined or the main place at which it is discussed.

Printed and bound by CPI Group (UK) Ltd, Croydon, CR0 4YY